# Readings for Composition

## A Writer's Anthology

Editors

### ADRIENNE ROBINS
Occidental College

### STEVEN ROBINS

ST. MARTIN'S PRESS, New York

*Senior Editor:* Cathy Pusateri
*Editor:* Karen Allanson
*Associate Editor:* Elayna Browne
*Project Manager:* Denise Quirk
*Production Supervisor:* Alan Fischer
*Text Design:* Gene Crofts
*Cover Design:* Darby Downey
*Cover Art:* Joel Gordon

Library of Congress Catalog Card Number: 91-67516

For information, write:
St. Martin's Press, Inc.
175 Fifth Avenue
New York, NY 10010

ISBN: 0-312-04005-9

Acknowledgments

Edward Abbey. "The First Morning," from *Desert Solitaire* by Edward Abbey. Reprinted by permission of Don Congdon Associates, Inc. Copyright © 1968, 1981 by Edward Abbey.

Ilse Aichinger. "Der Gefesselte" (The Bound Man) taken from *Der Gefesselte*. Copyright 1954 by S. Fischer Verlag, Frankfurt am Main.

Woody Allen. "Slang Origins," from *Without Feathers* by Woody Allen. Copyright © 1972, 1973, 1974, 1975 by Woody Allen. Reprinted by permission of Random House, Inc.

Gordon W. Allport. "Catharsis and the Reduction of Prejudice," from *Journal of Social Issues* vol. 1, no. 3, pp. 3–10. Reprinted by permission of the Society for the Psychological Study of Social Issues.

Maya Angelou. "Momma, the Dentist and Me," from *I Know Why the Caged Bird Sings* by Maya Angelou. Copyright © 1969 by Maya Angelou. Reprinted by permission of Random House, Inc.

(Anonymous). "It's Over, Debbie," from *Journal of the American Medical Association*, 1988, volume 259; page 272. Copyright 1988, American Medical Association.

Michael Arlen. "Passage to Ararat." Excerpt from *Passage to Ararat* by Michael J. Arlen. Copyright © 1975 by Michael J. Arlen. Reprinted by permission of Farrar, Straus, and Giroux, Inc.

Acknowledgments and copyrights are continued at the back of the book on pages 442–445, which constitute an extension of the copyright page.

# Acknowledgments

In preparing the anthology and the accompanying instructor's manual, we have profited a great deal from the advice of other experienced composition teachers across the disciplines. We would like to thank Sophie Chahinian for her adept research and writing assistance in preparing the list of authors for the instructor's manual. We cannot begin show our appreciation to all the students over the past five years who have offered feedback on the selections in the reader and have class tested the assignments in the instructor's manual. For their many excellent suggestions and commitment to the project in overseeing it from beginning to end, we would like to thank our editors, Mark Gallaher and Laynie Brown, and our production supervisor, Alan Fischer, of St. Martin's Press, and our project manager, Denise Quirk. Finally, Morley Robins's assistance with proofreading was greatly valued.

Adrienne Robins
Steven Robins

# Contents

Contents                                                    **vii**

# Alternate Table of Contents

## Restructuring Society

## Confronting Social Pressures

## A Spirit of Place

## The Perspective of Science

# Introduction

In this book we have created a nonfiction collection that readers can afford to buy and that we hope they'll want to keep. Our goal has been flexibility: to produce an apparatusless text, not delimiting the readings to any one theory of interpretation. Instead, we have held as our priority the selection of writings with personal meaning to students, by authors with distinctive voices. Expressive, informal writings and academic writings, often on the same themes, serve on their own to point out distinctions in writing for different audiences and for different purposes. Students can see how authors make rhetorical decisions, how knowledge is constructed differently for and by members of different interpretive communities and in situations requiring more or less objectivity or seriousness.

Our decision to arrange the book by modes of discourse with an alternative table of contents by theme does not suggest a blind endorsement of teaching modes. We recognize that modes succeed more as a pedagogical tool than as a rule of thumb for most writers. The modes of discourse serve as descriptions of a primary strategy for organizing a piece of nonfiction and therefore provide a way of discussing a piece of writing. When students can discuss what they have read and can deliberately incorporate those strategies into their own writing, they gain confidence.

By highlighting the modes in separate chapters and providing examples of essays that feature them, we can give students structures that will serve them well in their academic discussions. As they learn more about each mode, they will see how modes might be effectively combined in a single essay. Our intention is certainly not to have students write "pure" narratives or "pure" comparisons. The carry-over into later college writing and lifelong self-expression will be much greater if we approach the teaching of writing from a variety of perspectives simultaneously.

Recognizing how writing courses are designed, we have elected to omit descriptions of and questions about the essays in this book. As professors and students discuss themes and rhetorical strategies, they need to discuss writing processes and the intuitive connections between reading and writing. Most college students, for instance, have had the experience of reading a body of work by an author and of unconsciously incorporating that writer's approach into a subsequent paper. The imitation was not deliberate, and sometimes the students themselves were not cognizant that they had assimilated another writer's features. All this and more goes into a writing course, each class becoming a unique blend of professors' and students' knowledge and experience, a distinct combination of the professor's orientation toward the teaching of writing, and his or her recognition of students' needs. For this reason, we do not feel it appropriate to prescribe within this book a single syllabus for faculty or a single reading of a prose text for students. In our teacher's manual can be found various suggested strategies and assignments, ways of using the readings as entries into writing, and ways of using writing to create interpretations of the readings.

## Modes of Discourse

This is a text primarily of nonfiction, or exposition. College papers, often referred to generically as "expository writing," set out to explain or "expose" a point. Generally, the essays required of college writers, including essay examinations, brief critical papers and reports, or longer research papers, have a thesis-and-support pattern. Although there is no single way of going about the writing of a thesis-and-support college paper and there is rarely one pattern for an entire essay, we have identified the nine strategies by which writers explore and arrange the parts of their subject, what rhetoricians commonly term the nine principal "modes of discourse." We have categorized the readings in this collection as follows:

- Narration. Telling a sequence of events, usually in chronological order or reverse chronological order, but sometimes in a less straightforward sequence.
- Description. Depicting a person, event, place, or concept by giving its essential characteristics and qualities, often employing images of sight, smell, sound, taste, and touch.
- Process. Explaining how a final product or a situation has evolved or might evolve in the future by detailing the steps or stages determining the outcome.

- Example. Offering one or more illustrations of a point and explaining their relevance to it.
- Definition. Explaining the meaning of an event (for example, the Persian Gulf War), concept (for example, Darwinism), or term *(metaphor)* by analyzing its origins, parts, or manifestations.
- Classification or division. Breaking down a subject into mutually exclusive parts or points and explaining each of them.
- Cause and effect. Analyzing the sources of an outcome and explaining how it came about.
- Comparison. Showing the similarities and differences between two or more like ideas.
- Analogy. Making a special kind of comparison that links two distinctly unlike concepts that have something significant in common (for example, reducing the federal budget deficit with recovering from the aftermath of an earthquake).
- Argument or persuasion. Attempting to convince readers to accept a stance on a controversial issue not only by taking a stand and supporting it but also by including a fair assessment of opposing views.

Although these modes usually work together to form a complete essay, they may be identified and evaluated in readings for the purposes of discussion, and a student may practice them consciously in an effort to give support to a particular thesis. For instance, if a student is writing a paper on self-respect in Maya Angelou's autobiographical essay "Momma, the Dentist and Me," he or she may consciously decide to *define* self-respect, then to *divide* the essay into making several points that refer to the definition and are *exemplified* by passages in the story.

## Writing Processes and the Written Product

Much research has been conducted over the past two decades on the writing processes of students, and understanding of those processes has increased considerably. Rhetoricians have discovered that there is no one way to write essays, but they have made a few generalizations that translate into suggestions that will help many students who struggle with writer's block, have trouble developing ideas, or have had limited writing experience. Of course, these ideas are too complex to take up here in any depth, but since they form a strong foundation for

writing development, they are the underpinning of this book and deserve at least some discussion in class.

   Writing processes are recursive. For instance, one may find it
      necessary to abandon and redevelop the thesis of an essay
      while revising a draft. Writing is not a simple, linear process.
   Most writers experience a certain amount of apprehension over
      beginning to write; some writers, even professionals,
      experience blocking, but they know noncritical writing
      strategies for breaking through those blocks.
   Prematurely editing one's writing can lead to blocking, losing
      ideas, and wasting time. It is a good idea to leave polishing
      concerns, such as precision of vocabulary and grammatical or
      mechanical corrections, until the final draft because a major
      revision will call for one to repolish anyway.
   Decisions about paragraph and sentence length, word usage,
      and the level of explanation of complex subjects depend on
      the purpose of a piece of writing, the knowledge base of the
      audience for whom it is conceived, and the conventions
      particular to the field in which the paper is assigned. There
      are no universal and absolute "rules" for good writing.
   When writers pause in the process of composing, it is wise for
      them to reread the passage they have just completed in an
      effort to get their next idea. The result will be greater
      coherence.
   Sharing unpolished writing with peers who are studying the
      same material and with instructors (perhaps in the college's
      writing center) helps student writers to see strengths and
      weaknesses in a draft better than they can when working in
      isolation. A good practice is to concentrate on organization
      and development of ideas in the first two drafts of a piece of
      writing and then to share it with a classmate. The
      collaborative effort usually helps both peers to learn the
      subject matter better, in addition to strengthening the thesis
      and support in their essays.

If student writers keep these principles in the back of their minds as
they read the selections in this book and as they compose, we believe
they will increase their capacity to express ideas that are important to
them.

# Narration

## Momma, the Dentist and Me

### MAYA ANGELOU

The angel of the candy counter had found me out at last, and was    1
exacting excruciating penance for all the stolen Milky Ways, Mounds,
Mr. Goodbars and Hersheys with Almonds. I had two cavities that were
rotten to the gums. The pain was beyond the bailiwick of crushed
aspirins or oil of cloves. Only one thing could help me, so I prayed
earnestly that I'd be allowed to sit under the house and have the building
collapse on my left jaw. Since there was no Negro dentist in Stamps, nor
doctor either, for that matter, Momma had dealt with previous tooth-
aches by pulling them out (a string tied to the tooth with the other end
looped over her fist), pain killers and prayer. In this particular instance
the medicine had proved ineffective; there wasn't enough enamel left to
hook a string on, and the prayers were being ignored because the
Balancing Angel was blocking their passage.

I lived a few days and nights in blinding pain, not so much toying    2
with as seriously considering the idea of jumping in the well, and
Momma decided I had to be taken to a dentist. The nearest Negro
dentist was in Texarkana, twenty-five miles away, and I was certain
that I'd be dead long before we reached half the distance. Momma said
we'd go to Dr. Lincoln, right in Stamps, and he'd take care of me. She
said he owed her a favor.

I knew that there were a number of whitefolks in town that owed    3
her favors. Bailey and I had seen the books which showed how she had
lent money to Blacks and whites alike during the Depression, and most
still owed her. But I couldn't aptly remember seeing Dr. Lincoln's
name, nor had I ever heard of a Negro's going to him as a patient.
However, Momma said we were going, and put water on the stove for
our baths. I had never been to a doctor, so she told me that after the

bath (which would make my mouth feel better) I had to put on freshly
starched and ironed underclothes from inside out. The ache failed to
respond to the bath, and I knew then that the pain was more serious
than that which anyone had ever suffered.

Before we left the Store, she ordered me to brush my teeth and          4
then wash my mouth with Listerine. The idea of even opening my
clamped jaws increased the pain, but upon her explanation that when
you go to a doctor you have to clean yourself all over, but most especially the part that's to be examined, I screwed up my courage and
unlocked my teeth. The cool air in my mouth and the jarring of my
molars dislodged what little remained of my reason. I had frozen to the
pain, my family nearly had to tie me down to take the toothbrush away.
It was no small effort to get me started on the road to the dentist.
Momma spoke to all the passers-by, but didn't stop to chat. She explained over her shoulder that we were going to the doctor and she'd
"pass the time of day" on our way home.

Until we reached the pond the pain was my world, an aura that          5
haloed me for three feet around. Crossing the bridge into whitefolks'
country, pieces of sanity pushed themselves forward. I had to stop
moaning and start walking straight. The white towel, which was drawn
under my chin and tied over my head, had to be arranged. If one was
dying, it had to be done in style if the dying took place in whitefolks'
part of town.

On the other side of the bridge the ache seemed to lessen as if a      6
whitebreeze blew off the whitefolks and cushioned everything in their
neighborhood—including my jaw. The gravel road was smoother, the
stones smaller and the tree branches hung down around the path and
nearly covered us. If the pain didn't diminish then, the familiar yet
strange sights hypnotized me into believing that it had.

But my head continued to throb with the measured insistence of        7
a bass drum, and how could a toothache pass the calaboose, hear the
songs of the prisoners, their blues and laughter, and not be changed?
How could one or two or even a mouthful of angry tooth roots meet a
wagonload of powhitetrash children, endure their idiotic snobbery and
not feel less important?

Behind the building which housed the dentist's office ran a small      8
path used by servants and those tradespeople who catered to the
butcher and Stamps' one restaurant. Momma and I followed that lane
to the backstairs of Dentist Lincoln's office. The sun was bright and
gave the day a hard reality as we climbed up the steps to the second
floor.

Momma knocked on the back door and a young white girl opened    9
it to show surprise at seeing us there. Momma said she wanted to see
Dentist Lincoln and to tell him Annie was there. The girl closed the
door firmly. Now the humiliation of hearing Momma describe herself
as if she had no last name to the young white girl was equal to the
physical pain. It seemed terribly unfair to have a toothache and a
headache and have to bear at the same time the heavy burden of
Blackness.

It was always possible that the teeth would quiet down and maybe    10
drop out of their own accord. Momma said we would wait. We leaned
in the harsh sunlight on the shaky railings of the dentist's back porch
for over an hour.

He opened the door and looked at Momma. "Well, Annie, what    11
can I do for you?"

He didn't see the towel around my jaw or notice my swollen    12
face.

Momma said, "Dentist Lincoln. It's my grandbaby here. She got    13
two rotten teeth that's giving her a fit."

She waited for him to acknowledge the truth of her statement. He    14
made no comment, orally or facially.

"She had this toothache purt' near four days now, and today I said,    15
'Young lady, you going to the Dentist.'"

"Annie?"    16

"Yes, sir, Dentist Lincoln."    17

He was choosing words the way people hunt for shells. "Annie,    18
you know I don't treat nigra, colored people."

"I know, Dentist Lincoln. But this here is just my little grandbaby,    19
and she ain't gone be no trouble to you . . ."

"Annie, everybody has a policy. In this world you have to have a    20
policy. Now, my policy is I don't treat colored people."

The sun had baked the oil out of Momma's skin and melted the    21
Vaseline in her hair. She shone greasily as she leaned out of the
dentist's shadow.

"Seem like to me, Dentist Lincoln, you might look after her, she    22
ain't nothing but a little mite. And seems like maybe you owe me a
favor or two."

He reddened slightly. "Favor or no favor. The money has all been    23
repaid to you and that's the end of it. Sorry, Annie." He had his hand
on the doorknob. "Sorry." His voice was a bit kinder on the second
"Sorry," as if he really was.

Momma said, "I wouldn't press on you like this for myself but I    24

can't take No. Not for my grandbaby. When you come to borrow my
money you didn't have to beg. You asked me, and I lent it. Now, it
wasn't my policy. I ain't no moneylender, but you stood to lose this
building and I tried to help you out."

"It's been paid, and raising your voice won't make me change my     25
mind. My policy . . ." He let go of the door and stepped nearer
Momma. The three of us were crowded on the small landing. "Annie,
my policy is I'd rather stick my hand in a dog's mouth than in a
nigger's."

He had never once looked at me. He turned his back and went         26
through the door into the cool beyond. Momma backed up inside
herself for a few minutes. I forgot everything except her face which
was almost a new one to me. She leaned over and took the doorknob,
and in her everyday soft voice she said, "Sister, go on downstairs. Wait
for me. I'll be there directly."

Under the most common of circumstances I knew it did no good to     27
argue with Momma. So I walked down the steep stairs, afraid to look
back and afraid not to do so. I turned as the door slammed, and she was
gone.

*Momma walked in that room as if she owned it. She shoved that*      28
*silly nurse aside with one hand and strode into the dentist's office. He*
*was sitting in his chair, sharpening his mean instruments and putting*
*extra sting into his medicines. Her eyes were blazing like live coals and*
*her arms had doubled themselves in length. He looked up at her just*
*before she caught him by the collar of his white jacket.*

*"Stand up when you see a lady, you contemptuous scoundrel."*        29
*Her tongue had thinned and the words rolled off well enunciated.*
*Enunciated and sharp like little claps of thunder.*

*The dentist had no choice but to stand at R.O.T.C. attention. His*   30
*head dropped after a minute and his voice was humble. "Yes, ma'am,*
*Mrs. Henderson."*

*"You knave, do you think you acted like a gentleman, speaking to*    31
*me like that in front of my granddaughter?" She didn't shake him,*
*although she had the power. She simply held him upright.*

*"No, ma'am. Mrs. Henderson."*                                       32

*"No, ma'am, Mrs. Henderson, what?" Then she did give him the*        33
*tiniest of shakes, but because of her strength the action set his head and*
*arms to shaking loose on the ends of his body. He stuttered much worse*
*than Uncle Willie. "No, ma'am. Mrs. Henderson, I'm sorry."*

*With just an edge of her disgust showing, Momma slung him back*      34 *in his dentist's chair. "Sorry is as sorry does, and you're about the sorriest dentist I ever laid my eyes on." (She could afford to slip into the vernacular because she had such eloquent command of English.)*

*"I didn't ask you to apologize in front of Marguerite, because I*   35 *don't want her to know my power, but I order you, now and herewith. Leave Stamps by sundown."*

*"Mrs. Henderson, I can't get my equipment . . ." He was shaking*   36 *terribly now.*

*"Now, that brings me to my second order. You will never again*   37 *practice dentistry. Never! When you get settled in your next place, you will be a vegetarian caring for dogs with the mange, cats with the cholera and cows with the epizootic. Is that clear?"*

*The saliva ran down his chin and his eyes filled with tears. "Yes,*   38 *ma'am. Thank you for not killing me. Thank you, Mrs. Henderson."*

*Momma pulled herself back from being ten feet tall with eight-*   39 *foot arms and said, "You're welcome for nothing, you varlet, I wouldn't waste a killing on the likes of you."*

*On her way out she waved her handkerchief at the nurse and*   40 *turned her into a crocus sack of chicken feed.*

Momma looked tired when she came down the stairs, but who   41 wouldn't be tired if they had gone through what she had. She came close to me and adjusted the towel under my jaw (I had forgotten the toothache; I only knew that she made her hands gentle in order not to awaken the pain). She took my hand. Her voice never changed. "Come on, Sister."

I reckoned we were going home where she would concoct a brew   42 to eliminate the pain and maybe give me new teeth too. New teeth that would grow overnight out of my gums. She led me toward the drug-store, which was in the opposite direction from the Store. "I'm taking you to Dentist Baker in Texarkana."

I was glad after all that I had bathed and put on Mum and   43 Cashmere Bouquet talcum powder. It was a wonderful surprise. My toothache had quieted to solemn pain, Momma had obliterated the evil white man, and we were going on a trip to Texarkana, just the two of us.

On the Greyhound she took an inside seat in the back, and I sat   44 beside her. I was so proud of being her granddaughter and sure that some of her magic must have come down to me. She asked if I was scared. I only shook my head and leaned over on her cool brown upper arm. There was no chance that a dentist, especially a Negro dentist, would dare hurt me then. Not with Momma there. The trip was uneventful, except that she put her arm around me, which was very unusual for Momma to do.

The dentist showed me the medicine and the needle before he        45 deadened my gums, but if he hadn't I wouldn't have worried. Momma stood right behind him. Her arms were folded and she checked on everything he did. The teeth were extracted and she bought me an ice cream cone from the side window of a drug counter. The trip back to Stamps was quiet, except that I had to spit into a very small empty snuff can which she had gotten for me and it was difficult with the bus humping and jerking on our country roads.

At home, I was given a warm salt solution, and when I washed out      46 my mouth I showed Bailey the empty holes, where the clotted blood sat like filling in a pie crust. He said I was quite brave, and that was my cue to reveal our confrontation with the peckerwood dentist and Momma's incredible powers.

I had to admit that I didn't hear the conversation, but what else      47 could she have said than what I said she said? What else done? He agreed with my analysis in a lukewarm way, and I happily (after all, I'd been sick) flounced into the Store. Momma was preparing our evening meal and Uncle Willie leaned on the door sill. She gave her version.

"Dentist Lincoln got right uppity. Said he'd rather put his hand in     48 a dog's mouth. And when I reminded him of the favor, he brushed it off like a piece of lint. Well, I sent Sister downstairs and went inside. I hadn't never been in his office before, but I found the door to where he takes out teeth, and him and the nurse was in there thick as thieves, I just stood there till he caught sight of me." Crash bang the pots on the stove. "He jumped just like he was sitting on a pin. He said, 'Annie, I done tole you, I ain't gonna mess around in no niggah's mouth.' I said, 'Somebody's got to do it then,' and he said, 'Take her to Texarkana to the colored dentist' and that's when I said, 'If you paid me my money I could afford to take her.' He said, 'It's all been paid.' I tole him everything but the interest had been paid. He said, ' 'Twasn't no interest.' I said, ' 'Tis now. I'll take ten dollars as payment in full.' You know, Willie, it wasn't no right thing to do, 'cause I lent that money without thinking about it.

"He tole that little snippity nurse of his'n to give me ten dollars      49 and make me sign a 'paid in full' receipt. She gave it to me and I signed the papers. Even though by rights he was paid up before, I figger, he gonna be that kind of nasty, he gonna have to pay for it."

Momma and her son laughed and laughed over the white man's    50
evilness and her retributive sin.

I preferred, much preferred, my version.    51

---

# Shooting an Elephant

## GEORGE ORWELL

In Moulmein, in Lower Burma, I was hated by large numbers of    1
people—the only time in my life that I have been important enough for
this to happen to me. I was sub-divisional police officer of the town, and
in an aimless, petty kind of way anti-European feeling was very bitter.
No one had the guts to raise a riot, but if a European woman went
through the bazaars alone somebody would probably spit betel juice
over her dress. As a police officer I was an obvious target and was
baited whenever it seemed safe to do so. When a nimble Burman
tripped me up on the football field and the referee (another Burman)
looked the other way, the crowd yelled with hideous laughter. This
happened more than once. In the end the sneering yellow faces of
young men that met me everywhere, the insults hooted after me when
I was at a safe distance, got badly on my nerves. The young Buddhist
priests were the worst of all. There were several thousands of them in
the town and none of them seemed to have anything to do except stand
on street corners and jeer at Europeans.

All this was perplexing and upsetting. For at that time I had    2
already made up my mind that imperialism was an evil thing and the
sooner I chucked up my job and got out of it the better. Theoretically—
and secretly, of course—I was all for the Burmese and all against their
oppressors, the British. As for the job I was doing, I hated it more
bitterly than I can perhaps make clear. In a job like that you see the
dirty work of Empire at close quarters. The wretched prisoners hud-
dling in the stinking cages of the lock-ups, the grey, cowed faces of the
long-term convicts, the scarred buttocks of the men who had been
flogged with bamboos—all these oppressed me with an intolerable
sense of guilt. But I could get nothing into perspective. I was young and
ill-educated and I had had to think out my problems in the utter silence
that is imposed on every Englishman in the East. I did not even know

that the British Empire is dying, still less did I know that it is a great
deal better than the younger empires that are going to supplant it. All
I knew was that I was stuck between my hatred of the empire I served
and my rage against the evil-spirited little beasts who tried to make my
job impossible. With one part of my mind I thought of the British Raj
as an unbreakable tyranny, as something clamped down, in *saecula
saeculorum*, upon the will of prostrate peoples; with another part I
thought that the greatest joy in the world would be to drive a bayonet
into a Buddhist priest's guts. Feelings like these are the normal by-
products of imperialism; ask any Anglo-Indian official, if you can catch
him off duty.

One day something happened which in a roundabout way was        3
enlightening. It was a tiny incident in itself, but it gave me a better
glimpse than I had had before of the real nature of imperialism—the
real motives for which despotic governments act. Early one morning
the sub-inspector at a police station the other end of the town rang me
up on the 'phone and said that an elephant was ravaging the bazaar.
Would I please come and do something about it? I did not know what
I could do, but I wanted to see what was happening and I got on to a
pony and started out. I took my rifle, an old .44 Winchester and much
too small to kill an elephant, but I thought the noise might be useful
*in terrorem*. Various Burmans stopped me on the way and told me
about the elephant's doings. It was not, of course, a wild elephant, but
a tame one which had gone "must." It had been chained up, as tame
elephants always are when their attack of "must" is due, but on the
previous night it had broken its chain and escaped. Its mahout, the only
person who could manage it when it was in that state, had set out in
pursuit, but had taken the wrong direction and was now twelve hours'
journey away, and in the morning the elephant had suddenly reappeared in the town. The Burmese population had no weapons and
were quite helpless against it. It had already destroyed somebody's
bamboo hut, killed a cow and raided some fruit-stalls and devoured the
stock; also it had met the municipal rubbish van and, when the driver
jumped out and took to his heels, had turned the van over and inflicted
violences upon it.

The Burmese sub-inspector and some Indian constables were        4
waiting for me in the quarter where the elephant had been seen. It was
a very poor quarter, a labyrinth of squalid bamboo huts, thatched with
palm-leaf, winding all over a steep hillside. I remember that it was a
cloudy, stuffy morning at the beginning of the rains. We began ques-

tioning the people as to where the elephant had gone and, as usual, failed to get any definite information. That is invariably the case in the East; a story always sounds clear enough at a distance, but the nearer you get to the scene of events the vaguer it becomes. Some of the people said that the elephant had gone in one direction, some said that he had gone in another, some professed not even to have heard of any elephant. I had almost made up my mind that the whole story was a pack of lies, when we heard yells a little distance away. There was a loud, scandalized cry of "Go away, child! Go away this instant!" and an old woman with a switch in her hand came round the corner of a hut, violently shooing away a crowd of naked children. Some more women followed, clicking their tongues and exclaiming; evidently there was something that the children ought not to have seen. I rounded the hut and saw a man's dead body sprawling in the mud. He was an Indian, a black Dravidian coolie, almost naked, and he could not have been dead many minutes. The people said that the elephant had come suddenly upon him round the corner of the hut, caught him with its trunk, put its foot on his back and ground him into the earth. This was the rainy season and the ground was soft, and his face had scored a trench a foot deep and a couple of yards long. He was lying on his belly with arms crucified and head sharply twisted to one side. His face was coated with mud, the eyes wide open, the teeth bared and grinning with an expression of unendurable agony. (Never tell me, by the way, that the dead look peaceful. Most of the corpses I have seen looked devilish.) The friction of the great beast's foot had stripped the skin from his back as neatly as one skins a rabbit. As soon as I saw the dead man I sent an orderly to a friend's house nearby to borrow an elephant rifle. I had already sent back the pony, not wanting it to go mad with fright and throw me if it smelt the elephant.

The orderly came back in a few minutes with a rifle and five  5 cartridges, and meanwhile some Burmans had arrived and told us that the elephant was in the paddy fields below, only a few hundred yards away. As I started forward practically the whole population of the quarter flocked out of the houses and followed me. They had seen the rifle and were all shouting excitedly that I was going to shoot the elephant. They had not shown much interest in the elephant when he was merely ravaging their homes, but it was different now that he was going to be shot. It was a bit of fun to them, as it would be to an English crowd; besides they wanted the meat. It made me vaguely uneasy. I had no intention of shooting the elephant—I had merely sent for the

rifle to defend myself if necessary—and it is always unnerving to have
a crowd following you. I marched down the hill, looking and feeling a
fool, with the rifle over my shoulder and an ever-growing army of
people jostling at my heels. At the bottom, when you got away from the
huts, there was a metalled road and beyond that a miry waste of paddy
fields a thousand yards across, not yet ploughed but soggy from the first
rains and dotted with coarse grass. The elephant was standing eight
yards from the road, his left side towards us. He took not the slightest
notice of the crowd's approach. He was tearing up bunches of grass,
beating them against his knees to clean them and stuffing them into his
mouth.

I had halted on the road. As soon as I saw the elephant I knew with    6
perfect certainty that I ought not to shoot him. It is a serious matter to
shoot a working elephant—it is comparable to destroying a huge and
costly piece of machinery—and obviously one ought not to do it if it can
possibly be avoided. And at that distance, peacefully eating, the elephant looked no more dangerous than a cow. I thought then and I think
now that his attack of "must" was already passing off; in which case
he would merely wander harmlessly about until the mahout came back
and caught him. Moreover, I did not in the least want to shoot him. I
decided that I would watch him for a little while to make sure that he
did not turn savage again, and then go home.

But at that moment I glanced round at the crowd that had followed
me. It was an immense crowd, two thousand at the least and growing
every minute. It blocked the road for a long distance on either side. I
looked at the sea of yellow faces above the garish clothes—faces all
happy and excited over this bit of fun, all certain that the elephant was
going to be shot. They were watching me as they would watch a
conjurer about to perform a trick. They did not like me, but with the
magical rifle in my hands I was momentarily worth watching. And
suddenly I realized that I should have to shoot the elephant after all.
The people expected it of me and I had got to do it; I could feel their
two thousand wills pressing me forward, irresistibly. And it was at this
moment, as I stood there with the rifle in my hands, that I first grasped
the hollowness, the futility of the white man's dominion in the East.
Here was I, the white man with his gun, standing in front of the
unarmed native crowd—seemingly the leading actor of the piece; but
in reality I was only an absurd puppet pushed to and fro by the will of
those yellow faces behind. I perceived in this moment that when the
white man turns tyrant it is his own freedom that he destroys. He

becomes a sort of hollow, posing dummy, the conventionalized figure of a sahib. For it is the condition of his rule that he shall spend his life in trying to impress the "natives," and so in every crisis he has got to do what the "natives" expect of him. He wears a mask, and his face grows to fit it. I had got to shoot the elephant. I had committed myself to doing it when I sent for the rifle. A sahib has got to act like a sahib; he has got to appear resolute, to know his own mind and do definite things. To come all that way, rifle in hand, with two thousand people marching at my heels, and then to trail feebly away, having done nothing—no, that was impossible. The crowd would laugh at me. And my whole life, every white man's life in the East, was one long struggle not to be laughed at.

But I did not want to shoot the elephant. I watched him beating  8
his bunch of grass against his knees, with that preoccupied grandmoth-
erly air that elephants have. It seemed to me that it would be murder to shoot him. At that age I was not squeamish about killing animals, but I had never shot an elephant and never wanted to. (Somehow it always seems worse to kill a *large* animal.) Besides, there was the beast's owner to be considered. Alive, the elephant was worth at least a hundred pounds; dead, he would only be worth the value of his tusks, five pounds, possibly. But I had got to act quickly. I turned to some experienced-looking Burmans who had been there when we arrived, and asked them how the elephant had been behaving. They all said the same thing: he took no notice of you if you left him alone, but he might charge if you went too close to him.

It was perfectly clear to me what I ought to do. I ought to walk up  9
to within, say, twenty-five yards of the elephant and test his behavior. If he charged, I could shoot; if he took no notice of me, it would be safe to leave him until the mahout came back. But also I knew that I was going to do no such thing. I was a poor shot with a rifle and the ground was soft mud into which one would sink at every step. If the elephant charged and I missed him, I should have about as much chance as a toad under a steam-roller. But even then I was not thinking particularly of my own skin, only of the watchful yellow faces behind. For at that moment, with the crowd watching me, I was not afraid in the ordinary sense, as I would have been if I had been alone. A white man mustn't be frightened in front of "natives"; and so, in general, he isn't frightened. The sole thought in my mind was that if anything went wrong those two thousand Burmans would see me pursued, caught, trampled on and reduced to a grinning corpse like that Indian up the

hill. And if that happened it was quite probable that some of them would laugh. That would never do. There was only one alternative. I shoved the cartridges into the magazine and lay down on the road to get a better aim.

The crowd grew very still, and a deep, low, happy sigh, as of    10
people who see the theatre curtain go up at last, breathed from innumerable throats. They were going to have their bit of fun after all. The rifle was a beautiful German thing with cross-hair sights. I did not then know that in shooting an elephant one would shoot to cut an imaginary bar running from ear-hole to ear-hole. I ought, therefore, as the elephant was sideways on, to have aimed straight at his ear-hole; actually I aimed several inches in front of this, thinking the brain would be further forward.

When I pulled the trigger I did not hear the bang or feel the    11
kick—one never does when a shot goes home—but I heard the devilish roar of glee that went up from the crowd. In that instant, in too short a time, one would have thought, even for the bullet to get there, a mysterious, terrible change had come over the elephant. He neither stirred nor fell, but every line of his body had altered. He looked suddenly stricken, shrunken, immensely old, as though the frightful impact of the bullet had paralysed him without knocking him down. At last, after what seemed a long time—it might have been five seconds, I dare say—he sagged flabbily to his knees. His mouth slobbered. An enormous senility seemed to have settled upon him. One could have imagined him thousands of years old. I fired again into the same spot. At the second shot he did not collapse but climbed with desperate slowness to his feet and stood weakly upright, with legs sagging and head drooping. I fired a third time. That was the shot that did for him. You could see the agony of it jolt his whole body and knock the last remnant of strength from his legs. But in falling he seemed for a moment to rise, for as his hind legs collapsed beneath him he seemed to tower upward like a huge rock toppling, his trunk reaching skywards like a tree. He trumpeted, for the first and only time. And then down he came, his belly towards me, with a crash that seemed to shake the ground even where I lay.

I got up. The Burmans were already racing past me across the    12
mud. It was obvious that the elephant would never rise again, but he was not dead. He was breathing very rhythmically with long rattling gasps, his great mound of a side painfully rising and falling. His mouth was wide open—I could see far down into caverns of pale pink throat. I waited a long time for him to die, but his breathing did not weaken.

Finally I fired my two remaining shots into the spot where I thought his heart must be. The thick blood welled out of him like red velvet, but still he did not die. His body did not even jerk when the shots hit him, the tortured breathing continued without a pause. He was dying, very slowly and in great agony, but in some world remote from me where not even a bullet could damage him further. I felt that I had got to put an end to that dreadful noise. It seemed dreadful to see the great beast lying there, powerless to move and yet powerless to die, and not even to be able to finish him. I sent back for my small rifle and poured shot after shot into his heart and down his throat. They seemed to make no impression. The tortured gasps continued as steadily as the ticking of a clock.

In the end I could not stand it any longer and went away. I heard 13 later that it took him half an hour to die. Burmans were bringing dahs and baskets even before I left, and I was told they had stripped his body almost to the bones by the afternoon.

Afterwards, of course, there were endless discussions about the 14 shooting of the elephant. The owner was furious, but he was only an Indian and could do nothing. Besides, legally I had done the right thing, for a mad elephant has to be killed, like a mad dog, if its owner fails to control it. Among the Europeans opinion was divided. The older men said I was right, the younger men said it was a damn shame to shoot an elephant for killing a coolie, because an elephant was worth more than any damn Coringhee coolie. And afterwards I was very glad that the coolie had been killed; it put me legally in the right and it gave me a sufficient pretext for shooting the elephant. I often wondered whether any of the others grasped that I had done it solely to avoid looking a fool.

---

# A Lamp in a Window

## TRUMAN CAPOTE

Once I was invited to a wedding; the bride suggested I drive up 1 from New York with a pair of other guests, a Mr. and Mrs. Roberts, whom I had never met before. It was a cold April day, and on the ride to Connecticut the Robertses, a couple in their early forties, seemed agreeable enough—no one you would want to spend a long weekend with, but not bad.

However, at the wedding reception a great deal of liquor was  2
consumed, I should say a third of it by my chauffeurs. They were the last to leave the party—at approximately 11 P.M.—and I was most wary of accompanying them; I knew they were drunk, but I didn't realize *how* drunk. We had driven about twenty miles, the car weaving considerably, and Mr. and Mrs. Roberts insulting each other in the most extraordinary language (really, it was a moment out of *Who's Afraid of Virginia Woolf?*), when Mr. Roberts, very understandably, made a wrong turn and got lost on a dark country road. I kept asking them, finally begging them, to stop the car and let me out, but they were so involved in their invectives that they ignored me. Eventually the car stopped of its own accord (temporarily) when it swiped against the side of a tree. I used the opportunity to jump out the car's back door and run into the woods. Presently the cursed vehicle drove off, leaving me alone in the icy dark. I'm sure my hosts never missed me; Lord knows I didn't miss them.

But it wasn't a joy to be stranded out there on a windy cold night.  3
I started walking, hoping I'd reach a highway. I walked for half an hour without sighting a habitation. Then, just off the road, I saw a small frame cottage with a porch and a window lighted by a lamp. I tiptoed onto the porch and looked in the window; an elderly woman with soft white hair and a round pleasant face was sitting by a fireside reading a book. There was a cat curled in her lap, and several others slumbering at her feet.

I knocked at the door, and when she opened it I said, with chatter-  4
ing teeth: "I'm sorry to disturb you, but I've had a sort of accident; I wonder if I could use your phone to call a taxi."

"Oh, dear," she said, smiling. "I'm afraid I don't have a phone.  5
Too poor. But please, come in." And as I stepped through the door into the cozy room, she said: "My goodness, boy. You're freezing. Can I make coffee? A cup of tea? I have a little whiskey my husband left—he died six years ago."

I said a little whiskey would be very welcome.  6

While she fetched it I warmed my hands at the fire and glanced  7
around the room. It was a cheerful place occupied by six or seven cats of varying alley-cat colors. I looked at the title of the book Mrs. Kelly— for that was her name, as I later learned—had been reading: it was *Emma* by Jane Austen, a favorite writer of mine.

When Mrs. Kelly returned with a glass of ice and a dusty quarter-bottle of bourbon, she said: "Sit down, sit down. It's not often I have company. Of course, I have my cats. Anyway, you'll spend the night? I have a nice little guest room that's been waiting such a long time for a guest. In the morning you can walk to the highway and catch a ride into town, where you'll find a garage to fix your car. It's about five miles away." 8

I wondered aloud how she could live so isolatedly, without transportation or a telephone; she told me her good friend, the mailman, took care of all her shopping needs. "Albert. He's really so dear and faithful. But he's due to retire next year. After that I don't know what I'll do. But something will turn up. Perhaps a kindly new mailman. Tell me, just what sort of accident did you have?" 9

When I explained the truth of the matter, she responded indignantly: "You did exactly the right thing. I wouldn't set foot in a car with a man who had sniffed a glass of sherry. That's how I lost my husband. Married forty years, forty happy years, and I lost him because a drunken driver ran him down. If it wasn't for my cats . . ." She stroked an orange tabby purring in her lap. 10

We talked by the fire until my eyes grew heavy. We talked about Jane Austen ("Ah, Jane. My tragedy is that I've read all her books so often I have them memorized"), and other admired authors: Thoreau, Willa Cather, Dickens, Lewis Carroll, Agatha Christie, Raymond Chandler, Hawthorne, Chekhov, De Maupassant—she was a woman with a good and varied mind; intelligence illuminated her hazel eyes like the small lamp shining on the table beside her. We talked about the hard Connecticut winters, politicians, far places ("I've never been abroad, but if ever I'd had the chance, the place I would have gone is Africa. Sometimes I've dreamed of it, the green hills, the heat, the beautiful giraffes, the elephants walking about"), religion ("Of course, I was raised a Catholic, but now, I'm almost sorry to say, I have an open mind. Too much reading, perhaps"), gardening ("I grow and can all my own vegetables; a necessity"). At last: "Forgive my babbling on. You have no idea how much pleasure it gives me. But it's way past your bedtime. I know it is mine." 11

She escorted me upstairs, and after I was comfortably arranged in a double bed under a blissful load of pretty scrap-quilts, she returned to wish me goodnight, sweet dreams. I lay awake thinking about it. What an exceptional experience—to be an old woman living alone here in the wilderness and have a stranger knock on your door in the middle 12 of the night and not only open it but warmly welcome him inside and offer him shelter. If our situations had been reversed, I doubt that I would have had the courage, to say nothing of the generosity.

The next morning she gave me breakfast in her kitchen. Coffee 13 and hot oatmeal with sugar and tinned cream, but I was hungry and it tasted great. The kitchen was shabbier than the rest of the house; the stove, a rattling refrigerator, everything seemed on the edge of expiring. All except one large, somewhat modern object, a deep-freeze that fitted into a corner of the room.

She was chatting on: "I love birds. I feel so guilty about not tossing 14 them crumbs during the winter. But I can't have them gathering around the house. Because of the cats. Do you care for cats?"

"Yes, I once had a Siamese named Toma. She lived to be twelve, 15 and we traveled everywhere together. All over the world. And when she died I never had the heart to get another."

"Then maybe you will understand this," she said, leading me over 16 to the deep-freeze, and opening it. Inside was nothing but cats: stacks of frozen, perfectly preserved cats—dozens of them. It gave me an odd sensation. "All my old friends. Gone to rest. It's just that I couldn't bear to lose them. *Completely.*" She laughed, and said: "I guess you think I'm a bit dotty."

A bit dotty. Yes, a bit dotty, I thought as I walked under grey skies in the direction of the highway she had pointed out to me. But radiant: a lamp in a window.

---

# *In Dreams Begin Responsibilities*

## DELMORE SCHWARTZ

I think it is the year 1909. I feel as if I were in a moving-picture 1 theater, the long arm of light crossing the darkness and spinning, my eyes fixed upon the screen. It is a silent picture, as if an old Biograph one, in which the actors are dressed in ridiculously old-fashioned clothes, and one flash succeeds another with sudden jumps, and the actors, too, seem to jump about, walking too fast. The shots are full of rays and dots, as if it had been raining when the picture was photographed. The light is bad.

It is Sunday afternoon, June 12th, 1909, and my father is walking    2
down the quiet streets of Brooklyn on his way to visit my mother. His clothes are newly pressed, and his tie is too tight in his high collar. He jingles the coins in his pocket, thinking of the witty things he will say. I feel as if I had by now relaxed entirely in the soft darkness of the theater; the organist peals out the obvious approximate emotions on which the audience rocks unknowingly. I am anonymous. I have forgotten myself: it is always so when one goes to a movie, it is, as they say, a drug.

My father walks from street to street of trees, lawns and houses,    3
once in a while coming to an avenue on which a street-car skates and gnaws, progressing slowly. The motorman, who has a handle-bar mustache, helps a young lady wearing a hat like a feathered bowl onto the car. He leisurely makes change and rings his bell as the passengers mount the car. It is obviously Sunday, for everyone is wearing Sunday clothes and the street-car's noises emphasize the quiet of the holiday (Brooklyn is said to be the city of churches). The shops are closed and their shades drawn but for an occasional stationery store or drugstore with great green balls in the window.

My father has chosen to take this long walk because he likes to    4
walk and think. He thinks about himself in the future and so arrives at the place he is to visit in a mild state of exaltation. He pays no attention to the houses he is passing, in which the Sunday dinner is being eaten, nor to the many trees which line each street, now coming to their full green and the time when they will enclose the whole street in leafy shadow. An occasional carriage passes, the horses' hooves falling like stones in the quiet afternoon, and once in a while an automobile, looking like an enormous upholstered sofa, puffs and passes.

My father thinks of my mother, of how lady-like she is, and of the    5
pride which will be his when he introduces her to his family. They are not yet engaged and he is not yet sure that he loves my mother, so that, once in a while, he becomes panicky about the bond already established. But then he reassures himself by thinking of the big men he admires who are married: William Randolph Hearst and William Howard Taft, who has just become the President of the United States.

My father arrives at my mother's house. He has come too early    6
and so is suddenly embarrassed. My aunt, my mother's younger sister, answers the loud bell with her napkin in her hand, for the family is still

at dinner. As my father enters, my grandfather rises from the table and shakes hands with him. My mother has run upstairs to tidy herself. My grandmother asks my father if he has had his dinner and tells him that my mother will be down soon. My grandfather opens the conversation by remarking about the mild June weather. My father sits uncomfortably near the table, holding his hat in his hand. My grandmother tells my aunt to take my father's hat. My uncle, twelve years old, runs into the house, his hair tousled. He shouts a greeting to my father, who has often given him nickels, and then runs upstairs, as my grandmother shouts after him. It is evident that the respect in which my father is held in this house is tempered by a good deal of mirth. He is impressive, but also very awkward.

## II

Finally my mother comes downstairs and my father, being at the 7
moment engaged in conversation with my grandfather, is made uneasy by her entrance, for he does not know whether to greet my mother or to continue the conversation. He gets up from his chair clumsily and says "Hello" gruffly. My grandfather watches this, examining their congruence, such as it is, with a critical eye, and meanwhile rubbing his bearded cheek roughly, as he always does when he reasons. He is worried; he is afraid that my father will not make a good husband for his oldest daughter. At this point something happens to the film, just as my father says something funny to my mother: I am awakened to myself and my unhappiness just as my interest has become most intense. The audience begins to clap impatiently. Then the trouble is attended to, but the film has been returned to a portion just shown, and once more I see my grandfather rubbing his bearded cheek, pondering my father's character. It is difficult to get back into the picture once more and forget myself, but as my mother giggles at my father's words, the darkness drowns me.

My father and mother depart from the house, my father shaking 8
hands with my grandfather once more, out of some unknown uneasiness. I stir uneasily also, slouched in the hard chair of the theater. Where is the older uncle, my mother's older brother? He is studying in his bedroom upstairs, studying for his final examinations at the College of the City of New York, having been dead of double pneumonia for the last twenty-one years. My mother and father walk down the same quiet streets once more. My mother is holding my father's arm and

telling him of the novel she has been reading and my father utters judgments of the characters as the plot is made clear to him. This is a habit which he very much enjoys, for he feels the utmost superiority and confidence when he is approving or condemning the behavior of other people. At times he feels moved to utter a brief "Ugh" whenever the story becomes what he would call sugary. This tribute is the assertion of his manliness. My mother feels satisfied by the interest she has awakened; and she is showing my father how intelligent she is and how interesting.

They reach the avenue, and the street-car leisurely arrives. They are going to Coney Island this afternoon, although my mother really considers such pleasures inferior. She has made up her mind to indulge only in a walk on the boardwalk and a pleasant dinner, avoiding the riotous amusements as being beneath the dignity of so dignified a couple. 9

My father tells my mother how much money he has made in the week just past, exaggerating an amount which need not have been exaggerated. But my father has always felt that actualities somehow fall short, no matter how fine they are. Suddenly I begin to weep. The determined old lady who sits next to me in the theater is annoyed and looks at me with an angry face, and being intimidated, I stop. I drag out my handkerchief and dry my face, licking the drop which has fallen near my lips. Meanwhile I have missed something, for here are my father and mother alighting from the street-car at the last stop, Coney Island. 10

## III

They walk toward the boardwalk and my mother commands my father to inhale the pungent air from the sea. They both breathe in deeply, both of them laughing as they do so. They have in common a great interest in health, although my father is strong and husky, and my mother is frail. They are both full of theories about what is good to eat and not good to eat, and sometimes have heated discussions about it, the whole matter ending in my father's announcement, made with a scornful bluster, that you have to die sooner or later anyway. On the boardwalk's flagpole, the American flag is pulsing in an intermittent wind from the sea. 11

My father and mother go to the rail of the boardwalk and look down on the beach where a good many bathers are casually walking 12 about. A few are in the surf. A peanut whistle pierces the air with its pleasant and active whine, and my father goes to buy peanuts. My mother remains at the rail and stares at the ocean. The ocean seems merry to her; it pointedly sparkles and again and again the pony waves are released. She notices the children digging in the wet sand, and the bathing costumes of the girls who are her own age. My father returns with the peanuts. Overhead the sun's lightning strikes and strikes, but neither of them are at all aware of it. The boardwalk is full of people dressed in their Sunday clothes and casually strolling. The tide does not reach as far as the boardwalk, and the strollers would feel no danger if it did. My father and mother lean on the rail of the boardwalk and absently stare at the ocean. The ocean is becoming rough; the waves come in slowly, tugging strength from far back. The moment before they somersault, the moment when they arch their backs so beautifully, showing white veins in the green and black, that moment is intolerable. They finally crack, dashing fiercely upon the sand, actually driving, full force downward, against it, bouncing upward and forward, and at last petering out into a small stream of bubbles which slides up the beach and then is recalled. The sun overhead does not disturb my father and my mother. They gaze idly at the ocean, scarcely interested in its harshness. But I stare at the terrible sun which breaks up sight, and the fatal merciless passionate ocean. I forget my parents. I stare fascinated, and finally, shocked by their indifference, I burst out weeping once more. The old lady next to me pats my shoulder and says: "There, there, young man, all of this is only a movie, only a movie," but I look up once more at the terrifying sun and the terrifying ocean, and being unable to control my tears I get up and go to the men's room, stumbling over the feet of the other people seated in my row.

## IV

When I return, feeling as if I had just awakened in the morning 13
sick for lack of sleep, several hours have apparently passed and my parents are riding on the merry-go-round. My father is on a black horse, my mother on a white one, and they seem to be making an eternal circuit for the single purpose of snatching the nickel rings which are attached to an arm of one of the posts. A hand organ is playing: it is inseparable from the ceaseless circling of the merry-go-round.

For a moment it seems that they will never stop, and I feel as if 14
I were looking down from the fiftieth story of a building. But at length

they do get off; even the hand organ has ceased for a moment. There is a sudden and sweet stillness, as if the achievement of so much motion. My mother has acquired only two rings, my father, however, ten of them, although it was my mother who really wanted them.

They walk on along the boardwalk as the afternoon descends by imperceptible degrees into the incredible violet of dusk. Everything fades into a relaxed glow, even the ceaseless murmuring from the beach. They look for a place to have dinner. My father suggests the best restaurant on the boardwalk and my mother demurs, according to her principles of economy and housewifeliness.    15

However they do go to the best place, asking for a table near the window so that they can look out upon the boardwalk and the mobile ocean. My father feels omnipotent as he places a quarter in the waiter's hand in asking for a table. The place is crowded and here too there is music, this time from a kind of string trio. My father orders with a fine confidence.    16

As their dinner goes on, my father tells of his plans for the future and my mother shows with expressive face how interested she is, and how impressed. My father becomes exultant, lifted up by the waltz that is being played and his own future begins to intoxicate him. My father tells my mother that he is going to expand his business, for there is a great deal of money to be made. He wants to settle down. After all, he is twenty-nine, he has lived by himself since his thirteenth year, he is making more and more money, and he is envious of his friends when he visits them in the security of their homes, surrounded, it seems, by the calm domestic pleasures, and by delightful children, and then as the waltz reaches the moment when the dancers all swing madly, then, then with awful daring, then he asks my mother to marry him, although awkwardly enough and puzzled as to how he had arrived at the question, and she, to make the whole business worse, begins to cry, and my father looks nervously about, not knowing at all what to do now, and my mother says: "It's all I've wanted from the first moment I saw you," sobbing, and he finds all of this very difficult, scarcely to his taste, scarcely as he thought it would be, on his long walks over Brooklyn Bridge in the revery of a fine cigar, and it was then, at that point, that I stood up in the theater and shouted: "Don't do it! It's not too late to change your minds, both of you. Nothing good will come of it, only remorse, hatred, scandal, and two children whose characters are monstrous." The whole audience turned to look at me, annoyed, the usher came hurrying down the aisle flashing his search-    17 light, and the old lady next to me tugged me down into my seat, saying: "Be quiet. You'll be put out, and you paid thirty-five cents to come in." And so I shut my eyes because I could not bear to see what was happening. I sat there quietly.


V

But after a while I begin to take brief glimpses and at length I 18 watch again with thirsty interest, like a child who tries to maintain his sulk when he is offered the bribe of candy. My parents are now having their picture taken in a photographer's booth along the boardwalk. The place is shadowed in the mauve light which is apparently necessary. The camera is set to the side on its tripod and looks like a Martian man. The photographer is instructing my parents in how to pose. My father has his arm over my mother's shoulder, and both of them smile emphatically. The photograpter brings my mother a bouquet of flowers to hold in her hand, but she holds it at the wrong angle. Then the photographer covers himself with the black cloth which drapes the camera and all that one sees of him is one protruding arm and his hand with which he holds tightly to the rubber ball which he squeezes when the picture is taken. But he is not satisfied with their appearance. He feels that somehow there is something wrong in their pose. Again and again he comes out from his hiding place with new directions. Each suggestion merely makes matters worse. My father is becoming impatient. They try a seated pose. The photographer explains that he has his pride, he wants to make beautiful pictures, he is not merely interested in all of this for the money. My father says: "Hurry up, will you? We haven't got all night." But the photographer only scurries about apologetically, issuing new directions. The photographer charms me, and I approve of him with all my heart, for I know exactly how he feels, and as he criticizes each revised pose according to some obscure idea of rightness, I become quite hopeful. But then my father says angrily: "Come on, you've had enough time, we're not going to wait any longer." And the photographer, sighing unhappily, goes back into the black covering, and holds out his hand, saying: "One, two, three, Now!," and the picture is taken, with my father's smile turned to a grimace and my mother's bright and false. It takes a few minutes for the picture to be developed and as my parents sit in the curious light they become depressed.

## VI

They have passed a fortune-teller's booth and my mother wishes     19
to go in, but my father does not. They begin to argue about it. My
mother becomes stubborn, my father once more impatient. What my
father would like to do now is walk off and leave my mother there, but
he knows that that would never do. My mother refuses to budge. She
is near tears, but she feels an uncontrollable desire to hear what the
palm-reader will say. My father consents angrily and they both go into
the booth which is, in a way, like the photographer's, since it is draped
in black cloth and its light is colored and shadowed. The place is too
warm, and my father keeps saying that this is all nonsense, pointing to
the crystal ball on the table. The fortune-teller, a short, fat woman
garbed in robes supposedly exotic, comes into the room and greets
them, speaking with an accent, but suddenly my father feels that the
whole thing is intolerable; he tugs at my mother's arm but my mother
refuses to budge. And then, in terrible anger, my father lets go of my
mother's arm and strides out, leaving my mother stunned. She makes
a movement as if to go after him, but the fortune-teller holds her and
begs her not to do so, and I in my seat in the darkness am shocked and
horrified. I feel as if I were walking a tight-rope one hundred feet over
a circus audience and suddenly the rope is showing signs of breaking,
and I get up from my seat and begin to shout once more the first words
I can think of to communicate my terrible fear, and once more the
usher comes hurrying down the aisle flashing his searchlight, and the
old lady pleads with me, and the shocked audience has turned to stare
at me, and I keep shouting: "What are they doing? Don't they know
what they are doing? Why doesn't my mother go after my father and
beg him not to be angry? If she does not do that, what will she do?
Doesn't my father know what he is doing?" But the usher has seized
my arm, and is dragging me away, and as he does so, he says: "What
are *you* doing? Don't you know you can't do things like this, you can't
do whatever you want to do, even if other people aren't about? You
will be sorry if you do not do what you should do. You can't carry on
like this, it is not right, you will find that out soon enough, everything
you do matters too much," and as he said that, dragging me through
the lobby of the theater, into the cold light, I woke up into the bleak
winter morning of my twenty-first birthday, the window-sill shining
with its lip of snow, and the morning already begun.

# from *Dispatches*

## MICHAEL HERR

*Name me someone that's not a parasite,*
*And I'll go out and say a prayer for him.*

Bob Dylan, "Visions of Johanna"

I keep thinking about all the kids who got wiped out by seventeen    1
years of war movies before coming to Vietnam to get wiped out for
good. You don't know what a media freak is until you've seen the way
a few of those grunts would run around during a fight when they knew
that there was a television crew nearby; they were actually making
war movies in their heads, doing little guts-and-glory Leatherneck tap
dances under fire, getting their pimples shot off for the networks. They
were insane, but the war hadn't done that to them. Most combat troops
stopped thinking of the war as an adventure after their first few fire-
fights, but there were always the ones who couldn't let that go, these
few who were up there doing numbers for the cameras. A lot of
correspondents weren't much better. We'd all seen too many movies,
stayed too long in Television City, years of media glut had made
certain connections difficult. The first few times that I got fired at or
saw combat deaths, nothing really happened, all the responses got
locked in my head. It was the same familiar violence, only moved over
to another medium; some kind of jungle play with giant helicopters
and fantastic special effects, actors lying out there in canvas body bags
waiting for the scene to end so they could get up again and walk it off.
But that was some scene (you found out), there was no cutting it.

A lot of things had to be unlearned before you could learn anything    2
at all, and even after you knew better you couldn't avoid the ways in
which things got mixed, the war itself with those parts of the war that
were just like the movies, just like *The Quiet American* or *Catch-22* (a
Nam standard because it said that in a war everybody thinks that
everybody else is crazy), just like all that combat footage from television ("We're taking fire from the treeline!" "Where?" "There!"
"Where?" "Over *there!*" "Over WHERE?" "Over THERE!!" Flynn

heard that go on for fifteen minutes once; we made it an epiphany), your vision blurring, images jumping and falling as though they were being received by a dropped camera, hearing a hundred horrible sounds at once—screams, sobs, hysterical shouting, a throbbing inside your head that threatened to take over, quavering voices trying to get the orders out, the dulls and sharps of weapons going off (Lore: When they're near they whistle, when they're really near they crack), the thud of helicopter rotors, the tinny, clouded voice coming over the radio, "Uh, that's a Rog, we mark your position, over." And out. Far out.

That feedback stalked you all over Vietnam, it often threatened    3
you with derangement, but somehow it always left you a little saner than you had any right to expect. Sometimes its intrusions could be subtle and ferocious. One afternoon during the battle for Hue, I was with David Greenway, a correspondent for *Time*, and we found it necessary to move from one Marine position to another. We were directly across from the south wall of the Citadel and airstrikes had dropped much of it down into the street, bringing with it torn, stinking portions of some North Vietnamese who had been dug in there. We had to make a run of something like 400 meters up that street, and we knew that the entire way was open to sniper fire, either from the standing sections of the wall on our right or from the rooftops on our left. When we'd run to our present position an hour earlier, David had gone first, and it was my turn now. We were crouching among some barren shrubbery with the Marines, and I turned to the guy next to me, a black Marine, and said, "Listen, we're going to cut out now. Will you cover us?" He gave me one of those amazed, penetrating looks. "You can go out there if you want to, baby, but shee-it . . ." and he began putting out fire. David and I ran all doubled over, taking cover every forty meters or so behind boulder-sized chunks of smashed wall, and halfway through it I started to laugh, looking at David and shaking my head. David was the most urbane of correspondents, a Bostonian of good family and impeccable education, something of a patrician even though he didn't care anything about it. We were pretty good friends, and he was willing to take my word for it that there was actually something funny, and he laughed too.

"What is it?" he said.                                              4

"Oh man, do you realize that I just asked that guy back there to    5
*cover us*?"

He looked at me with one eyebrow faintly cocked. "Yes," he said.   6
"Yes, you did. Oh, isn't that *marvelous!*"

And we would have laughed all the way up the street, except that   7
toward the end of it we had to pass a terrible thing, a house that had
been collapsed by the bombing, bringing with it a young girl who lay
stretched out dead on top of some broken wood. The whole thing was
burning, and the flames were moving closer and closer to her bare feet.
In a few minutes they were going to reach her, and from our conceal-
ment we were going to have to watch it. We agreed that anything was
better than that and we finished the run, but only after David spun
around, dropped to one knee and took a picture of it.

A few days after that, David's file from Hue appeared in *Time*,   8
worked over into that uni-prose which all news magazines and papers
maintained, placed somewhere among five or six other Vietnam stories
that had come in that week from the five or six other reporters *Time*
kept in Vietnam. About five months after that, a piece I'd written about
the battle appeared in *Esquire*, turning up like some lost dispatch from
the Crimea. I saw it in print for the first time on the day that we
returned from Mutter's Ridge, while the issue of *Time* which carried
David's story was on sale in Saigon and Danang within a week of the
events described. (I remember that issue in particular because General
Giap was on the cover and the South Vietnamese would not allow it to
be sold until a black X was scrawled over each copy, disfiguring but
hardly concealing Giap's face. People were doing weird things that
Tet.) What all of this means is that, no matter how much I love the
sound of it, there's no way that I can think of myself as a war correspondent without stopping to acknowledge the degree to which it's
pure affectation. I never had to run back to any bureau office to file (or,
worse, call it in from Danang over the knotted clot of military wires,
"Working, operator, I said working, hello, working. . . . Oh, you moron,
*working!*"). I never had to race out to the Danang airfield to get my
film on the eight-o'clock scatback to Saigon; there wasn't any bureau,
there wasn't any film, my ties to New York were as slight as my
assignment was vague. I wasn't really an oddity in the press corps, but
I was a peculiarity, an extremely privileged one. (An oddity was someone like the photographer John Schneider, who fixed a white flag to his
handlebars and took a bike from the top of Hill 881 North over to Hill
881 South during a terrible battle, in what came to be known as
Schneider's Ride; or the Korean cameraman who had spent four years

in Spain as a matador, who spoke exquisite, limpid Castilian and whom we called El Taikwando; or the Portuguese novelist who arrived at Khe Sanh in sports clothes, carrying a plaid suitcase, under the impression that field gear could be bought there.)

I'd run into Bernie Weinraub in Saigon, on his way to *The New York Times* bureau carrying a bunch of papers in his hand. He'd be coming back from a meeting with some of "the beautiful people" of the Joint U.S. Public Affairs Office, and he'd say, "I'm having a low-grade nervous breakdown right now. You can't really see it, but it's there. After you've been here awhile, you'll start having them too," laughing at the little bit of it that was true as much as at the part of it that had become our running joke. Between the heat and the ugliness and the pressures of filing, the war out there and the JUSPAO flacks right here, Saigon could be overwhelmingly depressing, and Bernie often looked possessed by it, so gaunt and tired and underfed that he could have brought out the Jewish mother in a Palestinian guerrilla.

"Let's have a drink," I'd say.

"No, no, I can't. You know how it is, we on the *Times* . . ." He'd start to laugh. "I mean, *we* have to file every day. It's a terrible responsibility, there's so little time. . . . I hope you'll understand."

"Of course. I'm sorry, I just wasn't thinking."

"Thank you, thank you."

But it was fine for me to laugh; he was going back to work, to write a story that would be published in New York hours later, and I was going across the street to the terrace bar of the Continental Hotel for a drink, possibly to write a few leisurely notes, probably not. I was spared a great deal, and except for a small handful of men who took their professional responsibilities very solemnly, no one ever held that against me. Whatever they came to know about the war was one thing; I know how they tried to get it into their stories, how generous they were as teachers and how embittering it all could become.

Because they worked in the news media, for organizations that were ultimately reverential toward the institutions involved: the Office of the President, the Military, America at war and, most of all, the empty technology that characterized Vietnam. There is no way of remembering good friends without remembering the incredible demands put on them from offices thousands of miles away. (Whenever the news chiefs and network vice-presidents and foreign editors would dress up in their Abercrombie & Fitch combat gear and come by for a firsthand look, a real story would develop, Snow In The Tropics, and after three days of high-level briefings and helicopter rides, they'd go home convinced that the war was over, that their men in the field were damned good men but a little too close to the story.) Somewhere on the periphery of that total Vietnam issue whose daily reports made the morning papers too heavy to bear, lost in the surreal contexts of television, there was a story that was as simple as it had always been, men hunting men, a hideous war and all kinds of victims. But there was also a Command that didn't feel this, that rode us into attrition traps on the back of fictional kill ratios, and an Administration that believed the Command, a cross-fertilization of ignorance, and a press whose tradition of objectivity and fairness (not to mention self-interest) saw that all of it got space. It was inevitable that once the media took the diversions seriously enough to report them, they also legitimized them. The spokesmen spoke in words that had no currency left as words, sentences with no hope of meaning in the sane world, and if much of it was sharply queried by the press, all of it got quoted. The press got all the facts (more or less), it got too many of them. But it never found a way to report meaningfully about death, which of course was really what it was all about. The most repulsive, transparent gropes for sanctity in the midst of the killing received serious treatment in the papers and on the air. The jargon of Progress got blown into your head like bullets, and by the time you waded through all the Washington stories and all the Saigon stories, all the Other War stories and the corruption stories and the stories about brisk new gains in ARVN effectiveness, the suffering was somehow unimpressive. And after enough years of that, so many that it seemed to have been going on forever, you got to a point where you could sit there in the evening and listen to the man say that American casualties for the week had reached a six-week low, only eighty GI's had died in combat, and you'd feel like you'd just gotten a bargain.

If you ever saw stories written by Peter Kann, William Touhy, 16 Tom Buckley, Bernie Weinraub, Peter Arnett, Lee Lescaze, Peter Braestrup, Charles Mohr, Ward Just or a few others, you'd know that most of what the Mission wanted to say to the American public was a psychotic vaudeville; that Pacification, for example, was hardly anything more than a swollen, computerized tit being forced upon an already violated population, a costly, valueless program that worked only in press conferences. Yet in the year leading up to the Tet Offensive ("1967—Year of Progress" was the name of an official year-end report) there were more stories about Pacification than there were about combat—front page, prime time, just as though it was really happening.

This was all part of a process which everyone I knew came grudg-          17
ingly to think of as routine, and I was free of it. What an incredible
hassle it would have been, having to run out to the airport to watch the
Mayor of Los Angeles embrace Mayor Cua of Saigon. (L.A. had declared Saigon its Sister City, dig it, and Yorty was in town to collect. If
there had been no newspapers or television, Cua and Yorty never
would have met.) I never had to cover luncheons given for members
of the Philippine Civic Action Group or laugh woodenly while the
Polish delegate to the International Control Commission lobbed a joke
on me. I never had to follow the Command to the field for those
interminable get-togethers with the troops. ("Where are you from,
son?" "Macon, Georgia, Sir." "Real fine. Are you getting your mail
okay, plenty of hot meals?" "Yes, Sir." "That's fine, where you from,
son?" "Oh, I don't know, God, I don't know, I don't *know!*" "That's
fine, real fine, where you from, son?") I never had to become familiar
with that maze of government agencies and sub-agencies, I never had
to deal with the Spooks. (They were from the real Agency, the CIA.
There was an endless Vietnam game played between the grunts and
the Spooks, and the grunts always lost.) Except to pick up my mail and
get my accreditation renewed, I never had to frequent JUSPAO unless
I wanted to. (That office had been created to handle press relations and
psychological warfare, and I never met anyone there who seemed to
realize that there was a difference.) I could skip the daily briefings, I
never had to cultivate Sources. In fact, my concerns were so rarefied
that I had to ask other correspondents what they ever found to ask
Westmoreland, Bunker, Komer and Zorthian. (Barry Zorthian was the
head of JUSPAO; for more than five years he *was* Information.) What
did anybody ever expect those people to *say?* No matter how highly
placed they were, they were still officials, their views were well established and well known, famous. It could have rained frogs over Tan Son
Nhut and they wouldn't have been upset; Cam Ranh Bay could have
dropped into the South China Sea and they would have found some
way to make it sound good for you; the Bo Doi Division (Ho's Own)
could have marched by the American embassy and they would have
characterized it as "desperate"—what did even the reporters closest to
the Mission Council ever find to write about when they'd finished their
interviews? (My own interview with General Westmoreland had been
hopelessly awkward. He'd noticed that I was accredited to *Esquire* and

asked me if I planned to be doing "humoristical" pieces. Beyond that, very little was really said. I came away feeling as though I'd just had a conversation with a man who touches a chair and says, "This is a chair," points to a desk and says, "This is a desk." I couldn't think of anything to ask him, and the interview didn't happen.) I honestly wanted to know what the form was for those interviews, but some of the reporters I'd ask would get very officious, saying something about "Command postures," and look at me as though I was insane. It was probably the kind of look that I gave one of them when he asked me once what I found to talk about with the grunts all the time, expecting me to confide (I think) that I found them as boring as he did.

And just-like-in-the-movies, there were a lot of correspondents 18 who did their work, met their deadlines, filled the most preposterous assignments the best they could and withdrew, watching the war and all its hideous secrets, earning their cynicism the hard way and turning their self-contempt back out again in laughter. If New York wanted to know how the troops felt about the assassination of Robert Kennedy, they'd go out and get it. ("Would you have voted for him?" "Yeah, he was a real good man, a real good man. He was, uh, young." "Who will you vote for now?" "Wallace, I guess.") They'd even gather troop reflections on the choice of Paris as the site of the peace talks. ("Paris? I dunno, sure, why not? I mean, they ain't gonna hold 'em in Hanoi, now are they?"), but they'd know how funny that was, how wasteful, how profane. They knew that, no matter how honestly they worked, their best work would somehow be lost in the wash of news, all the facts, all the Vietnam stories. Conventional journalism could no more reveal this war than conventional firepower could win it, all it could do was take the most profound event of the American decade and turn it into a communications pudding, taking its most obvious, undeniable history and making it into a secret history. And the very best correspondents knew even more than that.

There was a song by the Mothers of Invention called "Trouble 19 Comin' Every Day" that became a kind of anthem among a group of around twenty young correspondents. We'd play it often during those long night gatherings in Saigon, the ashtrays heaped over, ice buckets full of warm water, bottles empty, the grass all gone, the words running, "You know I watch that rotten box until my head begin to hurt, From checkin' out the way the newsmen say they get the dirt" (bitter funny looks passing around the room), "And if another woman driver gets machine-gunned from her seat, They'll send some joker with a

Brownie and you'll see it all complete" (lip-biting, flinching, nervous laughter), "And if the place blows up, we'll be the first to tell, 'Cause the boys we got downtown are workin' hard and doin' swell . . ." That wasn't really about *us*, no, we were *so* hip, and we'd laugh and wince every time we heard it, all of us, wire-service photographers and senior correspondents from the networks and special-assignment types like myself, all grinning together because of what we knew together, that in back of every column of print you read about Vietnam there was a dripping, laughing death-face; it hid there in the newspapers and magazines and held to your television screens for hours after the set was turned off for the night, an after-image that simply wanted to tell you at last what somehow had not been told.

On an afternoon shortly before the New Year, a few weeks before Tet, a special briefing was held in Saigon to announce the latest revisions in the hamlet-rating system of the Pacification program, the A-B-C-D profiling of the country's security and, by heavy inference, of the government's popular support "in the countryside," which meant any place outside of Saigon, the boonies. A lot of correspondents went, many because they had to, and I spent the time with a couple of photographers in one of the bars on Tu Do, talking to some soldiers from the 1st Infantry Division who had come down from their head-quarters at Lai Khe for the day. One of them was saying that Americans treated the Vietnamese like animals. 20

"How's that?" someone asked. 21

"Well, you know what we do to animals . . . kill 'em and hurt 'em and beat on 'em so's we can train 'em. Shit, we don't treat the Dinks no different than that." 22

And we knew that he was telling the truth. You only had to look at his face to see that he really knew what he was talking about. He wasn't judging it, I don't think that he was even particularly upset about it, it was just something he'd observed. We mentioned it later to some people who'd been at the Pacification briefing, someone from the *Times* and someone from the AP, and they both agreed that the kid from the Big Red One had said more about the Hearts-and-Minds program than they'd heard in over an hour of statistics, but their bureaus couldn't use his story, they wanted Ambassador Komer's. And they got it and you got it. 23

# Description

## Getting the Vegas Willies

### JOAN DIDION

Las Vegas hotels all smell alike. The Sands smells like the Fla- 1
mingo and the Flamingo smells like the Riviera and the Riviera smells
like the Dunes and the Dunes smells like the Stardust and also like the
Thunderbird, the Frontier, the Desert Inn, Caesars, the Hilton and the
MGM Grand. I had never set foot in the MGM Grand before last night
but I should have known how it would smell. This smell is sharp and
thin and chemical, not exactly the smell of air freshener and not exactly
the smell of air conditioning but acrid and a little stale and specific to
Vegas: I have never smelled it in the hotels of other cities, nor can I
duplicate it. The nearest I came was once when I threw a perfume box
on a fire that would not catch, but that smell went away, and the Vegas
smell does not. The Vegas smell permeates hair follicles and locked
suitcases and sealed packets of Kleenex and even the baggage carrou-
sels at LAX after a flight comes in from Vegas. The Vegas smell sticks.

The Vegas smell is with me today, and so is the Vegas fright, which 2
is what I am talking about here. This is a fright as particular and
specific to Las Vegas as the smell is particular and specific to Las Vegas,
and I have never gotten through a night there without catching it, like
a cold. Last night I thought I might. Last night I went to Las Vegas, for
the first time in six years, under the most benign and protected conditions possible: a friend, Helen Reddy, was opening at the MGM
Grand, and she and her husband, Jeffrey Wald, had invited seventy or
so people to fly in for the midnight show. Actually this kind of thing is
called a celebrity opening (CELEB OP is how the code reads on the
envelope with the room keys) and is a relatively fixed feature of life
among big-room Vegas headliners, but since Helen Reddy Wald is the
only friend I have who happens also to be a big-room Vegas headliner,

the details of the evening seemed to me entirely novel, and exotic, and to leave no time for the fright.

In the first place there was, for the hour's flight over, a chartered 3 Boeing 737. In the second place there were, when this Boeing 737 touched down at McCarran Field in Las Vegas, thirty limousines waiting on the tarmac, thirty Cadillac and Lincoln engines idling at wing tip, thirty drivers standing around in a light rain opening doors and holding umbrellas and waiting for the police escort to move the convoy out. The name HELEN REDDY blazed from a lighted marquee just off the tarmac. The name HELEN REDDY blazed from billboards every twenty yards on the drive from McCarran to the Grand. The police stopped traffic. Walkie-talkies crackled. The limos proceeded in formation through green lights and red. In front of the Grand there were crowds, cordoned off, and a red carpet and banks of blinding theatrical lights and, on top of every taxi, on every marquee, everywhere the eye rested, the name HELEN REDDY, and her face. So hallucinatory was the power of all this celebrity and all these arrangements that it was three in the morning, in a vast CELEB OP suite with a mirrored walk-in bathtub in the middle of the bedroom, before I caught the Vegas smell, the Vegas fright, the craven apprehension that I had to get out. On less benign nights in Vegas the fright has found me before I checked in. On this particular night, this three A.M., last night, this morning, it found me when I called room service, and was put on hold for fifty-eight minutes.

I suppose the fright comes because I do not understand. I did not 4 understand, for example, what the guests at a Strip hotel did ordinarily that gave them the psychic will and physical stamina to tie up room service for fifty-eight minutes at three A.M. I did not understand why so many men I had seen downstairs appeared to have nineteen-inch necks. I did not understand why anyone would arrive with his wife in Vegas for the weekend and rent a pink Cadillac Coupe De Ville, but I had watched such a rental arranged. I did not quite see why a woman visiting the Grand might decide to get some cosmetic breast surgery done and charge it to her room, but it was possible to do this, at the office of a Dr. Tippit, on the arcade level. I thought I knew why all the hookers in all the bars seemed gotten up for a Princeton weekend in 1956—their sweaters and skirts and little black dresses appeared, in situ, theatrical and seductive and slightly outrageous—but in that case I did not entirely understand the market for rhinestone brassieres in

the hotel shops. Nor did I understand, in the hotel shops, a certain rage
for large objects made entirely of spun glass: spun-glass whaling ships,
spun-glass caravans, spun-glass Washington monuments and spun-
glass dogs.

Q: *How do you get a three-foot spun-glass dog home from Vegas?*     5
A: *Rent it a pink Cadillac Coupe De Ville.*                          6

There is a great deal I never understand, out there on the Mojave     7
with the spun-glass dogs. I have never understood the ability of large
numbers of solid citizens to land at McCarran and enter cheerfully into
the spirit of a Genet brothel. I have never understood why the point
of the exercise is believed to be money, when the place is in fact
profoundly immaterial, all symbol, all light and shadow and metaphor,
a tableau vivant of lust and greed. I know Law Vegas to be a theater
dedicated to the immediate gratification of every impulse, but I also
know it to be a theater designed to numb those very impulses it
promises to gratify. Nobody in this theater rushes the stage. Nobody
handles the actual money. I know Las Vegas to be The Entertainment
Capital of the World, but I also know it to be a capital of the willies,
a place where the promise is everything and the payoff elusive, a place
where the level of frustration and nervous boredom is so pronounced
that a crowd will form around the search for a dropped dime. I recall
once drawing a crowd in the lobby of the Stardust simply by asking to
see the assistant manager. Certain tables will attract crowds and then,
with no perceptible change in the play, lose them. Lights flash and no
one blinks.

A glaze of overstimulation hangs over these crowds that form and     8
dissolve. A kind of electrical charging and recharging replaces all one's
notions of cause and effect. The name "Carl Cohen" on a Vegas paging
system will always draw a crowd. All I know about Carl Cohen is that
he used to manage the Sands casino and that he once hit Frank Sinatra
and that, on the evidence, watching him take a telephone call is considered something to do. Those crowds cordoned off in front of the Grand
last night appeared to have gathered and to disperse with no particular
rise and fall in expectations: watching a couple of William Morris
agents get out of a limousine and watching Olivia Newton-John get out
of a limousine seemed equally to satisfy the watchers, resolve the
moment, discharge the electricity and fill the time. Time is a great
presence in Vegas, since the only obligation is to fill it. People filling
time move around the Strip in waves, flowing from casino to casino,
swirling through a keno lounge here, eddying around a showroom door

there, flooding on out to wait a moment under the bright cold crosswalk lights and then, as if programmed to some lunar pull, surging on to fill another keno lounge, watch Carl Cohen take another call. The place is a hydraulic model of human tedium.

*Vegas notes.* (1) At a party in Beverly Hills I was once seated next    9
to a stranger who played the Riviera several times a year. I asked him how he filled the day in Vegas. He looked at me as if I were demented. He said filling the day was "no problem at the Riv." He said he got up, ordered breakfast, played nine holes, took some steam and did the dinner show. He did not understand me any better than I understand Vegas. (2) When my mother first saw the Las Vegas Strip she was surprised and disappointed. She had been hearing for years about these hotels, she said, and she had imagined places more along the lines of the Broadmoor or the Greenbrier. "Caesars Palace has no lawn," my mother said. My mother does not understand Vegas any better than I do. (3) My husband wrote a book in Vegas and for a year and a half maintained a furnished duplex apartment just off the Strip. I bought dishes and wastebaskets and three changes of king-size sheets for this apartment but saw it only once, the day he vacated it. I say "vacated" rather than "moved out" because he never exactly lived in this apartment: during the eighteen months of his tenancy he slept in the king-size bed only two or three times. Sometimes he would take a look at the apartment and then check into a motel. Later on he began skipping the look. He says that he does not understand Vegas any better than I do but I believe he does: anyone who could keep an empty duplex apartment off the Las Vegas Strip and sleep in a motel a few blocks away has some instinct for the radical immateriality of the place, and also for the willies.

Fly out of Vegas and the lights go off. The hallucination vanishes.    10
I recall a night in 1968 when my husband happened to be in New York and I happened to be in Las Vegas, reporting a piece and having a bad time. To be a woman alone in Vegas is usually to have a bad time, to be made immediately aware of one's class position. We are all "sweetie" and "sweetheart" and "dear" to the Vegas management. We are all out for something: a comped meal, an angle. They have seen us before. They have our number. On this particular night in 1968 I had checked into the Sands and ordered a sandwich and the room-service waiter had advised me that there was no need for me to be

alone: there were a lot of lonely people around, and he knew where.
I recognize now that this was on the part of the waiter no more than
a reflex, a Vegas tic, but at the time it unnerved me, and I called my
husband for solace. Never mind that, he said when I finally got him in
New York: he had just visited a circle of New York hell. He had just
come from the Oak Room of The Plaza, where he had seen, having
dinner together at the table next to his, Clay Felker, Gloria Steinem,
Arthur Schlesinger Jr. and Leonard Lyons.

I said what about me.                                                11

He said what about you?                                              12

I said quite frankly I would rather be having dinner at The Plaza    13
with Clay Felker, Gloria Steinem, Arthur Schlesinger Jr. and Leonard
Lyons than having a sandwich alone at the Sands with the room-
service waiter trying to fix me up.

"That's just Vegas, it doesn't figure," my husband said, and of      14
course he was right. Vegas figures only in the minds of those who are
there. I know for a fact that Ann-Margaret is playing the Hilton to-
night. I know that Bobbie Gentry is playing the Frontier. I know that
Helen Reddy is sold out at the Grand and I know that someone is
paging Carl Cohen and I know that outside the blackout curtains in the
vast CELEB OP suite where I slept last night there is still this view: the
roof of the jai alai palace and an empty lot where the sand is blowing.
I know that at the airport the taped voices of Liberace and Joan Rivers
and Jan Murray are even now advising travelers to take it easy on the
moving sidewalk, stand to the right and pass to the left "and come see
my show." I know the place is out there, but all that sticks now is the
smell.

---

# Nameless, Tennessee

## WILLIAM LEAST HEAT MOON

Nameless, Tennessee, was a town of maybe ninety people if you        1
pushed it, a dozen houses along the road, a couple of barns, same
number of churches, a general merchandise store selling Fire Chief
gasoline, and a community center with a lighted volleyball court. Behind the center was an open-roof, rusting metal privy with PAINT ME

on the door; in the hollow of a nearby oak lay a full pint of Jack Daniel's Black Label. From the houses, the odor of coal smoke.

Next to a red tobacco barn stood the general merchandise with a poster of Senator Albert Gore, Jr., smiling from the window. I knocked. The door opened partway. A tall, thin man said, "Closed up. For good." and started to shut the door.                                       2

"Don't want to buy anything. Just a question for Mr. Thurmond Watts."                                                                          3

The man peered through the slight opening. He looked me over. "What question would that be?"                                                 4

"If this is Nameless, Tennessee, could he tell me how it got that name?"                                                                        5

The man turned back into the store and called out, "Miss Ginny! Somebody here wants to know how Nameless come to be Nameless."       6

Miss Ginny edged to the door and looked me and my truck over. Clearly, she didn't approve. She said, "You know as well as I do, Thurmond. Don't keep him on the stoop in the damp to tell him." Miss Ginny, I found out, was Mrs. Virginia Watts, Thurmond's wife.   7

I stepped in and they both began telling the story, adding a detail here, the other correcting a fact there, both smiling at the foolishness of it all. It seems the hilltop settlement went for years without a name. Then one day the Post Office Department told the people if they wanted mail up on the mountain they would have to give the place a name you could properly address a letter to. The community met; there were only a handful, but they commenced debating. Some wanted patriotic names, some names from nature, one man recommended in all seriousness his own name. They couldn't agree, and they ran out of names to argue about. Finally, a fellow tired of the talk; he didn't like the mail he received anyway. "Forget the durn Post Office," he said. "This here's a nameless place if I ever seen one, so leave it be." And that's just what they did.                                            8

Watts pointed out the window. "We used to have signs on the road, but the Halloween boys keep tearin' them down."                           9

"You think Nameless is a funny name," Miss Ginny said. "I see it plain in your eyes. Well, you take yourself up north a piece to Difficult or Defeated or Shake Rag. Now them are silly names."                       10

The old store, lighted only by three fifty-watt bulbs, smelled of coal oil and baking bread. In the middle of the rectangular room, where the oak floor sagged a little, stood an iron stove. To the right was a wooden table with an unfinished game of checkers and a stool made from an    11 apple-tree stump. On shelves around the walls sat earthen jugs with corncob stoppers, a few canned goods, and some of the two thousand old clocks and clockworks Thurmond Watts owned. Only one was ticking; the others he just looked at. I asked how long he'd been in the store.

"Thirty-five years, but we closed the first day of the year. We're hopin' to sell it to a churchly couple. Upright people. No athians." 12

"Did you build this store?" 13

"I built this one, but it's the third general store on the ground. I fear it'll be the last. I take no pleasure in that. Once you could come in here for a gallon of paint, a pickle, a pair of shoes, and a can of corn." 14

"Or horehound candy," Miss Ginny said. "Or corsets and slaves. We had cough syrups and all that for the body. In season, we'd buy and sell blackberries and walnuts and chestnuts, before the blight got them. And outside, Thurmond milled corn and sharpened plows. Even shoed a horse sometimes." 15

"We could fix up a horse or a man or a baby," Watts said. 16

"Thurmond, tell him we had a doctor on the ridge in them days." 17

"We had a doctor on the ridge in them days. As good as any doctor alivin'. He'd cut a crooked toenail or deliver a woman. Dead these last years." 18

"I got some bad ham meat one day," Miss Ginny said, "and took to vomitin'. All day, all night. Hangin' on the drop edge of yonder. I said to Thurmond, Thurmond, unless you want shut of me, call the doctor.'" 19

"I studied on it," Watts said. 20

"You never did. You got him right now. He come over and put three drops of iodeen in half a glass of well water. I drank it down and the vomitin' stopped with the last swallow. Would you think iodeen could do that?" 21

"He put Miss Ginny on one teaspoon of spirits of ammonia in well water for her nerves. Ain't nothin' works better for her to this day." 21

"Calms me like the hand of the Lord." 22

Hilda, the Wattses' daughter, came out of the backroom. "I remember him," she said. "I was just a baby. Y'all were talkin' to him, and he lifted me up on the counter and gave me a stick of Juicy Fruit and a piece of cheese." 23

"Knew the old medicines," Watts said. "Only drugstore he needed was a good kitchen cabinet. None of them antee-beeotics that hit you worsen your ailment. Forgotten lore now, the old medicines, because they ain't profit in iodeen." 24

Miss Ginny started back to the side room where she and her sister     25
Marilyn were taking apart a duck-down mattress to make bolsters. She
stopped at the window for another look at Ghost Dancing. "How do
you sleep in that thing? Ain't you all cramped and cold?"

"How does the clam sleep in his shell?" Watts said in my defense.     26

"Thurmond, get the boy a piece of buttermilk pie afore he goes         27
on."

"Hilda, get him some buttermilk pie." He looked at me. "You           28
like good music?" I said I did. He cranked up an old Edison phono-
graph, the kind with the big morning-glory blossom for a speaker,
and put on a wax cylinder. "This will be 'My Mother's Prayer,' " he
said.

While I ate buttermilk pie, Watts served as disc jockey of Name-      29
less, Tennessee. "Here's 'Mountain Rose.' " It was one of those moments that you know at the time will stay with you to the grave: the
sweet pie, the gaunt man playing the old music, the coals in the stove
glowing orange, the scent of kerosene and hot bread. "Here's 'Evening
Rhapsody.' " The music was so heavily romantic we both laughed. I
thought: It is for this I have come.

Feathered over and giggling, Miss Ginny stepped from the side         30
room. She knew she was a sight. "Thurmond, give him some lunch. Still
looks hungry."

Hilda pulled food off the woodstove in the backroom: home-            31
butchered and canned whole-hog sausage, home-canned June apples,
turnip greens, cole slaw, potatoes, stuffing, hot cornbread. All delicious.

Watts and Hilda sat and talked while I ate. "Wish you would join      32
me."

"We've ate," Watts said. "Cain't beat a woodstove for flavorful       33
cookin'."

He told me he was raised in a one-hundred-fifty-year-old cabin        34
still standing in one of the hollows. "How many's left," he said, "that
grew up in a log cabin? I ain't the last surely, but I must be climbin'
on the list."

Hilda cleared the table. "You Watts ladies know how to cook."         35

"She's in nursin' school at Tennessee Tech. I went over for one       36
of them football games last year there at Coevul." To say *Cookeville*,
you let the word collapse in upon itself so that it comes out "Coevul."

"Do you like football?" I asked.                                      37

◊     ◊     ◊

"Don't know. I was so high up in that stadium, I never opened my   38
eyes."

Watts went to the back and returned with a fat spiral notebook   39
that he set on the table. His expression had changed. "Miss Ginny's
*Deathbook.*"

The thing startled me. Was it something I was supposed to sign?   40
He opened it but said nothing. There were scads of names written in
a tidy hand over pages incised to crinkliness by a ballpoint. Chronologi-
cally, the names had piled up: wives, grandparents, a stillborn infant,
relatives, friends close and distant. Names, names. After each, the date
of *the* unknown finally known and transcribed. The last entry bore
yesterday's date.

"She's wrote out twenty years' worth. Every day she listens to the   41
hospital report on the radio and puts the names in. Folks come by to
check a date. Or they just turn through the books. Read them like a
scrapbook."

Hilda said, "Like Saint Peter at the gates inscribin' the names."   42

Watts took my arm. "Come along." He led me to the fruit cellar   43
under the store. As we went down, he said, "Always take a newborn
baby upstairs afore you take him downstairs, otherwise you'll incline
him downwards."

The cellar was dry and full of cobwebs and jar after jar of home-   44
canned food, the bottles organized as a shopkeeper would: sausage,
pumpkin, sweet pickles, tomatoes, corn relish, blackberries, peppers,
squash, jellies. He held a hand out toward the dusty bottles. "Our
tomorrows."

Upstairs again, he said, "Hope to sell the store to the right folk. I   45
see now, though, it'll be somebody offen the ridge. I've studied on it,
and maybe it's the end of our place." He stirred the coals. "This store
could give a comfortable livin', but not likely get you rich. But just
gettin' by is dice rollin' to people nowadays. I never did see my day
guaranteed."

When it was time to go, Watts said, "If you find anyone along your   46
way wants a good store—on the road to Cordell Hull Lake—tell them
about us."

I said I would. Miss Ginny and Hilda and Marilyn came out to say   47
goodbye. It was cold and drizzling again. "Weather to give a man the
weary dismals," Watts grumbled. "Where you headed from here?"

"I don't know."   48

"Cain't get lost then."   49

Miss Ginny looked again at my rig. It had worried her from the   50
first as it had my mother. "I hope you don't get yourself kilt in that durn
thing gallivantin' around the country."

"Come back when the hills dry off," Watts said. "We'll go lookin'   51
for some of them round rocks all sparkly inside."

I thought a moment. "Geodes?"   52

"Them's the ones. The country's properly full of them."   53

---

# The First Morning

## EDWARD ABBEY

This is the most beautiful place on earth.   1

There are many such places. Every man, every woman, carries in   2
heart and mind the image of the ideal place, the right place, the one
true home, known or unknown, actual or visionary. A houseboat in
Kashmir, a view down Atlantic Avenue in Brooklyn, a gray gothic
farmhouse two stories high at the end of a red dog road in the Al-
legheny Mountains, a cabin on the shore of a blue lake in spruce and
fir country, a greasy alley near the Hoboken waterfront, or even,
possibly, for those of a less demanding sensibility, the world to be seen
from a comfortable apartment high in the tender, velvety smog of
Manhattan, Chicago, Paris, Tokyo, Rio or Rome—there's no limit to
the human capacity for the homing sentiment. Theologians, sky pilots,
astronauts have even felt the appeal of home calling to them from up
above, in the cold black outback of intersteller space.

For myself I'll take Moab, Utah. I don't mean the town itself, of   3
course, but the country which surrounds it—the canyonlands. The
slickrock desert. The red dust and the burnt cliffs and the lonely
sky—all that which lies beyond the end of the roads.

The choice became apparent to me this morning when I stepped   4
out of a Park Service housetrailer—my caravan—to watch for the first
time in my life the sun come up over the hoodoo stone of Arches
National Monument.

I wasn't able to see much of it last night. After driving all day from   5
Albuquerque—450 miles—I reached Moab after dark in cold, windy,

clouded weather. At park headquarters north of town I met the superintendent and the chief ranger, the only permanent employees, except
for one maintenance man, in this particular unit of America's national
park system. After coffee they gave me a key to the housetrailer and
directions on how to reach it; I am required to live and work not at
headquarters but at this one-man station some twenty miles back in
the interior, on my own. The way I wanted it, naturally, or I'd never
have asked for the job.

Leaving the headquarters area and the lights of Moab, I drove    6
twelve miles farther north on the highway until I came to a dirt road
on the right, where a small wooden sign pointed the way: Arches
National Monument Eight Miles. I left the pavement, turned east into
the howling wilderness. Wind roaring out of the northwest, black
clouds across the stars—all I could see were clumps of brush and
scattered junipers along the roadside. Then another modest signboard:

WARNING: QUICKSAND
DO NOT CROSS WASH
WHEN WATER IS RUNNING

The wash looked perfectly dry in my headlights. I drove down,    7
across, up the other side and on into the night. Glimpses of weird
humps of pale rock on either side, like petrified elephants, dinosaurs,
stone-age hobgoblins. Now and then something alive scurried across
the road: kangaroo mice, a jackrabbit, an animal that looked like a
cross between a raccoon and a squirrel—the ringtail cat. Farther on a
pair of mule deer started from the brush and bounded obliquely
through the beams of my lights, raising puffs of dust which the wind,
moving faster than my pickup truck, caught and carried ahead of me
out of sight into the dark. The road, narrow and rocky, twisted sharply
left and right, dipped in and out of tight ravines, climbing by degrees
toward a summit which I would see only in the light of the coming day.

Snow was swirling through the air when I crossed the unfenced    8
line and passed the boundary marker of the park. A quarter-mile
beyond I found the ranger station—a wide place in the road, an infor-
mational display under a lean-to shelter, and fifty yards away the little
tin government housetrailer where I would be living for the next six
months.

A cold night, a cold wind, the snow falling like confetti. In the    9
lights of the truck I unlocked the housetrailer, got out bedroll and

baggage and moved in. By flashlight I found the bed, unrolled my sleeping bag, pulled off my boots and crawled in and went to sleep at once. The last I knew was the shaking of the trailer in the wind and the sound, from inside, of hungry mice scampering around with the good news that their long lean lonesome winter was over—their friend and provider had finally arrived.

This morning I awake before sunrise, stick my head out of the sack,   10 peer through a frosty window at a scene dim and vague with flowing mists, dark fantastic shapes looming beyond. An unlikely landscape.

I get up, moving about in long underwear and socks, stooping   11 carefully under the low ceiling and the lower doorways of the house-trailer, a machine for living built so efficiently and compactly there's hardly room for a man to breathe. An iron lung it is, with windows and venetian blinds.

The mice are silent, watching me from their hiding places, but the   12 wind is still blowing and outside the ground is covered with snow. Cold as a tomb, a jail, a cave; I lie down on the dusty floor, on the cold linoleum sprinkled with mouse turds, and light the pilot on the butane heater. Once this thing gets going the place warms up fast, in a dense unhealthy way, with a layer of heat under the ceiling where my head is and nothing but frigid air from the knees down. But we've got all the indispensable conveniences: gas cookstove, gas refrigerator, hot water heater, sink with running water (if the pipes aren't frozen), storage cabinets and shelves, everything within arm's reach of everything else. The gas comes from two steel bottles in a shed outside; the water comes by gravity flow from a tank buried in a hill close by. Quite luxurious for the wilds. There's even a shower stall and a flush toilet with a dead rat in the bowl. Pretty soft. My poor mother raised five children without any of these luxuries and might be doing without them yet if it hadn't been for Hitler, war and general prosperity.

Time to get dressed, get out and have a look at the lay of the land,   13 fix a breakfast. I try to pull on my boots but they're stiff as iron from the cold. I light a burner on the stove and hold the boots upside down above the flame until they are malleable enough to force my feet into. I put on a coat and step outside. In the center of the world, God's navel, Abbey's country, the red wasteland.

The sun is not yet in sight but signs of the advent are plain to see.   14 Lavender clouds sail like a fleet of ships across the pale green dawn; each cloud, planed flat on the wind, has a base of fiery gold. Southeast, twenty miles by line of sight, stand the peaks of the Sierra La Sal,

twelve to thirteen thousand feet above sea level, all covered with snow
and rosy in the morning sunlight. The air is dry and clear as well as
cold; the last fogbanks left over from last night's storm are scudding
away like ghosts, fading into nothing before the wind and the sunrise.

The view is open and perfect in all directions except to the west      15
where the ground rises and the skyline is only a few hundred yards
away. Looking toward the mountains I can see the dark gorge of the
Colorado River five or six miles away, carved through the sandstone
mesa, though nothing of the river itself down inside the gorge. South-
ward, on the far side of the river, lies the Moab valley between thou-
sand-foot walls of rock, with the town of Moab somewhere on the
valley floor, too small to be seen from here. Beyond the Moab valley
is more canyon and tableland stretching away to the Blue Mountains
fifty miles south. On the north and northwest I see the Roan Cliffs and
the Book Cliffs, the two-level face of the Uinta Plateau. Along the foot
of those cliffs, maybe thirty miles off, invisible from where I stand, runs
U.S. 6–50, a major east-west artery of commerce, traffic and rubbish,
and the main line of the Denver–Rio Grande Railroad. To the east,
under the spreading sunrise, are more mesas, more canyons, league on
league of red cliff and arid tablelands, extending through purple haze
over the bulging curve of the planet to the ranges of Colorado—a sea
of desert.

Within this vast perimeter, in the middle ground and foreground     16
of the picture, a rather personal demesne, are the 33,000 acres of
Arches National Monument of which I am now sole inhabitant, usu-
fructuary, observer and custodian.

What are the Arches? From my place in front of the housetrailer     17
I can see several of the hundred or more of them which have been
discovered in the park. These are natural arches, holes in the rock,
windows in stone, no two alike, as varied in form as in dimension. They
range in size from holes just big enough to walk through to openings
large enough to contain the dome of the Capitol building in Washington, D.C. Some resemble jug handles or flying buttresses, others natural bridges but with this technical distinction: a natural bridge spans a
watercourse—a natural arch does not. The arches were formed
through hundreds of thousands of years by the weathering of the huge
sandstone walls, or fins, in which they are found. Not the work of a
cosmic hand, nor sculptured by sand-bearing winds, as many people
prefer to believe, the arches came into being and continue to come into
being through the modest wedging action of rainwater, melting snow,

frost, and ice, aided by gravity. In color they shade from off-white through buff, pink, brown and red, tones which also change with the time of day and the moods of the light, the weather, the sky.

Standing there, gaping at this monstrous and inhuman spectacle of rock and cloud and sky and space, I feel a ridiculous greed and possessiveness come over me. I want to know it all, possess it all, embrace the entire scene intimately, deeply, totally, as a man desires a beautiful woman. An insane wish? Perhaps not—at least there's nothing else, no one human, to dispute possession with me. 18

The snow-covered ground glimmers with a dull blue light, reflecting the sky and the approaching sunrise. Leading away from me the narrow dirt road, an alluring and primitive track into nowhere, meanders down the slope and toward the heart of the labyrinth of naked stone. Near the first group of arches, looming over a bend in the road, is a balanced rock about fifty feet high, mounted on a pedestal of equal height; it looks like a head from Easter Island, a stone god or a petrified ogre. 19

Like a god, like an ogre? The personification of the natural is exactly the tendency I wish to suppress in myself, to eliminate for good. I am here not only to evade for a while the clamor and filth and confusion of the cultural apparatus but also to confront, immediately and directly if it's possible, the bare bones of existence, the elemental and fundamental, the bedrock which sustains us. I want to be able to look at and into a juniper tree, a piece of quartz, a vulture, a spider, and see it as it is in itself, devoid of all humanly ascribed qualities, anti-Kantian, even the categories of scientific description. To meet God or Medusa face to face, even if it means risking everything human in myself. I dream of a hard and brutal mysticism in which the naked self merges with a non-human world and yet somehow survives still intact, individual, separate. Paradox and bedrock. 20

Well—the sun will be up in a few minutes and I haven't even begun to make coffee. I take more baggage from my pickup, the grub box and cooking gear, go back in the trailer and start breakfast. Simply breathing, in a place like this, arouses the appetite. The orange juice is frozen, the milk slushy with ice. Still chilly enough inside the trailer to turn my breath to vapor. When the first rays of the sun strike the cliffs I fill a mug with steaming coffee and sit in the doorway facing the sunrise, hungry for the warmth. 21

Suddenly it comes, the flaming globe, blazing on the pinnacles and minarets and balanced rocks, on the canyon walls and through the 22 windows in the sandstone fins. We greet each other, sun and I, across the black void of ninety-three million miles. The snow glitters between us, acres of diamonds almost painful to look at. Within an hour all the snow exposed to the sunlight will be gone and the rock will be damp and steaming. Within minutes, even as I watch, melting snow begins to drip from the branches of a juniper nearby; drops of water streak slowly down the side of the trailerhouse.

I am not alone after all. Three ravens are wheeling near the      23
balanced rock, squawking at each other and at the dawn. I'm sure they're as delighted by the return of the sun as I am and I wish I knew the language. I'd sooner exchange ideas with the birds on earth than learn to carry on intergalactic communications with some obscure race of humanoids on a satellite planet from the world of Betelgeuse. First things first. The ravens cry out in husky voices, blue-black wings flapping against the golden sky. Over my shoulder comes the sizzle and smell of frying bacon.

That's the way it was this morning.                               24

---

# The Wedding

## ANDREA LEE

Rima and Vasia got married a few days ago, on a sunny morning      1
when a green mist of budding foliage hung around the trees all over the city. We met them at a Palace of Weddings in northwest Moscow, a nineteenth-century mansion on a quiet tree-lined street; they entered with a sizable group of friends and family. Rima was wearing an embroidered gauze dress with slightly medieval lines that suited her austere beauty. Her face was waxen with excitement, and her eyes, the overvivid eyes of icons and Early Christian paintings, had a tearful glaze. She came up to me and whispered, "My dress—it's still damp! Nadia and I washed it last night, but had no way to get it dry. Does it look awful?"

"You look beautiful," I said, turning her around to tighten her   2
sash. "And Vasia does too."

"Oh, he's always a wonder," she said, smiling radiantly across the 3 room to where Vasia stood talking to some friends. Vasia wore a brownish suit, the first I'd ever seen him in, and he had tied back his long hair. His handsome fair-skinned face looked absurdly ruddy and clean, as if he'd scrubbed it for hours, and this, coupled with an expression of determined solemnity, made him look far younger than his nineteen years—a bit like a Sunday School student about to give a speech. His mother hovered around him, straightening his collar, and he batted her away impatiently.

We all stood around making strained conversation in the waiting    4
room, which was one of several in the Palace of Weddings, all of them high-ceilinged, painted in institutional pastels, and furnished, in a grisly attempt at elegance, with faded-pink banquettes, a few uncomfortable straight-backed chairs, lace curtains, and several rubber plants of alarming size and vigor. To promote a festive spirit, there was a loudspeaker playing some selections from the popular disco group Boney M.: unbelievably, the song most often repeated was "Love for Sale." Other bridal parties stood nearby, the brides dressed in white gowns and clutching bouquets of gladioli wrapped in cellophane. As people often do in restaurants here, when they are forced to double up at tables with strangers, each wedding party was politely pretending that the others didn't exist. In a corner of the big room, a buxom girl of seventeen or eighteen wearing a wedding dress she'd obviously sewn herself and a stiff ruffle with cloth daisies pinned to her head, sat alone, clasping and unclasping her hands and peering tensely at the door. She looked as if she were about to burst into tears. All the wedding parties had been assigned a time for the brief ceremony that would take place in what must have been the central reception room of the old mansion. Even now we could hear parties entering the room; each time, a bossy female voice ordered them to line up, and when the door opened, there was the same burst of music—the first few bars of Mendelssohn's "Wedding March," played either on a recording or by a trio of live musicians. The live music cost extra, Vasia told me.

We heard the burst of Mendelssohn about five times before we    5
lined up, and then suddenly the tall doors had opened for us, and we were entering the wedding chamber, a red-carpeted, high-ceilinged room, with ornate plaster moldings and a set of large windows overlooking a garden full of the light green of budding lilac bushes. Rima and Vasia had paid for live music, and so the trio—two glum violinists and a pianist—leaped into a sprightly rendition of the Mendelssohn, stopping abruptly at the fifth bar as if their throats had been cut. From

behind an immense, ornate wooden desk, a ruddy-faced woman wearing a red shoulder sash adorned with a large metal seal beckoned to
Vasia and Rima, and they advanced to stand in front of her. The
ceremony was as brief and routine as any performed by an American
justice of the peace. When it was finished, Vasia and Rima signed the
register with a pen that for some reason had an elaborate curling
plume at least three feet high. A little lame-footed official photographer took pictures of the signing, and the bridal pair with all of us.
Then the long-nosed woman who had shepherded us into the room
said, "Come on, comrades! Let's go, citizens!"—and we moved out
through a side door into a small room where the picture-taking continued. As the door to the wedding chamber closed, I caught sight of
the woman behind the desk stifling a yawn. In a minute the musicians
raced once more into the Mendelssohn march.

  "Well, now begins the fun part of the wedding," murmured    6
Rima's friend Larisa as we all stood in line to embrace Rima. "At least
they're not going to lay flowers on the Tomb of the Unknown Soldier."
The patriotic custom of leaving a bridal bouquet at the Tomb of the
Unknown Soldier in Red Square is so widespread that on any pleasant
day in the fall or spring, one can see five or six brides heading in that
direction, their white veils floating like foam on the wave of pedestri-
ans passing the Kremlin. The next leg of a typical bridal journey is the
classic trip to the Lenin Hills to drink champagne and be photographed
against the view; this is such a standard excursion that the bridal
limousines rented for the day automatically make both stops—there's
no avoiding them. Rima, as a bride for the second time and an artistic
free spirit, had, as far as she could, avoided this standard route. Now
all of us were headed out to a party at a friend's apartment in the
country, where the food and toasts and company would make up for
anything the ceremony had lacked. Coming down the steps of the
Palace of Weddings into the light sweet air of the April morning, I
didn't feel as if I'd just witnessed the joining of two loving hearts;
instead I felt melancholy and slightly foot-weary, as if I'd just finished
touring a factory. I watched four more wedding parties approach the
entrance, and thought what a curious country this was, that could join
the socialist spirit of mass production so unbeautifully to bourgeois
frills—limousines, white dresses, Mendelssohn. Rima and Vasia had
looked like a young king and queen at each other's side, and I wished
that they had had a worthy setting—a bower, perhaps, decked out with
lilies and cloth-of-silver, with music—a triumphal march—played all

the way through. As I paused on the sidewalk, Rima's beautiful friend
Nadia came up to me, wearing a homemade peach-colored dress and
a pair of plastic sandals so ill-fitting that they should never have been
allowed on her feet. Looking at her, I thought how many lovely things
in this country were destined never to receive their due. Her red lips
wore a quizzical half-smile that reflected my own mixed feelings about
the wedding, and the message she leaned over to whisper in my ear
was not one of the usual light-hearted sentiments that people share on
such festive occasions. "I'm so glad for Rima," she said. "So relieved!
Now that she's married again, they can no longer condemn her as a
parasite. She's a wife now, and if she doesn't have official work, that's
all right. She's respectable—she's safe."

---

# Entering the Conversation of the University

## MIKE ROSE

If you walked out the back door of 9116 South Vermont and across 1
our narrow yard, you would run smack into those four single-room
rentals and, alongside them, an old wooden house-trailer. The trailer
had belonged to Mrs. Jolly, the woman who sold us the property. It was
locked and empty, and its tires were flat and fused into the asphalt
driveway. Rusted dairy cases had been wedged in along its sides and
four corners to keep it balanced. Two of its eight windows were broken, the frames were warped, and the door stuck. I was getting way
too old to continue sharing a room with my mother, so I began to eye
that trailer. I decided to refurbish it. It was time to have a room of my
own.

Lou Minton had, by now, moved in with us, and he and I fixed the 2
windows and realigned the door. I painted the inside by combining
what I could find in our old shed with what I could afford to buy: The
ceiling became orange, the walls yellow, the rim along the windows flat
black. Lou redid the wiring and put in three new sockets. I got an old
record player from the second-hand store for five dollars. I had Roy

Herweck, the illustrator of our high school annual, draw women in
mesh stockings and other objets d'redneck art on the yellow walls, and
I put empty Smirnoff and Canadian Club bottles on the ledges above
the windows. I turned the old trailer into the kind of bachelor digs a
seventeen-year-old in South L.A. would fancy. My friends from high
school began congregating there. When she could, my mother would
make us a pot of spaghetti or pasta fasul'. And there was a clerk across
the street at Marty's Liquor who would sell to us: We would run back
across Vermont Avenue laughing and clutching our bags and seal
ourselves up in the trailer. We spun fantasies about the waitress at the
Mexican restaurant and mimicked our teachers and caught touchdown
passes and, in general, dreamed our way through adolescence. It was
a terrible time for rock 'n' roll—Connie Francis and Bobby Rydell were
headliners in 1961—so we found rhythm and blues on L.A.'s one black
station, played the backroom ballads of troubadour Oscar Brand, and
discovered Delta and Chicago blues on Pacifica's KPFK:

I'm a man
I'm a full-grown man

    As I fell increasingly under Mr. MacFarland's spell, books began      3
replacing the liquor bottles above the windows: *The Trial* and *Waiting
for Godot* and *No Exit* and *The Stranger.* Roy sketched a copy of the
back cover of *Exile and the Kingdom,* and so the pensive face of Albert
Camus now looked down from that patch of wall on which a cartoon
had once pressed her crossed legs. My mother found a quilt that my
grandmother had sewn from my father's fabric samples. It was dark
and heavy, and I would lie under it and read Rimbaud and not understand him and feel very connected to the life I imagined Jack MacFarland's life to be: a subterranean ramble through Bebop and breathless
poetry and back-alley revelations.

    In 1962, John Connor moved into dank, old Apartment 1. John had     4
also grown up in South L.A., and he and I had become best friends. His
parents moved to Oregon, and John—who was a good black-top basketball player and an excellent student—wanted to stay in Los Angeles
and go to college. So he rented an apartment for forty dollars a month,
and we established a community of two. Some nights, John and I and
Roy the artist and a wild kid named Gaspo would drive into downtown
L.A.—down to where my mother had waited fearfully for a bus years
before—and roam the streets and feel the excitement of the tender-
loin: the flashing arrows, the blue-and-orange beer neon, the bur-

lesque houses, the faded stairwell of Roseland—which we would inch up and then run down—brushing past the photos of taxi dancers, glossy and smiling in a glass display. Cops would tell us to go home, and that intensified this bohemian romance all the more.

About four months after John moved in, we both entered Loyola University. Loyola is now coeducational; its student center houses an Asian Pacific Students Association, Black Student Alliance, and Chicano Resource Center; and its radio station, KXLU, plays the most untamed rock 'n' roll in Los Angeles. But in the early sixties, Loyola was pretty much a school for white males from the middle and upper middle class. It was a sleepy little campus—its undergraduate enrollment was under two thousand—and it prided itself on providing spiritual as well as intellectual guidance for its students: Religion and Christian philosophy courses were a required part of the curriculum. It defined itself as a Catholic intellectual community—promotional brochures relied on phrases like "the social, intellectual, and spiritual aspects of our students"—and made available to its charges small classes, a campus ministry, and thirty-six clubs (the Chess Club, Economics Society, Fine Arts Circle, Debate Squad, and more). There were also six fraternities and a sports program that included basketball, baseball, volleyball, rugby, soccer, and crew. Loyola men, it was assumed, shared a fairly common set of social and religious values, and the university provided multiple opportunities for them to develop their minds, their spirits, and their social networks. I imagine that parents sent their boys to Loyola with a sigh of relief: God and man strolled together out of St. Robert Bellarmine Hall and veered left to Sacred Heart Chapel. There was an occasional wild party at one of the off-campus fraternity houses, but, well, a pair of panties in the koi pond was not on a par with crises of faith and violence against the state.

John and I rattled to college in his '53 Plymouth. Loyola Boulevard was lined with elms and maples, and as we entered the campus we could see the chapel tower rising in the distance. The chapel and all the early buildings had been constructed in the 1920s and were white and separated by broad sweeps of very green grass. Palm trees and stone pines grew in rows and clumps close to the buildings, and long concrete walkways curved and angled and crossed to connect everything, proving that God, as Plato suspected, is always doing geometry.

Most freshman courses were required, and I took most of mine in St. Robert Bellarmine Hall. Saint Robert was a father of the church who wrote on papal power and censored Galileo: The ceiling in his hallway was high, and dim lights hung down from it. The walls were beige up to about waist level, then turned off-white. The wood trim was dark and worn. The floor combined brown linoleum with brown and black tile. Even with a rush of students, the building maintained its dignity. We moved through it, and its old, clanking radiators warmed us as we did, but it was not a warmth that got to the bone. I remember a dream in which I climbed up beyond the third floor—up thin, narrow stairs to a bell tower that held a small, dusky room in which a priest was playing church music to a class of shadows.

My first semester classes included the obligatory theology and ROTC and a series of requirements: biology, psychology, speech, logic, and a language. I went to class and usually met John for lunch: We'd bring sandwiches to his car and play the radio while we ate. Then it was back to class, or the library, or the student union for a Coke. This was the next step in Jack MacFarland's plan for me—and I did okay for a while. I had learned enough routines in high school to act like a fairly typical student, but—except for the historical sketch I received in Senior English—there wasn't a solid center of knowledge and assurance to all this. When I look back through notes and papers and various photographs and memorabilia, I begin to remember what a disengaged, half-awake time it really was. I'll describe two of the notebooks I found. The one from English is a small book, eight by seven, and only eleven pages of it are filled. The notes I did write consist of book titles, dates of publication, names of characters, pointless summaries of books that were not on our syllabus and that I had never read (*"The Alexandria Quartet:* 5 or 6 characters seen by different people in different stages of life"), and quotations from the teacher ("Perception can bring sorrow"). The notes are a series of separate entries. I can't see any coherence. My biology lab notes are written on green-tint quadrille. They, too, are sparse. There is an occasional poorly executed sketch of a tiny organism or of a bone and muscle structure. Some of the formulas and molecular models sit isolated on the page, bare of any explanatory discussion. The lecture notes are fragmented; a fair number of sentences remain incomplete.

By the end of the second semester my grades were close to dipping below a C average, and since I had been admitted provisionally, that would have been that. Jack MacFarland had oriented me to Western intellectual history and had helped me develop my writing, but he had worked with me for only a year, and I needed more than twelve months of his kind of instruction. Speech and Introductory Psychology presented no big problems. General Biology had midterm and final examinations that required a good deal of memorizing, and I could do that, but the textbook—particularly the chapters covered in the second semester—was much, much harder than what I read in high school, and I was so ill-adept in the laboratory that I failed that portion of the class. We had to set up and pursue biological problems, not just memorize—and at the first sign of doing rather than memorizing, I would automatically assume the problem was beyond me and distance myself from it. Logic, another requirement, spooked me with its syllogisms and Venn diagrams—they were just a step away from more formal mathematics—so I memorized what I could and squirmed around the rest. Theology was god-awful; ROTC was worse. And Latin, the language I elected on the strength of Jack MacFarland's one piece of bad advice, had me suffocating under the dust of a dead civilization. Freshman English was taught by a frustrated novelist with glittering eyes who had us, among other things, describing the consumption of our last evening's meal using the images of the battlefield.

I was out of my league.                                                      10

Faculty would announce office hours. If I had had the sense, I     11
would have gone, but they struck me as aloof and somber men, and I felt stupid telling them I was . . . well—stupid. I drifted through the required courses, thinking that as soon as these requirements were over, I'd never have to face anything even vaguely quantitative again. Or anything to do with foreign languages. Or ROTC. I fortified myself with defiance: I worked up an imitation of the old priest who was my Latin teacher, and I kept my ROTC uniform crumpled in the greasy trunk of John's Plymouth.

Many of my classmates came from and lived in a world very     12
different from my own. The campus literary magazine would publish excerpts from the journals of upperclassmen traveling across Europe, standing before the Berlin Wall or hiking through olive groves toward Delphi. With the exception of one train trip back to Altoona, I had never been out of Southern California, and this translated, for me, into some personal inadequacy. Fraternities seemed exclusive and a little strange. I'm not sure why I didn't join any of Loyola's three dozen societies and clubs, though I do know that things like the Debate Squad were way too competitive. Posters and flyers and squibs in the campus newspaper gave testament to a lot of connecting activity, but John and I pretty much kept to ourselves, ragging on the "Loyola man," reading

the literary magazine aloud with a French accent, simultaneously feeling contempt for and exclusion from a social life that seemed to work with the mystery and enclosure of the clockwork in a music box.

It is an unfortunate fact of our psychic lives that the images that    13
surround us as we grow up—no matter how much we may scorn them later—give shape to our deepest needs and longings. Every year Loyola men elected a homecoming queen. The queen and her princesses were students at the Catholic sister schools: Marymount, Mount St. Mary's, St. Vincent's. They had names like Corinne and Cathy, and they came from the Sullivan family or the Mitchells or the Ryans. They were taught to stand with toe to heel, their smiles were inviting, and the photographer's flash illuminated their eyes. Loyola men met them at fraternity parties and mixers and "CoEd Day," met them according to rules of manner and affiliation and parental connection as elaborate as a Balinese dance. John and I drew mustaches on their photographs, but something about them reached far back into my life.

Growing up in South L.A. was certainly not a conscious misery.    14
My neighborhood had its diversions and its mysteries, and I felt loved and needed at home. But all in all there was a dreary impotence to the years, and isolation, and a deep sadness about my father. I protected myself from the harsher side of it all through a life of the mind. And while that interior life included spaceships and pink chemicals and music and the planetary moons, it also held the myriad television images of the good life that were piped into my home: Robert Young sitting down to dinner, Ozzie Nelson tossing the football with his sons, the blond in a Prell commercial turning toward the camera. The images couldn't have been more trivial—all sentimental phosphorescence—but as a child tucked away on South Vermont, they were just about the only images I had of what life would be without illness and dead ends. I didn't realize how completely their message had seeped into my being, what loneliness and sorrow was being held at bay— didn't realize it until I found myself in the middle of Loyola's social life without a guidebook, feeling just beyond the superficial touch of the queen and her princesses, those smiling incarnations of a television promise. I scorned the whole silly show and ached to be embraced by one of these mythic females under the muted light of a paper moon.

So I went to school and sat in class and memorized more than    15
understood and whistled past the academic graveyard. I vacillated

between the false potency of scorn and feelings of ineptitude. John and I would get in his car and enjoy the warmth of each other and laugh and head down the long strip of Manchester Boulevard, away from Loyola, away from the palms and green, green lawns, back to South L.A. We'd throw the ball in the alley or lag pennies on Vermont or hit Marty's Liquor. We'd leave much later for a movie or a football game at Mercy High or the terrible safety of downtown Los Angeles. Walking, then, past the *discotecas* and pawnshops, past the windows full of fried chicken and yellow lamps, past the New Follies, walking through hustlers and lost drunks and prostitutes and transvestites with rouge the color of bacon—stopping, finally, before the musty opening of a bar where two silhouettes moved around a pool table as though they were underwater.

I don't know what I would have found if the flow of events hadn't 16 changed dramatically. Two things happened. Jack MacFarland privately influenced my course of study at Loyola, and death once again ripped through our small family.

The coterie of MacFarland's students—Art Mitz, Mark Denver, 17 and me—were still visiting our rumpled mentor. We would stop by his office or his apartment to mock our classes and the teachers and all that " 'Loyola man' bullshit." Nobody had more appreciation for burlesque than Jack MacFarland, but I suppose he saw beneath our caustic performances and knew we were headed for trouble. Without telling us, he started making phone calls to some of his old teachers at Loyola—primarily to Dr. Frank Carothers, the chairman of the English Department—and, I guess, explained that these kids needed to be slapped alongside the head with a good novel. Dr. Carothers volunteered to look out for us and agreed to some special studies courses that we could substitute for a few of the more traditional requirements, courses that would enable us to read and write a lot under the close supervision of a faculty member. In fact, what he promised were tutorials—and that was exceptional, even for a small college. All this would start up when we returned from summer vacation. Our sophomore year, Jack MacFarland finally revealed, would be different.

When Lou Minton rewired the trailer, he rigged a phone line 18 from the front house: A few digits and we could call each other. One night during the summer after my freshman year, the phone rang while I was reading. It was my mother and she was screaming. I ran into the house to find her standing in the kitchen hysterical—both hands pressed to her face—and all I could make out was Lou's name. I didn't see him in the front of the house, so I ran back through the kitchen to the bedroom. He had fallen back across the bed, a hole right at his sideburn, his jaw still quivering. They had a fight, and some ugly depth of pain convulsed within him. He left the table and walked to the bedroom. My mother heard the light slam of a .22. Nothing more.

That summer seems vague and distant. I can't remember any specifics, though I had to take care of my mother and handle the affairs of the house. I probably made do by blunting a good deal of what I saw and navigating with intuitive quadrants. But though I cannot remember details, I do recall feelings and recognitions: Lou's suicide came to represent the sadness and dead time I had protected myself against, the personal as well as public oppressiveness of life in South Los Angeles. I began to see that my escape to the trailer and my isolationist fantasies of the demi-monde would yield another kind of death, a surrender to the culture's lost core. An alternative was somehow starting to take shape around school and knowledge. Knowledge seemed . . . was it empowering? No, that's a word I would use now. Then I felt freed, as if I were untying fetters. There simply were times when the pain and confusion of that summer would give way to something I felt more than I knew: a lightness to my body, an ease in breathing. Three or four months later I took an art history course, and one day during a slide show on Gothic architecture I felt myself rising up within the interior light of Mont-Saint-Michel. I wanted to be released from the despair that surrounded me on South Vermont and from my own troubled sense of exclusion.

Jack MacFarland had saved me at one juncture—caught my fancy and revitalized my mind—what I felt now was something further, some tentative recognition that an engagement with ideas could foster competence and lead me out into the world. But all this was very new and fragile, and given what I know now, I realize how easily it could have been crushed. My mother, for as long as I can remember, always added onto any statement of intention—hers or others'—the phrase *se vuol Dio*, if God wants it. The fulfillment of desire, no matter how trivial, required the blessing of the gods, for the world was filled with threat. "I'll plant the seeds this weekend," I might say. "*Se vuol Dio*," she would add. *Se vuol Dio*. The phrase expressed several lifetimes of ravaged hope: my grandfather's lost leg, the failure of the Rose Spaghetti House, my father laid low, Lou Minton, the landscapes of South L.A. *Se vuol Dio.* For those who live their lives on South Vermont, tomorrow doesn't beckon to be defined from a benign future. It's up to the gods, not you, if any old thing turns out right. I carried within me no history of assurances that what I was feeling would lead to anything.

Because of its size and because of the kind of teacher who is drawn   21
to small liberal arts colleges, Loyola would turn out to be a very good place for me. For even with MacFarland's yearlong tour through ideas and language, I was unprepared. English prose written before the twentieth century was difficult, sometimes impossible, for me to comprehend. The kind of reasoning I found in logic was very foreign. My writing was okay, but I couldn't hold a candle to Art Mitz or Mark Dever or to those boys who came from good schools. And my fears about science and mathematics prevailed: Pereira Hall, the Math and Engineering Building, was only forty to fifty yards from the rear entrance to the English Department but seemed an unfriendly mirage, a malevolent castle floating in the haze of a mescaline dream.

We live, in America, with so many platitudes about motivation and   22
self-reliance and individualism—and myths spun from them, like those of Horatio Alger—that we find it hard to accept the fact that they are serious nonsense. To live your early life on the streets of South L.A.— or Homewood or Spanish Harlem or Chicago's South Side or any one of hundreds of other depressed communities—and to journey up through the top levels of the American educational system will call for support and guidance at many, many points along the way. You'll need people to guide you into conversations that seem foreign and threatening. You'll need models, lots of them, to show you how to get at what you don't know. You'll need people to help you center yourself in your own developing ideas. You'll need people to watch out for you. There is much talk these days about the value of a classical humanistic education, a call for an immersion in the humanities, a return to the great books. These appeals raise lots of suspicions, for such curricula have traditionally served to exclude working-class people from the classroom. It doesn't, of necessity, have to be that way. The teachers that fate and Jack MacFarland's crisis intervention sent my way worked at making the humanities truly human. What transpired between us was the essence of humane liberal education, and it enabled me to move far beyond the cognitive charade of my freshman year.

# Bring on the Lions

## ANNIE DILLARD

"Bring on the lions!" I cried.                                             1

But there were no lions. I spent every day in the company of one    2
dog and one cat whose every gesture emphasized that this was a day
throughout whose duration intelligent creatures intended to sleep. I
would have to crank myself up.

To crank myself up I stood on a jack and ran myself up. I tightened   3
myself like a bolt. I inserted myself in a vise-clamp and wound the
handle till the pressure built. I drank coffee in titrated doses. It was a
tricky business, requiring the finely tuned judgment of a skilled anes-
thesiologist. There was a tiny range within which coffee was effective,
short of which it was useless, and beyond which, fatal.

I pointed myself. I walked to the water. I played the hateful      4
recorder, washed dishes, drank coffee, stood on a beach log, watched
bird. That was the first part; it could take all morning, or all month.
Only the coffee counted, and I knew it. It was boiled Colombian coffee:
raw grounds brought just to boiling in cold water and stirred. Now I
smoked a cigarette or two and read what I wrote yesterday. What I
wrote yesterday needed to be slowed down. I inserted words in one
sentence and hazarded a new sentence. At once I noticed that I was
writing—which, as the novelist Frederick Buechner noted, called for a
break, if not a full-scale celebration.

On break, I usually read Conrad Aiken's poetry aloud. It was pure    5
sound unencumbered by sense. If I ever caught a poem's sense by
accident, I could never use that poem again. I often read the Senlin
poems, and "Sea Holly." Some days I read part of any poetry anthology's index of first lines. The parallels sounded strong and suggestive.
They could set me off, perhaps.

This morning, as on so many mornings, I lacked sufficient fuel for    6
liftoff. I looked at the legal pad pages again. A new section must be
begun in the book, and a place found to put it. I wrote four or five
sentences on a gamble, smoked more to stimulate the brain or stop the
heart, whichever came first, and reheated a fourth mug of coffee. After

the first boiling, the grounds sink to the coffeepot's bottom. When you reheat it, you call it refried coffee. I already felt like the empty kettle on a hot burner, the thin kettle whose water had boiled away. The top of my stomach felt bruised or burned—was this how mustard gas tasted? I drank the fourth mug without looking at it, any more than you look at the needle in a doctor's hand.

Now, alas, I had cranked too far. I could no longer play the re-  7
corder; I would need a bugle. I would break a piano. What could I do around the cabin? There was no wood to split. There was something I needed to fix with a hacksaw, but I rejected the work as too fine. Why not adopt a baby, design a curriculum, go sailing?

The dog opened one eye, cocked it at me, and rolled it up  8
before her lids closed. People should not feed moralistic animals. If they're so holy, where are their books? I was starving, but eating was out of the question. Nausea might temper this energy, but eating would kill it.

I read it again. Reading, I drew all over it. This was usual. Now my  9
drawings tightened and darkened; I pressed them into the paper. They were digging through the paper and into the desk. Where next? I knew where next. It was within my possibilities. If only I could concentrate. I must quit. I was too young to be living at a desk. Many fine people were out there living, people whose consciences permitted them to sleep at night despite their not having written a decent sentence that day, or ever.

Let's dance. I could not draw the lamp any more; it was too little.  10
I walked out on the beach unseeing and fell back in the door, sick, dead, dying. I heated a bowl of soup which I ate blinded by coffee and nicotine, unremembering. I returned to the papers and enclosed a paragraph in parentheses; it meant that tomorrow I would delete the few sentences I wrote today. Too many days of this, I thought, too many days of this.

I do not so much write a book as sit up with it, as with a dying  11
friend. During visiting hours, I enter its room with dread and sympathy for its many disorders. I hold its hand and hope it will get better.

This tender relationship can change in a twinkling. If you skip a  12
visit or two, a work in progress will turn on you.

A work in progress quickly becomes feral. It reverts to a wild state  13
overnight. It is barely domesticated, a mustang on which you one day

fastened a halter, but which now you cannot catch. It is a lion you cage in your study. As the work grows, it gets harder to control; it is a lion growing in strength. You must visit it every day and reassert your mastery over it. If you skip a day, you are, quite rightly, afraid to open the door to its room. You enter its room with bravura, holding a chair at the thing and shouting, "Simba!"

# Process

## Nuclear Peril: The Choice

### JONATHAN SCHELL

The peril that the scientists have brought into our lives stems from 1
hitherto unknown properties of the physical universe, but it is not an
external, self-propelled peril—as though they had discovered that
forces in the interior of the earth were one day going to blow it up, or
that a huge asteroid was one day going to collide with it. Rather, the
peril comes from our own actions—from within us—and if we had
never sought to harm one another the energy latent in matter would
have remained locked up there, without posing any threat to anybody.
Thus, the peril of extinction by nuclear arms is doubly ours: first,
because we have it in our power to prevent the catastrophe, and,
second, because the catastrophe cannot occur unless, by pursuing our
political aims through violence, we bring it about. Since military action
is the one activity through which we deliberately threaten to employ
our new mastery over nature to destroy ourselves, nothing could be
more crucial to an understanding of the practical dimensions of the
nuclear predicament than a precise understanding of what nuclear
weapons have done to war, and, through war, to the system of sover-
eignty of which war has traditionally been an indispensable part. All
war is violent, but not all violence is war. War is a violent means
employed by a nation to achieve an end, and, like all mere means, is
subject to Aristotle's rule "The means to the end are not unlimited, for
the end itself sets the limit in each case." The possible ends of war are
as varied as the desires and hopes of men, having ranged from the
recovery of a single beautiful woman from captivity to world conquest,
but every one of them would be annihilated in a nuclear holocaust.
War is destructive, but it is also a human phenomenon—complex,
carefully wrought, and, in its way, fragile and delicate, like its maker—

but nuclear weapons, if they were ever used in large numbers, would simply blow war up, just as they would blow up everything else that is human.

One of the respects in which war is unique among the uses to which mankind's steadily increasing technical skills have been put is that in war no benefit is obtained and no aim achieved unless the powers involved exert themselves to the limit, or near-limit, of their strength. In the words of Clausewitz: "War is an act of violence pushed to its utmost bounds; as one side dictates to the other, there arises a sort of reciprocal action which logically must lead to an extreme." For only at the extremes are victory and defeat—the results of war— brought about. Even when victory and defeat are not absolute, the terms of the disengagement are determined by the nearness of one side to defeat. In this case, the antagonists, like chess players near the end of the game, see the inevitable outcome and spare themselves the trouble of actually going through the final moves. As Clausewitz writes, "everything is subject to a supreme law: which is the *decision by arms.*" Therefore, "all action . . . takes place on the supposition that if the solution by force of arms which lies at its foundation should be realized, it will be a favorable one." For "the decision by arms is, for all operations, great and small, what cash payment is in bill transactions," and "however remote from each other these relations, however seldom the realization may take place, still it can never entirely fail to occur." Nuclear arms ruin war by making the decision by arms impossible. The decision by arms can occur only when the strength of one side or the other is exhausted, or when its exhaustion is approached. But in nuclear "war" no one's strength fails until *both* sides have been annihilated. There cannot be a victor without a vanquished, the collapse of whose military efforts signals the end of the hostilities, permitting the victor to collect his spoils. But when both adversaries have nuclear arms that moment of collapse never comes, and the military forces— the missiles—of both countries go on "fighting" after the countries themselves have disappeared. From the point of view of a power contemplating war in the pre-nuclear world, war appeared to depend on the possession of great strength, since the side that possessed the greater strength had the better chance of being victorious. But when war is seen from the point of view of the nuclear world it becomes clear that as an institution—as the mechanism with which sovereign states settled their disputes—war depended, above all, on weakness: the weakness of the defeated party, whose collapse made the decision by arms (the whole purpose of war) possible. And this weakness, in turn, depended on the presence of certain technical limitations on the ability of mankind in general to avail itself of natural forces for destructive purposes. When science made the energy in mass available to man, the crucial limits were removed, for everybody, forever, and the exhaustion of the defeated party—and so the triumph of the victor—was rendered impossible. War itself has thus proved to be a casualty of the tremendous means that were put at its disposal by science. We are now in a position to see that helplessness has always been the specific product of war, and weakness its essential ingredient. War has never been anything but unilateral disarmament—the disarmament of one side by the other. But now, before the exhaustion of either party can be reached, everyone will be dead, and all human aims—the aims pursued in the "war" and all others—will have been nullified. In a nuclear conflict between the United States and the Soviet Union—the holocaust—not only the adversaries but also the world's bystanders will vanish. In this "war," instead of one side winning and the other losing, it is as though all human beings lost and all the weapons won. Clausewitz writes, "War can never be separated from political intercourse, and if, in the consideration of the matter, this is done in any way, all the threads of the different relations are, to a certain extent, broken, and we have before us a senseless thing without an object." War can, for example, decline into mere looting or banditry or some other form of aimless violence. But, of all the "senseless things" that can ever occur when war's violence (its means) is severed from its political purposes (its ends), a nuclear holocaust is the most senseless. To call this senseless thing "war" is, in fact, simply a misnomer, and to go on speaking of "nuclear war," and the like, can only mislead and confuse us. Thus, while the Soviet Union and the United States are perfectly free to fire their thousands of nuclear weapons at one another, the result would not be war, for no end could be served by it. It would be comprehensive destruction—a "senseless thing." With the invention of nuclear weapons, it became impossible for violence to be fashioned into war, or to achieve what war used to achieve. Violence can no longer break down the opposition of the adversary; it can no longer produce victory and defeat; it can no longer attain its ends. It can no longer be war.

It must be emphasized that what nuclear weapons have ruined is 3 not only "nuclear war" but all war (that is, all war between nuclear powers). "Conventional war," which in fact encompasses everything that deserves to be called war, is ruined because as long as nuclear weapons are held in reserve by the combatants, in accordance with the supposedly agreed-upon rules of some "limited war," the hostilities have not run to that extreme of violence at which the essential helplessness of one side or the other has been produced. If a decision were to be reached while the "defeated" party held potentially decisive means of violence in its possession, then that decision would be not "by arms" but by something else. We have to imagine that this power would accept its defeat while knowing that the use of its bombs would reverse it. A current example illustrates how little willingness there is among nuclear powers to accept such an outcome. For some time, it has been widely believed that the Soviet Union enjoys a preponderance in conventional forces over the NATO powers in Europe, and the United States has reserved for itself the right to resort to nuclear weapons in Europe rather than accept a conventional defeat there. Thus, the United States has already publicly discarded the notion of abiding by any rules of "limited war" if those rules should prove to mean a defeat for the United States. And there is certainly very little reason to suppose that the Soviet Union is any more willing to volunteer for defeat than the United States. That being the likely state of things, there seems little chance that a conventional war between nuclear powers could stay limited. And this means that a conventional war between nuclear powers must not even be begun, since it threatens the same holocaust that the limited use of nuclear weapons threatens. As a practical matter, this rule has up to now been followed by the statesmen of the nuclear world. Disregarding theoretical treatises on the possibility of "limited war" between nuclear powers, including "limited nuclear war," they have held back from any war; thus, in our thirty-six years of experience with nuclear weapons no two nuclear powers have ever entered into even conventional hostilities. The same cannot be said, of course, of hostilities between nuclear powers and non-nuclear powers, such as the Vietnam War or the Soviet-Afghanistan war. These remain possible—although, for reasons that I shall not go into here, they are not, it would seem, profitable.

It is often said that nuclear arms have made war obsolete, but this [4] is a misunderstanding. Obsolescence occurs when a means to some end is superseded by a new and presumably better means—as when it was discovered that vehicles powered by internal-combustion engines were more efficient than vehicles pulled by horses at transporting people and goods from one place to another. But war has not been superseded by some better means to its end, which is to serve as the final arbiter of disputes among sovereign states. On the contrary, war has gone out of existence without leaving behind any means at all—whether superior or inferior—to that end. The more than three decades of jittery peace between the nuclear superpowers which the world has experienced since the invention of nuclear weapons is almost certainly the result of this lack. There is thus no need to "abolish war" among the nuclear powers; it is already gone. The choices don't include war any longer. They consist now of peace, on the one hand, and annihilation, on the other. And annihilation—or "assured destruction"—is as far from being war as peace is, and the sooner we recognize this the sooner we will be able to save our species from self-extermination.

---

# On Natural Death

## LEWIS THOMAS

There are so many new books about dying that there are now special shelves set aside for them in bookshops, along with the health-diet and home-repair paperbacks and the sex manuals. Some of them are so packed with detailed information and step-by-step instructions for performing the function that you'd think this was a new sort of skill which all of us are now required to learn. The strongest impression the casual reader gets, leafing through, is that proper dying has become an extraordinary, even an exotic experience, something only the specially trained get to do.   1

Also, you could be led to believe that we are the only creatures capable of the awareness of death, that when all the rest of nature is being cycled through dying, one generation after another, it is a different kind of process, done automatically and trivially, more "natural," as we say.   2

An elm in our backyard caught the blight this summer and dropped stone dead, leafless, almost overnight. One weekend it was a normal-looking elm, maybe a little bare in spots but nothing alarming, and the next weekend it was gone, passed over, departed, taken. Taken is right, for the tree surgeon came by yesterday with his crew   3 of young helpers and their cherry picker, and took it down branch by branch and carted it off in the back of a red truck, everyone singing.

The dying of a field mouse, at the jaws of an amiable household    4
cat, is a spectacle I have beheld many times. It used to make me wince. Early in life I gave up throwing sticks at the cat to make him drop the mouse, because the dropped mouse regularly went ahead and died anyway, but I always shouted unaffections at the cat to let him know the sort of animal he had become. Nature, I thought, was an abomination.

Recently I've done some thinking about that mouse, and I wonder    5
if his dying is necessarily all that different from the passing of our elm. The main difference, if there is one, would be in the matter of pain. I do not believe that an elm tree has pain receptors, and even so, the blight seems to me a relatively painless way to go even if there were nerve endings in a tree, which there are not. But the mouse dangling tail-down from the teeth of a gray cat is something else again, with pain beyond bearing, you'd think, all over his small body.

There are now some plausible reasons for thinking it is not like that    6
at all, and you can make up an entirely different story about the mouse and his dying if you like. At the instant of being trapped and penetrated by teeth, peptide hormones are released by cells in the hypothalamus and the pituitary gland; instantly these substances, called endorphins, are attached to the surface of other cells responsible for pain perception; the hormones have the pharmacologic properties of opium; there is no pain. Thus it is that the mouse seems always to dangle so languidly from the jaws, lies there so quietly when dropped, dies of his injuries without a struggle. If a mouse could shrug, he'd shrug.

I do not know if this is true or not, nor do I know how to prove    7
it if it is true. Maybe if you could get in there quickly enough and administer naloxone, a specific morphine antagonist, you could turn off the endorphins and observe the restoration of pain, but this is not something I would care to do or see. I think I will leave it there, as a good guess about the dying of a cat-chewed mouse, perhaps about dying in general.

Montaigne had a hunch about dying, based on his own close call    8
in a riding accident. He was so badly injured as to be believed dead by his companions, and was carried home with lamentations, "all bloody, stained all over with the blood I had thrown up." He remembers the entire episode, despite having been "dead, for two full hours," with wonderment:

It seemed to me that my life was hanging only by the tip of my lips. I closed my eyes in order, it seemed to me, to help push it out, and took pleasure in growing languid and letting myself go. It was an idea that was only floating on the surface of my soul, as delicate and feeble as all the rest, but in truth not only free from distress but mingled with that sweet feeling that people have who have let themselves slide into sleep. I believe that this is the same state in which people find themselves whom we see fainting in the agony of death, and I maintain that we pity them without cause. . . . In order to get used to the idea of death, I find there is nothing like coming close to it.

Later, in another essay, Montaigne returns to it:

If you know not how to die, never trouble yourself; Nature will in a moment fully and sufficiently instruct you; she will exactly do that business for you; take you no care for it.

The worst accident I've ever seen was in Okinawa, in the early days of the invasion, when a jeep ran into a troop carrier and was crushed nearly flat. Inside were two young MPs, trapped in bent steel, both mortally hurt, with only their heads and shoulders visible. We had a conversation while people with the right tools were prying them free. Sorry about the accident, they said. No, they said, they felt fine. Is everyone else okay, one of them said. Well, the other one said, no hurry now. And then they died.    9

Pain is useful for avoidance, for getting away when there's time to get away, but when it is end game, and no way back, pain is likely to be turned off, and the mechanisms for this are wonderfully precise and quick. If I had to design an ecosystem in which creatures had to live off each other and in which dying was an indispensable part of living, I could not think of a better way to manage.    10

---

# It's Over, Debbie

## (ANONYMOUS)

The call came in the middle of the night. As a gynecology resident rotating through a large, private hospital, I had come to detest telephone calls, because invariably I would be up for several hours and    1 would not feel good the next day. However, duty called, so I answered the phone. A nurse informed me that a patient was having difficulty getting rest, could I please see her. She was on 3 North. That was the gynecologic-oncology unit, not my usual duty station. As I trudged along, bumping sleepily against walls and corners and not believing I was up again, I tried to imagine what I might find at the end of my walk. Maybe an elderly woman with an anxiety reaction, or perhaps something particularly horrible.

I grabbed the chart from the nurses station on my way to the      2
patient's room, and the nurse gave me some hurried details: a 20-year-old girl named Debbie was dying of ovarian cancer. She was having unrelenting vomiting apparently as the result of an alcohol drip administered for sedation. Hmm, I thought. Very sad. As I approached the room I could hear loud, labored breathing. I entered and saw an emaciated, dark-haired woman who appeared much older than 20. She was receiving nasal oxygen, had an IV, and was sitting in bed suffering from what was obviously severe air hunger. The chart noted her weight at 80 pounds. A second woman, also dark-haired but of middle-age, stood at her right, holding her hand. Both looked up as I entered. The room seemed filled with the patient's desperate effort to survive. Her eyes were hollow, and she had suprasternal and intercostal retractions with her rapid inspirations. She had not eaten or slept in two days. She had not responded to chemotherapy and was being given supportive care only. It was a gallows scene, a cruel mockery of her youth and unfulfilled potential. Her only words to me were, "Let's get this over with."

I retreated with my thoughts to the nurses station. The patient was      3
tired and needed rest. I could not give her health, but I could give her rest. I asked the nurse to draw 20 mg of morphine sulfate into a syringe. Enough, I thought, to do the job. I took the syringe into the room and told the two women I was going to give Debbie something that would let her rest and to say good-bye. Debbie looked at the syringe, then laid her head on the pillow with her eyes open, watching what was left of the world. I injected the morphine intravenously and watched to see if my calculations on its effects would be correct. Within seconds her breathing slowed to a normal rate, her eyes closed, and her features softened as she seemed restful at last. The older woman stroked the hair of the now-sleeping patient. I waited for the inevitable next effect of depressing the respiratory drive. With clocklike certainty, within four minutes the breathing rate slowed even more, then became

irregular, then ceased. The dark-haired woman stood erect and seemed relieved.

It's over, Debbie.    4

---

# Moving Alaska's Capital

## JOHN McPHEE

One morning in the Alaskan autumn, a small sharp-nosed helicop-    1
ter, on its way to a rendezvous, flew south from Fairbanks with three passengers. They crossed the fast, silted water of the Tanana River and whirred along over low black-spruce land with streams too numerous for names. The ground beneath them began to rise, and they with it, until they were crossing broad benchlands and high hills increasingly jagged in configuration as they stepped up to the Alaska Range.

At about the same time, another and somewhat larger group took    2
off from Anchorage in a de Havilland Twin Otter, and this sturdy vehicle, firm as iron in the air, flew north up the valley of the Big Su—Susitna River, a big river in a land of big rivers—and on up over alpine tundra that now, in the late season, was as red as wine. After moving over higher and higher hills, the plane moved in among mountains: great, upreaching things, gray on the rockface and then—above the five-thousand-foot contour and far on up, too high to see without pressing to the window—covered with fresh snow.

"Is the mountain out?" someone on the right side of the plane    3
wanted to know. In so many mountains, there was one mountain. "Is the mountain out?"

"It surer than hell is."    4

"It never looks the same."    5

The mountain was a megahedron—its high white facets doming in    6
the air. Long snow banners, extending eastward, were pluming from the ridges above twenty thousand feet.

"What would you call that mountain, Willie?"    7

"Denali. I'll go along with the Indians that far."    8

Everyone aboard was white but Willie (William Iġiaġruq Hens-    9
ley), of Arctic Alaska, and he said again, "Denali. What the hell did McKinley ever do?"

The Twin Otter by now was so deep in the Alaska Range that   10
nothing could be seen but walls of mountain in a pass. Then, finally, the
pass widened the way to the north. Banking over terraces and high
riverine bluffs—Nenana River—the plane landed on gravel near a
small group of buildings, a mining town. The helicopter from Fairbanks was already there. Handshakes all around. Brisk, nippy morning, right? Won't be long now. And then, in threes and fours, the group
made successive flights in the small helicopter—down the right bank of
the Nenana over the broad high benchland, back and forth in loosely
patterned flight. Four grizzly bears—large and small, perhaps a ton or
so of bear—were grazing a meadow below, eating blueberry bushes
rich with fruit. The helicopter ignored the bears. It crossed the river
and flew back to the north in vectors, as if looking for something. A
small lake. Then a larger lake. This was indeed a hunt, and what the
people in the air were hunting for was a new capital of Alaska.

When states move their capitals, as most of them have done at one   11
time or another, the usual aim is to have a seat of government somewhere near the centers of geography and population—criteria that
distinctly fail to describe Juneau. Juneau, capital of Alaska since 1900,
is in the eccentric region that Alaskans call Southeastern—a long,
archipelagic claw that dangles toward Seattle and is knuckled to the
main body of Alaska by a glacier the size of Rhode Island. Southeastern
Alaska reaches so far east that all the land north of it is Canadian.
British Columbia. Yukon Territory. Juneau is two time zones from
Anchorage, from Fairbanks, from the center of the state. It is twenty-
five hundred miles from the other end of Alaska. Many Alaskans do not
regard Southeastern as part of Alaska but, rather, as an appendage of
inconvenience, because Juneau is there. Juneau is an outpost—cannot
be reached, or even approached, by road. Juneau was the site of a gold
strike that attracted people enough to make a town, and the town's
importance increased when strikes of bonanza quantity were made in
mountains to the north, along the Klondike River and other tributaries
of the upper Yukon. Juneau, already a mining town, was also a way
station on trips to the Klondike, and it became—for the duration of the
gold boom—a center of Alaskan commerce.

Anchorage is the commercial center now, and roughly half of   12
political Alaska. As a result of a petition signed by sixteen thousand, an
initiative appeared on the 1974 primary ballot through which the voters could indicate a wish to move their capital. Similar initiatives in
1960 and 1962 had been defeated, perhaps in part because Alaskans

elsewhere in the state did not want to see even more power concentrated in Anchorage. Anchorage, for its part, wished to yield nothing to Fairbanks. Their rivalry is intense to the point of unseemliness. So the 1974 initiative was written to exclude both cities—the new capital could not be within thirty miles of either one—and in strong majority (fifty-seven per cent) the voters went for it.

The state is more or less broke—if that term can be used to describe a budget that regularly expends a great deal more than it ingests. For this reason, it might seem an act of bravado to contemplate building anything at all, let alone a new capital city. Bravado, on the other hand, is a synonym for Alaska. A high proportion of the white people who have tried to make their way in Alaska have lived from boom to boom. The first boom was in fur, and then came gold, followed by war, and now oil. How could it matter that the treasury was atilt when the Alyeska Pipeline Service Company was moving toward completion of a tube that would draw so much oil out of the north of Alaska that the state government alone would collect in royalties as much as three and a half million dollars a day? Some Alaskans were already spending the money. Others were dreaming of ways to spend it. One of the dreams was of a new capital, in a wild setting, preferably within sight of the summits of North America's highest massif.  `13`

Following the terms of the initiative, the governor of Alaska appointed a Capital Site Selection Committee, most of whose nine members had been—like the governor himself—opponents of the initiative. One might think that only Gilbert and Sullivan could work out the story from there. The committee, though—representing a geographical spread of the state, including Southeastern—had taken up its work with a seriousness Alaskan in grandeur, and would spend well over a million dollars to narrow its choices down.

The move to move the capital has "bestirred the community," as one Alaska senator has put it, and from the community has come a chorus of comment. The dialogue assembled here contains voices from Seward, Sitka, Fort Yukon, Kotzebue, Fairbanks, Juneau, Anchorage.  `14`

"Despite the terms of the initiative, Anchorage is the logical place for the capital. The move would cost the least, and Anchorage would serve best. Anchorage should *be* the capital."  `15`

"There are more state-government employees in Anchorage now than there are in Juneau."  `16`

"Everyone is afraid of, and is envious of, Anchorage."  `17`

"Anchorage has got enough."  `18`

"People don't want the Anchorage scourge to spread."                    19
"The initiative was a vendetta."                                        20
"The capital move started with people in Anchorage who thought          21
they were getting screwed by the legislature in Juneau."
"Make no mistake. Anchorage wants the capital in Anchorage and          22
will somehow get it."
"Anchorage works hard to get things from other towns. It has from       23
the start. When Anchorage was just a few people in tents, they tried
to take the headquarters of the railroad from Seward and the U.S.
District Court from Valdez. In both instances, they succeeded. Recently, they have tried hard to take the university from Fairbanks.
They have part of it already. They wooed the U.S. land office away
from Juneau. 'Proud' is a word still used here in Alaska—but not about
Anchorage."
A single voice can be particularly audible in Alaska, because there     24
are so few people. Much is made of Alaska's great size. It is worth
remembering, as well, how small Alaska is—a handful of people clinging to a subcontinent. There are nearly twice as many people in the
District of Columbia as there are in the State of Alaska. In ten square
miles of the eastern state I live in are more people than there are in the
five hundred and eighty-six thousand square miles of Alaska.
"The capital must be a new city."                                       25
"Pipeline or no pipeline, the state would go broke buying land in       26
Anchorage. On top of that, because everybody in Alaska hates Anchorage it is politically expedient to put the capital in a new place, an
undeveloped place."
"The land out there is of no great value. It's just wilderness,         27
standing there."

---

# Casualties of Commitment

## ELLEN GOODMAN

—The announcement comes over the phone, from West Coast to           1
East, a long-distance obituary to a longtime relationship.
I listen as my old friend, a poet, mourns her loss, eulogizes her     2
broken connection. Her words are so familiar to me that they might

have been uttered at a hundred other such wakes: "In the end, he couldn't make a commitment."

This is the third time recently that I have been called upon as     3
pallbearer to a love affair. Some strange spring fever seems to have proved fatal to these couplings.

In each case, the man came up to the threshold of promise. In each     4
case, he experienced it less as a doorway than as a line drawn in the sand. A line he couldn't cross.

By the time I hang up the phone this long evening, I share my     5
friends' pain and frustration. I want to say something about men and their troubles with the thing we call commitment.

I know that three life stories do not make a class action or even a     6
generalization about men. I am surrounded by exceptions, in my home, my family, my friends, my reading.

Yet when I look back over space and time, I see more men who     7
were skittish about permanent connections than women, more men who were frightened about commitment, more men who were anxious about marriage.

I am not talking about men who subscribe to *Playboy* magazine     8
and its philosophy. I am not talking about musical comedy "guys" who fear being housebroken by marriage-minded "dolls." I am not just talking about 1950s bachelors who try to avoid the tender traps.

These are men who have relationships on which they work. These     9
are men who may regard their reluctance to make a commitment as a problem. When pressed though, they may tell themselves that the problem will disappear with "the right woman."

Nor do the women in their lives lay traps anymore. They do not fill     10
hope chests or talk about men as good catches. They, too, have relationships on which they work.

Still, sometimes I wonder how much things have changed between     11
men and women. The dimensions of the commitment problem, the description of it may be different than in the days of the tender trap, but what about the origins, what about the feelings?

We still, men and women, grow up differently. It's not just a     12
matter of dolls and building blocks, though there is some of that. We are taught in this country that people have to break away to become mature. People have to become independent, a condition we confuse with being alone. In real life, these people are men.

We teach men in a thousand ways that relationships are encum-     13
brances that hold them back, trap them, catch them. It's the men, almost always, who become our lone rangers.

Women learn another double message. We are both urged toward    14
independence and encouraged toward caretaking. We try to grow up
without growing away, thinking of ourselves and our lives as connected. And fearing isolation.

What happens then when we come together expecting love? Men    15
who equate maturity with independence meet women who equate it
with connections. Our fears collide.


Most of us break through this difference, but not all or always or    16
without pain. Often, there are casualties along the way.

I spoke with one of the three men who had caught this spring    17
fever. It was hard, he said, but he would get through it, tough it out.
I had the sense that he regarded this breakup as a challenge.

Reenacting some primal scene, he was again a real man, alone. In    18
some odd way the new bad feelings felt right.

In the next few weeks or months, this man will use his considerable    19
strength. He will use it to prevent himself from crossing the threshold.
He will use it to deal with his loneliness. It will be easier for him that
way, making no commitments.

# Example

## Aria: A Memoir of a Bilingual Childhood

### RICHARD RODRIGUEZ

I remember to start with that day in Sacramento—a California 1
now nearly thirty years past—when I first entered a classroom, able to
understand some fifty stray English words.

The third of four children, I had been preceded to a neighborhood 2
Roman Catholic school by an older brother and sister. But neither of
them had revealed very much about their classroom experiences. Each
afternoon they returned, as they left in the morning, always together,
speaking in Spanish as they climbed the five steps of the porch. And
their mysterious books, wrapped in shopping-bag paper, remained on
the table next to the door, closed firmly behind them.

An accident of geography sent me to a school where all my class- 3
mates were white, many the children of doctors and lawyers and
business executives. All my classmates certainly must have been uneasy on that first day of school—as most children are uneasy—to find
themselves apart from their families in the first institution of their lives.
But I was astonished.

The nun said, in a friendly but oddly impersonal voice, "Boys and 4
girls, this is Richard Rodriguez." (I heard her sound out: *Rich-heard
Road-ree-guess.*) It was the first time I had heard anyone name me in
English. "Richard," the nun repeated more slowly, writing my name
down in her black leather book. Quickly I turned to see my mother's
face dissolve in a watery blur behind the pebbled glass door.

Many years later there is something called bilingual education—a 5
scheme proposed in the late 1960s by Hispanic-American social acti-
vists, later endorsed by a congressional vote. It is a program that seeks

to permit non-English-speaking children, many from lower-class homes, to use their family language as the language of school. (Such is the goal its supporters announce.) I hear them and am forced to say no: It is not possible for a child—any child—ever to use his family's language in school. Not to understand this is to misunderstand the public uses of schooling and to trivialize the nature of intimate life—a family's "language."

Memory teaches me what I know of these matters; the boy reminds the adult. I was a bilingual child, a certain kind—socially disadvantaged—the son of working-class parents, both Mexican immigrants. 6

In the early years of my boyhood, my parents coped very well in America. My father had steady work. My mother managed at home. They were nobody's victims. Optimism and ambition led them to a house (our home) many blocks from the Mexican south side of town. We lived among *gringos* and only a block from the biggest, whitest houses. It never occurred to my parents that they couldn't live wherever they chose. Nor was the Sacramento of the fifties bent on teaching them a contrary lesson. My mother and father were more annoyed than intimidated by those two or three neighbors who tried initially to make us unwelcome. ("Keep your brats away from my sidewalk!") But despite all they achieved, perhaps because they had so much to achieve, any deep feeling of ease, the confidence of "belonging" in public was withheld from them both. They regarded the people at work, the faces in crowds, as very distant from us. They were the others, *los gringos*. That term was interchangeable in their speech with another, even more telling, *los americanos*. 7

I grew up in a house where the only regular guests were my relations. For one day, enormous families of relatives would visit and there would be so many people that the noise and the bodies would spill out to the backyard and front porch. Then, for weeks, no one came by. (It was usually a salesman who rang the doorbell.) Our house stood apart. A gaudy yellow in a row of white bungalows. We were the people with the noisy dog. The people who raised pigeons and chickens. We were the foreigners on the block. A few neighbors smiled and waved. We waved back. But no one in the family knew the names of the old couple who lived next door; until I was seven years old, I did not know the names of the kids who lived across the street. 8

In public, my father and mother spoke a hesitant, accented, not always grammatical English. And they would have to strain—their 9 bodies tense—to catch the sense of what was rapidly said by *los grin-gos*. At home they spoke Spanish. The language of their Mexican past sounded in counterpoint to the English of public society. The words would come quickly, with ease. Conveyed through those sounds was the pleasing, soothing, consoling reminder of being at home.

During those years when I was first conscious of hearing, my mother and father addressed me only in Spanish; in Spanish I learned to reply. By contrast, English *(inglés)*, rarely heard in the house, was the language I came to associate with *gringos*. I learned my first words of English overhearing my parents speak to strangers. At five years of age, I knew just enough English for my mother to trust me on errands to stores one block away. No more.

I was a listening child, careful to hear the very different sounds of Spanish and English. Wide-eyed with hearing, I'd listen to sounds more than words. First, there were English *(gringo)* sounds. So many words were still unknown that when the butcher or the lady at the drugstore said something to me, exotic polysyllabic sounds would bloom in the midst of their sentences. Often, the speech of people in public seemed to me very loud, booming with confidence. The man behind the counter would literally ask, "What can I do for you?" But by being so firm and so clear, the sound of his voice said that he was a *gringo;* he belonged in public society.

I would also hear then the high nasal notes of middle-class Ameri-can speech. The air stirred with sound. Sometimes, even now, when I have been traveling abroad for several weeks, I will hear what I heard as a boy. In hotel lobbies or airports, in Turkey or Brazil, some Ameri-cans will pass, and suddenly I will hear it again—the high sound of American voices. For a few seconds I will hear it with pleasure, for it is now the sound of *my* society—a reminder of home. But inevitably—already on the flight headed for home—the sound fades with repeti-tion. I will be unable to hear it anymore.

When I was a boy, things were different. The accent of *los gringos* was never pleasing nor was it hard to hear. Crowds at Safeway or at bus stops would be noisy with sound. And I would be forced to edge away from the chirping chatter above me.

I was unable to hear my own sounds, but I knew very well that I spoke English poorly. My words could not stretch far enough to form complete thoughts. And the words I did speak I didn't know well enough to make into distinct sounds. (Listeners would usually lower their heads, better to hear what I was trying to say.) But it was one thing for *me* to speak English with difficulty. It was more troubling for me to hear my parents speak in public: their high-whining vowels and guttural consonants; their sentences that got stuck with "ch" and "ah" sounds; the confused syntax; the hesitant rhythm of sounds so different from the way *gringos* spoke. I'd notice, moreover, that my parents' voices were softer than those of *gringos* we'd meet.

I am tempted now to say that none of this mattered. In adulthood    15
I am embarrassed by childhood fears. And, in a way, it didn't matter very much that my parents could not speak English with ease. Their linguistic difficulties had no serious consequences. My mother and father made themselves understood at the county hospital clinic and at government offices. And yet, in another way, it mattered very much— it was unsettling to hear my parents struggle with English. Hearing them, I'd grow nervous, my clutching trust in their protection and power weakened.

There were many times like the night at a brightly lit gasoline    16
station (a blaring white memory) when I stood uneasily, hearing my father. He was talking to a teenaged attendant. I do not recall what they were saying, but I cannot forget the sounds my father made as he spoke. At one point his words slid together to form one word—sounds as confused as the threads of blue and green oil in the puddle next to my shoes. His voice rushed through what he had left to say. And, toward the end, reached falsetto notes, appealing to his listener's understanding. I looked away to the lights of passing automobiles. I tried not to hear anymore. But I heard only too well the calm, easy tones in the attendant's reply. Shortly afterward, walking toward home with my father, I shivered when he put his hand on my shoulder. The very first chance that I got, I evaded his grasp and ran on ahead into the dark, skipping with feigned boyish exuberance.

But then there was Spanish. *Español:* my family's language. *Es-*    17
*pañol:* the language that seemed to me a private language. I'd hear strangers on the radio and in the Mexican Catholic church across town speaking in Spanish, but I couldn't really believe that Spanish was a public language, like English. Spanish speakers, rather, seemed related to me, for I sensed that we shared—through our language—the experience of feeling apart from *los gringos*. It was thus a ghetto Spanish that I heard and I spoke. Like those whose lives are bound by a barrio, I was reminded by Spanish of my separateness from *los otros, los gringos* in power. But more intensely than for most barrio children—because I did not live in a barrio—Spanish seemed to me the language of home.

(Most days it was only at home that I'd hear it.) It became the language of joyful return.

A family member would say something to me and I would feel myself specially recognized. My parents would say something to me and I would feel embraced by the sounds of their words. Those sounds said: *I am speaking with ease in Spanish. I am addressing you in words I never use with los gringos. I recognize you as someone special, close, like no one outside. You belong with us. In the family.*

*(Ricardo.)*

At the age of five, six, well past the time when most other children no longer easily notice the difference between sounds uttered at home and words spoken in public, I had a different experience. I lived in a world magically compounded of sounds. I remained a child longer than most; I lingered too long, poised at the edge of language—often frightened by the sounds of *los gringos,* delighted by the sounds of Spanish at home. I shared with my family a language that was startlingly different from that used in the great city around us.

For me there were none of the gradations between public and private society so normal to a maturing child. Outside the house was public society; inside the house was private. Just opening or closing the screen door behind me was an important experience. I'd rarely leave home all alone or without reluctance. Walking down the sidewalk, under the canopy of tall trees, I'd warily notice the—suddenly—silent neighborhood kids who stood warily watching me. Nervously, I'd arrive at the grocery store to hear there the sounds of the *gringo*—foreign to me—reminding me that in this world so big, I was a foreigner. But then I'd return. Walking back toward our house, climbing the steps from the sidewalk, when the front door was open in summer, I'd hear voices beyond the screen door talking in Spanish. For a second or two, I'd stay, linger there, listening. Smiling, I'd hear my mother call out, saying in Spanish (words): "Is that you, Richard?" All the while her sounds would assure me: *You are home now; come closer; inside. With us.*

"Sí," I'd reply.

Once more inside the house I would resume (assume) my place in the family. The sounds would dim, grow harder to hear. Once more at home, I would grow less aware of that fact. It required, however, no more than the blurt of the doorbell to alert me to listen to sounds all over again. The house would turn instantly still while my mother went to the door. I'd hear her hard English sounds. I'd wait to hear her voice return to soft-sounding Spanish, which assured me, as surely as did the clicking tongue of the lock on the door, that the stranger was gone.

Plainly, it is not healthy to hear such sounds so often. It is not    24 healthy to distinguish public words from private sounds so easily. I remained cloistered by sounds, timid and shy in public, too dependent on voices at home. And yet it needs to be emphasized: I was an extremely happy child at home. I remember many nights when my father would come back from work, and I'd hear him call out to my mother in Spanish, sounding relieved. In Spanish, he'd sound light and free notes he never could manage in English. Some nights I'd jump up just at hearing his voice. With *mis hermanos* I would come running into the room where he was with my mother. Our laughing (so deep was the pleasure!) became screaming. Like others who know the pain of public alienation, we transformed the knowledge of our public separateness and made it consoling—the reminder of intimacy. Excited, we joined our voices in a celebration of sounds. *We are speaking now the way we never speak out in public. We are alone—together,* voices sounded, surrounded to tell me. Some nights, no one seemed willing to loosen the hold sounds had on us. At dinner, we invented new words. (Ours sounded Spanish, but made sense only to us.) We pieced together new words by taking, say, an English verb and giving it Spanish endings. My mother's instructions at bedtime would be lacquered with mock-urgent tones. Or a word like *sí* would become, in several notes, able to convey added measures of feeling. Tongues explored the edges of words, especially the fat vowels. And we happily sounded that military drum roll, the twirling roar of the Spanish *r*. Family language: my family's sounds. The voices of my parents and sisters and brother. Their voices insisting: *You belong here. We are family members. Related. Special to one another. Listen!* Voices singing and sighing, rising, straining, then surging, teeming with pleasure that burst syllables into fragments of laughter. At times it seemed there was steady quiet only when, from another room, the rustling whispers of my parents faded and I moved closer to sleep.

Supporters of bilingual education today imply that students like    25 me miss a great deal by not being taught in their family's language. What they seem not to recognize is that, as a socially disadvantaged child, I considered Spanish to be a private language. What I needed to learn in school was that I had the right—and the obligation—to speak the public language of *los gringos*. The odd truth is that my first-grade classmates could have become bilingual, in the conventional sense of that word, more easily than I. Had they been taught (as upper-middle-class children are often taught early) a second language like Spanish or French, they could have regarded it simply as that: another public language. In my case such bilingualism could not have been so quickly achieved. What I did not believe was that I could speak a single public language.

Without question, it would have pleased me to hear my teachers 26 address me in Spanish when I entered the classroom. I would have felt much less afraid. I would have trusted them and responded with ease. But I would have delayed—for how long postponed?—having to learn the language of public society. I would have evaded—and for how long could I have afforded to delay?—learning the great lesson of school, that I had a public identity.

Fortunately, my teachers were unsentimental about their respon- 27 sibility. What they understood was that I needed to speak a public language. So their voices would search me out, asking me questions. Each time I'd hear them, I'd look up in surprise to see a nun's face frowning at me. I'd mumble, not really meaning to answer. The nun would persist, "Richard, stand up. Don't look at the floor. Speak up. Speak to the entire class, not just to me!" But I couldn't believe that the English language was mine to use. (In part, I did not want to believe it.) I continued to mumble. I resisted the teacher's demands. (Did I somehow suspect that once I learned public language my pleas-ing family life would be changed?) Silent, waiting for the bell to sound, I remained dazed, diffident, afraid.

Because I wrongly imagined that English was intrinsically a public 28 language and Spanish an intrinsically private one, I easily noted the difference between classroom language and the language of home. At school, words were directed to a general audience of listeners. ("Boys and girls.") Words were meaningfully ordered. And the point was not self-expression alone but to make oneself understood by many others. The teacher quizzed: "Boys and girls, why do we use that word in this sentence? Could we think of a better word to use there? Would the sentence change its meaning if the words were differently arranged? And wasn't there a better way of saying much the same thing?" (I couldn't say. I wouldn't try to say.)

Three months. Five. Half a year passed. Unsmiling, ever watchful, 29 my teachers noted my silence. They began to connect my behavior with the difficult progress my older sister and brother were making. Until one Saturday morning three nuns arrived at the house to talk to

our parents. Stiffly, they sat on the blue living room sofa. From the
doorway of another room, spying the visitors, I noted the incongruity—
the clash of two worlds, the faces and voices of school intruding upon
the familiar setting of home. I overheard one voice gently wondering,
"Do your children speak only Spanish at home, Mrs. Rodriguez?"
While another voice added, "That Richard especially seems so timid
and shy."

*That Rich-heard!*                                                    30

With great tact the visitors continued, "Is it possible for you and    31
your husband to encourage your children to practice their English
when they are home?" Of course, my parents complied. What would
they not do for their children's well-being? And how could they have
questioned the Church's authority which those women represented? In
an instant, they agreed to give up the language (the sounds) that had
revealed and accentuated our family's closeness. The moment after the
visitors left, the change was observed. *"Ahora,* speak to us *en inglés,"*
my father and mother united to tell us.

At first, it seemed a kind of game. After dinner each night, the       32
family gathered to practice "our" English. (It was still then *inglés,* a
language foreign to us, so we felt drawn as strangers to it.) Laughing,
we would try to define words we could not pronounce. We played with
strange English sounds, often over-anglicizing our pronunciations. And
we filled the smiling gaps of our sentences with familiar Spanish
sounds. But that was cheating, somebody shouted. Everyone laughed.
In school, meanwhile, like my brother and sister, I was required to
attend a daily tutoring session. I needed a full year of special attention.
I also needed my teachers to keep my attention from straying in class
by calling out, *Rich-heard*—their English voices slowly prying loose my
ties to my other name, its three notes, *Ri-car-do.* Most of all I needed
to hear my mother and father speak to me in a moment of seriousness
in broken—suddenly heartbreaking—English. The scene was inevitable: One Saturday morning I entered the kitchen where my parents
were talking in Spanish. I did not realize that they were talking in
Spanish however until, at the moment they saw me, I heard their
voices change to speak English. Those *gringo* sounds they uttered
startled me. Pushed me away. In that moment of trivial misunderstanding and profound insight, I felt my throat twisted by unsounded
grief. I turned quickly and left the room. But I had no place to escape
to with Spanish. (The spell was broken.) My brother and sisters were
speaking English in another part of the house.

Again and again in the days following, increasingly angry, I was   33
obliged to hear my mother and father: "Speak to us *en inglés.*"
*(Speak.)* Only then did I determine to learn classroom English. Weeks
after, it happened: One day in school I raised my hand to volunteer an
answer. I spoke out in a loud voice. And I did not think it remarkable
when the entire class understood. That day, I moved very far from the
disadvantaged child I had been only days earlier. The belief, the
calming assurance that I belonged in public, had at last taken hold.

Shortly after, I stopped hearing the high and loud sounds of *los*   34
*gringos.* A more and more confident speaker of English, I didn't trouble
to listen to *how* strangers sounded, speaking to me. And there simply
were too many English-speaking people in my day for me to hear
American accents anymore. Conversations quickened. Listening to
persons who sounded eccentrically pitched voices, I usually noted their
sounds for an initial few seconds before I concentrated on *what* they
were saying. Conversations became content-full. Transparent. Hearing someone's *tone* of voice—angry or questioning or sarcastic or
happy or sad—I didn't distinguish it from the words it expressed.
Sound and word were thus tightly wedded. At the end of a day, I was
often bemused, always relieved, to realize how "silent," though
crowded with words, my day in public had been. (*This* public silence
measured and quickened the change in my life.)

At last, seven years old, I came to believe what had been techni-   35
cally true since my birth: I was an American citizen.

But the special feeling of closeness at home was diminished by   36
then. Gone was the desperate, urgent, intense feeling of being at
home; rare was the experience of feeling myself individualized by
family intimates. We remained a loving family, but one greatly
changed. No longer so close; no longer bound tight by the pleasing and
troubling knowledge of our public separateness. Neither my older
brother nor sister rushed home after school anymore. Nor did I. When
I arrived home there would often be neighborhood kids in the house.
Or the house would be empty of sounds.

Following the dramatic Americanization of their children, even   37
my parents grew more publicly confident. Especially my mother. She
learned the names of all the people on our block. And she decided we
needed to have a telephone installed in the house. My father continued
to use the word *gringo.* But it was no longer charged with the old
bitterness or distrust. (Stripped of any emotional content, the word
simply became a name for those Americans not of Hispanic descent.)

Hearing him, sometimes, I wasn't sure if he was pronouncing the Spanish word *gringo* or saying gringo in English.

Matching the silence I started hearing in public was a new quiet    38
at home. The family's quiet was partly due to the fact that, as we children learned more and more English, we shared fewer and fewer words with our parents. Sentences needed to be spoken slowly when a child addressed his mother or father. (Often the parent wouldn't understand.) The child would need to repeat himself. (Still the parent misunderstood.) The young voice, frustrated, would end up saying, "Never mind"—the subject was closed. Dinners would be noisy with the clinking of knives and forks against dishes. My mother would smile softly between her remarks; my father at the other end of the table would chew and chew at his food, while he stared over the heads of his children.

My *mother!* My *father!* After English became my primary lan-    39
guage, I no longer knew what words to use in addressing my parents. The old Spanish words (those tender accents of sound) I had used earlier—*mamá* and *papá*—I couldn't use anymore. They would have been too painful reminders of how much had changed in my life. On the other hand, the words I heard neighborhood kids call *their* parents seemed equally unsatisfactory. *Mother* and *Father; Ma, Papa, Pa, Dad, Pop* (how I hated the all-American sound of that last word especially)—all these terms I felt were unsuitable, not really terms of address for *my* parents. As a result, I never used them at home. Whenever I'd speak to my parents, I would try to get their attention with eye contact alone. In public conversations, I'd refer to "my parents" or "my mother and father."

My mother and father, for their part, responded differently, as    40
their children spoke to them less. She grew restless, seemed troubled and anxious at the scarcity of words exchanged in the house. It was she who would question me about my day when I came home from school. She smiled at small talk. She pried at the edges of my sentences to get me to say something more. (What?) She'd join conversations she overheard, but her intrusions often stopped her children's talking. By contrast, my father seemed reconciled to the new quiet. Though his English improved somewhat, he retired into silence. At dinner he spoke very little. One night his children and even his wife helplessly giggled at his garbled English pronunciation of the Catholic Grace before Meals. Thereafter he made his wife recite the prayer at the start of each meal, even on formal occasions, when there were guests in the

house. Hers became the public voice of the family. On official business, it was she, not my father, one would usually hear on the phone or in stores, talking to strangers. His children grew so accustomed to his silence that, years later, they would speak routinely of his shyness. (My mother would often try to explain: Both his parents died when he was eight. He was raised by an uncle who treated him like little more than a menial servant. He was never encouraged to speak. He grew up alone. A man of few words.) But my father was not shy, I realized, when I'd watch him speaking Spanish with relatives. Using Spanish, he was quickly effusive. Especially when talking with other men, his voice would spark, flicker, flare alive with sounds. In Spanish, he expressed ideas and feelings he rarely revealed in English. With firm Spanish sounds, he conveyed confidence and authority English would never allow him.

The silence at home, however, was finally more than a literal    41
silence. Fewer words passed between parent and child, but more profound was the silence that resulted from my inattention to sounds. At about the time I no longer bothered to listen with care to the sounds of English in public, I grew careless about listening to the sounds family members made when they spoke. Most of the time I heard someone speaking at home and didn't distinguish his sounds from the words people uttered in public. I didn't even pay much attention to my parents' accented and ungrammatical speech. At least not at home. Only when I was with them in public would I grow alert to their accents. Though, even then, their sounds caused me less and less concern. For I was increasingly confident of my own public identity.

I would have been happier about my public success had I not    42
sometimes recalled what it had been like earlier, when my family had conveyed its intimacy through a set of conveniently private sounds. Sometimes in public, hearing a stranger, I'd hark back to my past. A Mexican farmworker approached me downtown to ask directions to somewhere. "*¿Hijito . . . ?*" he said. And his voice summoned deep longing. Another time, standing beside my mother in the visiting room of a Carmelite convent, before the dense screen which rendered the nuns shadowy figures, I heard several Spanish-speaking nuns—their busy, singsong overlapping voices—assure us that yes, yes, we were remembered, all our family was remembered in their prayers. (Then voices echoed faraway family sounds.) Another day, a dark-faced old woman—her hand light on my shoulder—steadied herself against me as she boarded a bus. She murmured something I couldn't quite com-

prehend. Her Spanish voice came near, like the face of a never-before-seen relative in the instant before I was kissed. Her voice, like so many of the Spanish voices I'd hear in public, recalled the golden age of my youth. Hearing Spanish then, I continued to be a careful, if sad, listener to sounds. Hearing a Spanish-speaking family walking behind me, I turned to look. I smiled for an instant, before my glance found the Hispanic-looking faces of strangers in the crowd going by.

Today I hear bilingual educators say that children lose a degree of 43 "individuality" by becoming assimilated into public society. (Bilingual schooling was popularized in the seventies, that decade when middle-class ethnics began to resist the process of assimilation—the American melting pot.) But the bilingualists simplistically scorn the value and necessity of assimilation. They do not seem to realize that there are *two* ways a person is individualized. So they do not realize that while one suffers a diminished sense of *private* individuality by becoming assimilated into public society, such assimilation makes possible the achievement of *public* individuality.

The bilingualists insist that a student should be reminded of his 44 difference from others in mass society, his heritage. But they equate mere separateness with individuality. The fact is that only in private—with intimates—is separateness from the crowd a prerequisite for individuality. (An intimate draws me apart, tells me that I am unique, unlike all others.) In public, by contrast, full individuality is achieved, paradoxically, by those who are able to consider themselves members of the crowd. Thus it happened for me: Only when I was able to think of myself as an American, no longer an alien in *gringo* society, could I seek the rights and opportunities necessary for full public individuality. The social and political advantages I enjoy as a man result from the day that I came to believe that my name, indeed, is *Rich-heard Road-ree-guess.* It is true that my public society today is often impersonal. (My public society is usually mass society.) Yet despite the anonymity of the crowd and despite the fact that the individuality I achieve in public is often tenuous—because it depends on my being one in a crowd—I celebrate the day I acquired my new name. Those middle-class ethnics who scorn assimilation seem to me filled with decadent self-pity, obsessed by the burden of public life. Dangerously, they romanticize public separateness and they trivialize the dilemma of the socially disadvantaged.

My awkward childhood does not prove the necessity of bilingual 45 education. My story discloses instead an essential myth of childhood—inevitable pain. If I rehearse here the changes in my private life after my Americanization, it is finally to emphasize the public gain. The loss implies the gain: The house I returned to each afternoon was quiet. Intimate sounds no longer rushed to the door to greet me. There were other noises inside. The telephone rang. Neighborhood kids ran past the door of the bedroom where I was reading my schoolbooks—covered with shopping-bag paper. Once I learned public language, it would never again be easy for me to hear intimate family voices. More and more of my day was spent hearing words. But that may only be a way of saying that the day I raised my hand in class and spoke loudly to an entire roomful of faces, my childhood started to end.

I grew up victim to a disabling confusion. As I grew fluent in   46
English, I no longer could speak Spanish with confidence. I continued to understand spoken Spanish. And in high school, I learned how to read and write Spanish. But for many years I could not pronounce it. A powerful guilt blocked my spoken words; an essential glue was missing whenever I'd try to connect words to form sentences. I would be unable to break a barrier of sound, to speak freely. I would speak, or try to speak, Spanish, and I would manage to utter halting, hiccuping sounds that betrayed my unease.

When relatives and Spanish-speaking friends of my parents came   47
to the house, my brother and sisters seemed reticent to use Spanish, but at least they managed to say a few necessary words before being excused. I never managed so gracefully. I was cursed with guilt. Each time I'd hear myself addressed in Spanish, I would be unable to respond with any success. I'd know the words I wanted to say, but I couldn't manage to say them. I would try to speak, but everything I said seemed to me horribly anglicized. My mouth would not form the words right. My jaw would tremble. After a phrase or two, I'd cough up a warm, silvery sound. And stop.

It surprised my listeners to hear me. They'd lower their heads,   48
better to grasp what I was trying to say. They would repeat their questions in gentle, affectionate voices. But by then I would answer in English. No, no, they would say, we want you to speak to us in Spanish. (". . . *en español*.") But I couldn't do it. *Pocho* then they called me. Sometimes playfully, teasingly, using the tender diminutive—*mi pochito*. Sometimes not so playfully, mockingly, *Pocho*. (A Spanish dictionary defines that word as an adjective meaning "colorless" or "bland."

But I heard it as a noun, naming the Mexican-American who, in becoming an American, forgets his native society.) *"¡Pocho!"* the lady in the Mexican food store muttered, shaking her head. I looked up to the counter where red and green peppers were strung like Christmas tree lights and saw the frowning face of the stranger. My mother laughed somewhere behind me. (She said that her children didn't want to practice "our Spanish" after they started going to school.) My mother's smiling voice made me suspect that the lady who faced me was not really angry at me. But, searching her face, I couldn't find the hint of a smile.

Embarrassed, my parents would regularly need to explain their   49
children's inability to speak flowing Spanish during those years. My mother met the wrath of her brother, her only brother, when he came up from Mexico one summer with his family. He saw his nieces and nephews for the very first time. After listening to me, he looked away and said what a disgrace it was that I couldn't speak Spanish, *"su proprio idioma."* He made that remark to my mother; I noticed, how-ever, that he stared at my father.

I clearly remember one other visitor from those years. A long-time   50
friend of my father from San Francisco would come to stay with us for several days in late August. He took great interest in me after he realized that I couldn't answer his questions in Spanish. He would grab me as I started to leave the kitchen. He would ask me something. Usually he wouldn't bother to wait for my mumbled response. Know-ingly, he'd murmur: *"¿Ay Pocho, Pocho, adónde vas?"* And he would press his thumbs into the upper part of my arms, making me squirm with currents of pain. Dumbly, I'd stand there, waiting for his wife to notice us, for her to call him off with a benign smile. I'd giggle, hoping to deflate the tension between us, pretending that I hadn't seen the glittering scorn in his glance.

I remember that man now, but seek no revenge in this telling. I   51
recount such incidents only because they suggest the fierce power Spanish had for many people I met at home; the way Spanish was associated with closeness. Most of those people who called me a *pocho* could have spoken English to me. But they would not. They seemed to think that Spanish was the only language we could use, that Spanish alone permitted our close association. (Such persons are vulnerable always to the ghetto merchant and the politician who have learned the value of speaking their clients' family language to gain immediate trust.) For my part, I felt that I had somehow committed a sin of

betrayal by learning English. But betrayal against whom? Not against visitors to the house exactly. No, I felt that I had betrayed my immediate family. I *knew* that my parents had encouraged me to learn English. I *knew* that I had turned to English only with angry reluctance. But once I spoke English with ease, I came to *feel* guilty. (This guilt defied logic.) I felt that I had shattered the intimate bond that had once held the family close. This original sin against my family told whenever anyone addressed me in Spanish and I responded, confounded.

But even during those years of guilt, I was coming to sense certain consoling truths about language and intimacy. I remember playing with a friend in the backyard one day, when my grandmother appeared at the window. Her face was stern with suspicion when she saw the boy (the *gringo*) I was with. In Spanish she called out to me, sounding the whistle of her ancient breath. My companion looked up and watched her intently as she lowered the window and moved, still visible, behind the light curtain, watching us both. He wanted to know what she had said. I started to tell him, to say—to translate her Spanish words into English. The problem was, however, that though I knew how to translate exactly *what* she had told me, I realized that any translation would distort the deepest meaning of her message: It had been directed only to me. This message of intimacy could never be translated because it was not *in* the words she had used but passed *through* them. So any translation would have seemed wrong; her words would have been stripped of an essential meaning. Finally, I decided not to tell my friend anything. I told him that I didn't hear all she had said.

This insight unfolded in time. Making more and more friends outside my house, I began to distinguish intimate voices speaking through *English*. I'd listen at times to a close friend's confidential tone or secretive whisper. Even more remarkable were those instances when, for no special reason apparently, I'd become conscious of the fact that my companion was speaking only to me. I'd marvel just hearing his voice. It was a stunning event: to be able to break through his words, to be able to hear this voice of the other, to realize that it was directed only to me. After such moments of intimacy outside the house, I began to trust hearing intimacy conveyed through my family's English. Voices at home at last punctured sad confusion. I'd hear myself addressed as an intimate at home once again. Such moments were never as raucous with sound as past times had been when we had had "private" Spanish to use. (Our English-sounding house was never to be as noisy as our Spanish-speaking house had been.) Intimate moments were usually soft moments of sound. My mother was in the dining room while I did my homework nearby. And she looked over at me. Smiled. Said something—her words said nothing very important. But her voice sounded to tell me *(We are together)* I was her son.

    *(Richard!)*                                                                54

    Intimacy thus continued at home; intimacy was not stilled by   55
English. It is true that I would never forget the great change of my life, the diminished occasions of intimacy. But there would also be times when I sensed the deepest truth about language and intimacy: *Intimacy is not created by a particular language; it is created by intimates.* The great change in my life was not linguistic but social. If, after becoming a successful student, I no longer heard intimate voices as often as I had earlier, it was not because I spoke English rather than Spanish. It was because I used public language for most of the day. I moved easily at last, a citizen in a crowded city of words.

---

# Split at the Root: An Essay on Jewish Identity

## ADRIENNE RICH

    For about fifteen minutes I have been sitting chin in hand in front   1
of the typewriter, staring out at the snow. Trying to be honest with myself, trying to figure out why writing this seems to be so dangerous an act, filled with fear and shame, and why it seems so necessary. It comes to me that in order to write this I have to be willing to do two things: I have to claim my father, for I have my Jewishness from him and not from my gentile mother; and I have to break his silence, his taboos; in order to claim him I have in a sense to expose him.

    And there is, of course, the third thing: I have to face the sources   2
and the flickering presence of my own ambivalence as a Jew; the daily, mundane anti-Semitisms of my entire life.

    These are stories I have never tried to tell before. Why now? Why,   3
I asked myself sometime last year, does this question of Jewish identity

float so impalpably, so ungraspably around me, a cloud I can't quite see the outlines of, which feels to me to be without definition?

And yet I've been on the track of this longer than I think.     4

In a long poem written in 1960, when I was thirty-one years old,     5
I described myself as "Split at the root, neither Gentile nor Jew, / Yankee nor Rebel." I was still trying to have it both ways: to be neither / nor, trying to live (with my Jewish husband and three children more Jewish in ancestry than I) in the predominantly gentile Yankee academic world of Cambridge, Massachusetts.

But this begins, for me, in Baltimore, where I was born in my     6
father's workplace, a hospital in the Black ghetto, whose lobby contained an immense white marble statue of Christ.

My father was then a young teacher and researcher in the depart-     7
ment of pathology at the Johns Hopkins Medical School, one of the very few Jews to attend or teach at that institution. He was from Birmingham, Alabama; his father, Samuel, was Ashkenazic, an immigrant from Austria-Hungary and his mother, Hattie Rice, a Sephardic Jew from Vicksburg, Mississippi. My grandfather had had a shoe store in Birmingham, which did well enough to allow him to retire comfortably and to leave my grandmother income on his death. The only souvenirs of my grandfather, Samuel Rich, were his ivory flute, which lay on our living-room mantel and was not to be played with; his thin gold pocket watch, which my father wore; and his Hebrew prayer book, which I discovered among my father's books in the course of reading my way through his library. In this prayer book there was a newspaper clipping about my grandparents' wedding, which took place in a synagogue.

My father, Arnold, was sent in adolescence to a military school in     8
the North Carolina mountains, a place for training white southern Christian gentlemen. I suspect that there were few, if any, other Jewish boys at Colonel Bingham's, or at "Mr. Jefferson's university" in Charlottesville, where he studied as an undergraduate. With whatever conscious forethought, Samuel and Hattie sent their son into the dominant southern WASP culture to become an "exception," to enter the professional class. Never, in describing these experiences, did he speak of having suffered—from loneliness, cultural alienation, or outsiderhood. Never did I hear him use the word *anti-Semitism*.

❖     ❖     ❖

It was only in college, when I read a poem by Karl Shapiro begin-    9
ning "To hate the Negro and avoid the Jew / is the curriculum," that
it flashed on me that there was an untold side to my father's story of
his student years. He looked recognizably Jewish, was short and slender in build with dark wiry hair and deep-set eyes, high forehead and
curved nose.

My mother is a gentile. In Jewish law I cannot count myself a Jew.    10
If it is true that "we think back through our mothers if we are women"
(Virginia Woolf)—and I myself have affirmed this—then even accord-
ing to lesbian theory, I cannot (or need not?) count myself a Jew.

The white southern Protestant woman, the gentile, has always    11
been there for me to peel back into. That's a whole piece of history in
itself, for my gentile grandmother and my mother were also frustrated
artists and intellectuals, a lost writer and a lost composer between
them. Readers and annotators of books, note takers, my mother a good
pianist still, in her eighties. But there was also the obsession with
ancestry, with "background," the southern talk of family, not as people
you would necessarily know and depend on, but as heritage, the guarantee of "good breeding." There was the inveterate romantic heterosexual fantasy, the mother telling the daughter how to attract men (my
mother often used the word "fascinate"); the assumption that relations
between the sexes could only be romantic, that it was in the woman's
interest to cultivate "mystery," conceal her actual feelings. Survival
tactics of a kind, I think today, knowing what I know about the white
woman's sexual role in the southern racist scenario. Heterosexuality as
protection, but also drawing white women deeper into collusion with
white men.

It would be easy to push away and deny the gentile in me—that    12
white southern woman, that social christian. At different times in my
life I have wanted to push away one or the other burden of inheritance,
to say merely *I am a woman; I am a lesbian.* If I call myself a Jewish
lesbian, do I thereby try to shed some of my southern gentile white
woman's culpability? If I call myself only through my mother, is it
because I pass more easily through a world where being a lesbian often
seems like outsiderhood enough?

According to Nazi logic, my two Jewish grandparents would have    13
made me a *Mischling, first-degree*—nonexempt from the Final Solution.

                              ✧         ✧         ✧

The social world in which I grew up was christian virtually without   14
needing to say so—christian imagery, music, language, symbols, assumptions everywhere. It was also a genteel, white, middle-class world
in which "common" was a term of deep opprobrium. "Common"
white people might speak of "niggers"; *we* were taught never to use
that word—*we* said "Negroes" (even as we accepted segregation, the
eating taboo, the assumption that Black people were simply of a separate species). Our language was more polite, distinguishing us from the
"red-necks" or the lynch-mob mentality. But so charged with negative
meaning was even the word "Negro" that as children we were taught
never to use it in front of Black people. We were taught that any
mention of skin color in the presence of colored people was treacherous, forbidden ground. In a parallel way, the word "Jew" was not used
by polite gentiles. I sometimes heard my best friend's father, a Presbyterian minister, allude to "the Hebrew people" or "people of the
Jewish faith." The world of acceptable folk was white, gentile (christian, really), and had "ideals" (which colored people, white "common"
people, were not supposed to have). "Ideals" and "manners" included
not hurting someone's feelings by calling her or him a Negro or a
Jew—naming the hated identity. This is the mental framework of the
1930s and 1940s in which I was raised.

(Writing this, I feel dimly like the betrayer: of my father, who did   15
not speak the word; of my mother, who must have trained me in the
messages; of my caste and class; of my whiteness itself.)

*Two memories:* I am in a play reading at school of *The Merchant*   16
*of Venice.* Whatever Jewish law says, I am quite sure I was *seen* as
Jewish (with a reassuringly gentile mother) in that double vision that
bigotry allows. I am the only Jewish girl in the class, and I am playing
Portia. As always, I read my part aloud for my father the night before,
and he tells me to convey, with my voice, more scorn and contempt
with the word "Jew": "Therefore, Jew . . ." I have to say the word out,
and say it loudly. I was encouraged to pretend to be a non-Jewish child
acting a non-Jewish character who has to speak the word "Jew" emphatically. Such a child would not have had trouble with the part. But
*I* must have had trouble with the part, if only because the word itself
was really taboo. I can see that there was a kind of terrible, bitter
bravado about my father's way of handling this. And who would not
dissociate from Shylock in order to identify with Portia? As a Jewish
child who was also a female, I loved Portia—and, like every other
Shakespearean heroine, she proved a treacherous role model.

A year or so later I am in another play, *The School for Scandal*, in    17
which a notorious spendthrift is described as having "many excellent
friends . . . among the Jews." In neither case was anything explained,
either to me or to the class at large, about this scorn for Jews and the
disgust surrounding Jews and money. Money, when Jews wanted it,
had it, or lent it to others, seemed to take on a peculiar nastiness; Jews
and money had some peculiar and unspeakable relation.

At this same school—in which we had Episcopalian hymns and    18
prayers, and read aloud through the Bible morning after morning—I
gained the impression that Jews were in the Bible and mentioned in
English literature, that they had been persecuted centuries ago by the
wicked Inquisition, but that they seemed not to exist in everyday life.
These were the 1940s, and we were told a great deal about the Battle
of Britain, the noble French Resistance fighters, the brave, starving
Dutch—but I did not learn of the resistance of the Warsaw ghetto until
I left home.

I was sent to the Episcopal church, baptized and confirmed, and    19
attended it for about five years, though without belief. That religion
seemed to have little to do with belief or commitment; it was liturgy
that mattered, not spiritual passion. Neither of my parents ever entered that church, and my father would not enter *any* church for any
reason—wedding or funeral. Nor did I enter a synagogue until I left
Baltimore. When I came home from church, for a while, my father
insisted on reading aloud to me from Thomas Paine's *The Age of
Reason*—a diatribe against institutional religion. Thus, he explained, I
would have a balanced view of these things, a choice. He—they—did
not give me the choice to be a Jew. My mother explained to me when
I was filling out forms for college that if any question was asked about
"religion," I should put down "Episcopalian" rather than "none"—to
seem to have no religion was, she implied, dangerous.

But it was white social christianity, rather than any particular    20
christian sect, that the world was founded on. The very word *Christian*
was used as a synonym for virtuous, just, peace-loving, generous, etc.,
etc.[1] The norm was christian: "religion: none" was indeed not acceptable. Anti-Semitism was so intrinsic as not to have a name. I don't
recall exactly being taught that the Jews killed Jesus—"Christ killer"
seems too strong a term for the bland Episcopal vocabulary—but certainly we got the impression that the Jews had been caught out in a
terrible mistake, failing to recognize the true Messiah, and were
thereby less advanced in moral and spiritual sensibility. The Jews had

actually allowed *moneylenders in the Temple* (again, the unexplained obsession with Jews and money). They were of the past, archaic, primitive, as older (and darker) cultures are supposed to be primitive; christianity was lightness, fairness, peace on earth, and combined the feminine appeal of "The meek shall inherit the earth" with the masculine stride of "Onward, Christian Soldiers."

Sometime in 1946, while still in high school, I read in the newspaper that a theater in Baltimore was showing films of the Allied liberation of the Nazi concentration camps. Alone, I went downtown after school one afternoon and watched the stark, blurry, but unmistakable newsreels. When I try to go back and touch the pulse of that girl of sixteen, growing up in many ways so precocious and so ignorant, I am overwhelmed by a memory of despair, a sense of inevitability more enveloping than any I had ever known. Anne Frank's diary and many other personal narratives of the Holocaust were still unknown or unwritten. But it came to me that every one of those piles of corpses, mountains of shoes and clothing had contained, simply, individuals, who had believed, as I now believed of myself, that they were intended to live out a life of some kind of meaning, that the world possessed some kind of sense and order; yet *this* had happened to them. And I, who believed my life was intended to be so interesting and meaningful, was connected to those dead by something—not just mortality but a taboo name, a hated identity. Or was I—did I really have to be? Writing this now, I feel belated rage that I was so impoverished by the family and social worlds I lived in, that I had to try to figure out by myself what this did indeed mean for me. That I had never been taught about resistance, only about passing. That I had no language for anti-Semitism itself.

When I went home and told my parents where I had been, they were not pleased. I felt accused of being morbidly curious, not healthy, sniffing around death for the thrill of it. And since, at sixteen, I was often not sure of the sources of my feelings or of my motives for doing what I did, I probably accused myself as well. One thing was clear: there was nobody in my world with whom I could discuss those films. Probably at the same time, I was reading accounts of the camps in magazines and newspapers; what I remember were the films and having questions that I could not even phrase, such as *Are those men and women "them" or "us"?*

To be able to ask even the child's astonished question *Why do they*

21

22

23

*hate us so?* means knowing how to say "we." The guilt of not knowing, the guilt of perhaps having betrayed my parents or even those victims, those survivors, through mere curiosity—these also froze in me for years the impulse to find out more about the Holocaust.

1947: I left Baltimore to go to college in Cambridge, Massachu-   24
setts, left (I thought) the backward, enervating South for the intellectual, vital North. New England also had for me some vibration of
higher moral rectitude, of moral passion even, with its seventeenth-
century Puritan self-scrutiny, its nineteenth-century literary "flower-
ing," its abolitionist righteousness, Colonel Shaw and his Black Civil
War regiment depicted in granite on Boston Common. At the same
time, I found myself, at Radcliffe, among Jewish women. I used to sit
for hours over coffee with what I thought of as the "real" Jewish
students, who told me about middle-class Jewish culture in America.
I described my background—for the first time to strangers—and they
took me on, some with amusement at my illiteracy, some arguing that
I could never marry into a strict Jewish family, some convinced I didn't
"look Jewish," others that I did. I learned the names of holidays and
foods, which surnames are Jewish and which are "changed names";
about girls who had had their noses "fixed," their hair straightened.
For these young Jewish women, students in the late 1940s, it was
acceptable, perhaps even necessary, to strive to look as gentile as
possible; but they stuck proudly to being Jewish, expected to marry a
Jew, have children, keep the holidays, carry on the culture.

I felt I was testing a forbidden current, that there was danger in   25
these revelations. I bought a reproduction of a Chagall portrait of a
rabbi in striped prayer shawl and hung it on the wall of my room. I was
admittedly young and trying to educate myself, but I was also doing
something that *is* dangerous: I was flirting with identity.

One day that year I was in a small shop where I had bought a dress   26
with a too-long skirt. The shop employed a seamstress who did alterations, and she came in to pin up the skirt on me. I am sure that she was
a recent immigrant, a survivor. I remember a short, dark woman
wearing heavy glasses, with an accent so foreign I could not understand her words. Something about her presence was very powerful and
disturbing to me. After marking and pinning up the skirt, she sat back
on her knees, looked up at me, and asked in a hurried whisper: "You
Jewish?" Eighteen years of training in assimilation sprang into the
reflex by which I shook my head, rejecting her, and muttered, "No."

What was I actually saying "no" to? She was poor, older, struggling    27
with a foreign tongue, anxious; she had escaped the death that had been
intended for her, but I had no imagination of her possible courage and
foresight, her resistance—I did not see in her a heroine who had perhaps
saved many lives, including her own. I saw the frightened immigrant, the
seamstress hemming the skirts of college girls, the wandering Jew. But I
was an American college girl having her skirt hemmed. And I was
frightened myself, I think, because she had recognized me ("It takes one
to know one," my friend Edie at Radcliffe had said) even if I refused to
recognize myself or her, even if her recognition was sharpened by
loneliness or the need to feel safe with me.

But why should she have felt safe with me? I myself was living    28
with a false sense of safety.

There are betrayals in my life that I have known at the very    29
moment were betrayals: this was one of them. There are other betrayals committed so repeatedly, so mundanely, that they leave no memory
trace behind, only a growing residue of misery, of dull, accreted self-
hatred. Often these take the form not of words but of silence. Silence
before the joke at which everyone is laughing: the anti-woman joke,
the racist joke, the anti-Semitic joke. Silence and then amnesia. Blocking it out when the oppressor's language starts coming from the lips of
one we admire, whose courage and eloquence have touched us: *She
didn't really mean that; he didn't really say that.* But the accretions
build up out of sight, like scale inside a kettle.

1948: I come home from my freshman year at college, flaming with    30
new insights, new information. I am the daughter who has gone out
into the world, to the pinnacle of intellectual prestige, Harvard, fulfill-
ing my father's hopes for me, but also exposed to dangerous influences.
I have already been reproved for attending a rally for Henry Wallace
and the Progressive party. I challenge my father: "Why haven't you
told me that I am Jewish? Why do you never talk about being a Jew?"
He answers measuredly, "You know that I have never denied that I am
a Jew. But it's not important to me. I am a scientist, a deist. I have no
use for organized religion. I choose to live in a world of many kinds of
people. There are Jews I admire and others whom I despise. I am a
person, not simply a Jew." The words are as I remember them, not
perhaps exactly as spoken. But that was the message. And it contained
enough truth—as all denial drugs itself on partial truth—so that it
remained for the time being unanswerable, leaving me high and dry,
split at the root, gasping for clarity, for air.

At that time Arnold Rich was living in suspension, waiting to be    31
appointed to the professorship of pathology at Johns Hopkins. The
appointment was delayed for years, no Jew ever having held a professional chair in that medical school. And he wanted it badly. It must
have been a very bitter time for him, since he had believed so greatly
in the redeeming power of excellence, of being the most brilliant,
inspired man for the job. With enough excellence, you could presumably make it stop mattering that you were Jewish; you could become
the *only* Jew in the gentile world, a Jew so "civilized," so far from
"common," so attractively combining southern gentility with European cultural values that no one would ever confuse you with the raw,
"pushy" Jews of New York, the "loud, hysterical" refugees from eastern Europe, the "overdressed" Jews of the urban South.

We—my sister, mother, and I—were constantly urged to speak    32
quietly in public, to dress without ostentation, to repress all vividness
or spontaneity, to assimilate with a world which might see us as too
flamboyant. I suppose that my mother, pure gentile though she was,
could be seen as acting "common" or "Jewish" if she laughed too
loudly or spoke aggressively. My father's mother, who lived with us
half the year, was a model of circumspect behavior, dressed in dark
blue or lavender, retiring in company, ladylike to an extreme, wearing
no jewelry except a good gold chain, a narrow brooch, or a string of
pearls. A few times, within the family, I saw her anger flare, felt the
passion she was repressing. But when Arnold took us out to a restaurant or on a trip, the Rich women were always tuned down to some
WASP level my father believed, surely, would protect us all—maybe
also make us unrecognizable to the "real Jews" who wanted to seize
us, drag us back to the *shtetl*, the ghetto, in its many manifestations.

For, yes, that *was* a message—that some Jews would be after you,    33
once they "knew," to rejoin them, to re-enter a world that was messy,
noisy, unpredictable, maybe poor—"even though," as my mother once
wrote me, criticizing my largely Jewish choice of friends in college,
"some of them will be the most brilliant, fascinating people you'll ever
meet." I wonder if that isn't one message of assimilation—of America—that the unlucky or the unachieving want to pull you backward,
that to identify with them is to court downward mobility, lose the
precious chance of passing, of token existence. There was always
within this sense of Jewish identity a strong class discrimination. Jews
might be "fascinating" as individuals but came with huge unruly families who "poured chicken soup over everyone's head" (in the phrase of

a white southern male poet). Anti-Semitism could thus be justified by the bad behavior of certain Jews; and if you did not effectively deny family and community, there would always be a remote cousin claiming kinship with you who was the "wrong kind" of Jew.

*I have always believed his attitude toward other Jews depended*     34
*on who they were. . . . It was my impression that Jews of this back-*
*ground looked down on Eastern European Jews, including Polish Jews*
*and Russian Jews, who generally were not as well educated.* This from
a letter written to me recently by a gentile who had worked in my father's department, whom I had asked about anti-Semitism there and in particular regarding my father. This informant also wrote me that it was hard to perceive anti-Semitism in Baltimore because the racism made so much more intense an impression: *I would almost have to think that blacks went to a different heaven than the whites, because the bodies were kept in a separate morgue, and some white persons did not even want blood transfusions from black donors.* My father's mind was predictably racist and misogynist; yet as a medical student he noted in his journal that southern male chivalry stopped at the point of any white man in a streetcar giving his seat to an old, weary Black woman standing in the aisle. Was this a Jewish insight—an outsider's insight, even though the outsider was striving to be on the inside?

Because what isn't named is often more permeating than what is,     35
I believe that my father's Jewishness profoundly shaped my own identity and our family existence. They were shaped both by external anti-Semitism and my father's self-hatred, and by his Jewish pride. What Arnold did, I think, was call his Jewish pride something else: achievement, aspiration, genius, idealism. Whatever was unacceptable got left back under the rubric of Jewishness or the "wrong kind" of Jews—uneducated, aggressive, loud. The message I got was that we were really superior: nobody else's father had collected so many books, had traveled so far, knew so many languages. Baltimore was a musical city, but for the most part, in the families of my school friends, culture was for women. My father was an amateur musician, read poetry, adored encyclopedic knowledge. He prowled and pounced over my school papers, insisting I use "grown-up" sources; he criticized my poems for faulty technique and gave me books on rhyme and meter and form. His investment in my intellect and talent was egotistical, tyrannical, opinionated, and terribly wearing. He taught me, nevertheless, to believe in hard work, to mistrust easy inspiration, to write and rewrite; to feel that I *was* a person of the book, even though a woman;

to take ideas seriously. He made me feel, at a very young age, the power of language and that I could share in it.

The Riches were proud, but we also had to be very careful. Our  36
behavior had to be more impeccable than other people's. Strangers were not to be trusted, nor even friends; family issues must never go beyond the family; the world was full of potential slanderers, betrayers, *people who could not understand.* Even within the family, I realize that I never in my whole life knew what my father was really feeling. Yet he spoke—monologued—with driving intensity. You could grow up in such a house mesmerized by the local electricity, the crucial meanings assumed by the merest things. This used to seem to me a sign that we were all living on some high emotional plane. It was a difficult force field for a favored daughter to disengage from.

Easy to call that intensity Jewish; and I have no doubt that passion  37
is one of the qualities required for survival over generations of persecution. But what happens when passion is rent from its original base, when the white gentile world is softly saying "Be more like us and you can be almost one of us"? What happens when survival seems to mean closing off one emotional artery after another? His forebears in Europe had been forbidden to travel or expelled from one country after another, had special taxes levied on them if they left the city walls, had been forced to wear special clothes and badges, restricted to the poorest neighborhoods. He had wanted to be a "free spirit," to travel widely, among "all kinds of people." Yet in his prime of life he lived in an increasingly withdrawn world, in his house up on a hill in a neighborhood where Jews were not supposed to be able to buy property, depending almost exclusively on interactions with his wife and daughters to provide emotional connectedness. In his home, he created a private defense system so elaborate that even as he was dying, my mother felt unable to talk freely with his colleagues or others who might have helped her. Of course, she acquiesced in this.

The loneliness of the "only," the token, often doesn't feel like  38
loneliness but like a kind of dead echo chamber. Certain things that ought to don't resonate. Somewhere Beverly Smith writes of women of color "inspiring the behavior" in each other. When there's nobody to "inspire the behavior," act out of the culture, there is an atrophy, a dwindling, which is partly invisible.

Sometimes I feel I have seen too long from too many discon-  39
nected angles: white, Jewish, anti-Semite, racist, anti-racist, once-

married, lesbian, middle-class, feminist, exmatriate southerner, *split at the root*—that I will never bring them whole. I would have liked, in this essay, to bring together the meanings of anti-Semitism and racism as I have experienced them and as I believe they intersect in the world beyond my life. But I'm not able to do this yet. I feel the tension as I think, make notes: *If you really look at the one reality, the other will waver and disperse.* Trying in one week to read Angela Davis and Lucy Davidowicz[2]; trying to hold throughout to a feminist, a lesbian, perspective—what does this mean? Nothing has trained me for this. And sometimes I feel inadequate to make any statement as a Jew; I feel the history of denial within me like an injury, a scar. For assimilation has affected *my* perceptions; those early lapses in meaning, those blanks, are with me still. My ignorance can be dangerous to me and to others.

Yet we can't wait for the undamaged to make our connections for us; we can't wait to speak until we are perfectly clear and righteous. There is no purity and, in our lifetime, no end to this process.       40

This essay, then, has no conclusions: it is another beginning for me. Not just a way of saying, in 1982 Right Wing America, *I, too, will wear the yellow star.* It's a moving into accountability, enlarging the range of accountability. I know that in the rest of my life, the next half century or so, every aspect of my identity will have to be engaged. The middle-class white girl taught to trade obedience for privilege. The Jewish lesbian raised to be a heterosexual gentile. The woman who first heard oppression named and analyzed in the Black Civil Rights struggle. The woman with three sons, the feminist who hates male violence. The woman limping with a cane, the woman who has stopped bleeding are also accountable. The poet who knows that beautiful language can lie, that the oppressor's language sometimes sounds beautiful. The woman trying, as part of her resistance, to clean up her act.       41

### Notes

1. In a similar way the phrase "That's white of you" implied that you were behaving with the superior decency and morality expected of white but not of Black people. [Author's note]
2. Angela Y. Davis, *Women, Race and Class* (New York: Random House, 1981); Lucy S. Davidowicz, *The War against the Jews 1933–1945* (1975) (New York: Bantam, 1979). [Author's note]

# A Few Words about Breasts

## NORA EPHRON

I have to begin with a few words about androgyny. In grammar     1
school, in the fifth and sixth grades, we were all tyrannized by a rigid
set of rules that supposedly determined whether we were boys or girls.
The episode in *Huckleberry Finn* where Huck is disguised as a girl and
gives himself away by the way he threads a needle and catches a
ball—that kind of thing. We learned that the way you sat, crossed your
legs, held a cigarette and looked at your nails, your wristwatch, the
way you did these things instinctively was absolute proof of your sex.
Now obviously most children did not take this literally, but I did. I
thought that just one slip, just one incorrect cross of my legs or flick of
an imaginary cigarette ash would turn me from whatever I was into the
other thing; that would be all it took, really. Even though I was out-
wardly a girl and had many of the trappings generally associated with
the field of girldom—a girl's name, for example, and dresses, my own
telephone, an autograph book—I spent the early years of my adolescence absolutely certain that I might at any point gum it up. I did not
feel at all like a girl. I was boyish. I was athletic, ambitious, outspoken,
competitive, noisy, rambunctious. I had scabs on my knees and my
socks slid into my loafers and I could throw a football. I wanted
desperately not to be that way, not to be a mixture of both things but
instead just one, a girl, a definite indisputable girl. As soft and as pink
as a nursery. And nothing would do that for me, I felt, but breasts.

I was about six months younger than everyone in my class, and so     2
for about six months after it began, for six months after my friends had
begun to develop—that was the word we used, develop—I was not
particularly worried. I would sit in the bathtub and look down at my
breasts and know that any day now, any second now, they would start
growing like everyone else's. They didn't. "I want to buy a bra," I said
to my mother one night. "What for?" she said. My mother was really
hateful about bras, and by the time my third sister had gotten to the
point where she was ready to want one, my mother had worked the
whole business into a comedy routine. "Why not use a Band-Aid

instead?" she would say. It was a source of great pride to my mother that she had never even had to wear a brassiere until she had her fourth child, and then only because her gynecologist made her. It was incomprehensible to me that anyone could ever be proud of something like that. It was the 1950's, for God's sake. Jane Russell. Cashmere sweaters. Couldn't my mother see that? *"I am too old to wear an undershirt."* Screaming. Weeping. Shouting. "Then don't wear an undershirt," said my mother. "But I want to buy a bra." "What for?"

I suppose that for most girls, breasts, brassieres, that entire    3
thing, has more trauma, more to do with the coming of adolescence, with becoming a woman, than anything else. Certainly more than getting your period, although that too was traumatic, symbolic. But you could *see* breasts; they were there; they were visible. Whereas a girl could claim to have her period for months before she actually got it and nobody would ever know the difference. Which is exactly what I did. All you had to do was make a great fuss over having enough nickels for the Kotex machine and walk around clutching your stomach and moaning for three to five days a month about The Curse and you could convince anybody. There is a school of thought somewhere in the women's lib/women's mag/gynecology establishment that claims that menstrual cramps are purely psychological, and I lean toward it. Not that I didn't have them finally. Agonizing cramps, heating-pad cramps, go-down-to-the-school-nurse-and-lie-on-the-cot cramps. But unlike any pain I had ever suffered, I adored the pain of cramps, welcomed it, wallowed in it, bragged about it. "I can't go. I have cramps." "I can't do that. I have cramps." And most of all, gigglingly, blushingly: "I can't swim. I have cramps." Nobody ever used the hard-core word. Menstruation. God, what an awful word. Never that. "I have cramps."

The morning I first got my period, I went into my mother's bed-    4
room to tell her. And my mother, my utterly-hateful-about-bras mother, burst into tears. It was really a lovely moment, and I remember it so clearly not just because it was one of the two times I ever saw my mother cry on my account (the other was when I was caught being a six-year-old kleptomaniac), but also because the incident did not mean to me what it meant to her. Her little girl, her first-born, had finally become a woman. That was what she was crying about. My reaction to the event, however, was that I might well be a woman in some scientific, textbook sense (and could at least stop faking every month and stop wasting all those nickels). But in another sense—in a

visible sense—I was as androgynous and as liable to tip over into
boyhood as ever.

I started with a 28AA bra. I don't think they made them any   5
smaller in those days, although I gather that now you can buy bras for
five year olds that don't have any cups whatsoever in them; trainer
bras they are called. My first brassiere came from Robinson's Department Store in Beverly Hills. I went there alone, shaking; positive they
would look me over and smile and tell me to come back next year. An
actual fitter took me into the dressing room and stood over me while
I took off my blouse and tried the first one on. The little puffs stood out
on my chest. "Lean over," said the fitter (to this day I am not sure what
fitters in bra departments do except to tell you to lean over). I leaned
over, with the fleeting hope that my breasts would miraculously fall out
of my body and into the puffs. Nothing.
   "Don't worry about it," said my friend Libby some months later,   6
when things had not improved. "You'll get them after you're married."
   "What are you talking about?" I said.                              7
   "When you get married," Libby explained, "your husband will        8
touch your breasts and rub them and kiss them and they'll grow."
   That was the killer. Necking I could deal with. Intercourse I could  9
deal with. But it had never crossed my mind that a man was going to
touch my breasts, that breasts had something to do with all that,
petting, my God they never mentioned petting in my little sex manual
about the fertilization of the ovum. I became dizzy. For I knew instantly—as naïve as I had been only a moment before—that only part
of what she was saying was true: the touching, rubbing, kissing part,
not the growing part. And I knew that no one would ever want to
marry me. I had no breasts. I would never have breasts.


   My best friend in school was Diana Raskob. She lived a block from  10
me in a house full of wonders. English muffins, for instance. The
Raskobs were the first people in Beverly Hills to have English muffins
for breakfast. They also had an apricot tree in the back, and a badmin-
ton court, and a subscription to *Seventeen* magazine, and hundreds of
games like Sorry and Parcheesi and Treasure Hunt and Anagrams.
Diana and I spent three or four afternoons a week in their den reading
and playing and eating. Diana's mother's kitchen was full of the most
colossal assortment of junk food I have ever been exposed to. My house

was full of apples and peaches and milk and homemade chocolate-chip cookies—which were nice, and good for you, but-not-right-before-dinner-or-you'll-spoil-your-appetite. Diana's house had nothing in it that was good for you, and what's more, you could stuff it in right up until dinner and nobody cared. Bar-B-Q potato chips (they were the first in them, too), giant bottles of ginger ale, fresh popcorn with melted butter, hot fudge sauce on Baskin-Robbins jamoca ice cream, powdered-sugar doughnuts from Van de Kamp's. Diana and I had been best friends since we were seven; we were about equally popular in school (which is to say, not particularly), we had about the same success with boys (extremely intermittent) and we looked much the same. Dark. Tall. Gangly.

It is September, just before school begins. I am eleven years old,   11 about to enter the seventh grade, and Diana and I have not seen each other all summer. I have been to camp and she has been somewhere like Banff with her parents. We are meeting, as we often do, on the street midway between our two houses and we will walk back to Diana's and eat junk and talk about what has happened to each of us that summer. I am walking down Walden Drive in my jeans and my father's shirt hanging out and my old red loafers with the socks falling into them and coming toward me is . . . I take a deep breath . . . a young woman. Diana. Her hair is curled and she has a waist and hips and a bust and she is wearing a straight skirt, an article of clothing I have been repeatedly told I will be unable to wear until I have the hips to hold it up. My jaw drops, and suddenly I am crying, crying hysterically, can't catch my breath sobbing. My best friend has betrayed me. She has gone ahead without me and done it. She has shaped up.

Here are some things I did to help:   12

> Bought a Mark Eden Bust Developer.
> Slept on my back for four years.
> Splashed cold water on them every night because some French actress said in *Life* magazine that that was what *she* did for her perfect bustline.

Ultimately, I resigned myself to a bad toss and began to wear   13 padded bras. I think about them now, think about all those years in high school I went around in them, my three padded bras, every single one of them with different sized breasts. Each time I changed bras I changed sizes: one week nice perky but not too obtrusive breasts, the next medium-sized slightly pointy ones, the next week knockers, true

knockers; all the time, whatever size I was, carrying around this rub-
berized appendage on my chest that occasionally crashed into a wall
and was poked inward and had to be poked outward—I think about all
that and wonder how anyone kept a straight face through it. My
parents, who normally had no restraints about needling me—why did
they say nothing as they watched my chest go up and down? My
friends, who would periodically inspect my breasts for signs for growth
and reassure me—why didn't they at least counsel consistency?

And the bathing suits. I die when I think about the bathing suits.      14
That was the era when you could lay an uninhabited bathing suit on
the beach and someone would make a pass at it. I would put one on,
an absurd swimsuit with its enormous bust built into it, the bones from
the suit stabbing me in the rib cage and leaving little red welts on my
body, and there I would be, my chest plunging straight downward
absolutely vertically from my collarbone to the top of my suit and then
suddenly, wham, out came all that padding and material and wiring
absolutely horizontally.


Buster Klepper was the first boy who ever touched them. He was       15
my boyfriend my senior year of high school. There is a picture of him
in my high-school yearbook that makes him look quite attractive in a
Jewish, horn-rimmed glasses sort of way, but the picture does not show
the pimples, which were air-brushed out, or the dumbness. Well, that
isn't really fair. He wasn't dumb. He just wasn't terribly bright. His
mother refused to accept it, refused to accept the relentlessly average
report cards, refused to deal with her son's inevitable destiny in some
junior college or other. "He was tested," she would say to me, apropos
of nothing, "and it came out 145. That's near-genius." Had the word
underachiever been coined, she probably would have lobbed that one
at me, too. Anyway, Buster was really very sweet—which is, I know,
damning with faint praise, but there it is. I was the editor of the front
page of the high-school newspaper and he was editor of the back page;
we had to work together, side by side, in the print shop, and that was
how it started. On our first date, we went to see *April Love* starring Pat
Boone. Then we started going together. Buster had a green coupe, a
1950 Ford with an engine he had hand-chromed until it shone, dazzled,
reflected the image of anyone who looked into it, anyone usually being
Buster polishing it or the gas-station attendants he constantly asked to
check the oil in order for them to be overwhelmed by the sparkle on

the valves. The car also had a boot stretched over the back seat for reasons I never understood; hanging from the rearview mirror, as was the custom, was a pair of angora dice. A previous girl friend named Solange who was famous throughout Beverly Hills High School for having no pigment in her right eyebrow had knitted them for him. Buster and I would ride around town, the two of us seated to the left of the steering wheel. I would shift gears. It was nice.

There was necking. Terrific necking. First in the car, overlooking 16 Los Angeles from what is now the Trousdale Estates. Then on the bed of his parents' cabana at Ocean House. Incredibly wonderful, frustrating necking, I loved it, really, but no further than necking, please don't, please, because there I was absolutely terrified of the general implications of going-a-step-further with a near-dummy and also terrified of his finding out there was next to nothing there (which he knew, of course; he wasn't that dumb).

I broke up with him at one point. I think we were apart for about 17 two weeks. At the end of that time I drove down to see a friend at a boarding school in Palos Verdes Estates and a disc jockey played *April Love* on the radio four times during the trip. I took it as a sign. I drove straight back to Griffith Park to a golf tournament Buster was playing in (he was the sixth-seeded teen-age golf player in Southern California) and presented myself back to him on the green of the 18th hole. It was all very dramatic. That night we went to a drive-in and I let him get his hand under my protuberances and onto my breasts. He really didn't seem to mind at all.

*"Do you want to marry my son?" the woman asked me.* 18
*"Yes," I said.* 19
*I was nineteen years old, a virgin, going with this woman's son, this* 20 *big strange woman who was married to a Lutheran minister in New Hampshire and pretended she was Gentile and had this son, by her first husband, this total fool of a son who ran the hero-sandwich concession at Harvard Business School and whom for one moment one December in New Hampshire I said—as much out of politeness as anything else—that I wanted to marry.*
*"Fine," she said. "Now, here's what you do. Always make sure* 21 *you're on top of him so you won't seem so small. My bust is very large, you see, so I always lie on my back to make it look smaller, but you'll have to be on top most of the time."*
*I nodded. "Thank you," I said.* 22

*"I have a book for you to read,"* she went on. *"Take it with you*   23
*when you leave. Keep it." She went to the bookshelf, found it, and*
*gave it to me. It was a book on frigidity.*

*"Thank you,"* I said.                                                          24

That is a true story. Everything in this article is a true story, but I feel   25
I have to point out that that story in particular is true. It happened on
December 30, 1960. I think about it often. When it first happened, I
naturally assumed that the woman's son, my boyfriend, was responsible.
I invented a scenario where he had had a little heart-to-heart with his
mother and had confessed that his only objection to me was that my
breasts were small; his mother then took it upon herself to help out. Now
I think I was wrong about the incident. The mother was acting on her
own, I think: that was her way of being cruel and competitive under the
guise of being helpful and maternal. You have small breasts, she was
saying; therefore you will never make him as happy as I have. Or you
have small breasts; therefore you will doubtless have sexual problems.
Or you have small breasts; therefore you are less woman than I am. She
was, as it happens, only the first of what seems to me to be a never-ending
string of women who have made competitive remarks to me about breast
size. "I would love to wear a dress like that," my friend Emily says to me,
"but my bust is too big." Like that. Why do women say these things to
me? Do I attract these remarks the way other women attract married
men or alcoholics or homosexuals? This summer, for example. I am at a
party in East Hampton and I am introduced to a woman from Washington. She is a minor celebrity, very pretty and Southern and blonde and
outspoken and I am flattered because she has read something I have
written. We are talking animatedly, we have been talking no more than
five minutes, when a man comes up to join us. "Look at the two of us," the
woman says to the man, indicating me and her. "The two of us together
couldn't fill an A cup." Why does she say that? It isn't even true, dammit,
so why? Is she even more addled than I am on this subject? Does she
honestly believe there is something wrong with her size breasts, which,
it seems to me, now that I look hard at them, are just right. Do I
unconsciously bring out competitiveness in women? In that form? What
did I do to deserve it?

As for men.                                                                     26

There were men who minded and let me know that they minded.   27
There were men who did not mind. In any case, I always minded.

And even now, now that I have been countlessly reassured that my   28
figure is a good one, now that I am grown-up enough to understand that
most of my feelings have very little to do with the reality of my shape, I

am nonetheless obsessed by breasts. I cannot help it. I grew up in the terrible Fifties—with rigid stereotypical sex roles, the insistence that men be men and dress like men and women be women and dress like women, the intolerance of androgyny—and I cannot shake it, cannot shake my feelings of inadequacy. Well, that time is gone, right? All those exaggerated examples of breast worship are gone, right? Those women were freaks, right? I know all that. And yet, here I am, stuck with the psychological remains of it all, stuck with my own peculiar version of breast worship. You probably think I am crazy to go on like this: here I have set out to write a confession that is meant to hit you with the shock of recognition and instead you are sitting there thinking I am thoroughly warped. Well, what can I tell you? If I had had them, I would have been a completely different person. I honestly believe that.

After I went into therapy, a process that made it possible for me 29 to tell total strangers at cocktail parties that breasts were the hang-up of my life, I was often told that I was insane to have been bothered by my condition. I was also frequently told, by close friends, that I was extremely boring on the subject. And my girl friends, the ones with nice big breasts, would go on endlessly about how their lives had been far more miserable than mine. Their bra straps were snapped in class. They couldn't sleep on their stomachs. They were stared at whenever the word "mountain" cropped up in geography. And *Evangeline*, good God what they went through every time someone had to stand up and recite the Prologue to Longfellow's *Evangeline: ". . . stand like druids of eld . . . / With beards that rest on their bosoms."* It was much worse for them, they tell me. They had a terrible time of it, they assure me. I don't know how lucky I was, they say.

I have thought about their remarks, tried to put myself in their 30 place, considered their point of view. I think they are full of shit.

---

# Science and Imagination

## JACOB BRONOWSKI

What is the insight with which the scientist tries to see into nature? 1 Can it indeed be called either imaginative or creative? To the literary man the question may seem merely silly. He has been taught that science is a large collection of facts; and if this is true, then the only seeing which scientists need do is, he supposes, seeing the facts. He pictures them, the colorless professionals of science, going off to work in the morning into the universe in a neutral, unexposed state. They then expose themselves like a photographic plate. And then in the darkroom or laboratory they develop the image; so that suddenly and startlingly it appears, printed in capital letters, as a new formula for atomic energy.

Men who have read Balzac and Zola are not deceived by the   2
claims of these writers that they do no more than record the facts. The readers of Christopher Isherwood do not take him literally when he writes "I am a camera." Yet the same readers solemnly carry with them from their schooldays this foolish picture of the scientist fixing by some mechanical process the facts of nature. I have had of all people a historian tell me that science is a collection of facts, and his voice had not even the ironic rasp of one filing cabinet reproving another.

It seems impossible that this historian had ever studied the begin-   3
nings of a scientific discovery. The Scientific Revolution can be held to begin in the year 1543 when there was brought to Copernicus, perhaps on his deathbed, the first printed copy of the book he had finished about a dozen years earlier. The thesis of this book is that the earth moves around the sun. When did Copernicus go out and record this fact with his camera? What appearance in nature prompted his outrageous guess? And in what odd sense is this guess to be called a neutral record of fact?

Less than a hundred years after Copernicus, Kepler published   4
(between 1609 and 1619) the three laws which describe the paths of the planets. The work of Newton and with it most of our mechanics spring from these laws. They have a solid, matter of fact sound. For example, Kepler says that if one squares the year of a planet, one gets a number which is proportional to the cube of its average distance from the sun. Does anyone think that such a law is found by taking enough readings and then squaring and cubing everything in sight? If he does then, as a scientist, he is doomed to a wasted life; he has as little prospect of making a scientific discovery as an electronic brain has.

It was not this way that Copernicus and Kepler thought, or that   5
scientists think today. Copernicus found that the orbits of the planets would look simpler if they were looked at from the sun and not from the earth. But he did not in the first place find this by routine calculation. His first step was a leap of imagination—to lift himself from the

earth, and put himself wildly, speculatively into the sun. "The earth conceives from the sun," he wrote; and "the sun rules the family of stars." We catch in his mind an image, the gesture of the virile man standing in the sun, with arms outstretched, overlooking the planets. Perhaps Copernicus took the picture from the drawings of the youth with outstretched arms which the Renaissance teachers put into their books on the proportions of the body. Perhaps he had seen Leonardo's drawings of his loved pupil Salai. I do not know. To me, the gesture of Copernicus, the shining youth looking outward from the sun, is still vivid in a drawing which William Blake in 1780 based on all these: the drawing which is usually called *Glad Day*.

Kepler's mind, we know, was filled with just such fanciful analo-   6
gies; and we know what they were. Kepler wanted to relate the speeds of the planets to the musical intervals. He tried to fit the five regular solids into their orbits. None of these likenesses worked, and they have been forgotten; yet they have been and they remain the stepping stones of every creative mind. Kepler felt for his laws by way of metaphors, he searched mystically for likenesses with what he knew in every strange corner of nature. And when among these guesses he hit upon his laws, he did not think of their numbers as the balancing of a cosmic bank account, but as a revelation of the unity in all nature. To us, the analogies by which Kepler listened for the movement of the planets in the music of the spheres are farfetched. Yet are they more so than the wild leap by which Rutherford and Bohr in our own century found a model for the atom in, of all places, the planetary system?

---

# The Fate of the Dinosaur

### ELLEN GOODMAN

Boston—I became a dinosaur groupie when I was eight years old.   1
I still remember the colossal reconstructed skeleton of a brontosaurus in the science museum that first captured my imagination.

This wasn't a dramatic, life-changing event. I didn't go off to   2
become a paleontologist. Nor did I run off with a paleontologist. But I

was hooked. Over the years, when other members of my family worried about the extinction of whales and seals, I stuck to dinosaurs.

I suppose it was their size and fate that grabbed my attention. Children tend to equate the huge with the powerful. The larger something or someone is, the more impressive to a childish mind. These creatures were, by any definition, grown-ups, the biggest animals on earth. Yet they had all died. Here was a mystery that challenged my preconceptions.   3

Over time, I read all sorts of explanations for their extinction. The dinosaurs were big, but their brains were small. The dinosaurs couldn't adapt. Slowly, they died out while humans, the adaptable, thinking species, prospered.   4

There was a charming egocentricity to these theories. My dinosaurs were evolution's failure and we were its successes. There was some comfort in it, too. In the nineteenth century, Darwin's theory of gradual evolution upset the religious orthodoxy, but it offered an orderliness of its own.   5

Evolution drew a reasonable pattern in the universe. Over time, species grew better and better. In the rough justice of nature, the fittest survived.   6

But the theory didn't survive intact. A few years ago, another generation of scientists offered up evidence about my extinct subjects. The dinosaurs didn't gradually die of their evolutionary flaws. The scientists speculated that sixty-five million years ago an asteroid struck the earth and produced a worldwide crop failure that did them in. My giant vegetarian, the brontosaurus, was the victim of a climatic disaster, a cosmic accident.   7

Then, more recently, two scientists at the University of Chicago reported that such disasters have occurred like cosmic clockwork every 26 million years over the past 250 million years, wiping out huge numbers of life forms. The dinosaurs were just the biggest, most memorable of the victims.   8

Now when I look at the evolution of these theories, I wonder whether every era gets the dinosaur story it deserves. I don't mean to suggest that science is trendy. All theories are not equal. They are built on real, measurable knowledge.   9

Yet scientists are also part of their culture, their times. At one moment or another they are open to a certain line of questioning, a path of inquiry that would have been unlikely earlier on.   10

The scientists of the nineteenth century—a time full of belief in   11 progress—saw evolution as part of the planet's plan of self-improvement. The rugged individualists of that century blamed the victims for their own failure. Those who lived in a competitive economy valued the "natural" competition of species. The best man won.

The latest theories may reflect our own contemporary world view. 12 Surely we are now more sensitive to cosmic catastrophe, to accident. Surely we are more conscious of the shared fate of the whole species.

Today the astronauts travel into space and report back that they 13 see no national borders. Environmentalists remind us that the acid from one nations' chimneys rains down on another. Most significantly, another group of scientists warns us that a nuclear war between two great powers would bring a universal and wintry death. One hemisphere is no longer immune from the mistakes of the other hemisphere.

In that sense, the latest dinosaur theory fits us uncomfortably well. 14 "Our" dinosaurs died together in some meteoric winter, the victims of a global catastrophe. As humans, we fear a similar shared fate.

The difference is that their world was hit by a giant asteroid while 15 we—the large-brained, adaptable creatures who inherited the earth— may produce our own extinction.

In these times, what a luxury it would be to only worry about the 16 next "natural" catastrophe. It's due in fifteen million years.

---

# Four-Letter Words Can Hurt You

## BARBARA LAWRENCE

Why should any words be called obscene? Don't they all describe 1 natural human functions? Am I trying to tell them, my students demand, that the "strong, earthy, gut-honest"—or, if they are fans of Norman Mailer, the "rich, liberating, existential"—language they use to describe sexual activity isn't preferable to "phony-sounding, middle-class words like 'intercourse' and 'copulate' "? "Cop You Late!" they say with fancy inflections and gagging grimaces. "Now, what is *that* supposed to mean?"

       °     °     °

Well, what is it supposed to mean? And why indeed should one    2
group of words describing human functions and human organs be
acceptable in ordinary conversation and another, describing presumably the same organs and functions, be tabooed—so much so, in fact,
that some of these words still cannot appear in print in many parts of
the English-speaking world?

The argument that these taboos exist only because of "sexual    3
hangups" (middle-class, middle-age, feminist), or even that they are a
result of class oppression (the contempt of the Norman conquerors for
the language of their Anglo-Saxon serfs), ignores a much more likely
explanation, it seems to me, and that is the sources and functions of the
words themselves.

The best known of the tabooed sexual verbs, for example, comes    4
from the German *ficken,* meaning "to strike"; combined, according to
Partridge's etymological dictionary *Origins,* with the Latin sexual verb
*futuere;* associated in turn with the Latin *fustis,* "a staff or cudgel";
the Celtic *buc,* "a point, hence to pierce"; the Irish "bot, "the male
member"; the Latin *battuere,* "to beat"; the Gaelic *batair,* "a cud-
geller"; the Early Irish *bualaim,* "I strike"; and so forth. It is one of
what etymologists sometimes call "the sadistic group of words for the
man's part in copulation."

The brutality of this word, then, and its equivalents ("screw,"    5
"bang," etc.), is not an illusion of the middle class or a crotchet of
Women's Liberation. In their origins and imagery these words carry
undeniably painful, if not sadistic, implications, the object of which is
almost always female. Consider, for example, what a "screw" actually
does to the wood it penetrates; what a painful, even mutilating, activity this kind of analogy suggests. "Screw" is particularly interesting in
this context, since the noun, according to Partridge, comes from words
meaning "groove," "nut," "ditch," "breeding sow," "scrofula" and
"swelling," while the verb, besides its explicit imagery, has antecedent
associations to "write on," "scratch," "scarify," and so forth—a revealing fusion of a mechanical or painful action with an obviously deni-
grated object.

Not all obscene words, of course, are as implicitly sadistic or deni-    6
grating to women as these, but all that I know seem to serve a similar
purpose: to reduce the human organism (especially the female organism) and human functions (especially sexual and procreative) to their
least organic, most mechanical dimension; to substitute a trivializing or
deforming resemblance for the complex human reality of what is being
described.

Tabooed male descriptives, when they are not openly denigrating 7
to women, often serve to divorce a male organ or function from any
significant interaction with the female. Take the word "testes," for
example, suggesting "witnesses" (from the Latin *testis*) to the sexual
and procreative strengths of the male organ; and the obscene counter-
part of this word, which suggests little more than a mechanical shape.
Or compare almost any of the "rich," "liberating" sexual verbs, so
fashionable today among male writers, with that much-derided Latin
word "copulate" ("to bind or join together") or even that Anglo-Saxon
phrase (which seems to have had no trouble surviving the Norman
Conquest) "make love."

How arrogantly self-involved the tabooed words seem in compari- 8
son to either of the other terms, and how contemptuous of the female
partner. Understandably so, of course, if she is only a "skirt," a
"broad," a "chick," a "pussycat" or a "piece." If she is, in other words,
no more than her skirt, or what her skirt conceals; no more than a
breeder, or the broadest part of her; no more than a piece of a human
being or a "piece of tail."

The most severely tabooed of all the female descriptives, inciden- 9
tally, are those like a "piece of tail," which suggest (either explicitly or
through antecedents) that there is no significant difference between
the female channel through which we are all conceived and born and
the anal outlet common to both sexes—a distinction that pornogra-
phers have always enjoyed obscuring.

This effort to deny women their biological identity, their individu- 10
ality, their humanness, is such an important aspect of obscene language that one can only marvel at how seldom, in an era preoccupied
with definitions of obscenity, this fact is brought to our attention. One
problem, of course, is that many of the people in the best position to
do this (critics, teachers, writers) are so reluctant today to admit that
they are angered or shocked by obscenity. Bored, maybe, unimpressed,
aesthetically displeased, but—no matter how brutal or denigrating the
material—never angered, never shocked.

And yet how eloquently angered, how piously shocked many of 11
these same people become if denigrating language is used about any
minority group other than women; if the obscenities are racial or
ethnic, that is, rather than sexual. Words like "coon," "kike," "spic,"
"wop," after all, deform identity, deny individuality and humanness in
almost exactly the same way that sexual vulgarisms and obscenities do.

No one that I know, least of all my students, would fail to question 12
the values of a society whose literature and entertainment rested

heavily on racial or ethnic pejoratives. Are the values of a society whose literature and entertainment rest as heavily as ours on sexual pejoratives any less questionable?

---

# Slang Origins

## WOODY ALLEN

How many of you have ever wondered where certain slang expres-    1
sions come from? Like "She's the cat's pajamas," or to "take it on the
lam." Neither have I. And yet for those who are interested in this sort
of thing I have provided a brief guide to a few of the more interesting
origins.

Unfortunately, time did not permit consulting any of the estab-    2
lished works on the subject, and I was forced to either obtain the
information from friends or fill in certain gaps by using my own common sense.

Take, for instance, the expression "to eat humble pie." During the    3
reign of Louis the Fat, the culinary arts flourished in France to a
degree unequaled anywhere. So obese was the French monarch that
he had to be lowered onto the throne with a winch and packed into the
seat itself with a large spatula. A typical dinner (according to DeRochet) consisted of a thin crêpe appetizer, some parsley, an ox, and
custard. Food became the court obsession, and no other subject could
be discussed under penalty of death. Members of a decadent aristoc-
racy consumed incredible meals and even dressed as foods. DeRochet
tells us that M. Monsant showed up at the coronation as a weiner, and
Etienne Tisserant received papal dispensation to wed his favorite cod-
fish. Desserts grew more and more elaborate and pies grew larger and
larger until the minister of justice suffocated trying to eat a seven-foot
"Jumbo Pie." *Jumbo* pie soon became *jumble* pie and "to eat a jumble
pie" referred to any kind of humiliating act. When the Spanish seamen
heard the word *jumble,* they pronounced it "humble," although many
preferred to say nothing and simply grin.

Now, while "humble pie" goes back to the French, "take it on the    4
lam" is English in origin. Years ago, in England, "lamming" was a
game played with dice and a large tube of ointment. Each player in

turn threw dice and then skipped around the room until he hemorrhaged. If a person threw seven or under he would say the word "quintz" and proceed to twirl in a frenzy. If he threw over seven, he was forced to give every player a portion of his feathers and was given a good "lamming." Three "lammings" and a player was "kwirled" or declared a moral bankrupt. Gradually any game with feathers was called "lamming" and feathers became "lams." To "take it on the lam" meant to put on feathers and later, to escape, although the transition is unclear.

Incidentally, if two of the players disagreed on the rules, we might say they "got into a beef." This term goes back to the Renaissance when a man would court a woman by stroking the side of her head with a slab of meat. If she pulled away, it meant she was spoken for. If, however, she assisted by clamping the meat to her face and pushing it all over head, it meant she would marry him. The meat was kept by the bride's parents and worn as a hat on special occasions. If, however, the husband took another lover, the wife could dissolve the marriage by running with the meat to the town square and yelling, "With thine own beef, I do reject thee. Aroo! Aroo!" If a couple "took to the beef" or "had a beef" it meant they were quarreling.

Another marital custom gives us that eloquent and colorful expression of disdain, "to look down one's nose." In Persia it was considered a mark of great beauty for a woman to have a long nose. In fact, the longer the nose, the more desirable the female, up to a certain point. Then it became funny. When a man proposed to a beautiful woman he awaited her decision on bended knee as she "looked down her nose at him." If her nostrils twitched, he was accepted, but if she sharpened her nose with pumice and began pecking him on the neck and shoulders, it mean she loved another.

Now, we all know when someone is very dressed up, we say he looks "spiffy." The term owes its origin to Sir Oswald Spiffy, perhaps the most renowned fop of Victorian England. Heir to treacle millions, Spiffy squandered his money on clothes. It was said that at one time he owned enough handkerchiefs for all the men, women and children in Asia to blow their noses for seven years without stopping. Spiffy's sartorial innovations were legend, and he was the first man ever to wear gloves on his head. Because of extra-sensitive skin, Spiffy's underwear had to be made of the finest Nova Scotia salmon, carefully sliced by one particular tailor. His libertine attitudes involved him in several notorious scandals, and he eventually sued the government over the right to wear earmuffs while fondling a dwarf. In the end, Spiffy died a broken man in Chichester, his total wardrobe reduced to kneepads and a sombrero.

Looking "spiffy," then, is quite a compliment, and one who does 8 is liable to be dressed "to beat the band," a turn-of-the-century expression that originated from the custom of attacking with clubs any symphony orchestra whose conductor smiled during Berlioz. "Beating the band" soon became a popular evening out, and people dressed up in their finest clothes, carrying with them sticks and rocks. The practice was finally abandoned during a performance of the *Symphonie Fantastique* in New York when the entire string section suddenly stopped playing and exchanged gunfire with the first ten rows. Police ended the melee but not before a relative of J. P. Morgan's was wounded in the soft palate. After that, for a while at least, nobody dressed "to beat the band."

If you think some of the above derivations questionable, you might 9 throw up your hands and say, "Fiddlesticks." This marvelous expression originated in Austria many years ago. Whenever a man in the banking profession announced his marriage to a circus pinhead, it was the custom for friends to present him with a bellows and a three-year supply of wax fruit. Legend has it that when Leo Rothschild made known his betrothal, a box of cello bows was delivered to him by mistake. When it was opened and found not to contain the traditional gift, he exclaimed, "What are these? Where are my bellows and fruit? Eh? All I rate is fiddlesticks!" The term "fiddlesticks" became a joke overnight in the taverns amongst the lower classes, who hated Leo Rothschild for never removing the comb from his hair after combing it. Eventually "fiddlesticks" meant any foolishness.

Well, I hope you've enjoyed some of these slang origins and that 10 they stimulate you to investigate some on your own. And in case you were wondering about the term used to open this study, "the cat's pajamas," it goes back to an old burlesque routine of Chase and Rowe's, the two nutsy German professors. Dressed in oversized tails, Bill Rowe stole some poor victim's pajamas. Dave Chase, who got great mileage out of his "hard of hearing" speciality, would ask him:

CHASE: Ach, Herr Professor. Vot is dot bulge under your pocket?
ROWE: Dot? Dot's de chap's pajamas.
CHASE: The cat's pajamas? Ut mein Gott?

Audiences were convulsed by this sort of repartee and only a premature death of the team by strangulation kept them from stardom.

# Definition

## Passage to Ararat

### MICHAEL ARLEN

At a particular time in my life, I set out on a voyage to discover   1
for myself what it is to be Armenian. For although I myself am Armenian, or part Armenian, until then I knew nothing about either
Armenians or Armenia. That is, almost nothing. My father had been
Armenian—a child born of Armenian parents—but he had been
brought up in England and educated in English schools. His citizenship had been English and, later, American. More to the point, he
seemed to have virtually no connection with Armenia. At home, he
never spoke the language. He rarely talked about Armenia. Professionally, he was a writer of romantic novels that were set for the
most part in English society, and with hardly more than one or two
exceptions he never wrote about Armenia—or Armenians. The exceptions were mainly deprecatory or amusing. One of his lines went
"Now who would claim he was an Armenian if he was not?" Indeed,
at the age of twenty-one he had changed his name from Dikran
Kouyoumjian to Michael Arlen.

My mother (who was American and Greek) sometimes called my   2
father Dikran in private, and this was the only way I knew as a child
that he was something other than—or in addition to—English. "It's an
Armenian name," she explained to me one long-ago afternoon. For a
while, I thought this referred to the kind of name—a private name. I
understood that some of my far-off uncles were called Kouyoumjian—
an odd and difficult word for a child to scrawl on a thank-you letter. But
my father, while he was well disposed toward the uncles, evidently
detached himself from the name. Reluctantly, and usually with a grimace, he would tell me again how to spell it. "It's ridiculous and un-
pronounceable," he once said, and I had reason to agree. For the most
part, my father's Armenianness was a hazy and remote matter that

rarely intruded into family conversation: a youthful stage of his life
that he had apparently long since passed through—had passed through
successfully, as if with a school degree—and now there was clearly no
point in talking further about it.

It was at an English boarding school, when I was nine, that I first    4
realized that I was myself in any way Armenian—or, at least, half
Armenian. Before the Second World War, we lived in Europe—English expatriates in the South of France. But if in those days I thought
at all about identity I thought that I was English. *We* were English. We
spoke English. We traveled on English passports.

At school, I was assigned to room with a cheerful, towheaded        5
Scottish boy, MacGregor.

"Are you French, or what?" MacGregor asked me one day.              6

"Of course I'm not French," I said.                                 7

"You have to be French. You live in France."                        8

"I'm English," I said.                                              9

"You *can't* be English!" said MacGregor.                          10

The headmaster's wife helped set us straight. We sat at her table   11
in the school dining room—a chill and drafty chamber where ancient
uniformed waitresses clattered in with trays of dry toast and sardines,
or sometimes baked beans, and on Sundays with silver platters holding
pieces of bread covered with gravy. The headmaster's wife was a lady
of cultured interests, who was active in the local theater group, and
who often discoursed to us on the larger life that she glimpsed through
avid reading of the London magazines and sometimes through abrupt,
disastrous excursions to audition for historical pageants in the county
seat. On this occasion, she announced that she had read somewhere
that my father had recently published a new book. I never had much
to say to such announcements. I knew that my father "wrote books"
in his office, but writing in general, and his in particular, was another
subject on which very little family conversation existed or was encouraged. She had not read any of his other novels, she continued, but she
was sure they were very interesting. Wasn't *The Green Hat* the famous one? She had heard many good things about it. It must be
fascinating, she said, to have a father who was a well-known writer.
Did I, too, speak Armenian?

This last question took me by surprise. "No, I don't speak Ar-    12
menian," I said. I think I added, "I've never heard anyone speak
Armenian"—which was true.

"But I know I read somewhere that your father was Armenian,"      13 she said, with a bright smile. "I thought all Armenians spoke Armenian."

Later, in our small room, MacGregor glanced up from the comic   14
he was reading. *"Har-meenian?"* he said. "What kind of sports do they
play there?"

"I don't know," I said. "I've never been there. Probably the same   15
sports as here."

"Not cricket," said MacGregor.   16

"Yes, cricket," I said. "Anyway, I'm English."   17

"You can't be *English*," said MacGregor.   18

At midterm, my father came alone to visit me, arriving in a chauf-   19
feur-driven car and carrying a box of chocolates. For the first time in
my life, I thought him strange—almost a stranger. I remember looking
at him surreptitiously, sneaking glances at his face—looking for what?
I don't know. I wanted him to tell me that we were really English, but
I didn't know how to ask.

Months later, home on vacation, I asked my mother instead. "Are   20
we Armenian?" I felt that it was a daring question.

"Of course not," she replied, her tone kindly but brisk. "Your   21
father's family have Armenian blood, but he is English and so are you."
She showed me his passport.

As time went by, I went to other schools. In fact, as a result of the   22
war, we moved to America, and I became more and more American,
finally, at twenty-one, becoming an American citizen. I felt generally
American, or perhaps for a while Anglo-American, but, clearly, there
was also something missing. Something missing or added. I became
conscious of being accompanied by a kind of shadow of "being Armenian," which other people sometimes noticed, or casually commented on, but which my father had said, in effect, did not exist. And
so I, too, said that it did not exist.

I remember, as an older boy at school in New Hampshire, watch-   23
ing terrified from a fire escape while a gang of sixteen-year-olds
taunted and pushed about one of their classmates, a sallow, spidery
boy called Gordon, who was supposedly Jewish. What was I so terrified
of, I've later wondered—for it is not an enhancing memory. I think
probably this: I had gradually become aware that to be Jewish in
certain Anglo-Saxon milieus was to be "different"—that is, to be alien
and unprotected—and I knew that I, too, was "different," although I
was somewhat protected by the camouflage of an accepted Anglo-
American manner. But I felt that it was no more than a camouflage and

might disappear any day. I know that as I looked down from that fire escape at poor Gordon, I thought: There but for *them* go *we*. Who were *we?* The truth is that for most of my growing up, and for much of my life, I didn't try very hard to find out. There seemed to be something slightly dangerous or second-rate in being Armenian; otherwise, my father would not have been so determined to move beyond it. And so I took the hint and followed him. Armenians were somebody else.

I remember also, years ago, in New York, around the time of an     24 expected visit from my Uncle Krikor, who lived in Argentina, my father angrily brandishing some recent communication from Buenos Aires— probably a change in plans. "Why can't these Armenians ever do things simply?" he said. And "Now, isn't this just like an Armenian!" Evidently, Uncle Krikor was "just like an Armenian"; my father was something different. And, in fact, when Krikor finally arrived (a short, wiry man, with a definite nose and a face tanned by the Argentine sun) I felt him to be different from my father—darker, somehow more "Eastern"—although actually the two men were of the same size and build, had similar features (except for the Argentine suntan), and spoke impeccable English. At one point, Krikor addressed a few words to me in Armenian, which I naturally couldn't reply to. "Why, you haven't taught the boy any Armenian!" said Krikor, in genial reproof. We were having dinner in Krikor's hotel.

My father in those days had a carefully trimmed mustache and     25 wore a flower in his jacket. "Well, it's an impossible language," he said, scowling.

Krikor smiled good-naturedly. "Ah, Dikran," he said. He was the     26 elder brother.

In all my life, I never heard my father speak a single word of     27 Armenian, unless one counts the occasional times we went to an Armenian restaurant and he would read, with a certain offhand professionalism, from the exotic menu, with its kebabs and dolmas, which, I later found out, were mainly Turkish. On the whole, I met few Armenians in his company, and most of these I thought of as being associated with a particular Armenian restaurant in New York, which we went to *en famille* perhaps once or twice a year. It was called the Golden Horn and was a small place in the West Fifties. Its proprietor was a large, warm-hearted man—Aram Salisian, a former wrestler, as wide as he was tall, with immense, gnarled hands and a square, rough-hewn, kind face, which invariably seemed to be smiling. When we entered, he always embraced my father; I think he was just about the only man I ever saw do so. He bowed to the rest of us. He told me that someday he would teach me how to wrestle.

I liked the Golden Horn, because it was a nice place and because as a family we were generally happy there. I also had a special, secret feeling about it—and still have to this day, although the restaurant itself has disappeared—for it was the only region or territory in which I can recall my father's being at ease with his Armenian identity, even halfway accepting it. "So-and-So was here the other day," I can remember Salisian saying, stopping by our table, rattling off an Armenian name. 28

"Is that so?" I can hear my father's voice reply. "Well, how is he? Say hello to him from me." 29

Say hello to him from me. Not what one might describe as reckless bonhomie, but in those rare and periodic moments I believe he showed more affection for his Armenian background—our Armenian background—than most other times that I can remember. Now and then, other guests in the restaurant, or at the bar, would come over to chat for a few minutes. Talk of families, of sons and daughters in school. George, the bartender, I remember, had a son studying with Rudolf Serkin at the Curtis Institute of Music, who later became the pianist Eugene Istomin. 30

It was a strange and friendly time—strange because the men and women there for the most part looked to me so different, as if they were from another country, and yet for a moment we were part of them, their group, whatever *they* might be. I had a sense of "Armenia" as a fragile network of restaurants inhabited by people who seemed to live elsewhere—in somebody else's country. All that seemed real to me was the affection, the mysterious bond. On the walls of the restaurant, I remember, there were photographs of various Armenians who had "made good." One of them was a picture of my father with William Saroyan, the Armenian-American writer from California, whose plays had been appearing on Broadway and winning prizes. In the photograph, the two men were seated at a table with drinks in front of them, smoking cigarettes, staring rather glassily into the flashbulb—the usual night-club snapshot. It seemed to me a romantic and heroic moment: my father together with Mr. Saroyan. My eyes always turned to it— that glimpse of an Armenian comradeship. 31

But then after dinner we all walked out of the Golden Horn, saying goodbye to Mr. Salisian, leaving Aram Salisian and his world behind— 32

and were back in our own world. On a few occasions, perhaps encouraged by our moments at the restaurant, I later questioned my father
about Armenia, but I tried this rarely, because he so visibly wished not
to be connected with the subject—in fact, brushed off such simple
questions as I might have put—and because, indeed, I had no strong
wish to be connected with it myself. Once, I remember, I asked him to
come to the phone to take a call from a Mr. Hagopian, an Armenian
professor who wished to discuss a literary project. "Tell him I'm out,"
my father said coldly. Afterward, I asked him why, for Hagopian and
he had clearly never met. "He'll only want to talk about Armenian
problems," my father said. "He'll go on for hours. They end up boring
you to death." Later, more casually, he said, "They're a sweet people,
but you can't let them get too close."

For the most part, I was content to leave things as they were. I was     33
only slightly curious about my Armenian background—or so I thought,
although, if I had understood how to acknowledge such matters, I
might have known that I was haunted by it. Mostly, I was afraid of it.
(What *were* "Armenian problems"? I supposed they must have to do
with "Turkish massacres" and "starving Armenians," and such—distant and repellent events that I had vaguely heard about and that
obviously had little or nothing to do with us.) What was I afraid of? It's
difficult to remember now. Probably of being exposed in some way, or
pulled down by the connection: that association of "difference," one's
own "difference," with something deeply pejorative, with sin. I can't
say that I felt sinful in any explicit sense, but I felt somehow marked—
even to the extent, for much of my life, of considering myself unnaturally dark, so that a few years ago I was astonished to hear a skin doctor
describe my skin as "light." And in the end (as perhaps in the beginning) I came to hate my father for my fear. It was not the only emotion
I felt toward him, for I loved him, too; though he was seldom an
emotionally expressive man, I knew, he was kind to me. He was my
father. But also I was afraid of him. Something always lay between
us—something unspoken and (it seemed) unreachable. We were strangers.

When my father died, nineteen years ago, I felt we were no closer.     34
Even as on his deathbed he talked with me amiably and we held each
other's hands. Even as, later, I wrote about him—for I myself had
become a writer, although not a novelist, and tried to make a kind of
contact with him, and with my mother, by writing about their life

together and his career. As I remember, his funeral service was held in a Greek Orthodox church (my mother's church), rather than in an Armenian church. "All his life, he wanted to be free of the Armenians," my mother said. I missed him, although it was a relief to me in some ways that he was gone. Absent. In truth, I dreamed about him often, usually in the same scenario, or in dreams with the same feel to them: a feeling of distance between us. Sometimes he called to me and I couldn't hear what he was saying. Sometimes he merely stood apart—a solitary and somehow disapproving figure. We were still strangers.

---

# The Superior Virtue of the Oppressed

## BERTRAND RUSSELL

One of the persistent delusions of mankind is that some sections of the human race are morally better or worse than others. This belief has many different forms, none of which has any rational basis. It is natural to think well of ourselves, and thence, if our mental processes are simple, of our sex, our class, our nation, and our age. But among writers, especially moralists, a less direct expression of self-esteem is common. They tend to think ill of their neighbors and acquaintances, and therefore to think well of the sections of mankind to which they themselves do not belong. Lao-tse admired the "pure men of old," who lived before the advent of Confucian sophistication. Tacitus and Madame de Staël admired the Germans because they had no emperor. Locke thought well of the "intelligent American" because he was not led astray by Cartesian sophistries. 1

A rather curious form of this admiration for groups to which the admirer does not belong is the belief in the superior virtue of the oppressed: subject nations, the poor, women, and children. The eighteenth century, while conquering America from the Indians, reducing the peasantry to the condition of pauper laborers, and introducing the cruelties of early industrialism, loved to sentimentalize about the "noble savage" and the "simple annals of the poor." Virtue, it was 2

said, was not to be found in courts: but court ladies could *almost* secure
it by masquerading as shepherdesses. And as for the male sex:

Happy the man whose wish and care
A few paternal acres bound.

Nevertheless, for himself Pope preferred London and his villa at
Twickenham.

At the French Revolution the superior virtue of the poor became        3
a party question, and has remained so ever since. To reactionaries they
became the "rabble" or the "mob." The rich discovered, with surprise,
that some people were so poor as not to own even "a few paternal
acres." Liberals, however, still continued to idealize the rural poor,
while intellectual Socialists and Communists did the same for the
urban proletariat—a fashion to which, since it only became important
in the twentieth century, I shall return later.

Nationalism introduced, in the nineteenth century, a substitute for    4
the noble savage—the patriot of an oppressed nation. The Greeks until
they had achieved liberation from the Turks, the Hungarians until the
*Ausgleich* of 1867, the Italians until 1870, and the Poles until after the
1914–18 war were regarded romantically as gifted poetic races, too
idealistic to succeed in this wicked world. The Irish were regarded by
the English as possessed of a special charm and mystical insight until
1921, when it was found that the expense of continuing to oppress them
would be prohibitive. One by one these various nations rose to independence, and were found to be just like everybody else; but the
experience of those already liberated did nothing to destroy the illusion
as regards those who were still struggling. English old ladies still sentimentalize about the "wisdom of the East" and American intellectuals
about the "earth consciousness" of the Negro.

Women, being the objects of the strongest emotions, have been          5
viewed even more irrationally than the poor or the subject nations. I
am thinking not of what poets have to say but of the sober opinions of
men who imagine themselves rational. The church had two opposite
attitudes: on the one hand, woman was the Temptress, who led monks
and others into sin; on the other hand, she was capable of saintliness
to an almost greater degree than man. Theologically, the two types
were represented by Eve and the Virgin. In the nineteenth century the
temptress fell into the background; there were, of course, "bad"
women, but Victorian worthies, unlike St. Augustine and his succes-
sors, would not admit that such sinners could tempt them, and did not

like to acknowledge their existence. A kind of combination of the Madonna and the lady of chivalry was created as the ideal of the ordinary married woman. She was delicate and dainty, she had a bloom which would be rubbed off by contact with the rough world, she had ideals which might be dimmed by contact with wickedness; like the Celts and the Slavs and the noble savage, but to an even greater degree, she enjoyed a spiritual nature, which made her the superior of man but unfitted her for business or politics or the control of her own fortune. This point of view is still not entirely extinct. Not long ago, in reply to a speech I had made in favor of equal pay for equal work, an English schoolmaster sent me a pamphlet published by a schoolmasters' association, setting forth the opposite opinion, which it supports with curious arguments. It says of woman: "We gladly place her first as a spiritual force; we acknowledge and reverence her as the 'angelic part of humanity'; we give her superiority in all the graces and refinements we are capable of as human beings; we wish her to retain all her winsome womanly ways." "This appeal"—that women should be content with lower rates of pay—"goes forth from us to them," so we are assured, "in no selfish spirit, but out of respect and devotion to our mothers, wives, sisters, and daughters. . . . Our purpose is a sacred one, a real spiritual crusade."

Fifty or sixty years ago such language would have roused no comment except on the part of a handful of feminists; now, since women have acquired the vote, it has come to seem an anachronism. The belief in their "spiritual" superiority was part and parcel of the determination to keep them inferior economically and politically. When men were worsted in this battle, they had to respect women, and therefore gave up offering them "reverence" as a consolation for inferiority.

A somewhat similar development has taken place in the adult view of children. Children, like women, were theologically wicked, especially among evangelicals. They were limbs of Satan, they were unregenerate; as Dr. Watts so admirably put it:

One stroke of His almighty rod
Can send young sinners quick to Hell.

It was necessary that they should be "saved." At Wesley's school "a general conversion was once effected, . . . one poor boy only excepted, who unfortunately resisted the influence of the Holy Spirit, for which he was severely flogged. . . ." But during the nineteenth century, when parental authority, like that of kings and priests and husbands, felt itself threatened, subtler methods of quelling insubordination came into vogue. Children were "innocent"; like good women they had a "bloom"; they must be protected from knowledge of evil lest their bloom should be lost. Moreover, they had a special kind of wisdom. Wordsworth made this view popular among English-speaking people. He first made it fashionable to credit children with

High instincts before which our mortal nature
Did tremble like a guilty thing surprised.

No one in the eighteenth century would have said to his little daughter, unless she were dead:

Thou liest in Abraham's bosom all the year
And worships't at the temple's inner shrine.

But in the nineteenth century this view became quite common; and respectable members of the Episcopal church—or even of the Catholic church—shamelessly ignored Original Sin to dally with the fashionable heresy that

. . . trailing clouds of glory do we come
    From God who is our home:
Heaven lies about us in our infancy.

This led to the usual development. It began to seem hardly right to spank a creature that was lying in Abraham's bosom, or to use the rod rather than "high instincts" to make it "tremble like a guilty thing surprised." And so parents and schoolmasters found that the pleasures they had derived from inflicting chastisement were being curtailed and a theory of education grew up which made it necessary to consider the child's welfare, and not only the adult's convenience and sense of power.

The only consolation the adults could allow themselves was the 8 invention of a new child psychology. Children, after being limbs of Satan in traditional theology and mystically illuminated angels in the minds of educational reformers, have reverted to being little devils— not theological demons inspired by the Evil One, but scientific Freudian abominations inspired by the Unconscious. They are, it must be said, far more wicked than they were in the diatribes of the monks; they display, in modern textbooks, an ingenuity and persistence in sinful imaginings to which in the past there was nothing comparable except St. Anthony. Is all this the objective truth at last? Or is it merely an adult imaginative compensation for being no longer allowed to wallop the little pests? Let the Freudians answer, each for the others.

As appears from the various instances that we have considered, the stage in which superior value is attributed to the oppressed is transient and unstable. It begins only when the oppressors come to have a bad conscience, and this only happens when their power is no longer secure. The idealizing of the victim is useful for a time: if virtue is the greatest of goods, and if subjection makes people virtuous, it is kind to refuse them power, since it would destroy their virtue. If it is difficult for a rich man to enter the kingdom of heaven, it is a noble act on his part to keep his wealth and so imperil his eternal bliss for the benefit of his poorer brethren. It was a fine self-sacrifice on the part of men to relieve women of the dirty work of politics. And so on. But sooner or later the oppressed class will argue that its superior virtue is a reason in favor of its having power, and the oppressors will find their own weapons turned against them. When at last power has been equalized, it becomes apparent to everybody that all the talk about superior virtue was nonsense, and that it was quite unnecessary as a basis for the claim to equality.

In regard to the Italians, the Hungarians, women, and children, we have run through the whole cycle. But we are still in the middle of it in the case which is of the most importance at the present time— namely, that of the proletariat. Admiration of the proletariat is very modern. The eighteenth century, when it praised "the poor," thought always of the rural poor. Jefferson's democracy stopped short at the urban mob; he wished America to remain a country of agriculturists. Admiration of the proletariat, like that of dams, power stations, and airplanes, is part of the ideology of the machine age. Considered in human terms, it has as little in its favor as belief in Celtic magic, the Slav soul, women's intuition, and children's innocence. If it were indeed the case that bad nourishment, little education, lack of air and sunshine, unhealthy housing conditions, and overwork produce better people than are produced by good nourishment, open air, adequate education and housing, and a reasonable amount of leisure, the whole case for economic reconstruction would collapse, and we could rejoice that such a large percentage of the population enjoys the conditions that make for virtue. But obvious as this argument is, many Socialist and Communist intellectuals consider it *de rigueur* to pretend to find the proletariat more amiable than other people, while professing a desire to abolish the conditions which, according to them, alone produce good human beings. Children were idealized by Wordsworth and un-idealized by Freud. Marx was the Wordsworth of the proletariat; its Freud is still to come.

---

# The Libido for the Ugly

## H. L. MENCKEN

On a Winter day some years ago, coming out of Pittsburgh on one   1
of the expresses of the Pennsylvania Railroad, I rolled eastward for an hour through the coal and steel towns of Westmoreland county. It was familiar ground; boy and man, I had been through it often before. But somehow I had never quite sensed its appalling desolation. Here was the very heart of industrial America, the center of its most lucrative and characteristic activity, the boast and pride of the richest and grand-est nation ever seen on earth—and here was a scene so dreadfully hideous, so intolerably bleak and forlorn that it reduced the whole aspiration of man to a macabre and depressing joke. Here was wealth beyond computation, almost beyond imagination—and here were human habitations so abominable that they would have disgraced a race of alley cats.

I am not speaking of mere filth. One expects steel towns to be   2
dirty. What I allude to is the unbroken and agonizing ugliness, the sheer revolting monstrousness, of every house in sight. From East Liberty to Greensburg, a distance of twenty-five miles, there was not one in sight from the train that did not insult and lacerate the eye. Some were so bad, and they were among the most pretentious— churches, stores, warehouses, and the like—that they were downright startling; one blinked before them as one blinks before a man with his face shot away. A few linger in memory, horrible even there: a crazy little church just west of Jeannette, set like a dormer-window on the side of a bare, leprous hill; the headquarters of the Veterans of Foreign Wars at another forlorn town, a steel stadium like a huge rat-trap somewhere further down the line. But most of all I recall the general effect—of hideousness without a break. There was not a single decent house within eye-range from the Pittsburgh suburbs to the Greensburg

yards. There was not one that was not misshapen, and there was not one that was not shabby.

The country itself is not uncomely, despite the grime of the endless 3 mills. It is, in form, a narrow river valley, with deep gullies running up into the hills. It is thickly settled, but not noticeably overcrowded. There is still plenty of room for building, even in the larger towns, and there are very few solid blocks. Nearly every house, big and little, has space on all four sides. Obviously, if there were architects of any professional sense or dignity in the region, they would have perfected a chalet to hug the hillsides—a chalet with a high-pitched roof, to throw off the heavy Winter snows, but still essentially a low and clinging building, wider than it was tall. But what have they done? They have taken as their model a brick set on end. This they have converted into a thing of dingy clapboards, with a narrow, low-pitched roof. And the whole they have set upon thin, preposterous brick piers. By the hundreds and thousands these abominable houses cover the bare hillsides, like gravestones in some gigantic and decaying cemetery. On their deep sides they are three, four and even five stories high; on their low sides they bury themselves swinishly in the mud. Not a fifth of them are perpendicular. They lean this way and that, hanging on to their bases precariously. And one and all they are streaked in grime, with dead and eczematous patches of paint peeping through the streaks.

Now and then there is a house of brick. But what brick! When it 4 is new it is the color of a fried egg. When it has taken on the patina of the mills it is the color of an egg long past all hope or caring. Was it necessary to adopt that shocking color? No more than it was necessary to set all of the houses on end. Red brick, even in a steel town, ages with some dignity. Let it become downright black, and it is still sightly, especially if its trimmings are of white stone, with soot in the depths and the high spots washed by the rain. But in Westmoreland they prefer that uremic yellow, and so they have the most loathsome towns and villages ever seen by mortal eye.

I award this championship only after laborious research and inces- 5 sant prayer. I have seen, I believe, all of the most unlovely towns of the world; they are all to be found in the United States. I have seen the mill towns of decomposing New England and the desert towns of Utah, Arizona and Texas. I am familiar with the back streets of Newark, Brooklyn and Chicago, and have made scientific explorations to Camden, N.J. and Newport News, Va., Safe in a Pullman, I have whirled through the gloomy, God-forsaken villages of Iowa and Kansas, and the malarious tide-water hamlets of Georgia. I have been to Bridgeport, Conn., and to Los Angeles. But nowhere on this earth, at home or abroad, have I seen anything to compare to the villages that huddle along the line of the Pennsylvania from the Pittsburgh yards to Greensburg. They are incomparable in color, and they are incomparable in design. It is as if some titanic and aberrant genius, uncompromisingly inimical to man, had devoted all the ingenuity of Hell to the making of them. They show grotesqueries of ugliness that, in retrospect, become almost diabolical. One cannot imagine mere human beings concocting such dreadful things, and one can scarcely imagine human beings bearing life in them.

Are they so frightful because the valley is full of foreigners—dull,    6
insensate brutes, with no love of beauty in them? Then why didn't these foreigners set up similar abominations in the countries that they come from? You will, in fact, find nothing of the sort in Europe—save perhaps in the more putrid parts of England. There is scarcely an ugly village on the whole Continent. The peasants, however poor, somehow manage to make themselves graceful and charming habitations, even in Spain. But in the American village and small town the pull is always toward ugliness, and in that Westmoreland valley it has been yielded to with an eagerness bordering upon passion. It is incredible that mere ignorance should have achieved such masterpieces of horror.

On certain levels of the American race, indeed, there seems to be    7
a positive libido for the ugly, as on other and less Christian levels there is a libido for the beautiful. It is impossible to put down the wallpaper that defaces the average American home of the lower middle class to mere inadvertence, or to the obscene humor of the manufacturers. Such ghastly designs, it must be obvious, give a genuine delight to a certain type of mind. They meet, in some unfathomable way, its obscure and unintelligible demands. They caress it as "The Palms" caresses it, or the art of the movie, or jazz. The taste for them is as enigmatical and yet as common as the taste for dogmatic theology and the poetry of Edgar A. Guest.

Thus I suspect (though confessedly without knowing) that the vast    8
majority of the honest folk of Westmoreland county, and especially the 100% Americans among them, actually admire the houses they live in, and are proud of them. For the same money they could get vastly better ones, but they prefer what they have got. Certainly there was no pressure upon the Veterans of Foreign Wars to choose the dreadful

edifice that bears their banner, for there are plenty of vacant buildings along the track-side, and some of them are appreciably better. They might, indeed, have built a better one of their own. But they chose that clapboarded horror with their eyes open, and having chosen it, they let it mellow into its present shocking depravity. They like it as it is: beside it, the Parthenon would no doubt offend them. In precisely the same way the authors of the rattrap stadium that I have mentioned made a deliberate choice. After painfully designing and erecting it, they made it perfect in their own sight by putting a completely impossible penthouse, painted a staring yellow, on top of it. The effect is that of a fat woman with a black eye. It is that of a Presbyterian grinning. But they like it.

Here is something that the psychologists have so far neglected: the   9
love of ugliness for its own sake, the lust to make the world intolerable. Its habitat is the United States. Out of the melting pot emerges a race which hates beauty as it hates truth. The etiology of this madness deserves a great deal more study than it has got. There must be causes behind it; it arises and flourishes in obedience to biological laws, and not as a mere act of God. What, precisely, are the terms of those laws? And why do they run stronger in America than elsewhere? Let some honest *Privat Dozent* in pathological sociology apply himself to the problem.

---

# *Vulnerability: A Feminine Emotion*

## SUSAN BROWNMILLER

A 1970 landmark study, known in the field as *Broverman and*   1
*Broverman,* reported that "Cries very easily" was rated by a group of professional psychologists as a highly feminine trait. "Very emotional," "Very excitable in a minor crises" and "Feelings easily hurt" were additional characteristics on the femininity scale. So were "Very easily influenced," "Very subjective," "Unable to separate feelings from ideas," "Very illogical" and "Very sneaky." As might be expected, masculinity was defined by opposing, sturdier values: "Very direct," "Very logical," "Can make decisions easily," "Never cries." The im-

portance of *Broverman and Broverman* was not in nailing down a set of popular assumptions and conventional perceptions—masculine-feminine scales were well established in the literature of psychology as a means of ascertaining normality and social adjustment—but in the authors' observation that stereotypic femininity was a grossly negative assessment of the female sex and, furthermore, that many so-called feminine traits ran counter to clinical descriptions of maturity and mental health.

Emotional femininity is a tough nut to crack, impossible to quantify    2
yet hard to ignore. As the task of conforming to a specified physical design is a gender mission that few women care to resist, conforming to a prepackaged emotional design is another imperative task of gender. To satisfy a societal need for sexual clarification, and to justify second-class status, an emblematic constellation of inner traits, as well as their outward manifestations, has been put forward historically by some of the world's great thinkers as proof of the "different" feminine nature.

"Woman," wrote Aristotle, "is more compassionate than man,    3
more easily moved to tears. At the same time, she is more jealous, more querulous, more apt to scold and to strike. She is, furthermore, more prone to despondency and less hopeful than man, more void of shame or self-respect, more false of speech, more deceptive and of more retentive memory. She is also more wakeful, more shrinking, more difficult to rouse to action, and she requires a smaller amount of nutriment."

Addressing a suffrage convention in 1855, Ralph Waldo Emerson    4
had kindlier words on the nature of woman, explicating the nine-teenth-century view that her difference was one of superior virtue. "Women," he extolled, "are the civilizers of mankind. What is civiliza-tion? I answer, the power of good women. . . . The starry crown of woman is in the power of her affection and sentiment, and the infinite enlargements to which they lead." (In less elevated language, the Emersonian view was perhaps what President Reagan had in mind when he cheerfully stated, "Why, if it wasn't for women, we men would still be walking around in skin suits carrying clubs.")

A clarification is in order. Are women believed to possess a wider    5
or deeper emotional range, a greater sensitivity, say, to the beauties of nature or to the infinite complexities of feeling? Any male poet, artist, actor, marine biologist or backpacker would strenuously object. Rather, it is commonly agreed that women are tossed and buffeted on

the high seas of emotion, while men have the tough mental fiber, the intellectual muscle, to stay in control. As for the civilizing influence, surely something more is meant than sophistication, culture and taste, using the correct fork or not belching after dinner. The idealization of emotional femininity, as women prefer to see themselves affirmed, is more exquisitely romantic: a finer temperament in a more fragile vessel, a gentler nature ruled by a twin need to love and to be protected: one who appreciates—without urgency to create—good art, music, literature and other public expressions of the private soul; a flame-bearer of spiritual values by whose shining example the men of the world are inspired to redemption and to accomplish great things.

Two thousand years ago *Dominus flevit,* Jesus wept as he beheld   6 Jerusalem. "Men ceased weeping," proposed Simone de Beauvoir, "when it became unfashionable." Now it is Mary, *Mater Dolorosa,* who weeps with compassion for mankind. In mystical visions, in the reliquaries of obscure churches and miraculous shrines, the figure of the Virgin, the world's most feminine woman, has been seen to shed tears. There are still extant cultures in which men are positively lachrymose (and kissy-kissy) with no seeming detriment to their masculine image, but the Anglo-Saxon tradition, in particular, requires keeping a stiff upper lip. Weeping, keening women shrouded in black are an established fixture in mourning rites in many nations. Inconsolable grief is a feminine role, at least in its unquiet representations. In what has become a stock photograph in the national news magazines, women weep for the multitudes when national tragedy (a terrorist bombing, an air crash, an assassination) strikes.

The catharsis of tears is encouraged in women—"There, there,   7 now, let it all out"—while a man may be told to get a grip on himself, or to gulp down a double Scotch. Having "a good cry" in order to feel better afterward is not usually recommended as a means of raising the spirits of men, for the cathartic relief of succumbing to tears would be tempered by the uncomfortable knowledge that the loss of control was hardly manly. In the 1972 New Hampshire Presidential primary, Senator Edmund Muskie, then the Democratic front-runner, committed political suicide when he publicly cried during a campaign speech. Muskie had been talking about some harsh press comments directed at his wife when the tears filled his eyes. In retrospect it was his watershed moment: Could a man who became tearful when the going got rough in a political campaign be expected to face the Russians? To a nation that had delighted in the hatless, overcoatless macho posturing of John F. Kennedy, the military successes of General Ike and the irascible outbursts of "Give 'em hell" Harry Truman, the answer was No. Media accounts of Muskie's all-too-human tears were merciless. In the summer of 1983 the obvious and unshakable grief displayed by Israeli prime minister Menachem Begin after the death of his wife was seized upon by the Israeli and American press as evidence that a tough old warrior had lost his grip. Sharing this perception of his own emotional state, perhaps, Begin shortly afterward resigned.

Expressions of anger and rage are not a disqualifying factor in the    8
masculine disposition. Anger in men is often understood, or excused, as reasonable or just. Anger in men may even be cast in a heroic mold—a righteous response to an insult against honor that will prelude a manly, aggressive act. Because competitive acts of personal assertion, not to mention acts of outright physical aggression, are known to flow from angry feelings, anger becomes the most unfeminine emotion a woman can show.

Anger in a woman isn't "nice." A woman who seethes with anger    9
is "unattractive." An angry woman is hard, mean and nasty; she is unreliably, unprettily out of control. Her face contorts into unpleasant lines: the jaw juts, the eyes are narrowed, the teeth are bared. Anger is a violent snarl and a hostile threat, a declaration of war. The endless forbearance demanded of women, described as the feminine virtue of patience, prohibits an angry response. Picture a charming old-fashioned scene: The mistress of the house bends low over her needlework, cross-stitching her sampler: "Patience is a virtue, possess it if you can/Seldom seen in women, never seen in man." Does the needle jab through the cloth in uncommon fury? Does she prick her thumb in frustration?

Festering without a permissible release, women's undissolved    10
anger has been known to seep out in petty, mean-spirited ways—fits of jealousy, fantasies of retaliation, unholy plots of revenge. Perhaps, after all, it is safer to cry. "Woman's aptitude for facile tears," wrote Beauvoir, "comes largely from the fact that her life is built upon a foundation of impotent revolt."[1]

Beauvoir hedged her bet, for her next words were these: "It is also    11
doubtless true that physiologically she has less nervous control than a man." Is this "doubtless true," or is it more to the point, as Beauvoir continues, that "her education has taught her to let herself go more readily"?

Infants and children cry out of fear, frustration, discomfort, hun-    12 ger, anxiety at separation from a parent, and rage. Surveying all available studies of crying newborns and little children, psychologists Eleanor Maccoby and Carol Jacklin found no appreciable sexual difference. If teenage girls and adult women are known to cry more than men—and there is no reason to question the popular wisdom in this regard—should the endocrine changes of adolescence be held to account? What of those weepy "blue days" of premenstrual tension that genuinely afflict so many women? What about mid-life depression, known in some circles as "the feminine malady"? Are these conditions, as some men propose, a sign of "raging hormonal imbalance" that incapacitates the cool, logical functioning of the human brain? Or does feminine depression result, as psychiatrist Willard Gaylin suggests, when confidence in one's coping mechanism is lost?

Belief in a biological basis for the instability of female emotions has   13
a notorious history in the development of medical science. Hippocrates the physician held that hysteria was caused by a wandering uterus that remained unfulfilled. Discovery in the seventeenth century that the thyroid gland was larger in women inspired that proposition that the thyroid's function was to give added grace to the feminine neck, but other beliefs maintained that the gland served to flush impurities from the blood before it reached the brain. A larger thyroid "was necessary to guard the female system from the influence of the more numerous causes of irritation and vexation" to which the sex was unfortunately disposed. Nineteenth-century doctors averred that womb-related disorders were the cause of such female complaints as "nervous prostration." For those without money to seek out a physician's care, Lydia E. Pinkham's Vegetable Compound and other patent medicines were available to give relief. In the 1940s and '50s, prefrontal lobotomy was briefly and tragically in vogue for a variety of psychiatric disorders, particularly among women, since the surgical procedure had a flattening effect on raging emotions. Nowadays Valium appears to suffice.

Beginning in earnest in the 1960s, one line of research has at-   14
tempted to isolate premenstrual tension as a contributing cause of accidents, suicide, admittance to mental hospitals and the commission of violent crimes. Mood swings, irritability and minor emotional upsets probably do lead to more "acting out" by females at a cyclical time in the month, but what does this prove beyond the increasingly accepted fact that the endocrine system has a critical influence on the human emotional threshold? Suicide, violent crime and dangerous psychiatric disorders are statistically four to nine times more prevalent in men.

Should we theorize, then, that "raging hormonal imbalance" is a chronic, year-round condition in males? A disqualifying factor? By any method of calculation and for whatever reason—hormonal effects, the social inhibitions of femininity, the social pleasure of the masculine role, or all of these—the female gender is indisputably less prone to irrational, antisocial behavior. The price of inhibited anger and a non-violent temperament may well be a bucketful of tears.

Like the emotion of anger, exulting in personal victory is a harshly 15 unfeminine response. Of course, good winners of either sex are sup-posed to display some degree of sportsmanlike humility, but the merest hint of gloating triumph—"Me, me, me, I did it!"—is completely at odds with the modesty and deference expected of women and girls. Arm raised in a winner's salute, the ritualized climax of a prizefight, wrestling match or tennis championship, is unladylike, to say the least. The powerful feeling that victory engenders, the satisfaction of climb-ing to the top of the heap or clinching a deal, remains an inappropriate emotion. More appropriate to femininity are the predictable tears of the new Miss America as she accepts her crown and scepter. Trem-bling lip and brimming eyes suggest a Cinderella who has stumbled upon good fortune through unbelievable, undeserved luck. At her moment of victory the winner of America's favorite pageant appears overcome, rather than superior in any way. A Miss America who raised her scepter high like a trophy would not be in keeping with the femi-nine ideal.

The maidenly blush, that staple of the nineteenth-century lady's 16 novel, was an excellent indicator of innocent virginal shyness in con-trast to the worldliness and sophistication of men. In an age when a variety of remarks, largely sexual, were considered uncouth and not for the ears of virtuous women, the feminine blush was an expected re-sponse. On the other side of the ballroom, men never blushed, at least not in romantic fiction, since presumably they were knowledgeable and sexually practiced. Lowered eyes, heightened color, breathless-ness and occasional swooning were further proofs of a fragile and innocent feminine nature that required protection in the rough, indeli-cate masculine world. (In the best-selling Harlequin and Silhouette books devoured by romance addicts who need the quick fix, the maid-enly blush is alive and well.)

In a new age of relative sexual freedom, or permissiveness, at any 17 rate, squeals and moans replace the blush and the downcast eye. Screaming bobbysoxers who fainted in the aisle at the Paramount

Theater when a skinny young Frank Sinatra crooned his love ballads during the 1940s (reportedly, the first wave of fainting girls was staged by promoters) presaged the whimpering orgasmic ecstasy at rock concerts in huge arenas today. By contrast, young men in the audience automatically rise to their feet and whistle and shout when the band starts to play, but they seldom appear overcome.

Most emphatically, feminine emotion has gotten louder. The ribald squeal of the stereotypic serving wench in Elizabethan times, a supposed indicator of loose, easy ways, seem to have lost its lower-class stigma. One byproduct of our media-obsessed society, in which privacy is considered a quaint and rather old-fashioned human need, has been the reproduction of the unmistakable sounds of female orgasm on a record (Donna Summer's "Love to Love You Baby," among other hits). More than commercialization of sex is operative here. Would the sounds of male orgasm suffice for a recording, and would they be unmistakable? Although I have seen no studies on this interesting sex difference, I believe it can be said that most women do vocalize more loudly and uncontrollably than men in the throes of sexual passion. Is this response physiological, compensatory or merely symptomatic of the feminine mission to display one's feelings (and the corresponding masculine mission to keep their feelings under control)? 18

Feminine emotion specializes in sentimentality, empathy and admissions of vulnerability—three characteristics that most men try to avoid. Linking these traits to female anatomy became an article of faith in the Freudian school. Erik Erikson, for one, spoke of an "inner space" (he meant the womb) that yearns for fulfillment through maternal love. Helene Deutsch, the grande dame of Freudian feminine psychology, spoke of psychic acceptance of hurt and pain; menstrual cramps, defloration and the agonies of childbirth called for a masochistic nature she believed was innate. 19

Love of babies, any baby and all babies, not only one's own, is a celebrated and anticipated feminine emotion, and a woman who fails to ooh and ahh at the snapshot of a baby or cuddle a proffered infant in her arms is instantly suspect. Evidence of a maternal nature, of a certain innate competence when handling a baby or at least some indication of maternal longing, becomes a requirement of gender. Women with no particular feeling for babies are extremely reluctant to admit their private truth, for the entire weight of woman's place in the biological division of labor, not to mention the glorification of motherhood as woman's greatest and only truly satisfactory role, has kept 20

alive the belief that all women yearn to fulfill their biological destiny
out of a deep emotional need. That a sizable number of mothers have
no genuine aptitude for the job is verified by the records of hospitals,
family courts and social agencies where cases of battery and neglect
are duly entered—and perhaps also by the characteristic upper-class
custom of leaving the little ones to the care of the nanny. But despite
this evidence that day-to-day motherhood is not a suitable or a stimu-
lating occupation for all, the myth persists that a woman who prefers
to remain childless must be heartless or selfish or less than complete.

Books have been written on maternal guilt and its exploitation, on    21
the endemic feeling that whatever a mother does, her loving care may
be inadequate or wrong, with consequences that can damage a child
for life. Trends in child care (bottle feeding, demand feeding, not
picking up the crying baby, delaying the toilet training or giving up an
outside job to devote one's entire time to the family) illuminate the fear
of maternal inadequacy as well as the variability or "expert" opinion
in each generation. Advertising copywriters successfully manipulate
this feminine fear when they pitch their clients' products. A certain
cereal, one particular brand of packaged white bread, must be bought
for the breakfast table or else you have failed to love your child sufficiently and denied him the chance to "build a strong body twelve
ways." Until the gay liberation movement began to speak for itself, it
was a commonplace of psychiatric wisdom that a mother had it within
her power to destroy her son's heterosexual adjustment by failing to
cut his baby curls, keep him away from dance class or encourage his
interest in sports.

A requirement of femininity is that a woman devote her life to      22
love—to mother love, to romantic love, to religious love, to amorphous,
undifferentiated caring. The territory of the heart is admittedly a province that is open to all, but women alone are expected to make an
obsessional career of its exploration, to find whatever adventure,
power, fulfillment or tragedy that life has to offer within its bounds.
There is no question that a woman is apt to feel most feminine, most
confident of her interior gender makeup, when she is reliably within
some stage of love—even the girlish crush or the stage of unrequited
love or a broken heart. Men have suffered for love, and men have
accomplished great feats in the name of love, but what man has ever
felt at the top of his masculine form when he is lovesick or suffering
from heartache?

Gloria Steinem once observed that the heart is a sex-distinctive    23 symbol of feminine vulnerability in the marketing of fashion. Heart-shaped rings and heart-shaped gold pendants and heart-shaped frames on red plastic sunglasses announce an addiction to love that is beyond the pale of appropriate design for masculine ornamentation. (A man does not wear his heart on his sleeve.) The same observation applies a little less stringently to flowers.

Rare is the famous girl singer, whatever her age, of popular music   24
(blues, country, Top Forty, disco or rock) who is not chiefly identified with some expression of love, usually its downside. Torchy bittersweet ballads and sad, suffering laments mixed with vows of eternal fidelity to the rotten bastard who done her wrong communicate the feminine message of love at any cost. Almost unique to the female singer, I think, is the poignant anthem of battered survival, from Fanny Brice's "My Man" to Gloria Gaynor's "I Will Survive," that does not quite shut the door on further emotional abuse if her man should return.

But the point is not emotional abuse (except in extreme, aberrant   25
cases); the point is feeling. Women are instructed from childhood to be keepers of the heart, keepers of the sentimental memory. In diaries, packets of old love letters and family albums, in slender books of poetry in which a flower is pressed, a woman's emotional history is preserved. Remembrance of things past—the birthday, the anniversary, the death—is a feminine province. In the social division of labor, the wife is charged with maintaining the emotional connection, even with the husband's side of the family. Her thoughtful task is to make the long-distance call, select the present and write the thank-you note (chores that secretaries are asked to do by their bosses). Men are busy; they move forward. A woman looks back. It is significant that in the Biblical parable it was Lot's wife who looked back for one last precious glimpse of their city, their home, their past (and was turned into a pillar of salt).

Love confirms the feminine psyche. A celebrated difference be-   26
tween men and women (either women's weakness or women's strength, depending on one's values) is the obstinate reluctance, the emotional inability of women to separate sex from love. Understandably. Love makes the world go round, and women are supposed to get dizzy—to rise, to fall, to feel alive in every pore, to be undone. In place of a suitable attachment, an unlikely or inaccessible one may have to do. But more important, sex for a woman, even in an age of accessible contraception, has reproductive consequences that render the act a serious affair. Casual sex can have a most uncasual resolution. If a young girl thinks of love and marriage while a boy thinks of getting

laid, her emotional commitment is rooted not only in her different upbringing but in her reproductive biology as well. Love, then, can become an alibi for thoughtless behavior, as it may also become an identity, or a distraction, à la Emma Bovary or Anna Karenina, from the frustrations of a limited life.[2]

Christian houses of worship, especially in poor neighborhoods, are   26 filled disproportionately by women. This phenomenon may not be entirely attributable to the historic role of the Catholic and Protestant religions in encouraging the public devotions of women (which Judaism and Islam did not), or because women have more time for prayer, or because in the Western world they are believed to be more religious by nature. Another contributing factor may be that the central article of Christian faith, "Jesus loves you," has particular appeal for the gender that defines itself through loving emotions.

Women's special interest in the field of compassion is catered to   28 and promoted. Hollywood "weepies," otherwise known as four-hand-kerchief movies, were big-studio productions that were tailored to bring in female box-office receipts. Columns of advice to the lovelorn, such as the redoubtable "Dear Dorothy Dix" and the current "Dear Abby," were by tradition a woman's slot on daily newspapers, along with the coverage of society births and weddings, in the days when females were as rare in a newsroom as they were in a coal mine. In the heyday of the competitive tabloids, sob-sister journalism, that news-room term for a human-interest story told with heart-wrenching pathos (usually by a tough male reporter who had the formula down pat), was held in contempt by those on the paper who covered the "hard stuff" of politics, crime and war. (Nathanael West's famous antihero labored under the byline of Miss Lonelyhearts.) Despite its obvious audience appeal, "soft stuff" was, and is, on the lower rungs of journalism— trivial, weak and unmanly.

In Government circles during the Vietnam war, it was considered   29 a sign of emotional softness, of lily-livered liberals and nervous nellies, to suggest that Napalmed babies, fire-bombed villages and defoliated crops were reason enough to pull out American forces. The peace movement, went the charge, was composed of cowards and fuzzy thinkers. Suspicion of an unmanly lack of hard practical logic always haunts those men who espouse peace and nonviolence, but women, the weaker sex, are permitted a certain amount of emotional leeway. Feminine logic, after all, is reputedly governed by the heartstrings. Compassion and sentiment are the basis for its notorious "subjectivity" compared to the "objectivity" of men who use themselves as the objective standard.

As long as the social division of labor ordains that women should bear the chief emotional burden of caring for human life from the cradle to the grave while men may demonstrate their dimorphic difference through competitive acts of physical aggression, emblematic compassion and fear of violence are compelling reasons for an aversion to war and other environmental hazards. When law and custom deny the full range of public expression and economic opportunity that men claim for themselves, a woman must place much of her hopes, her dreams, her feminine identity and her social importance in the private sphere of personal relations, in the connective tissue of marriage, family, friendship and love. In a world out of balance, where men are taught to value toughness and linear vision as masculine traits that enable them to think strategically from conquest to conquest, from campaign to campaign without looking back, without getting sidetracked by vulnerable feelings, there is, and will be, an emotional difference between the sexes, a gender gap that may even appear on a Gallup poll.

If a true shape could emerge from the shadows of historic oppression, would the gender-specific experience of being female still suggest a range of perceptions and values that differ appreciably from those of men? It would be premature to offer an answer. Does a particular emotion ultimately resist separation from its historic deployment in the sexual balance of power? In the way of observation, this much can be said: The entwining of anatomy, history and culture presents such a persuasive emotional argument for a "different nature" that even the best aspects of femininity collaborate in its perpetuation.

### Notes

1. "Facile" is the English translator's match for the French *facile*, more correctly rendered as "easy." Beauvoir did not mean to ascribe a stereotypic superficiality to women in her remark.
2. The overwhelming influence of feminine love is frequently offered as a mitigating explanation by women who do unfeminine things. Elizabeth Bentley, the "Red Spy Queen" of the cold war Fifties, attributed her illegal activities to her passion for the Russian master spy Jacob Golos. Judith Coplon's defense for stealing Government documents was love for another Russian, Valentin Gubichev. More recently, Jean Harris haplessly failed to convince a jury that her love for "Scarsdale diet" Doctor Herman Tarnower was so great that she could not possibly have intended to kill him.

# Classification and Division

## Thinking as a Hobby

### WILLIAM GOLDING

While I was still a boy, I came to the conclusion that there were 1
three grades of thinking; and since I was later to claim thinking as my
hobby, I came to an even stranger conclusion—namely, that I myself
could not think at all.

I must have been an unsatisfactory child for grownups to deal 2
with. I remember how incomprehensible they appeared to me at first,
but not, of course, how I appeared to them. It was the headmaster of
my grammar school who first brought the subject of thinking before
me—though neither in the way, nor with the result he intended. He
had some statuettes in his study. They stood on a high cupboard behind
his desk. One was a lady wearing nothing but a bath towel. She seemed
frozen in an eternal panic lest the bath towel slip down any farther;
and since she had no arms, she was in an unfortunate position to pull
the towel up again. Next to her, crouched the statuette of a leopard,
ready to spring down at the top drawer of a filing cabinet labeled
A-AH. My innocence interpreted this as the victim's last, despairing
cry. Beyond the leopard was a naked, muscular gentleman, who sat,
looking down, with his chin on his fist and his elbow on his knee. He
seemed utterly miserable.

Some time later, I learned about these statuettes. The headmaster 3
had placed them where they would face delinquent children, because
they symbolized to him the whole of life. The naked lady was the
Venus of Milo. She was Love. She was not worried about the towel.
She was just busy being beautiful. The leopard was Nature, and he was
being natural. The naked, muscular gentleman was not miserable. He

148

was Rodin's Thinker, an image of pure thought. It is easy to buy small plaster models of what you think life is like.

I had better explain that I was a frequent visitor to the headmaster's study, because of the latest thing I had done or left undone. As we now say, I was not integrated. I was, if anything, disintegrated; and I was puzzled. Grownups never made sense. Whenever I found myself in a penal position before the headmaster's desk, with the statuettes glimmering whitely above him, I would sink my head, clasp my hands behind my back and writhe one shoe over the other.

The headmaster would look opaquely at me through flashing spectacles.

"What are we going to do with you?"

Well, what *were* they going to do with me? I would writhe my shoe some more and stare down at the worn rug.

"Look up, boy! Can't you look up?"

Then I would look up at the cupboard, where the naked lady was frozen in her panic and the muscular gentleman contemplated the hindquarters of the leopard in endless gloom. I had nothing to say to the headmaster. His spectacles caught the light so that you could see nothing human behind them. There was no possibility of communication.

"Don't you ever think at all?"

No, I didn't think, wasn't thinking, couldn't think—I was simply waiting in anguish for the interview to stop.

"Then you'd better learn—hadn't you?"

On one occasion the headmaster leaped to his feet, reached up and plonked Rodin's masterpiece on the desk before me.

"That's what a man looks like when he's really thinking."

I surveyed the gentleman without interest or comprehension.

"Go back to your class."

Clearly there was something missing in me. Nature had endowed the rest of the human race with a sixth sense and left me out. This must be so, I mused, on my way back to the class, since whether I had broken a window, or failed to remember Boyle's Law, or been late for school, my teachers produced me one, adult answer: "Why can't you think?"

As I saw the case, I had broken the window because I had tried to hit Jack Arney with a cricket ball and missed him; I could not remember Boyle's Law because I had never bothered to learn it; and I was late for school because I preferred looking over the bridge into the river. In fact, I was wicked. Were my teachers, perhaps, so good that they could not understand the depths of my depravity? Were they clear, untormented people who could direct their every action by this mysterious business of thinking? The whole thing was incomprehensible. In my earlier years, I found even the statuette of the Thinker confusing. I did not believe any of my teachers were naked, ever. Like someone born deaf, but bitterly determined to find out about sound, I watched my teachers to find out about thought.

There was Mr. Houghton. He was always telling me to think. With  19
a modest satisfaction, he would tell me that he had thought a bit himself. Then why did he spend so much time drinking? Or was there more sense in drinking than there appeared to be? But if not, and if drinking were in fact ruinous to health—and Mr. Houghton was ruined, there was no doubt about that—why was he always talking about the clean life and the virtues of fresh air? He would spread his arms wide with the action of a man who habitually spent his time striding along mountain ridges.

"Open air does me good, boys—I know it!"                          20

Sometimes, exalted by his own oratory, he would leap from his   21
desk and hustle us outside into a hideous wind.

"Now, boys! Deep breaths! Feel it right down inside you—huge    22
draughts of God's good air!"

He would stand before us, rejoicing in his perfect health, an open-  23
air man. He would put his hands on his waist and take a tremendous breath. You could hear the wind, trapped in the cavern of his chest and struggling with all the unnatural impediments. His body would reel with shock and his ruined face go white at the unaccustomed visitation. He would stagger back to his desk and collapse there, useless for the rest of the morning.

Mr. Houghton was given to high-minded monologues about the   24
good life, sexless and full of duty. Yet in the middle of one of these monologues, if a girl passed the window, tapping along on her neat little feet, he would interrupt his discourse, his neck would turn of itself and he would watch her out of sight. In this instance, he seemed to me ruled not by thought but by an invisible and irresistible spring in his nape.

His neck was an object of great interest to me. Normally it bulged  25
a bit over his collar. But Mr. Houghton had fought in the First World War alongside both Americans and French, and had come—by who knows what illogic?—to a settled detestation of both countries. If ei-

ther country happened to be prominent in current affairs, no argument could make Mr. Houghton think well of it. He would bang the desk, his neck would bulge still further and go red. "You can say what you like," he would cry, "but I've thought about this—and I know what I think!"

Mr. Houghton thought with his neck.                                    26

There was Miss Parsons. She assured us that her dearest wish was    27
our welfare, but I knew even then, with the mysterious clairvoyance of childhood, that what she wanted most was the husband she never got. There was Mr. Hands—and so on.

I have dealt at length with my teachers because this was my    28
introduction to the nature of what is commonly called thought. Through them I discovered that thought is often full of unconscious prejudice, ignorance and hypocrisy. It will lecture on disinterested purity while its neck is being remorselessly twisted toward a skirt. Technically, it is about as proficient as most businessmen's golf, as honest as most politicians' intentions, or—to come near my own preoc- cupation—as coherent as most books that get written. It is what I came to call grade-three thinking, though more properly, it is feeling, rather than thought.

True, often there is a kind of innocence in prejudices, but in those    29
days I viewed grade-three thinking with an intolerant contempt and an incautious mockery. I delighted to confront a pious lady who hated the Germans with the proposition that we should love our enemies. She taught me a great truth in dealing with grade-three thinkers; because of her, I no longer dismiss lightly a mental process which for nine- tenths of the population is the nearest they will ever get to thought. They have immense solidarity. We had better respect them, for we are outnumbered and surrounded. A crowd of grade-three thinkers, all shouting the same thing, all warming their hands at the fire of their own prejudices, will not thank you for pointing out the contradictions in their beliefs. Man is a gregarious animal, and enjoys agreement as cows will graze all the same way on the side of a hill.

Grade-two thinking is the detection of contradictions. I reached    30
grade two when I trapped the poor, pious lady. Grade-two thinkers do not stampede easily, though often they fall into the other fault and lag behind. Grade-two thinking is a withdrawal, with eyes and ears open. It became my hobby and brought satisfaction and loneliness in either hand. For grade-two thinking destroys without having the power to create. It set me watching the crowds cheering His Majesty the King and asking myself what all the fuss was about, without giving me

anything positive to put in the place of that heady patriotism. But there were compensations. To hear people justify their habit of hunting foxes and tearing them to pieces by claiming that the foxes liked it. To hear our Prime Minister talk about the great benefit we conferred on India by jailing people like Pandit Nehru and Gandhi. To hear American politicians talk about peace in one sentence and refuse to join the League of Nations in the next. Yes, there were moments of delight.

But I was growing toward adolescence and had to admit that Mr.   31
Houghton was not the only one with an irresistible spring in his neck. I, too, felt the compulsive hand of nature and began to find that pointing out contradiction could be costly as well as fun. There was Ruth, for example, a serious and attractive girl. I was an atheist at the time. Grade-two thinking is a menace to religion and knocks down sects like skittles. I put myself in a position to be converted by her with an hypocrisy worthy of grade three. She was a Methodist—or at least, her parents were, and Ruth had to follow suit. But, alas, instead of relying on the Holy Spirit to convert me, Ruth was foolish enough to open her pretty mouth in argument. She claimed that the Bible (King James Version) was literally inspired. I countered by saying that the Catholics believed in the literal inspiration of Saint Jerome's *Vulgate,* and the two books were different.

At last she remarked that there were an awful lot of Methodists,   32
and they couldn't be wrong, could they—not all those millions? That was too easy, said I restively (for the nearer you were to Ruth, the nicer she was to be near to) since there were more Roman Catholics than Methodists anyway; and they couldn't be wrong, could they—not all those hundreds of millions? An awful flicker of doubt appeared in her eyes. I slid my arm round her waist and murmured breathlessly that if we were counting heads, the Buddhists were the boys for my money. But Ruth had *really* wanted to do me good, because I was so nice. She fled. The combination of my arm and those countless Buddhists was too much for her.

That night her father visited my father and left, red-cheeked and   33
indignant. I was given the third degree to find out what had happened. It was lucky we were both of us only fourteen. I lost Ruth and gained an undeserved reputation as a potential libertine.

So grade-two thinking could be dangerous. It was in this knowl-   34
edge, at the age of fifteen, that I remember making a comment from the heights of grade two, on the limitations of grade three. One evening I found myself alone in the schoolhall, preparing it for a party. The

door of the headmaster's study was open. I went in. The headmaster
had ceased to thump Rodin's Thinker down on the desk as an example
to the young. Perhaps he had not found any more candidates, but the
statuettes were still there, glimmering and gathering dust on top of the
cupboard. I stood on a chair and rearranged them. I stood Venus in her
bath towel on the filing cabinet, so that now the top drawer caught its
breath in a gasp of sexy excitement. "A-ah!" The portentous Thinker
I placed on the edge of the cupboard so that he looked down at the bath
towel and waited for it to slip.

Grade-two thinking, though it filled life with fun and excitement,          35
did not make for content. To find out the deficiencies of our elders
bolsters the young ego but does not make for personal security. I found
that grade two was not only the power to point out contradictions. It
took the swimmer some distance from the shore and left him there, out
of his depth. I decided that Pontius Pilate was a typical grade-two
thinker. "What is truth?" he said, a very common grade-two thought,
but one that is used always as the end of an argument instead of the
beginning. There is a still higher grade of thought which says, "What
is truth?" and sets out to find it.

But these grade-one thinkers were few and far between. They did          36
not visit my grammar school in the flesh though they were there in
books. I aspired to them, partly because I was ambitious and partly
because I now saw my hobby as an unsatisfactory thing if it went no
further. If you set out to climb a mountain, however high you climb,
you have failed if you cannot reach the top.

I *did* meet an undeniably grade-one thinker in my first year at          37
Oxford. I was looking over a small bridge in Magdalen Deer Park, and
a tiny mustached and hatted figure came and stood by my side. He was
a German who had just fled from the Nazis to Oxford as a temporary
refuge. His name was Einstein.

But Professor Einstein knew no English at that time and I knew          38
only two words of German. I beamed at him, trying wordlessly to
convey by my bearing all the affection and respect that the English felt
for him. It is possible—and I have to make the admission—that I felt
here were two grade-one thinkers standing side by side; yet I doubt if
my face conveyed more than a formless awe. I would have given my
Greek and Latin and French and a good slice of my English for enough
German to communicate. But we were divided; he was as inscrutable
as my headmaster. For perhaps five minutes we stood together on the
bridge, undeniable grade-one thinker and breathless aspirant. With

true greatness, Professor Einstein realized that any contact was better
than none. He pointed to a trout wavering in midstream.

He spoke: *"Fisch."*                                                    39

My brain reeled. Here I was, mingling with the great, and yet        40
helpless as the veriest grade-three thinker. Desperately I sought for
some sign by which I might convey that I, too, revered pure reason. I
nodded vehemently. In a brilliant flash I used up half of my German
vocabulary. *"Fisch. Ja. Ja."*

For perhaps another five minutes we stood side by side. Then          41
Professor Einstein, his whole figure still conveying good will and amia-
bility, drifted away out of sight.

I, too, would be a grade-one thinker. I was irreverent at the best    42
of times. Political and religious systems, social customs, loyalties and
traditions, they all came tumbling down like so many rotten apples off
a tree. This was a fine hobby and a sensible substitute for cricket, since
you could play it all the year round. I came up in the end with what
must always remain the justification for grade-one thinking, its sign,
seal and charter. I devised a coherent system for living. It was a moral
system, which was wholly logical. Of course, as I readily admitted,
conversion of the world to my way of thinking might be difficult, since
my system did away with a number of trifles, such as big business,
centralized government, armies, marriage. . . .

It was Ruth all over again. I had some very good friends who stood   43
by me, and still do. But my acquaintances vanished, taking the girls
with them. Young women seemed oddly contented with the world as
it was. They valued the meaningless ceremony with a ring. Young men,
while willing to concede the chaining sordidness of marriage, were
hesitant about abandoning the organizations which they hoped would
give them a career. A young man on the first rung of the Royal Navy,
while perfectly agreeable to doing away with big business and marriage, got as red-necked as Mr. Houghton when I proposed a world
without any battleships in it.

Had the game gone too far? Was it a game any longer? In those        44
prewar days I stood to lose a great deal for the sake of a hobby.

Now you are expecting me to describe how I saw the folly of my       45
ways and came back to the warm nest, where prejudices are so often
called loyalties, where pointless actions are hallowed into custom by
repetition, where we are content to say we think when all we do is feel.

But you would be wrong. I dropped my hobby and turned profes-        46
sional.

If I were to go back to the headmaster's study and find the dusty 47
statuettes still there, I would arrange them differently. I would dust
Venus and put her aside, for I have come to love her and know her for
the fair thing she is. But I would put the Thinker, sunk in his desperate
thought, where there were shadows before him and at his back, I
would put the leopard, crouched and ready to spring.

---

# College Pressures

## WILLIAM ZINSSER

DEAR CARLOS: I desperately need a dean's excuse for my chem midterm which
will begin in about 1 hour. All I can say is that I totally blew it this week. I've
fallen incredibly, inconceivably behind.

CARLOS: Help! I'm anxious to hear from you. I'll be in my room and won't leave
it until I hear from you. Tomorrow is the last day for . . .

CARLOS: I left town because I started bugging out again. I stayed up all night
to finish a take-home make-up exam & am typing it to hand in on the 10th. It
was due on the 5th. P.S. I'm going to the dentist. Pain is pretty bad.

CARLOS: Probably by Friday I'll be able to get back to my studies. Right now
I'm going to take a long walk. This whole thing has taken a lot out of me.

CARLOS: I'm really up the proverbial creek. The problem is I really *bombed* the
history final. Since I need that course for my major I . . .

CARLOS: Here follows a tale of woe. I went home this weekend, had to help
my Mom, & caught a fever so didn't have much time to study. My professor . . .

CARLOS: Aargh! Trouble. Nothing original but everything's piling up at once.
To be brief, my job interview . . .

Hey Carlos, good news! I've got mononucleosis.

Who are these wretched supplicants, scribbling notes so laden 1
with anxiety, seeking such miracles of postponement and balm? They
are men and women who belong to Branford College, one of the twelve
residential colleges at Yale University, and the messages are just a few
of the hundreds that they left for their dean, Carlos Hortas—often
slipped under his door at 4 A.M.—last year.

But students like the ones who wrote those notes can also be found    2
on campuses from coast to coast—especially in New England and at
many other private colleges across the country that have high academic
standards and highly motivated students. Nobody could doubt that the
notes are real. In their urgency and their gallows humor they are
authentic voices of a generation that is panicky to succeed.

My own connection with the message writers is that I am master    3
of Branford College. I live in its Gothic quadrangle and know the
students well. (We have 485 of them.) I am privy to their hopes and
fears—and also to their stereo music and their piercing cries in the
dead of night ("Does anybody *ca-a-are?*"). If they went to Carlos to ask
how to get through tomorrow, they come to me to ask how to get
through the rest of their lives.

Mainly I try to remind them that the road ahead is a long one and    4
that it will have more unexpected turns than they think. There will be
plenty of time to change jobs, change careers, change whole attitudes
and approaches. They don't want to hear such liberating news. They
want a map—right now—that they can follow unswervingly to career
security, financial security, Social Security and, presumably, a prepaid
grave.

What I wish for all students is some release from the clammy grip    5
of the future. I wish them a chance to savor each segment of their
education as an experience in itself and not as a grim preparation for
the next step. I wish them the right to experiment, to trip and fall, to
learn that defeat is as instructive as victory and is not the end of the
world.

My wish, of course, is naïve. One of the few rights that America    6
does not proclaim is the right to fail. Achievement is the national god,
venerated in our media—the million-dollar athlete, the wealthy executive—and glorified in our praise of possessions. In the presence of such
a potent state religion, the young are growing up old.

I see four kinds of pressure working on college students today:    7
economic pressure, parental pressure, peer pressure, and self-induced
pressure. It is easy to look around for villains—to blame the colleges for
charging too much money, the professors for assigning too much work,
the parents for pushing their children too far, the students for driving
themselves too hard. But there are no villains; only victims.

"In the late 1960s," one dean told me, "the typical question that    8
I got from students was 'Why is there so much suffering in the world?'
or 'How can I make a contribution?' Today it's 'Do you think it would

look better for getting into law school if I did a double major in history and political science, or just majored in one of them?'" Many other deans confirmed this pattern. One said: "They're trying to find an edge—the intangible something that will look better on paper if two students are about equal."

Note the emphasis on looking better. The transcript has become a      9
sacred document, the passport to security. How one appears on paper is more important than how one appears in person. A is for Admirable and B is for Borderline, even though, in Yale's official system of grading, A means "excellent" and B means "very good." Today, looking very good is no longer good enough, especially for students who hope to go on to law school or medical school. They know that entrance into the better schools will be an entrance into the better law firms and better medical practices where they will make a lot of money. They also know that the odds are harsh, Yale Law School, for instance, matriculates 170 students from an applicant pool of 3,700; Harvard enrolls 550 from a pool of 7,000.

It's all very well for those of us who write letters of recommenda-      10
tion for our students to stress the qualities of humanity that will make them good lawyers or doctors. And it's nice to think that admission officers are really reading our letters and looking for the extra dimension of commitment or concern. Still, it would be hard for a student not to visualize these officers shuffling so many transcripts studded with As that they regard a B as positively shameful.

The pressure is almost as heavy on students who just want to      11
graduate and get a job. Long gone are the days of the "gentleman's C," when students journeyed through college with a certain relaxation, sampling a wide variety of courses—music, art, philosophy, classics, anthropology, poetry, religion—that would send them out as liberally educated men and women. If I were an employer I would rather employ graduates who have this range and curiosity than those who narrowly pursued safe subjects and high grades. I know countless students whose inquiring minds exhilarate me. I like to hear the play of their ideas. I don't know if they are getting As or Cs, and I don't care. I also like them as people. The country needs them, and they will find satisfying jobs. I tell them to relax. They can't.

Nor can I blame them. They live in a brutal economy. Tuition,      12
room, and board at most private colleges now comes to at least $7,000, not counting books and fees. This might seem to suggest that the colleges are getting rich. But they are equally battered by inflation.

Tuition covers only 60 percent of what it costs to educate a student, and ordinarily the remainder comes from what colleges receive in endowments, grants, and gifts. Now the remainder keeps being swallowed by the cruel costs—higher every year—of just opening the doors. Heating oil is up. Insurance is up. Postage is up. Health-premium costs are up. Everything is up. Deficits are up. We are witnessing in America the creation of a brotherhood of paupers—colleges, parents, and students, joined by the common bond of debt.

Today it is not unusual for a student, even if he works part time    13 at college and full time during the summer, to accrue $5,000 in loans after four years—loans that he must start to repay within one year after graduation. Exhorted at commencement to go forth into the world, he is already behind as he goes forth. How could he not feel under pressure throughout college to prepare for this day of reckoning? I have used "he," incidentally, only for brevity. Women at Yale are under no less pressure to justify their expensive education to themselves, their parents, and society. In fact, they are probably under more pressure. For although they leave college superbly equipped to bring fresh leadership to traditionally male jobs, society hasn't yet caught up with this fact.

Along with economic pressure goes parental pressure. Inevitably,    14 the two are deeply intertwined.

I see many students taking pre-medical courses with joyless tenac-    15 ity. They go off to their labs as if they were going to the dentist. It saddens me because I know them in other corners of their life as cheerful people.

"Do you want to go to medical school?" I ask them.                    16

"I guess so," they say, without conviction, or "Not really."          17

"Then why are you going?"                                             18

"Well, my parents want me to be a doctor. They're paying all this     19 money and . . ."

Poor students, poor parents. They are caught in one of the oldest     20 webs of love and duty and guilt. The parents mean well; they are trying to steer their sons and daughters toward a secure future. But the sons and daughters want to major in history or classics or philosophy— subjects with no "practical" value. Where's the payoff on the humanities? It's not easy to persuade such loving parents that the humanities do indeed pay off. The intellectual faculties developed by studying subjects like history and classics—an ability to synthesize and relate, to weigh cause and effect, to see events in perspective—are just the faculties that make creative leaders in business or almost any general field. Still, many fathers would rather put their money on courses that point toward a specific profession—courses that are pre-law, pre-medical, pre-business, or, as I sometimes heard it put, "pre-rich."

But the pressure on students is severe. They are truly torn. One    21
part of them feels obligated to fulfill their parents' expectations; after all, their parents are older and presumably wiser. Another part tells them that the expectations that are right for their parents are not right for them.

I know a student who wants to be an artist. She is very obviously    22
an artist and will be a good one—she has already had several modest local exhibits. Meanwhile she is growing as a well-rounded person and taking humanistic subjects that will enrich the inner resources out of which her art will grow. But her father is strongly opposed. He thinks that an artist is a "dumb" thing to be. The student vacillates and tries to please everybody. She keeps up with her art somewhat furtively and takes some of the "dumb" courses her father wants her to take—at least they are dumb courses for her. She is a free spirit on a campus of tense students—no small achievement in itself—and she deserves to follow her muse.

Peer pressure and self-induced pressure are also intertwined, and    23
they begin almost at the beginning of freshman year.

"I had a freshman student I'll call Linda," one dean told me, "who    24
came in and said she was under terrible pressure because her roommate, Barbara, was much brighter and studied all the time. I couldn't tell her that Barbara had come in two hours earlier to say the same thing about Linda."

The story is almost funny—except that it's not. It's symptomatic of    25
all the pressures put together. When every student thinks every other student is working harder and doing better, the only solution is to study harder still. I see students going off to the library every night after dinner and coming back when it closes at midnight. I wish they would sometimes forget about their peers and go to a movie. I hear the clacking of typewriters in the hours before dawn. I see the tension in their eyes when exams are approaching and papers are due: *"Will I get everything done?"*

Probably they won't. They will get sick. They will get "blocked."    26
They will sleep. They will oversleep. They will bug out. *Hey Carlos, help!*

Part of the problem is that they do more than they are expected to    27
do. A professor will assign five-page papers. Several students will start
writing ten-page papers to impress him. Then more students will write
ten-page papers, and a few will raise the ante to fifteen. Pity the poor
student who is still just doing the assignment.

"Once you have twenty or thirty percent of the student population    28
deliberately overexerting," one dean points out, "it's bad for everybody. When a teacher gets more and more effort from his class, the
student who is doing normal work can be perceived as not doing well.
The tactic works, psychologically."

Why can't the professor just cut back and not accept longer pa-    29
pers? He can, and he probably will. But by then the term will be half
over and the damage done. Grade fever is highly contagious and not
easily reversed. Besides, the professor's main concern is with his
course. He knows his students only in relation to the course and doesn't
know that they are also overexerting in their other courses. Nor is it
really his business. He didn't sign up for dealing with the student as a
whole person and with all the emotional baggage the student brought
along from home. That's what deans, masters, chaplains, and psychiatrists are for.

To some extent this is nothing new: a certain number of professors    30
have always been self-contained islands of scholarship and shyness,
more comfortable with books than with people. But the new pauper-
ism has widened the gap still further, for professors who actually like
to spend time with students don't have as much time to spend. They
also are overexerting. If they are young, they are busy trying to publish
in order not to perish, hanging by their finger nails onto a shrinking
profession. If they are old and tenured, they are buried under the
duties of administering departments—as departmental chairmen or
members of committees—that have been thinned out by the budgetary
axe.

Ultimately it will be the students' own business to break the circles    31
in which they are trapped. They are too young to be prisoners of their
parents' dreams and their classmates' fears. They must be jolted into
believing in themselves as unique men and women who have the
power to shape their own future.

"Violence is being done to the undergraduate experience," says    32
Carlos Hortas. "College should be open-ended: at the end it should
open many, many roads. Instead, students are choosing their goal in
advance, and their choices narrow as they go along. It's almost as if

they think that the country has been codified in the type of jobs that exist—that they've got to fit into certain slots. Therefore, fit into the best-paying slot.

"They ought to take chances. Not taking chances will lead to a life      33
of colorless mediocrity. They'll be comfortable. But something in the spirit will be missing."

I have painted too drab a portrait of today's students, making them      34
seem a solemn lot. That is only half of their story; if they were so dreary I wouldn't so thoroughly enjoy their company. The other half is that they are easy to like. They are quick to laugh and to offer friendship. They are not introverts. They are unusually kind and are more considerate of one another than any student generation I have known.

Nor are they so obsessed with their studies that they avoid sports      35
and extracurricular activities. On the contrary, they juggle their crowded hours to play on a variety of teams, perform with musical and dramatic groups, and write for campus publications. But this in turn is one more cause of anxiety. There are too many choices. Academically, they have 1,300 courses to select from; outside class they have to decide how much spare time they can spare and how to spend it.

This means that they engage in fewer extracurricular pursuits than      36
their predecessors did. If they want to row on the crew and play in the symphony they will eliminate one; in the '60s they would have done both. They also tend to choose activities that are self-limiting. Drama, for instance, is flourishing in all twelve of Yale's residential colleges as it never has before. Students hurl themselves into these productions— as actors, directors, carpenters, and technicians—with a dedication to create the best possible play, knowing that the day will come when the run will end and they can get back to their studies.

They also can't afford to be the willing slave of organizations like      37
the *Yale Daily News*. Last spring at the one-hundredth anniversary banquet of that paper—whose past chairmen include such once and future kings as Potter Stewart, Kingman Brewster, and William F. Buckley, Jr.—much was made of the fact that the editorial staff used to be small and totally committed and that "newsies" routinely worked fifty hours a week. In effect they belonged to a club; Newsies is how they defined themselves at Yale. Today's student will write one or two articles a week, when he can, and he defines himself as a student. I've never heard the word Newsie except at the banquet.

✿   ✿   ✿

If I have described the modern undergraduate primarily as a   38
driven creature who is largely ignoring the blithe spirit inside who
keeps trying to come out and play, it's because that's where the crunch
is, not only at Yale but throughout American education. It's why I think
we should all be worried about the values that are nurturing a generation so fearful of risk and so goal-obsessed at such an early age.

I tell students that there is no one "right" way to get ahead—that   39
each of them is a different person, starting from a different point and
bound for a different destination. I tell them that change is a tonic and
that all the slots are not codified nor the frontiers closed. One of my
ways of telling them is to invite men and women who have achieved
success outside the academic world to come and talk informally with
my students during the year. They are heads of companies or ad
agencies, editors of magazines, politicians, public officials, television
magnates, labor leaders, business executives, Broadway producers,
artists, writers, economists, photographers, scientists, historians—a
mixed bag of achievers.

I ask them to say a few words about how they got started. The   40
students assume that they started in their present profession and knew
all along that it was what they wanted to do. Luckily for me, most of
them got into their field by a circuitous route, to their surprise, after
many detours. The students are startled. They can hardly conceive of
a career that was not pre-planned. They can hardly imagine allowing
the hand of God or chance to nudge them down some unforeseen trail.

---

# The Novice Writer

## JOSEPH WILLIAMS and GREGORY G. COLOMB

*Progress as Linear Movement.* Metaphors influence not only how   1
we think about experience, but how we deal with it. We speak of
anger, for example, with images of liquids boiling inside sealed con-
tainers: "I was so boiling mad that I blew my lid. After I let off steam,
though, I felt better" (Johnson, 1987). Had circumstances been different, our culture might have adopted the metaphor of the machine: "I
was so racing mad that I was already running too high for my specs,

so I knew I had to lower my rpms or burn out my bearings. After I cooled the system down, I operated better." Under our presiding metaphorical frame, we often encourage—or at least condone—the expression of anger because we consider its "release" therapeutic; under another metaphorical system, we might consider the expression of anger damaging because it could lead to systemic breakdown.

The metaphors we use to describe learning, particularly skills such   2
as reading, writing, and thinking, are metaphors of natural development and growth. When we develop normally, we grow "up." As we grow "up," we also "progress" left to right along a time scale (controlled by the tacit metaphor of reaching a "goal"). So we visually graph development from low to high and progress from a starting point on the lower left to a goal on the upper right. We picture normal growth as a curve (or stairstep, if we think growth has stages), from lower left to higher right. We typically combine this growth metaphor with construction metaphors: We have to "lay a solid foundation" and then "reinforce" what we learn so that we both "maintain" what we have learned and "build" on it toward mastery.

These metaphors of linear development and building up come so   3
naturally to us that we become particularly receptive to theories of learning expressible through them. So it is not surprising that administrators and teachers, particularly those who teach "generic" skills such as reading, writing, and thinking, should be attracted to the work of developmentalists such as Jean Piaget (Inhelder and Piaget, 1958), William Perry (1968), Lawrence Kohlberg (1984), and others whose models of development would seem to impose order on the more puzzling patterns of student behavior.

For Piaget, developing children move from concrete operational   4
thinking to formal operational thinking, not smoothly, but in ways that let us account for their early cognitive limitations not by IQ or diligence, but by a qualitative structure of mind. Young children are not yet able to manipulate the abstractions derived from sets of sets; they are not able to juggle multiple hypotheticals, think probabilistically, etc. To put it crudely, younger children are incapable of thinking abstractly, a cognitive constraint Piagetians explain not by intelligence or cultural background, but by genetic epistemology.

Perry found a roughly similar pattern of development in the social/   5
academic development of Harvard undergraduates: In their academic careers, students often appeared in his office at a stage he calls "dualistic"—the stage at which students simply want to know who the author-

ities are and what they know. When students "progress," they move to what he called the "multiple/relative" stage, that stage where students believe that since there are no final authorities and no final answers, then "everyone's opinion must be equally good." Perry claimed that the dualist stage regularly precedes the multiple/relative stage, and that these are followed by stages in which the student is increasingly able to handle ambiguities, to appreciate the legitimacy of different conclusions drawn from different premises, to understand the importance of the process of reasoning as opposed to its outcome, etc.

Kohlberg laid out a sequence of moral reasoning that begins at the   6 stage of preconventional moral reasoning involving immediate, concrete approval and disapproval; then moves up to conventional moral reasoning governed by socially established values and peer pressure; and culminates in postconventional moral reasoning, that stage where the mature moral reasoner comes to recognize that local systems in particular societies rest not on rules that govern, but on universal moral principles that guide. Again, this is movement from the concrete to the abstract.

All three of these models describe a pattern of cognitive growth   7 that begins with the immediate, concrete, rule-governed here and now, and that develops to more abstract, hypothetical forms of reasoning guided by principles. To be sure, these models differ profoundly, in ways our reductive description ignores. But to put it in a way that is not deceptively reductive, they describe a movement from relatively "lower-level" concreteness to relatively "higher-order" abstraction.

Like all models that reflect tacit metaphors, however, these models have consequences. One is that "regression" is bad. A student who   8 does not continue to perform at a level "reached" earlier has "fallen back" to a "lower" level of performance. And whoever taught the student at that "lower level"—teaching writing is a paradigm case— did not do the job right. The student failed to learn the "bas(e)ics."

It is a metaphoric scheme that motivates us to abuse those who   9 taught our students before they reach us. In the case of writing, teachers of first-year college students criticize the high schools; teachers of upper-class students criticize teachers of first-year composition; teachers in professional and graduate schools criticize the colleges; and professional organizations such as law firms and businesses criticize the whole educational system. A skill such as writing, the story goes, should follow a model of steady, linear development from lower-left to upper-right. When our students do not write as we expect, we feel empowered by our metaphors to decide that our predecessors must have failed to raise them to the level we think they should have achieved. A related consequence is that entire curricula are constructed to "raise" the student to achieve objectifiable levels of performance. If students are identifiably dualists when they enter the system, they should be measurably closer to being multiple relativists at the end of the first semester. That kind of thinking produces a system of testing that reductively categorizes students according to their cognitive/moral/social/academic development.

But the most problematical consequences come when we rely on these linear models to make policy decisions about education. Such decisions may be costly, because evidence suggests that these models may not entirely comport with reality. The evidence comes from three directions. First, some reports increasingly suggest that children who test at the concrete operational level of thinking can be induced to behave in ways that characterize formal operational thinking (Bryant, 1983). By manipulating the form of the test and particularly the kind of knowledge that the child controls about the materials of the test, one can "move" a concrete-operational-thinking child to a formal operational level of thinking.

A second line of evidence comes from an opposite direction. A number of researchers have asserted that up to half of first-year college students are still concrete operational thinkers, this long after Piaget's model would have had them move "up" to formal operational thinking (Dunlop and Fazio, 1976; Tomlinson-Keasey, 1972). And when the American Accounting Association studied a group of upper-class and graduate students, up to half were judged to be either concrete operational thinkers or in transition from concrete to formal operational thinking (Shute, 1979). Is it plausible that large numbers of graduate students think in ways generically similar to ten-year-olds? Possible, perhaps, but put together these two lines of evidence—young children can be taught to think in formal operational terms, and graduate students can seem to think in concrete operational terms—and a more likely hypothesis suggests itself. Perhaps what counts in "higher-level" cognitive processing is not only those abstract and generic operations, but also knowledge, experience, control over specific content (see Glaser, 1984). "Concrete" behavior may in fact indicate thin categories of knowledge, not some intrinsic quality of mind.

This hypothesis is encouraged by a third line of evidence emerging from research into expert vs. novice thinking. Most of the research into this matter involves what is called in cognitive psychology "well-structured" problems, problems that have a single right answer and a relatively clear-cut algorithm for getting there (Larkin, McDermott, Simon, and Simon, 1980; Chi, Feltovitch, and Glaser, 1981). Experts and novices solve well-structured problems in different ways. Most relevant is that novices (not "lower-level" thinkers, please note) are characterized by relatively concrete thinking, while experts tend to be characterized by more abstract thinking. For example, a novice problem solver in physics might look at a problem containing a picture of a spring and assume that the problem belongs to the category of "spring problems" and begin to think about what she knows about springs. The expert looks at the problem and categorizes the problem not on the basis of its most concrete, physically present feature, but by the abstract character of its intellectual content.

Still more interesting is the line of research into "ill-formed" problems, problems for which there is no obviously "correct" answer, much less obviously correct algorithms for a solution. Voss and others (1985) put the following problem to four groups of subjects: if you were in charge, how would you solve the problems of agriculture in the Soviet Union? The problem solvers were grouped as follows:     13

1. Novice/low-knowledge: students taking a first course in Soviet affairs
2. Novice/high-knowledge: graduate students in Soviet affairs
3. Expert/low-knowledge: senior chemistry professors
4. Expert/high-knowledge: senior faculty in Soviet affairs

The high-knowledge experts differed from the novices in three ways: *(a)* the high-knowledge experts spent more time decomposing the problem, defining the problem space, explaining why the problem was complex; *(b)* where the novices would propose solutions at a relatively concrete level—more fertilizer, better roads, better farm machinery, etc.—the high-knowledge experts began at a "higher," more abstract level—with the system, infrastructure, or history; *(c)* the novices constructed relatively shorter chains of arguments, moving from point to point without developing any one of them extensively. However, once the high-knowledge experts introduced a topic, they stayed with it, developing a chain of reasoning based on that argument.     14

The most salient outcome is that of the low-knowledge experts, the chemistry professors. They behaved in ways similar to the low-knowledge novices. This outcome suggests that while there may be some     15 generic quality of expert thinking that characterizes all experts *in their field,* its deployment is crucially linked both to the amount of knowledge one controls about the matter in question, and to the complexity of the structure of that knowledge. Confronting a problem in an unfamiliar area, experts in an alien field seem to behave in ways similar to generic novices.

It seems, then, that extensive, structured knowledge counts for   16
much in good thinking. Some suggest everything. Indeed, it may count for much in development in general. If formal thinking can be induced in a young child by providing substantial experience with the problem materials, if a dualist becomes a relativist once he or she accumulates multiple points of view and sees that all of them are at best intrinsically tentative, if a preconventional moral reasoner becomes a conventional reasoner when that person becomes part of a larger community and understands the shared and therefore abstract values of the community, then the notion of intellectual growth as biological or cognitive epistemology with its own teleology becomes an open question. And so does the model of learning represented by linear movement on a steady or staggered lower-left, upper-right curve.

*Progress as Joining the Community.* Another—and perhaps more   17
productive—metaphor for growth is the equally familiar one of an "outsider" trying to "get into" a community, a metaphor that models the movement of a learner situated outside a bounded field, who then "enters" the field and so "joins" the community by acting like its members. (This metaphor does *not* place any single community at the upper right of the chart as an ultimate goal.) To join a disciplinary community is, in part, to master a body of knowledge. But that knowledge does not exist "out there," independent of those who control it, just waiting to be acquired. Knowledge belongs to groups of people who have some shared stake in exploring, preserving, and expanding it. The outsider must acquire knowledge from insiders, usually through some form of an apprenticeship. Perhaps we should not, but we draw institutional boundaries around knowledge by locating it in communities defined by experts and by those novices who are trying to learn what experts know. We call those communities by different names— subjects, fields, areas, majors, departments, disciplines. They often overlap, and they consist of subcommunities that also overlap. That these names cut up the pie so differently only reflects the unruliness of communities.

Whatever we call these fields and however we define them, the   18 knowledge they bound is colored by the values, conventions, and styles of the communities that make that knowledge the object of their interest. While the novice is committed to mastering the knowledge that the community thinks is important, the novice is equally committed to acquiring the *ways* of thinking that characterize that community, the tone of voice that identifies one member to another, the required silences whose violation instantly identifies the outsider. However true it is that Shakespeare is a famous writer who wrote many plays, it is usually inappropriate for those trying to join the ranks of literary experts to express that sentiment, either in writing or in speech.

We want to use this metaphor to redescribe the concrete operational thinker or the dualist or the preconventional moral reasoner as a novice standing outside a knowledge community. Of course, our metaphor has its own consequences, particularly in regard to the central interest of this volume—projects that seek to extend writing "across the curriculum." But we believe that the consequences of our description do more justice to—and do more to help—the novice learner. [19]

Those new to a knowledge community often exhibit some characteristic patterns of learning behavior, patterns that teachers can learn to anticipate. First, we should expect from novices behavior that is relatively "concrete" (*not* "lower-level"). A moment of reflection suggests why. Abstraction is at least partially based on the number and variety of instances of a category. By definition, a novice's knowledge is simultaneously very thin and relatively unstructured, with categories defined by as few as a single instance. The student of architecture who knows only classical forms has a very thin category of "architectural style." From the point of view of someone who also knows romanesque, gothic, baroque, modern, etc., that less knowledgeable student's problem-solving behavior would seem concrete operational indeed. [20]

In regard to writing, we can predict a number of "concrete," "immature" forms of behavior: mapping the particular (concrete) language of the assignment into the opening paragraph of the paper; mapping any hint of organization in the assignment onto the paper itself; closely following the sequence of events or topics in an assigned text; and in particular, summarizing rather than analyzing. Novices will tend to say those things that are ordinarily left unsaid by insiders, things that can be left unsaid just because they are shared. Novices will [21] also seize on those features of the "voice" that seem most markedly to characterize the discourse of the field. In a field as stylistically marked as the law, for example, new students typically seize on the *heretofore*'s and *whereas*'s because they are among the most concretely obvious signals of legal language, the language of the tribe.

Second, this "concrete" behavior may be compounded by a predictable deterioration of performance in skills mastered earlier. Someone trying to enter a new community of discourse must bring under control a new body of knowledge, new ways of thinking, new ways of writing and speaking. So it is entirely predictable that some skills already mastered will deteriorate, often by default reliance on the most concrete forms of behavior. 22

Concrete, novice behavior appears in those aspects of writing that depend on the ability to analyze and synthesize. Here the consequences can be especially damaging because this failing is so often perceived as a sign that the learner cannot think. Because it is so important to our pedagogy, we will examine this behavior at more length and at three different levels: (1) professional school writing, (2) advanced upper-class undergraduate writing, and (3) first-year undergraduate writing. (We might have included professional writing by new attorneys.) 23

We begin with the mixed professional/academic setting of law school because we want to emphasize that "novice" behavior is not limited to the young and untalented—the effort to join a discourse community invites it even at very high levels of professional writing. Nor are inappropriate judgments of novice behavior limited to teachers of the young: even at "higher" levels, learners write in ways that can by the old, linear metaphor be described as "low-level," "immature," "unskilled," etc., but that we prefer to describe as the predictable response of the novice, independent of any level of development. 24

*Writing by First-year Law Students.* Most schools of law require a first-year legal-writing course, but most of those courses do not teach legal writing. They teach research, citation forms, some aspects of legal thinking. This is especially so at the most selective law schools. They understandably assume that students who had A − and B + averages in college are not merely competent, but proficient writers. And yet in their first weeks and months of law school, many of those writers display the very forms of behavior that characterize writers in their first year of college. 25

Let us describe a paper given to us by a legal-writing instructor as 26 an example of the work of a student who had not learned how to write well, a paper written by a law student in his fourth week. . . . This student attends one of the country's most selective law schools, has graduated from a prestigious college near the top of his class, and has produced laudatory letters of recommendation, high LSAT scores, and an articulate application essay. The assignment was to analyze how a jurist used precedent while deciding whether a person can be convicted of second-degree murder if that person was coerced into participating in a crime in which another participant commits murder in the first degree.

The faculty person teaching in the legal-writing program was led    27
by a linear conception of development to decide that this writer had never learned to write well. But the essay paradigmatically illustrates the behavior of a novice trying to deal with a new field. First, it precisely tracks the sequence of the jurist's text rather than abstracting from the text the principles of law that the jurist followed. Second, each of the student's middle, supposedly analytical paragraphs (see excerpts) corresponds to one section of the decision and precisely tracks the sequence of its section. It is not surprising, therefore, that the instructor considered this "mere summary." Third, although the conclusion begins to address the abstractions that the jurist considered, it merely lists them in the order in which they appeared in the original text and in the essay. Finally and most importantly, the middle, analytical paragraphs do not (with a few exceptions) specifically state the key analytical terms of the conclusion, terms first announced only at the end of the paper, where the writer seemed to discover them.

Like so many novice performances, this paper replicates the act of    28
discovery. The writer structured the paper on the narrative of his thinking, discovering the abstract terms of analysis only at the end, where he summarizes them in a list. On the one hand, this might be treated merely as an example of "writer-based prose" (Flower, 1979). But "writer-based prose" is not necessarily a sign of generic "novice writer," as Flower seemed at that time to suggest. It may reflect the concrete behavior of a very experienced writer who is a novice in the field.

The signs of concrete, novice behavior are also evident in the style    29
of that essay. This peculiarly awkward sentence presents the jurist's thinking in the writer's own words:

The final step in Lord Morris's **preparation** to introduce the precedents is his **consideration** of the idea of **conviction** despite the **presence** of duress and then immediate **pardon** for that crime as an unnecessary step which is in fact injurious for it creates the stigma of the criminal on a potentially blameless (or at least not criminal) individual.

Pervasive nominalization characterizes bad legal writing in particular and bad academic writing in general. But as we noted above, it also characterizes a kind of stylistic breakdown typical of mature writers trying to wrestle with difficult concepts. The student might have written

Before he **introduces** the precedents, Lord Morris **considers** a final issue: if a court first **convicts** a defendant who acted under duress and then immediately **pardons** that defendant, has the court taken an unnecessary step, a step that may even injure the defendant by stigmatizing him as criminal when he may be blameless?

This is a complex "if-then" question, involving two conditionals ("if a court convicts . . . and then pardons"), one of which contains an embedded conditional ("a defendant who acted under duress"), followed by a conclusion ("taken an unnecessary step") that itself becomes a cause ("may even injure the defendant") of a complex consequence ("by stigmatizing him as criminal when he may be blameless"). It is not surprising that a novice in legal reasoning should suffer a stylistic breakdown in the face of complex conditions and consequences. But note that his confused tangle of nominalizations is akin to an equally ponderous but professionally deliberate legal style:

Because the individualized assessment of the appropriateness of the death penalty is a moral inquiry into the culpability of the defendant, and not an emotional response to the mitigating evidence, I agree with the Court that an instruction informing the jury that they "must not be swayed by mere sentiment, conjecture, sympathy, passion, prejudice, public opinion or public feeling" does not by itself violate the Eighth and Fourteenth Amendments to the United States Constitution. (Sandra Day O'Connor, concurring, *California v. Albert Greenwood Brown, Jr.*)

As turgid as this is, it is not the turgidity of a novice unfamiliar with legal thinking. One of the great ironies of modern prose is that the turgid professional, most deeply socialized into the language of a profession, and the awkward novice can seem to have so much in common.

A related, though less turgid novice response is to concretize in the text too much of the writer's thinking process. In the following example, a new law student as academically distinguished as the previous one tries to adopt the voice of a judge. But in doing so he uses metadiscourse to raise to a level of textual concreteness the machinery of thinking and reasoning—"the main point supporting my point of view," etc.—that experts usually suppress. At the same time, this student raises to the same level of textual concreteness certain substantive matters that any expert would leave unsaid, such as the obvious assertion that a plaintiff must produce evidence against a defendant. (In this passage, we have boldfaced the metadiscourse and italicized the statements that anyone socialized into the world of the law would be unlikely to make.)

**It is my opinion that** *the ruling of the lower court concerning the case of* Haslem v. Lockwood **should be upheld, thereby denying** *the appeal of the plaintiff.* **The main point supporting my point of view** *on this case* **concerns** *the tenet of our court system which holds that in order to win his case, the plaintiff must prove that he was somehow wronged by the defendant. The burden of proof rests on the plaintiff. He must show enough evidence to convince the court that he is in the right.* **However, in this case, I do not believe that** *the plaintiff has satisfied this requirement. In order to prove that the defendant owes him recompense for the six loads of manure,* he must first show that he was the legal owner of those loads, and then show that the defendant removed the manure for his own use [the paper goes on for several more paragraphs].

A more professional (i.e., socialized, i.e., "expert") version would be, "Plaintiff has failed to show that he was the legal owner of the loads and that the defendant removed the manure for his own use. The court affirms *Haslem v. Lockwood.*"

In both cases, the instructors took these as examples of bad writing 31 and unskilled writers. In our terms, they are examples of novices trying to express themselves in a field that largely baffles them, and displaying the signs of novice behavior—concreteness, saying what can be left unsaid, and occasional breakdowns in stylistic performance in the direction of the most visible and concrete features of the "voice" that characterizes the prose of a field.

These examples illustrate forms of writing familiar to every 32 teacher of freshman composition: summary rather than analysis, thinking out loud, a conclusion discovered at the end, evident stylistic infelicity, etc. In neither case could we assert that the writers were in some general sense immature or unintelligent. And yet they display the generic shortcomings of novice, "concrete" writers.

*Writing by Upperclass Students.* As they move into a discipline, 33 undergraduates face many of the conceptual difficulties faced by new professional students. The next example comes from a paper by a third-year student taking a course in Western Civilization, a good student who had written excellent papers in his first-year humanities course, but who had had no preparation in historical thinking. By the concluding paragraph of his paper, he at last reached a point worth making:

> The Popes, Urban II and Gregory VII, used the concept of the Crusades as a means to achieve a form of unity important to them during their pontificate. During Urban's pontificate, he could establish his authority, fight the devil (Muslims), and control fighting amongst the Europeans and direct those energies elsewhere. Gregory VII wishes to achieve unification between the Roman Church and the Greek Orthodox Church. . . . Therefore the Crusade was not just a fight against the Muslims to recapture the Holy Land and to save God's faith, but it was an effort to save the Church and Europe from the dissensions which were tearing it apart.

This paper was given a C+ because it was considered "disorga-    34
nized," "largely summary," etc. Why? Because all of the first five and most of the next five paragraphs offered only a close summary of the assigned texts, so that the central concept of the conclusion—the Crusades achieving Christian unity—did not begin to emerge until about the tenth paragraph. The introduction was wholly summary and pointless:

> During the eleventh through thirteenth centuries, the Roman Catholic Church initiated several Crusades against the Muslims in the Holy Lands. The Pope would usually instigate and call for armament and support for this endeavor. Pope Urban II started the first Crusade in 1096. His predecessor, Gregory VII, had also petitioned to get support for a crusade in 1074 but did not succeed in launching his Crusade. There are written statements from these Popes concerning the Crusades. Pope Urban II in "Speech at the Council of Clermont" in the year 1095 calls for a Crusade and Pope Gregory VII in a Letter to King Henry IV during the year 1074 also proposes a Crusade.

This is the writing of a student gripped by novice concreteness. Since    35
he does not control the information from the sources well enough to hold it whole in his mind as he thinks through its implications, he predictably summarizes the source, closely following the structure of its text. Once the material is concretized in the form of a linear summary, he is able to draw from it some inferences that qualify as analysis.

*Writing by First-year Students.* By this point it is almost redundant    36

Classification and Division

to offer a typical first-year student paper that might illustrate these same features. Let us briefly look at one from a student with a VSAT well over 600. He was in his third week of college and writing about two speeches in Thucydides' history of the Peloponnesian war, a subject wholly strange to him. This was the assignment:

> In the second chapter of his history, Thucydides presents two speakers asking Athens for help against the other. As we know Thucydides wrote these speeches to represent what "probably would have been said." Compare and contrast the way Thucydides had the Corcyrans and Corinthians rhetorically appeal to the Athenians in different ways.

And here are some indicative excerpts from the paper:

### A Comparison of the Corcyran and Corinthian Speeches

The Corcyran and Corinthian speeches in Thucydides's *The Peloponnesian War* differ in several ways. The most important way that the two speeches differ is in the particular appeals each side gives to support its arguments. I will first discuss the Corcyran speech and then the Corinthian speech in order to show what we can learn from these differences.

The Corcyrans first apologize. . . . Then they give three reasons why the Athenians should help them and join in an alliance. They say that . . . Then they predict that . . . They say that . . . Finally, they emphasize that . . .

The Corinthians start out by attacking the Corcyrans. . . .

The Athenians decide to join with the Corcyrans against the Corinthians because they are sure that there is going to be a war between them soon and that they would have a good ally with the Corcyrans. The speeches are different in that the Corcyrans had the better argument because they understood the Athenians better than the Corinthians since the Athenians were very practical and self-interested at this time. Therefore, the Corcyran speech was a more clever appeal.

We need not dwell on the obvious here: Like the novice problem 37 solver who thinks that a concrete picture of a spring in the problem statement means the problem is a spring-type problem, the student here takes the concrete language of the problem statement—the assignment—and maps it directly into the opening paragraph. The writer takes the sequence of the speeches from the assignment and from the text. In each section, he marches through each speech in summary fashion, at the end discovering his conclusion. While the style of the paper is competent, the organization and thought reflect the student's "concrete" thinking, which is to say, his inexperience in thinking about matters of this kind.

In three cases (new law student, upper-class student new to a field, 38
new college student) we see the same generic pattern—the tyranny of
the concrete and the breakdown of control over skills mastered earlier.
If our narrative is plausible, the upward curve of growth is at best
misleading. While there must certainly be development of some kind,
it is not the kind of development that can be graphed like height and
weight. A metaphor more insightful and useful than the upward curve
is that of the outsider trying to get in, that of the novice trying to join
a community of experts, an experience that happens to our best students many times over.

---

# Catharsis and the Reduction of Prejudice

## GORDON W. ALLPORT

Everyone knows that if he wishes to mend an inner tube he has to 1
let out the air before he can make repairs. Some similar principle seems
to hold in the process of re-education. Gaseous pressure inside a person
often holds him rigid and resistant, interfering with the repair work
that he needs in order to improve his functioning in accordance with
his own purposes. . . .

### A Not Untypical Re-educative Situation

Not long ago I attempted to teach an eight-hour course in race 2
relations to a group of public officials in an eastern city of over 100,000
population. The circumstances, personnel, and content of the course
need not concern us here. The important feature of the experience for
our present purposes was the distressing fact that from start to finish
the forty members of the group indulged in aggressive, hostile, preju-
diced discourse aimed occasionally at me, the instructor, but more
often at various minority groups (whom we were seeking to understand!), and at other scapegoats, including the public press, intellectuals, parents, and even the citizenry at large. The discussion was almost

entirely defensive, projective, hostile. At no point was it purely objective. It is important to add, however, that the hostility *diminished* with time. According to impartial observers, the concluding hours "made an impression" on the class.

As a re-educative problem the experience, admittedly, was extreme because the conditions were unusual. The members of the course felt themselves to be under public attack, and their attendance in the course was compulsory. Furthermore, it is undoubtedly in the field of race relations that we encounter the most defensive, the most irrational, and the most obdurate of human sentiments. If we can succeed in re-educating adults in the region of their racial hates, I suspect that we can succeed in re-educating them in almost any other region of their personalities.    3

Granted that the re-educative situation was forbidding in its difficulty, it was not, I think, untypical of many situations where re-education is attempted. Just because the difficulties in this case were extreme, we may all the better learn from it some of the basic lessons of group dynamics.    4

I should add to my report that, in spite of the abusive torrent of released hostility, the course was not regarded as a failure by the participants or by the instructor. On the contrary, reasonably friendly relations prevailed within the course (especially in the concluding sessions), and after-effects of the course were considered wholesome. To be specific, race relations in the community improved, and some judges awarded the credit, at least in part, to our tempestuous experiment in re-education.    5

## The Dynamics of Catharsis

For purposes of this discussion, I am including under the term "catharsis" only verbal expressions of hostility—complaints, defensive remarks, griping—which seem to serve the function of letting the air out of the "inner tube." True, not all verbal aggression serves a therapeutic purpose. Far from it; in many verbal battles the last state of the participants is far worse than the first. By catharsis in the present connection I mean only the verbal release of emotional tensions in the presence of a consultant, which in some way seems to clear the channel for re-educative processes. I am not including the more subtle emotional release that comes in acting out feelings in role-playing or psychodrama as now used in individual and group education. These expe-    6 riences are also in a sense cathartic, but they go beyond the scope of the present discussion. Neither am I speaking of the relief that comes from giving vent in public or private to grief, joy, anxiety, and numerous other emotions. Taken as a whole, catharsis is a large subject and one not yet sufficiently explored by psychologists. But here we confine ourselves to hostile catharsis as it exists in certain group situations where re-education is the aim.

*Expressions of Hostility As a Means of Testing the Instructor.* A       7
newcomer to the group, especially if he is suspected of being a reformer, is in a tough spot. His authority is unclear, his motives are in question, and above all he is under the suspicion of feeling superior to the group he is presuming to re-educate—in a field, incidentally, where the group itself feels that it has superior competence. This complex threat to the status of the group is felt all the more keenly if its members are not voluntarily exposing themselves to the course of instruction.

There is, therefore, every reason why the new instructor should be       8
the target of critical remarks, most of which are designed to try his mettle and his patience. One of the members of the course revealed some of the motivation for the attack when after the eighth session he said, "At the beginning we were afraid you were going to look down your nose at us." As a consequence of the instructor's mode of response, the members came to know that he was essentially sympathetic with their legitimate gripes and that he himself was able to take as much abuse as they themselves had taken. As a matter of fact, it required a considerable portion of the course for the instructor by unemotional listening to establish his right and ability to carry on the assignment given him. What is more, he learned a new point of view. Indeed he *had* to learn it before the group would listen to *his*.

*Expressions of Hostility As a Means of Avoiding Threat to Personal Status.* It is not only the personality of the instructor that must be       9
tested. It is also the dignity of the class that must be established. Many remarks were made for the purpose of telling *favorable* things about the existing situation. Still more remarks were for the purpose of answering explicit and implicit charges and complaints which the members felt to be unjust. "We've never had any trouble. Why do we need this course?" was the burden of some remarks. "Who, precisely, is responsible for our having to be here?" was the tenor of others. "Why do they pick on us?" was the common theme.

It is an axiom that people cannot be taught who feel that they are       10 at the same time being attacked. It is also an axiom that they learn very little unless they want to learn. In the case I cite, so strong was the implied threat to personal status that the instructor spent much of his time for the first four hours assuring the group of his personal appreciation for their past accomplishments. It was necessary to make a factual review of these accomplishments and to show that most current complaints from the public concerning racial tension were in fact badly exaggerated. When due praise and reassurance had been given, it became possible to direct the attention of the class upon the *preventive* phase of their work, placing all emphasis upon developing skill against *future* needs, and assiduously avoiding any reference to past failures.

*Expressions of Hostility As Guilt Projection.* Behind the theme    11
"We've never had any trouble; there is no problem" lurks often a trace of guilt. Deep down, each member of the class knows that there have been difficulties. But to admit this fact would be to menace one's self-esteem and to admit the need for the re-educative process. For this reason much of the cathartic discourse takes the form of focusing blame upon some outside group. "If it hadn't been for the newspapers, there wouldn't have been any problem," said one. Another averred that if the Negro leaders would learn how to control their own people, all would be well. Still another offered the remark, "It's all the fault of the Jews; they complain too much. But I wouldn't say that outside this group because someone might think I was anti-Semitic."

In this type of catharsis, of course, we encounter the very heart of    12
prejudice itself, unadmitted by the individual, rationalized and justified at every step. There is present the universal tendency to evade personal guilt by that most curious of all quirks of the human mind, projection.

Often have I encountered this phenomenon in meetings presum-    13
ably devoted to enhancing interracial and interfaith understanding. It is so common that I am inclined to think prejudice *needs* a safety valve and catharsis may be a *necessary* step in the process of re-education. Everyone knows that straight lectures on the interests, rights, and virtues of minority groups accomplish very little. The listener is often so near to bursting with hostility that nothing new can come into his mind until something old comes out.

## Why Is Catharsis Valuable?

It may seem questionable to hold, as I do, that all these various    14
forms of catharsis may have a therapeutic effect. At first sight they look

to be ugly and destructive and likely to aggravate the difficulties already present. It is not my contention that *every* expression of hostility is beneficial, but that cathartic release under certain circumstances may be the essential preliminary step in re-education.

*Expressions of Hostility As "Complacency Shock."* In certain instances, to mix metaphors, the individual, given enough cathartic rope, proceeds to hang himself. He overdoes his stuff. He makes ridiculous statements. Then he subsides in confusion, his face red all over. He has convicted himself of gross exaggeration, one-sidedness, obvious injustice. Nor is it necessary for the leader to point out the limb where the luckless speaker dangles. It is more tactful not to do so. The speaker, having convicted himself of irrationality, finds himself both ashamed and deflated. Thus humbled, he is more ready to reconstruct his attitudes on a sounder line. 15

It would be simple if we could count on such a "complacency shock" for everyone who indulges in catharsis; but the phenomenon, unfortunately, is not common. It does exist, however, with sufficient frequency to brighten the path for the harassed instructor. 16

*Expressions of Hostility As a Talking Cure.* Originally Freud, who first introduced the doctrine of catharsis into psychotherapy, regarded it as a healing process in its own right. Somehow, he thought, the verbal act of relieving repressions serves to diminish their force. An emotional vent dissipates the emotion. The inner tube becomes deflated. 17

Later Freudian theory discarded this simple physical analogy for catharsis. Although the release of pent-up feelings might make the patient feel better, it was considered likely that the release merely channeled the aggressions against the analyst or in some way symbolized and masked the underlying disorder, that it did not in itself strengthen the ego, which must ultimately understand and control the hostile impulses. 18

Yet in the case under discussion it seems to me very likely that the process of expressing hostilities in the presence of an accepting listener served a genuinely therapeutic purpose. The fact is that the class was more receptive to the material of the course after telling its own biases and expressing its own point of view. 19

It is possible that some process related to fatigue or satiation is here involved. After a few hours the mere act of complaining becomes boring. We have all had the experience of listening to friends who fill us with their woes and who finally say, "Well now, that's enough of my troubles. I feel better after spilling them out to you. Let's go to the 20

movies." Or, instead of going to the movies, it may be that the friend
is ready to listen to the opposite point of view. But he could not have
done so until his own pressure was relieved. If the listener had crossed
swords with the complainer at the outset, tenseness and struggle,
rather than catharsis, would have been the result.

Freud is no doubt right in denying that *mere* talk effects a cure. Yet    21
preliminary catharsis does not often seem to be a necessary *vestibule*
to the process of re-education. Until the pent-up tension is relieved, the
corrective point of view cannot enter.

*Catharsis in Re-structuring Attitudes.* In recent years, thanks to    22
Dr. Carl Rogers, we have heard much of non-directive therapy. The
counselor is primarily a listener who at times summarizes the client's
feelings and lets him proceed to formulate his own evaluation of his
conflicts, and ultimately his own personal plans for the future. The
emphasis here differs from "complacency shock" and from mere "talking out" in that the client is encouraged to proceed beyond the point
of catharsis to the point of personal planning and re-orientation.

Non-directive counseling is used only with individuals and is not    23
immediately applicable to groups. Yet some of its values seemed to be
realized in the episode we are discussing. Though very little was said
in the class about "next steps," that is to say, about how the officials
might go about their jobs to improve racial and religious relations, still
it is highly probable that the minds of the members continually played
upon their daily work and the typical problems confronting them in
line of duty. They were silently reconstructing their own view of their
jobs. Toward the end of the course some official might have been
thinking as follows: "Well, I certainly have blown my top. Damn it, I
had a right to; it's terrible the way we are picked on. At the same time,
things aren't quite right; I ought not let my own prejudices get me
down. Sure, everybody's got them. But it *is* tough on some minority
groups. Sure, they have their faults. But I don't want any trouble in my
district. I better look out for so and so; he's awfully anti-Semitic and
hates Negroes. I guess I'll do so and so," and here he begins to con-
struct in imagination a plan for his future work.

I cannot prove that such was the mental process of the typical    24
member of the class, but I suspect something of the sort took place. It
probably was so if the reported improvement in race relations was due
in part to the course given.

The important lesson here is that the reconstruction of personal    25
attitudes may take place *after* the course of instruction is completed.
The class situation may be such that every session from start to finish

is cathartic, but the constructive lessons may persevere in their effects long after the course is ended.

## Guiding Catharsis

Practitioners in the field of group dynamics may vigorously criti-  26
cize my case report and point out the dangers of letting catharsis continue so long without guidance. They would say, with good reason, that unless catharsis is guided it may merely reinforce all the disordered tendencies. It may freeze the self-justifications and projections. The processes of re-education, they will insist, should have started at the first session.

To them I reply: the situation described was not suitable to the  27
technique currently recommended and employed. As I have pointed out, the course was not voluntary; it had no build-up; there was no history of democratic management or group decision among its members; the existence of a problem was denied; the participants felt under attack; the teacher was an outsider; and race prejudice is peculiarly resistant to change. In short, the most unfavorable conditions for re-education prevailed. Before starting the course I had intended to employ role-playing, but I found it wholly inapplicable to the group in question. Since I could not count on real participation from the members, all my methods had to be unilateral. Even so, I employed a minimum of lecturing and made as much use as possible of movies, case studies, maps, slides, pamphlets, and guest speakers from minority groups.

Under more favorable conditions, I agree, role-playing might have  28
guided the catharsis more efficiently. If the officials had been required to act out the parts of higher-ups, of minority group members, of recognized leaders, of the indignant and confused public, enlightening results would no doubt have been obtained. If the instructor could have turned aggressive remarks into a channel leading to insight, it would have been well. For example, one remark that was crying to be made throughout the course was: "Now, gentlemen, you are behaving precisely as minority groups behave when they feel themselves to be unjustly attacked. Don't you see?" But this salutary bit of insight could not be given from the outside for the reason that this particular group did not have sufficient foundation for such objectivity, and further, the relationship between the instructor and the group had not sufficiently developed in the eight-hour course.

Yet it is true that unless catharsis is guided and directed more than  29 was possible in this group, the best results cannot be expected. My point is simply that a particularly tough problem in re-education can be attacked hopefully (as in this case) if the instructor is persistent in presenting his material objectively and likewise able to listen without emotion to the carthartic tirade. If he meets the tide of reactive abuse with a mild but persistent backwash of objectivity, he finally changes his own role. No longer regarded as an ogre or a threat, he becomes accepted, and his teaching, if not enthusiastically received, lingers well after the course is concluded.

A corollary of what I am saying is that re-trainers who encounter    30
more resistance than they expect may need to provide more abundantly than they do for the free expression of hostility. Let them be willing targets for the emotional catharsis for as many hours as necessary. If they do so, they will probably find that the gains in the closing hours of the session are appreciable and that the subsequent gains are even greater. The cathartic process has led their listeners to admit some guilt even while evading some, or to shock themselves out of their complacency, or to exhaust their pent-up hostility until they are receptive to new facts and new points of view. It is only then that the restructuring of attitudes begins.

---

# Territorial Behavior

## DESMOND MORRIS

A territory is a defended space. In the broadest sense, there are    1
three kinds of human territory: tribal, family, and personal.

It is rare for people to be driven to physical fighting in defense of    2
these "owned" spaces, but fight they will, if pushed to the limit. The invading army encroaching on national territory, the gang moving into a rival district, the trespasser climbing into an orchard, the burglar breaking into a house, the bully pushing to the front of a queue, the driver trying to steal a parking space, all of these intruders are liable to be met with resistance varying from the vigorous to the savagely violent. Even if the law is on the side of the intruder, the urge to protect a territory may be so strong that otherwise peaceful citizens abandon

all their usual controls and inhibitions. Attempts to evict families from their homes, no matter how socially valid the reasons, can lead to siege conditions reminiscent of the defense of a medieval fortress.

The fact that these upheavals are so rare is a measure of the success of Territorial Signals as a system of dispute prevention. It is sometimes cynically stated that "all property is theft," but in reality it is the opposite. Property, as owned space which is *displayed* as owned space, is a special kind of sharing system which reduces fighting much more than it causes it. Man is a co-operative species, but he is also competitive, and his struggle for dominance has to be structured in some way if chaos is to be avoided. The establishment of territorial rights is one such structure. It limits dominance geographically. I am dominant in my territory and you are dominant in yours. In other words, dominance is shared out spatially, and we all have some. Even if I am weak and unintelligent and you can dominate me when we meet on neutral ground, I can still enjoy a thoroughly dominant role as soon as I retreat to my private base. Be it ever so humble, there is no place like a home territory.

Of course, I can still be intimidated by a particularly dominant individual who enters my home base, but his encroachment will be dangerous for him and he will think twice about it, because he will know that here my urge to resist will be dramatically magnified and my usual subservience banished. Insulted at the heart of my own territory, I may easily explode into battle—either symbolic or real—with a result that may be damaging to both of us.

In order for this to work, each territory has to be plainly advertised as such. Just as a dog cocks its leg to deposit its personal scent on the trees in its locality, so the human animal cocks its leg symbolically all over his home base. But because we are predominantly visual animals we employ mostly visual signals, and it is worth asking how we do this at the three levels: tribal, family, and personal.

First: the Tribal Territory. We evolved as tribal animals, living in comparatively small groups, probably of less than a hundred, and we existed like that for millions of years. It is our basic social unit, a group in which everyone knows everyone else. Essentially, the tribal territory consisted of a home base surrounded by extended hunting grounds. Any neighboring tribe intruding on our social space would be repelled and driven away. As these early tribes swelled into agricultural super-tribes, and eventually into industrial nations, their territorial defense systems became increasingly elaborate. The tiny, ancient home base of the hunting tribe became the great capital city, the primitive warpaint became the flags, emblems, uniforms, and regalia of the specialized military, and the war-chants became national anthems, marching songs, and bugle calls. Territorial boundary-lines hardened into fixed borders, often conspicuously patrolled and punctuated with defensive structures—forts and lookout posts, checkpoints and great walls, and, today, customs barriers.

Today each nation flies its own flag, a symbolic embodiment of its territorial status. But patriotism is not enough. The ancient tribal hunter lurking inside each citizen finds himself unsatisfied by membership in such a vast conglomeration of individuals, most of whom are totally unknown to him personally. He does his best to feel that he shares a common territorial defense with them all, but the scale of the operation has become inhuman. It is hard to feel a sense of belonging with a tribe of fifty million or more. His answer is to form sub-groups, nearer to his ancient pattern, smaller, and more personally known to him—the local club, the teenage gang, the union, the specialist society, the sports association, the political party, the college fraternity, the social clique, the protest group, and the rest. Rare indeed is the individual who does not belong to at least one of these splinter groups, and take from it a sense of tribal allegiance and brotherhood. Typical of all these groups is the development of Territorial Signals—badges, costumes, headquarters, banners, slogans, and all the other displays of group identity. This is where the action is, in terms of tribal territorialism, and only when a major war breaks out does the emphasis shift upwards to the higher group level of the nations.

Each of these modern pseudo-tribes sets up its own special kind of home base. In extreme cases non-members are totally excluded, in others they are allowed in as visitors with limited rights and under a control system of special rules. In many ways they are like miniature nations, with their own flags and emblems and their own border guards. The exclusive club has its own "customs barrier": the doorman who checks your "passport" (your membership card) and prevents strangers from passing in unchallenged. There is a government: the club committee; and often special displays of the tribal elders: the photographs or portraits of previous officials on the walls. At the heart of the specialized territories there is a powerful feeling of security and importance, a sense of shared defense against the outside world. Much of the club chatter, both serious and joking, directs itself against the rottenness of everything outside the club boundaries—in that "other world" beyond the protected portals.

In social organizations which embody a strong class system, such 9
as military units and large business concerns, there are many territorial
rules, often unspoken, which interfere with the official hierarchy.
High-status individuals, such as officers or managers, could in theory
enter any of the regions occupied by the lower levels in the peck order,
but they limit this power in a striking way. An officer seldom enters a
sergeant's mess or a barrack room unless it is for a formal inspection.
He respects those regions as alien territories even though he has the
power to go there by virtue of his dominant role. And in businesses,
part of the appeal of unions, over and above their obvious functions, is
that with their officials, headquarters, and meetings they add a sense
of territorial power for the staff workers. It is almost as if each military
organization and business concern consists of two warring tribes: the
officers versus the other ranks, and the management versus the workers. Each has its special home base within the system, and the territorial defense pattern thrusts itself into what, on the surface, is a pure
social hierarchy. Negotiations between managements and unions are
tribal battles fought out over the neutral ground of a boardroom table,
and are as much concerned with territorial display as they are with
resolving problems of wages and conditions. Indeed, if one side gives
in too quickly and accepts the other's demands, the victors feel
strangely cheated and deeply suspicious that it may be a trick. What
they are missing is the protracted sequence of ritual and counter-ritual
that keeps alive their group territorial identity.

Likewise, many of the hostile displays of sports fans and teenage 10
gangs are primarily concerned with displaying their group image to
rival fanclubs and gangs. Except in rare cases, they do not attack one
another's headquarters, drive out the occupants, and reduce them to
a submissive, subordinate condition. It is enough to have scuffles on the
borderlands between the two rival territories. This is particularly clear
at football matches, where the fan-club headquarters becomes temporarily shifted from the club-house to a section of the stands, and where
minor fighting breaks out at the unofficial boundary line between the
massed groups of rival supporters. Newspaper reports play up the few
accidents and injuries which do occur on such occasions, but when
these are studied in relation to the total numbers of displaying fans
involved it is clear that the serious incidents represent only a tiny
fraction of the overall group behavior. For every actual punch or kick
there are a thousand war-cries, war dances, chants, and gestures.

Second: the Family Territory. Essentially, the family is a breeding 11
unit and the family territory is a breeding ground. At the center of this

space, there is the nest—the bedroom—where, tucked up in bed, we feel at our most territorially secure. In a typical house the bedroom is upstairs, where a safe nest should be. This puts it farther away from the entrance hall, the area where contact is made, intermittently, with the outside world. The less private reception rooms, where intruders are allowed access, are the next line of defense. Beyond them, outside the walls of the building, there is often a symbolic remnant of the ancient feeding grounds—a garden. Its symbolism often extends to the plants and animals it contains, which cease to be nutritional and become merely decorative—flowers and pets. But like a true territorial space it has a conspicuously displayed boundary-line, the garden fence, wall, or railings. Often no more than a token barrier, this is the outer territorial demarcation, separating the private world for the family from the public world beyond. To cross it puts any visitor or intruder at an immediate disadvantage. As he crosses the threshold, his dominance wanes, slightly but unmistakably. He is entering an area where he senses that he must ask permission to do simple things that he would consider a right elsewhere. Without lifting a finger, the territorial owners exert their dominance. This is done by all the hundreds of small ownership "markers" they have deposited on their family territory: the ornaments, the "possessed" objects positioned in the rooms and on the walls; the furnishings, the furniture, the colors, the patterns, all owner-chosen and all making this particular home base unique to them.

It is one of the tragedies of modern architecture that there has been a standardization of these vital territorial living units. One of the most important aspects of a home is that it should be similar to other homes only in a general way, and that in detail it should have many differences, making it a *particular* home. Unfortunately, it is cheaper to build a row of houses, or a block of flats, so that all the family living-units are identical, but the territorial urge rebels against this trend and house-owners struggle as best they can to make their mark on their mass-produced properties. They do this with garden-design, with front-door colors, with curtain patterns, with wallpaper and all the other decorative elements that together create a unique and different family environment. Only when they have completed this nest-building do they feel truly "at home" and secure.     12

When they venture forth as a family unit they repeat the process in a minor way. On a day-trip to the seaside, they load the car with personal belongings and it becomes their temporary, portable territory.     13

Arriving at the beach they stake out a small territorial claim, marking it with rugs, towels, baskets, and other belongings to which they can return from their seaboard wanderings. Even if they all leave it at once to bathe, it retains a characteristic territorial quality and other family groups arriving will recognize this by setting up their own "home" bases at a respectful distance. Only when the whole beach has filled up with these marked spaces will newcomers start to position themselves in such a way that the inter-base distance becomes reduced. Forced to pitch between several existing beach territories they will feel a momentary sensation of intrusion, and the established "owners" will feel a similar sensation of invasion, even though they are not being directly inconvenienced.

The same territorial scene is being played out in parks and fields     14
and on riverbanks, wherever family groups gather in their clustered units. But if rivalry for spaces creates mild feelings of hostility, it is true to say that, without the territorial system of sharing and space-limited dominance, there would be chaotic disorder.

Third: the Personal Space. If a man enters a waiting-room and sits     15
at one end of a long row of empty chairs, it is possible to predict where the next man to enter will seat himself. He will not sit next to the first man, nor will he sit at the far end, right away from him. He will choose a position about halfway between these two points. The next man to enter will take the largest gap left, and sit roughly in the middle of that, and so on, until eventually the latest newcomer will be forced to select a seat that places him right next to one of the already seated men. Similar patterns can be observed in cinemas, public urinals, airplanes, trains, and buses. This is a reflection of the fact that we all carry with us, everywhere we go, a portable territory called a Personal Space. If people move inside this space, we feel threatened. If they keep too far outside it, we feel rejected. The result is a subtle series of spatial adjustments, usually operating quite unconsciously and producing ideal compromises as far as this is possible. If a situation becomes too crowded, then we adjust our reactions accordingly and allow our personal space to shrink. Jammed into an elevator, a rush-hour compartment, or a packed room, we give up altogether and allow body-to-body contact, but when we relinquish our Personal Space in this way, we adopt certain special techniques. In essence, what we do is to convert these other bodies into "nonpersons." We studiously ignore them, and they us. We try not to face them if we can possibly avoid it. We wipe all expressiveness from our faces, letting them go blank. We may look

up at the ceiling or down at the floor, and we reduce body movements to a minimum. Packed together like sardines in a tin, we stand dumbly still, sending out as few social signals as possible.

Even if the crowding is less severe, we still tend to cut down our   16
social interactions in the presence of large numbers. Careful observations of children in play groups revealed that if they are high-density groupings there is less social interaction between the individual children, even though there is theoretically more opportunity for such contacts. At the same time, the high-density groups show a higher frequency of aggressive and destructive behavior patterns in their play. Personal Space—"elbow room"—is a vital commodity for the human animal, and one that cannot be ignored without risking serious trouble.

Of course, we all enjoy the excitement of being in a crowd, and this   17
reaction cannot be ignored. But there are crowds and crowds. It is pleasant enough to be in a "spectator crowd," but not so appealing to find yourself in the middle of a rush-hour crush. The difference between the two is that the spectator crowd is all facing in the same direction and concentrating on a distant point of interest. Attending a theater, there are twinges of rising hostility toward the stranger who sits down immediately in front of you or the one who squeezes into the seat next to you. The shared armrest can become a polite, but distinct, territorial boundary-dispute region. However, as soon as the show begins, these invasions of Personal Space are forgotten and the attention is focused beyond the small space where the crowding is taking place. Now, each member of the audience feels himself spatially related, not to his cramped neighbors, but to the actor on the stage, and this distance is, if anything, too great. In the rush-hour crowd, by contrast, each member of the pushing throng is competing with his neighbors all the time. There is no escape to a spatial relation with a distant actor, only the pushing, shoving bodies all around.

Those of us who have to spend a great deal of time in crowded   18
conditions become gradually better able to adjust, but no one can ever become completely immune to invasions of Personal Space. This is because they remain forever associated with either powerful hostile or equally powerful loving feelings. All through our childhood we will have been held to be loved and held to be hurt, and anyone who invades our Personal Space when we are adults is, in effect, threatening to extend his behavior into one of these two highly charged areas of human interaction. Even if his motives are clearly neither hostile nor sexual, we still find it hard to suppress our reactions to his close ap-

proach. Unfortunately, different countries have different ideas about exactly how close is close. It is easy enough to test your own "space reaction": when you are talking to someone in the street or in any open space, reach out with your arm and see where the nearest point on his body comes. If you hail from western Europe, you will find that he is at roughly fingertip distance from you. In other words, as you reach out, your fingertips will just about make contact with his shoulder. If you come from eastern Europe you will find you are standing at "wrist distance." If you come from the Mediterranean region you will find that you are much closer to your companion, at little more than "elbow distance."

Trouble begins when a member of one of these cultures meets and    19
talks to one from another. Say a British diplomat meets an Italian or an Arab diplomat at an embassy function. They start talking in a friendly way, but soon the fingertips man begins to feel uneasy. Without knowing quite why, he starts to back away gently from his companion. The companion edges forward again. Each tries in his way to set up a Personal Space relationship that suits his own background. But it is impossible to do. Every time the Mediterranean diplomat advances to a distance that feels comfortable for him, the British diplomat feels threatened. Every time the Briton moves back, the other feels rejected. Attempts to adjust this situation often lead to a talking pair shifting slowly across a room, and many an embassy reception is dotted with western-European fingertip-distance men pinned against the walls by eager elbow-distance men. Until such differences are fully understood and allowances made, these minor differences in "body territories" will continue to act as an alienation factor which may interfere in a subtle way with diplomatic harmony and other forms of international transaction.

If there are distance problems when engaged in conversation, then    20
there are clearly going to be even bigger difficulties where people must work privately in a shared space. Close proximity of others, pressing against the invisible boundaries of our personal body-territory, makes it difficult to concentrate on nonsocial matters. Flat-mates, students sharing a study, sailors in the cramped quarters of a ship, and office staff in crowded work-places, all have to face this problem. They solve it by "cocooning." They use a variety of devices to shut themselves off from the others present. The best possible cocoon, of course, is a small private room—a den, a private office, a study, or a studio—which physically obscures the presence of other nearby territory-owners. This

is the ideal situation for non-social work, but the space-sharers cannot enjoy this luxury. Their cocooning must be symbolic. They may, in certain cases, be able to erect small physical barriers, such as screens and partitions, which give substance to their invisible Personal Space boundaries, but when this cannot be done, other means must be sought. One of these is the "favored object." Each space-sharer develops a preference, repeatedly expressed until it becomes a fixed pattern, for a particular chair, or table, or alcove. Others come to respect this, and friction is reduced. This system is often formally arranged (this is my desk, that is yours), but even where it is not, favored places soon develop. Professor Smith has a favorite chair in the library. It is not formally his, but he always uses it and others avoid it. Seats around a mess-room table, or a boardroom table, become almost personal property for specific individuals. Even in the home, father has his favorite chair for reading the newspaper or watching television. Another device is the blinkers-posture. Just as a horse that over-reacts to other horses and the distractions of the noisy race-course is given a pair of blinkers to shield its eyes, so people studying privately in a public place put on pseudo-blinkers in the form of shielding hands. Resting their elbows on the table, they sit with their hands screening their eyes from the scene on either side.

A third method of reinforcing the body-territory is to use personal 21 markers. Books, papers, and other personal belongings are scattered around the favored site to render it more privately owned in the eyes of companions. Spreading out one's belongings is a well-known trick in public-transport situations, where a traveler tries to give the impression that seats next to him are taken. In many contexts carefully arranged personal markers can act as an effective territorial display, even in the absence of the territory owner. Experiments in a library revealed that placing a pile of magazines on the table in one seating position successfully reserved that place for an average of 77 minutes. If a sports-jacket was added, draped over the chair, then the "reservation effect" lasted for over two hours.

In these ways, we strengthen the defenses of our Personal Spaces, 22 keeping out intruders with the minimum of open hostility. As with all territorial behavior, the object is to defend space with signals rather than with fists and at all three levels—the tribal, the family, and the personal—it is a remarkably efficient system of space-sharing. It does not always seem so, because newspapers and newscasts inevitably magnify the exceptions and dwell on those cases where the signals have failed and wars have broken out, gangs have fought, neighboring families have feuded, or colleagues have clashed, but for every territorial signal that has failed, there are millions of others that have not. They do not rate a mention in the news, but they nevertheless constitute a dominant feature of human society—the society of a remarkably territorial animal.

---

# About the House

## PAUL FUSSELL

When in one of his poems W. H. Auden indicated that *healers*  1
were to be found not only in city clinics but in

country houses at the end of drives,

he was hardly suggesting that they were proles, or even middle-class. An acute reader of class signals, he knew that the sort of driveway you have, if any, suggests virtually as much about you as the house it leads to.

If you're not able to find some people's driveways at all, you are  2
safe to infer that they're top-out-of-sight. It's only with the upper class that driveways become visible and available for study. In general, we can say that there, the longer the drive the higher the class, with the proviso that long and curved is grander than long and straight. The reason, as Veblen perceived, is that the curved driveway is more "futile," taking up more land. "The canon of futility," he notes, dictates that the best driveway is "a circuitous drive laid across level ground." (If the ground weren't level, there might be a utilitarian reason for the curve: as it is, it's pure play and show.) Even with the more modest upper-middle-class driveway, if it goes straight into the garage, it has less class than if it curves. The surface of the drive is important too. The most impressive surface you can have on an upper-middle-class driveway is gravel in some neutral or dark shade. Beige is best. White gravel is lower, violating as it does the axiom that bold effects and vivid contrasts are always to be avoided. Asphalt is lower

still—too utilitarian and economical. Gravel beats asphalt not just because it's more archaic but because it must be renewed often at considerable expense and inconvenience. Because the desire for privacy is a top-class sign, high walls—anything higher than six or seven feet—confer class, while low ones, or see-through fences, or none at all, proclaim the middle class. Unless the house is known to be very splendid and is out of sight from the road, entryway gates are pretentious.

But you can be pretentious merely with the way you display your house number. One form of vainglory is to spell the number out (you can do this on stationery too), like "Two Hundred Five" ("Two Hundred and Five" is even more offensive). Or you can plaster your family name on the façade or mailbox: "The Johnsons," as if you were an institution. Or you can name your house as if it were something like Windsor Castle and blazon the name somewhere on the front: "The Willows." There's almost no limit to how cute you can be here, especially if you are upper-middle-class and fancy British usages. But in England, house-naming is also popular among proles who want to signal the message that their premises are not public housing but are owned and (largely) paid for by the occupants.

Garages: the upper-middle-class and middle-class house used to act ashamed of its garage, concealing it well in back with other unseemly outbuildings. But now the garage is very much a part of the owner's class presentation, and it's been moved forward on the lot so that passersby can appreciate its two-car size and admire its basketball backboard and hoop (evidence that the house contains at least one member of the leisure class junior grade). The more visible from the street the garage is, the more its costly trick doors can be noted and envied. Three-car and larger garages are seldom seen, not because there aren't any but because they're part of the invisible residences of the top-out-of-sights.

Approaching any house, one is bombarded with class signals. The serious student will not panic but will take them one at a time. The lawn first. Its very existence is an announcement of Anglophilia, England being the place where the lawn came into its own. Finicky neatness here is usually a sign of social anxiety, a tip-off that we are approaching middle-class premises. If there's no crabgrass at all, we can infer an owner who spends much of his time worrying about slipping down a class or two, the lawn being, as Brooks notes, "a crucial arena for classical predatory indiviousness and its concomitant, anxiety." Neglect of one's lawn in middle-class neighborhoods can invite terrible retribution. "The sanctions are not obvious," says William H. Whyte, Jr., "but the look in the eye, the absence of a smile, the inflection of a hello, can be exquisite punishment, and they have brought more than one to a nervous breakdown." If you keep an animal to crop your lawn (only the upper class does this), it's essential that it not be something useful in other ways like a sheep or cow or even a goat, creatures which, as Veblen says, have about them "the vulgar suggestion of thrift," but an animal of a more wasteful and exotic kind, like a deer, something "not vulgarly lucrative either in fact or in suggestion," and thus a happy emblem of "futility."

In cold-weather areas a problem arises for the middle class when the lawn is snow-covered and thus unavailable for invidious display. Hence the middle-class Christmas light show as a form of compensation, with reindeer prancing on the asbestos shingles, jocose Santas entering chimneys, and, on pious lawns, plywood Nativities. No one has ever sufficiently studied the middle-class determination to avoid criticism by putting on, as John Brooks says, "the biggest Christmastime light show on the block," nor sufficiently investigated the relation of the light show to "lawn care." One suburb studied by Whyte for his book *The Organization Man* (1956) goes so wild lighting up at holiday time that every year 100,000 people (proles, surely) drive through to marvel at the effects.

When the front lawn becomes a showcase for permanent objects meant to be admired, we know that we are proceeding down toward the proles. High-prole items for lawn exhibition are urns painted blinding white, as well as front-yard "trees" consisting of some fifteen green-painted wrought-iron branches, each holding, in a ring at the tip, a flower pot. Some prole lawn objects are meant to be not just admired but actually worshiped, like a statue of the Blessed Virgin, which one sees sometimes presented inside an old-fashioned claw-footed bathtub propped upright. A slightly lower kind of class statement is that made by plaster gnomes and flamingos and Disney animals, and by blue or lavender basketball-size shiny spheres resting on fluted cast-concrete pedestals. Proceeding further downward (we're now at about low prole), we see things like defunct truck tires painted white with flowers planted inside. (Auto tires are a grade higher.) At the very class bottom are flower-bed enclosures made of rows of dead light bulbs or the butts of disused beer bottles. Down here, another bit of front-yard décor will be a rusty supermarket cart, waiting quietly for further employment.

Anyone imagining that just any sort of flowers can be presented in    8
the front of a house without status jeopardy would be wrong. Upper-
middle-class flowers are rhododendrons, tiger lilies, amaryllis, colum-
bine, clematis, and roses, except for bright-red ones. One way to learn
which flowers are vulgar is to notice the varieties favored on Sunday-
morning TV religious programs like Rex Humbard's or Robert
Schuller's. There you will see primarily geraniums (red are lower than
pink), poinsettias, and chrysanthemums, and you will know instantly,
without even attending to the quality of the discourse, that you are
looking at a high-prole setup. Other prole flowers include anything too
vividly red, like red tulips. Declassed also are phlox, zinnias, salvia,
gladioli, begonias, dahlias, fuchsias, and petunias. Members of the
middle class will sometimes hope to mitigate the vulgarity of bright-red
flowers by planting them in a rotting wheelbarrow or rowboat displayed on the front lawn, but seldom with success.

Advertising is a good way to ascertain what we might call the    9
social language of flowers. In her study of the American funeral business, *The American Way of Death* (1963), Jessica Mitford calls attention to an ad in an undertakers' trade journal celebrating the profits to
be realized in the traditional collusion between the cadaver embalmer
and the florist. In the ad a new young widow is being presented with
some flowers, and, as the picture caption says, "Softness comes back to
her face as sorrow begins to slip away." The acute reader will not need
to be told that the flowers in question are—chrysanthemums.

But what of the house we are approaching? If it is relatively new    10
it will be so commonplace and uniform and ugly that ascertaining the
exact class of its owner will be difficult. A sarcastic but perhaps not
unfair view of it is Russell Lynes's:

Today's house, however expensive, has become a box . . . , or a series of boxes.
Sometimes the box has a sharply peaked roof and is covered with white
clapboards, in which case it is called a Cape Cod. If it is a box longer than it
is wide and has a gently pitched roof, then it is a ranch house. If it is a square
box, it is . . . a bungalow. If it is a two-story box, it is "colonial." If it is two boxes
set next to each other but one a little above the other, then it is a split-level.
(It can be either a split-level Cape Cod or a split-level ranch.)

That is the upper-middle-class and middle-class house. The upper-
class version will be set back farther from the street, but if built in the
last twenty-five years it will be essentially little different. The prole
model, on the other hand, will be identifiable less because it's smaller

than because of the power boat, trailer, or "recreational vehicle" exhibited in the driveway, which will be, of course, straight and asphalted. This in addition to the one or more moribund automobiles disposed about the premises. These are most authentic if elevated on concrete blocks. If you remove these driveway or backyard vehicles and instead plant a fake white wooden well-house in the front yard, you instantly, all other things being equal, transform the prole house into middle-class. This well-house is a component of the New England look, which is one form taken by the snob archaizing impulse of the middles. Other elements of the New England look are brass or black-painted "coach" lanterns on either side of the front door, with a similar lamp on a tall white post to illuminate the front walk; a weather vane on a detachable white cupola imposed on the roof of the garage; and a gilded or black "colonial" eagle above the front door: it will be made of cast aluminum but painted to ape hand-carved wood. There seems no house too mean to display the eagle, although it gradually seems to be losing its power to convey the snob message "Early America": one upper-middle-class friend of mine who had noticed a lot of these eagles on rather mean little houses thought they designated the residences of naval aviators. Other archaic house styles favored by the middle class are the model imitating the nineteenth-century American farmhouse (virtuous and cozy) and the "Tudor," with a brave show of half-timber work on the front (solid, impeccably trustworthy).

Given the structural uniformity of the boxes constituting the current house, the owner must depend largely on front-porch and façade appliqués and decorations (like the eagle) to deliver the news about the social status he's claiming. In the 1950s this used to be the social function of both rooftop television aerials and protruding window air conditioners, but now of course both transmit entirely unhonorific status messages. The front porch and doorway area are to the house what the mouth is to the human face, like the mouth conveying ungainsayable class signals. Whether high or low, the domestic façade labors to extort respect, and it is thus one of the most pathetic of artifacts, bespeaking the universal human need to claim dignity and high consequence.

One middle-class way of doing this is through "neo-classic" effects of absolute symmetry, of the sort achieved by a potted small tree on either side of the front door or by the well-known emblem of the precisely equal side curtains pulled back from the ranch-house picture window to reveal a table lamp, the cellophane on its shade visibly inviolate, positioned exactly in the middle of a centered table. A similar symmetrical effect (saying, "We are instinctively neat") is aimed at by installing two outdoor chairs (metal, with pipe arms) as a "conversation group" on the front porch, in stubborn defiance of the traffic thundering past. The middle-class longing for dignity frequently expresses itself in columns or pilasters arguing the impressive weight of the edifice. In one model of a middle-class house, these often attenuate to mere white-painted sticks (four of them, usually) two stories tall, supporting a flyweight rooflet extending over the façade of a Tara-like "Southern mansion." This sort of fraudulent support is endemic in the middle-class dwelling, and it's visible in a socially slightly lower form in two massive square brick pillars holding up a light porch roof, or in obese porch columns made of large boulders stuck together with mortar, or in heavy wrought-iron supports pretending to be needed to prevent a thirty-pound jalousie from crashing to the ground.

Near where I live there's a middle-class house which beautifully illustrates the dangerous proximity of dignity to pomposity. The house is actually a modest bungalow, a one-story gray box covered with asbestos "shakes" and topped by a simple peaked roof. It looks very like a one-story army barracks—nothing at all fancy in the basic fabric. But the owner, gnawed by *folie de grandeur*, has equipped it with a fake brick front, with, on each side of the front door, white fluted Ionic columns holding up nothing at all. (The principle that curves are classier than straight lines operates with columns as with driveways, and has been understood by this aspirant. Square columns are the lowest; round ones the next highest; round and fluted highest of all.) Against this man's fake, bright-red brick facing we find a maximum of "colonial" white trim as a vivid contrast—sills, shutters, canopies, etc. The house begs the observer on no account to look at its honest sides and rear but only at its front. It nicely illustrates Veblen's acute point about the apartment houses built in his time: "The needless variety of fronts presented by the better class of tenements and apartment houses in our cities is an endless variety of architectural distress. . . . Considered as objects of beauty, the dead walls of the sides and back of these structures, left untouched by the hands of the artist, are commonly the best feature of the building."

Bright red juxtaposed with blinding white somehow connote elegance in that social place where middle class meets high prole. I'm thinking of a high-prole little house I know in a small city. It's sited very close to the sidewalk and approached by a short concrete stairway. On either side of the stairway is a small lion *couchant* made of cast concrete. The two lions are painted dead white with their mouths picked out in brightest red. You feel that some sort of quasi-"heraldic" message is being aimed at, although ascertaining exactly what it is would engage a staff of semioticians for some weeks. Another way of achieving the red-and-white effect is to paint the bricks bright red and the mortar pure white. You're likely to come upon this where you also see such prole signals as what can be called the Sheraton Effect—the front steps (three at least) covered with brilliant green outdoor carpeting, very neatly applied, with razor-sharp edges and hospital corners. On high-prole porches there will usually be a "glider," although on low-prole porches the backseat removed from an old auto will serve. The point is to have something to court on. And in Southern states there will be a refrigerator on the front porch, its curious position perhaps owing something to the nineteenth-century tradition that the proper place for the ice box is the back porch, so that the iceman (a member of a yet lower class) can be excluded from the house proper. The refrigerator on the prole front porch serves two purposes: it announces to passersby that you own a costly appliance, and it contains items you need to consume while courting on the glider—"soda" (or "dopes"), fruit, and similar refreshments.

Walking now around behind the house, we should consider the way windows manifest social standing. The principle applying is, as usual, archaism. Socially, the highest kind of windows are pseudo-eighteenth-century wooden sash windows, and the more panes per sash, the better: six is standard, twelve, distinguished. One would think that the archaistic principle would confer great class on the mock-Tudor leaded window with diamond-shaped panes, but it doesn't: these windows are too palpably fraudulent, theatrical, and Camp, simply absurd, like collegiate or church Gothic architecture, in a country founded only in the eighteenth century. Some proles aim for status by going in for "portholes" on their split-level ranch houses, circular openings a foot and a half in diameter with white surrounds suggesting archaic life rings. By this means they hope to suggest time spent in yachts. Few will be deceived. If you have storm windows fitted over your sash windows, for class purposes the wooden ones are better than metal, both because they honor the organic-materials principle and because, on a large house, they seem to presuppose a servant (or "outdoor man") to put them up and take them down.

If there were such he'd also be in charge of the outdoor furniture around in back. Organic materials are important here, dictating that the lowest you can sink is to folding chairs made of aluminum tubing with bright-green plastic-mesh webbing which, with wear, grows gradually looser. Wooden furniture is probably the classiest, with plenty of overstuffed cushions, for it's a top-class principle never (except on a yacht) to be in the slightest degree uncomfortable. If you wouldn't sit on stretched vinyl strips indoors, why do it outside? If there's a patio, for class purposes it should be much larger than needed, and on it should stand a table with a glass top. The glass should be clear, not wrinkled, for clear glass, being harder to keep clean, suggests a servant to clean it—hence, by the way, the desirability of lots of mirrors indoors. Breakfast at this clear-glass-topped table on the extra-large patio is an upper-class or upper-middle-class practice established by the films of the 1940s and 1950s. At a table like this, you sit on white wrought-iron chairs equipped with deep cushions, and you drink orange juice, freshly squeezed, of course, but certainly not by yourself. (White-painted wrought iron is one of the few permissible deviations from the organic-materials principle.)

The automobile, like the all-important domestic façade, is another      17
mechanism for outdoor class display. Or class lack of display we'd have to say, if we focus on the usages of the upper class, who, on the principle of archaism, affect to regard the automobile as very *nouveau* and underplay it consistently. Class understatement describes the technique: if your money and freedom and carelessness of censure allow you to buy any kind of car, you provide yourself with the meanest and most common to indicate that you're not taking seriously so easily purchasable and thus vulgar a class totem. You have a Chevy, Ford, Plymouth, or Dodge, and in the least interesting style and color. It may be clean, although slightly dirty is best. But it should be boring. The next best thing is to have a "good" car, like a Jaguar or BMW, but to be sure it's old and beat-up. You may not have a Rolls, a Cadillac, or a Mercedes. Especially a Mercedes, a car, Joseph Epstein reports in *The American Scholar* (Winter 1981–82), which the intelligent young in West Germany regard, quite correctly, as "a sign of high vulgarity, a car of the kind owned by Beverly Hills dentists or African cabinet ministers." The worst kind of upper-middle-class types own Mercedes, just as the best own elderly Oldsmobiles, Buicks, and Chryslers, and perhaps jeeps and Land Rovers, the latter conveying the Preppy suggestion that one of your residences is in a place so unpublic that the roads to it are not even paved, indeed are hardly passable by your

ordinary vulgar automobile. And the understatement canon determines that the higher your class, the slower you drive. Speeders are either young non-Anglo-Saxon high-school proles hoping to impress girls of a similar sort, or insecure, status-anxious middle-class men who have seen too many movies involving auto chases and as a result think cars romantic, sexy, exciting, etc. The requirements of class dictate that you drive slowly, steadily, and silently, and as near the middle of the road as possible.

The class expressiveness of a car doesn't stop with the kind and condition of car it is, or with the way you drive it. It involves also the things you display on or in it, all the way from the rack holding three rifles, shotguns, or carbines in the rear window of the pickup with the Southern Methodist University sticker to the upper-middle-class rear-window announcement "I'd Rather Be Sailing." Proles love to decorate their cars, not just with mock-leopard upholstery and things like dice and baby shoes dangling from front and rear windows but with bumper stickers (AUSABLE CHASM; SOUTH OF THE BORDER; AYATOLLAH—PIG'S ASSHOLAH; HONK IF YOU LOVE JESUS), and of course little plastic Saint Christophers and the like on the dashboard. The middle class likes bumper stickers too, but is more likely to go in for self-congratulatory messages like CAUTION: I BRAKE FOR SMALL ANIMALS. 18

Americans are the only people in the world known to me whose status anxiety prompts them to advertise their college and university affiliations in the rear windows of their automobiles. You can drive all over Europe without once seeing a rear-window sticker reading CHRIST CHURCH or UNIVERSITÉ DE PARIS. A convention in the United States is that the higher learning is so serious a matter that joking or parody are wholly inappropriate. Actually, there's hardly an artifact more universally revered by Americans of all classes than the rear-window college sticker. One would sooner defile the flag than mock the sticker or what it represents by, say, putting it on upside down or slantwise, or scratching ironic quotation marks around "College" or "University." I have heard of one young person who cut apart and rearranged the letters of his STANFORD sticker so that his rear window said SNODFART. But the very rarity of so scandalous a performance is significant. And no family fortunate enough to be associated with Harvard or Princeton, no matter how remotely, would fly a KUTZTOWN STATE COLLEGE sticker as an ironic jest. These stickers pose an ethical problem uniquely American: how long after a family member has ceased to attend a classy college may one display the sticker? One year? Ten years? Forever? The 19

American family would appreciate some authoritative guidance here, perhaps from the colleges themselves.

Just as you generally don't joke with the college sticker, you don't    20
joke with the furnishing and decorating of the rooms of the house likely to be seen by strangers. Especially the living room, "the family's best foot a few inches forward, or sometimes a few miles," as Russell Lynes says. An upper-middle-class and often a middle-class house can be identified immediately you're inside by the way it stints the space allotted to the bedrooms and backstage areas so that the living room can constitute a more ample theater of display. The kinds of cultural emblems exhibited there were the focus of an elaborate study by sociologist F. Stuart Chapin almost fifty years ago in his book *Contemporary American Institutions* (1935). "The attitude of friends and other visitors, and hence social status," as he said, "may be advantageously influenced by the selection and proper display of cultural objects in the living room." To assist in measuring the class message projected by a living room, Chapin devised what he called "The Living-Room Scale," awarding or subtracting points for various items exhibited. Thus, if you had an alarm clock in your living room, you forfeited 2 points, but if you had a "fireplace with three or more utensils," you gained 8. A hardwood floor brought you 10, each curtained window 2, each bookcase with books 8. Each displayed newspaper and magazine earned 8, but a sewing machine, if you were so thoughtless as to position it in your living room, cost you 2. Admirable as this idea is, there are a couple of weaknesses in it. Chapin's distinctions, for one thing, aren't fine enough. The displayed magazines, for example: it matters terribly what magazines they are. A *Reader's Digest* and a *Family Circle* should lower you considerably on the scale, but they can be counterbalanced by display of a *Smithsonian* or *Art News*. And secondly, Chapin failed to take into account the practice among some uppermiddles of parody display, a practice which has advanced dramatically since his day. All the regrettable items he notices, including even the sewing machine, could be advantageously exhibited today in a Camp or hi-tech-parody setting. I have tried to bring Chapin's Living-Room Scale up to date and make it a more trustworthy gauge for measuring the social class of your neighbors and friends. You'll find my version in the Appendix of this book.

The upper-class living room is very likely to have an eleven-to-    21
thirteen-foot ceiling, to contain wasteful curves—moldings on baseboards, door panels, and the like—and, if wood is visible, to feature

dark rather than light wood (more archaic-looking). There must be a hardwood floor—parquet is best—covered, but not entirely, with Orientals so old as to be almost threadbare, suggesting inheritance from a primeval past. (On the other hand, a new Oriental, no matter how visibly expensive, is an all but infallible middle-class sign.) In the upper-class living room there may be exquisite homemade petit-point chair seats or a brick doorstop covered in needlepoint—these suggest yards and yards of leisure on the part of the lady of the house. In general, the more allusions to European architectural décor, the higher the class: black-and-white marble entryways, balustrades and railings, brocaded wall coverings, brass door fittings (which imply daily polishing by someone, certainly not the owner)—all confer the air both of archaism and the un-American so essential for upper-class status. There is one item which, although not indispensable in an upper-class setting, is never found outside one. It's the tabletop obelisk made of marble or crystal, a sly allusion not to Egypt—there would be no class there—but to Paris. And also to Tiffany, known by the cognoscenti to be the main local outlet for these choice items. And flowers usually appear in upper living rooms. (*Fresh flowers,* the middle-class housewife will call them, to distinguish them from the plastic ones assumed in her world.)

As we move down a bit to the upper-middle class, certain features 22 begin to enter the picture. Like the middlebrow "oil portrait" of the head of the household or his wife or issue, executed by someone like Zita Davisson, "the noted portrait artist . . . celebrated throughout the world for her realistic, expressive style." You can book a sitting with her through Bergdorf-Goodman. If that's too costly, you can display a photographic portrait of yourself (as if you were Churchill) made by Yousuf Karsh, who advertises in *The New Yorker.* If you put it in an easel frame, the frame must be of silver, like the cedar-lined cigarette box on the coffee table. If your living room has come equipped with more bookcases than you need, you can always respond to the ad of a company calling itself Books by the Yard (601 Madison Avenue, New York City): "Leather Bound Books, 18th and 19th Century Fiction, Biography, Ecclesiastic, Essays, Shakespeare, Fielding, Carlyle, Swift, Pope, Johnson, Milton, etc. . . . Excellent source for interior decorators." In the genuine upper-middle-class living room nautical allusions will be visible somewhere, like a framed map of Nantucket, implying intimate familiarity with its waters. In this class, the Orientals will be worn but not threadbare.

If the living rooms of the top classes tend to ape art galleries and    23
museums, those of the middle class and below resemble motel rooms.
Socially crucial is the dividing line where original works of art or *virtu*
are replaced by reproductions. The Tiffany lamp is a case in point. It
lost caste fatally the moment reproductions with plastic "glass" began
showing up in middle-class houses and restaurants, and now one sees
the things even in prole settings. The middle-class living room may
display "louvers" somewhere, and the furniture (most likely in the
"colonial" style) will be of maple or pine. There may be cute wall
plates at the light switches—porcelain, with flowers, cartoon characters, imitation samplers, etc.—and hanging against a wall you may find
a rack soliciting admiration for a vast "collection" of outré items like
match folders or swizzle sticks. The floor will be carpeted wall to wall,
and there will be venetian blinds made not of wood but of metal, with
the slats curved. If potted plants are displayed, there may be cactuses
among them.

But the most notable characteristic of middle-class décor is the    24
flight from any sort of statement that might be interpreted as "controversial" or ideologically pointed. One can't be too careful. Pictures, for
example: safe are sailing vessels, small children and animals, and
pastoral scenes, unlike images that hint any ideological import, like
"France," "Civil War," "New York City," or "East European Immigration." Argument or even disagreement must be avoided at all costs.
In aid of this high-minded end, benign mottos and signs are useful, like
the favorite which reads,

Great Spirit, grant that I may not criticize my neighbor until I have walked a
mile in his moccasins.

Audubon prints on the wall are nicely nonideological, and "wall systems" are popular because they are more likely to contain stereos
and TVs than bookshelves, always a danger because they may display books with controversial spines. In the same way your real middle class refuses to show any but the most bland books and magazines on its coffee tables: otherwise, expressions of opinion, awkward
questions, or even ideas might result. Thus in lieu of conversation,
the photographic slide show—a pleasantly nonideological middle-
class fixture, almost as welcome as an antidote to ideas as the *National Geographic* itself. The middle-class anxiety about ideology is
strongly implied by a phrase popular among the middles, "good
taste," which means, as Russell Lynes notes, the "entirely inoffensive

and essentially characterless." (To do your living room in "good taste" you go to W. & J. Sloan in New York or Marshall Field in Chicago.) One reason for the absence of character in middle-class decorating is that the women get their ideas from national magazines and assume, as one woman told Lynes, that "if you've seen something in a magazine—well, people will nearly always like it." Hence the brass skillet hung against the brick wall, the "colonial" wallpaper, etc. And it's true too that much of this characterlessness can be imputed to the frequency with which the middle class is moved from suburb to suburb by the corporations which employ it. What works in one house must work in the next. As one middle-class wife told Vance Packard, "I settle for something that will move well."

To change a middle-class living room to a prole one, you'd add a 25 Naugahyde Barcalounger and reinvite ideology back into the pictures, but the ideology would be the sort conveyed in the popular chromo "Christ at the United Nations." Thick transparent plastic would cover the upholstery, fringe would appear around the bottom of the sofa, and little woolly balls would dangle from the lampshades, which might be tied with large bows. These things would satisfy the prole hunger for, as decorators put it, "lots of goop." The dining table would be of metal and Formica, and somewhere a bowling-ball carrier might be visible.

An observer with little time to spend in a house can make a fair 26 estimate of the class of the occupants by noting the position of the TV set. The principle is that the higher in class you are, the less likely it is that your TV will be exhibited in your living room. Openly and proudly, that is: if you want it there for convenience or because there's no other place to put it, you'll drain away some of its nastiness by an act of parody display—indicating that you're not taking the TV at all seriously by using the top as a shelf for ridiculous objects like hideous statuettes, absurd souvenirs, hilariously awful wedding presents, and the like.

(This is assuming you have a TV at all. The upper class tends not 27 to. In a recent book of one hundred photographs of upper-class people in their houses in Lake Forest, Illinois, only one TV set is to be seen. TV is distinctly, as one industry spokesman said recently, "not a patrician medium," and it's a startling fact that there are upper-class people who've never heard of Lucy or the Muppets.)

An upper-middle-class way to devulgarize the set is to have it 28 gussied up to look like something else, like "fine furniture" or a Gothic drinks cabinet in "valuable woods." Or you can have it hidden behind a two-way mirror, or behind a painting, which can slide up on tracks when it's necessary to disclose the small screen. Or, as the British critic Peter Conrad observes, "Often in highbrow households the set will be found snugly lodged in a wall of bookshelves, as if proximity could make an ersatz literary object of it."

Down among the middles and high proles the set ceases to be an    29
occasion of shame and becomes instead a specific glory of the family. Here you find sets flaunting their complicated technology, with control panels looking like fixtures from jet aircraft or space capsules. Here also you're likely to find two or more sets (color, of course), and the further down socially you proceed the more likely that they'll be on all the time. In fact, if you're in the presence of one or more sets that are seldom dark, you're either a prole, someone who works in the TV or news industry, someone who does public relations for the President of the United States, or a person who runs an appliance store. Among mid- and low proles, the set will probably be found in the dining room or kitchen, wherever the family gathers for meals. This allows the TV to replace conversation entirely, which is why these classes depend upon it.

And of course what you watch on the set betrays your class at once.    30
Or don't watch, for the upper-middle class, those whose sets are disguised as something else, watches little more than an occasional emission from National Educational Television or a news special, like coverage of the current political assassination. The middle class likes *MASH* and *All in the Family*, with the occasional dose of *Paper Chase*, but what it prefers most is sports viewing, although *viewing*'s not precisely the right word. That's what you'd be doing if you were present at the game. TV sports watching is "Indirect Spectatorism," as Roger Price says. "Someone else," he comments rather severely, "is even doing our *watching* for us." And of course the more violent the body contact of the sports you watch, the lower your class. Tennis and golf and even bowling are classier to watch than boxing, hockey, and pro football. TV news is also watched regularly by the middle class, the audience that deified Walter Cronkite and whose loyalty to the seven-o'clock news, even if that snotty Dan Rather is reading it, is the main cause of the death of afternoon papers all over the country.

The bottom stratum of the middle class, together with the high    31
proles, furnishes the audience for game shows, from the higher (like *Family Feud*), with their fairly sophisticated sexiness and venturesome jokes, to the lower (like *Tic Tac Dough*), with their nonhumiliating questions and nonthreatening emcees. The uglier the gamemaster, the

greater appeal of the show to proles. *Blockbusters* is an illustration. There's no chance of being patronized or put down by a person so unprepossessing as the just-folks emcee Bill Cullen, whose polyester clothes in addition make him seem quite one of us proles.

The lower proles will watch any of this stuff on occasion, because     32 as long as the set's on and playing, they're moderately satisfied, pleased with the subliminal message their TV's always conveying: "I Am Owned by a Family that Can Afford a Color TV." On their ostentatiously technological sets, mid- and low proles like to watch sitcoms based either on outright magic *(The Flying Nun)* or on some technological marvel *(The Hulk, The Bionic Woman, The Six Million Dollar Man)*. The Hulk's emanating from an overdose of gamma radiation (whatever that may be) is as attractive to proles as Superman's association with "Krypton." Science and technology have never quite made it socially (whatever Sebastian Flyte was studying at Oxford in *Brideshead Revisited*, it wasn't chemistry), partly, I suppose, because excitement over them—and the illusion of "progress" they propose—is a prole characteristic. Mid- and low proles also like sitcoms like *Love Boat* and *Gilligan's Island* with dialogue so untaxing that no one in the viewing family will be embarrassed by not getting it. Close to the bottom as a class indicator is *The Flintstones*, appealing as it does to the audience that takes in a paper only for the funnies. Watching news or sports interviews on TV, you doubtless have seen people, not all of them adolescents, who carefully position themselves just in the background and jump up and down and wave frantically while wearing theatrically broad smiles. Hoping to be distinguished if only for a moment by being caught by "a media" and recognized—glory!—by family and friends, they reveal that they are low proles.

Because most mid- and low proles work under supervision and     33 hate it, they identify readily with TV characters in similar predicaments, harassed like the viewer by superintendents and foremen and inspectors. One reason police shows are popular is that they involve such appealing elements as brutality and coercion, but they're popular also because the prole viewer can identify himself easily with characters who are constantly either disobeying a boss, "getting around him," or humoring him. Likewise with newspaper shows like *Lou Grant* and "employee" dramas like *Alice* and *Nine to Five*.

Proles like TV commercials. At times their conversation consists of     34 little more than allusions to them: "I can't believe I ate the whole thing"; "Don't leave home without them"; "How do *you* spell relief?"

Bottom-out-of-sights love TV, but the choice of what to watch belongs largely to institutional personnel like prison guards or nurses and orderlies at establishments for the senile. In prison any show is popular which depicts luscious girls and stimulates imagery of having to do with them. As one former inmate told Studs Terkel, "Your whole day was sitting in a room . . . watching television. *The Dating Game* was a big hit because it dealt with women."

So much for the living room and its main giveaway piece of furni-       35
ture, the TV. Although the living room is the most important conveyer of class signals, two other rooms should not be neglected, the kitchen and the bathroom. The upper-class kitchen, designed to be entered only by servants, is identifiable at once: it's beat-up, inconvenient, and out-of-date, with lots of wood, no Formica whatever, and a minimum of accessories and labor-saving appliances like dishwashers and garbage disposals. Why tolerate these noisy things when you can have a silent servant do precisely what they do? The upper-class kitchen does have a refrigerator, but so antique that it has rounded corners and a big white coil on top. Neatness and modernity enter as we move down toward the middle class, and the more your kitchen resembles a lab, the worse for you socially. An electric stove has less class than a gas one, the appearance of modernity and efficiency, here as everywhere, severely compromising one's status presentation. The "tech" kitchen, with lots of microwave and toaster ovens and coffeemakers, is socially as fatal as the TV set whose control panel suggests a youth misspent at a technical institute.

The bathroom: the upper-class one will resemble the upper-class       36
kitchen in its backwardness. A toilet seat in dark varnished wood is class-eloquent, and so is the absence of a shower, the latter deprivation being especially valuable because of its allusion to England. Two items infallibly found in top-class bathrooms, the Mason Pearson hairbrush and the Kent comb, are trustworthy status emblems, as expressive in their way as the scented toilet paper and pink acrylic johnny-rug of the middle class.

The high-prole bathroom reveals two contradictory impulses at       37
war: one is the desire to exhibit a "hospital" standard of cleanliness, which means splashing a lot of Lysol or Pine Oil around; the other is to display as much fanciness and luxury as possible, which means a lurch in the opposite direction, toward fur toilet-seat covers and towels which don't work not merely because they are made largely of Dacron but also because a third of the remaining threads are "gold." The prole bathroom is a place for enacting the fantasy "What I'd Do If I Were

Really Rich." It's a conventional showcase for a family's aspirations toward the finer things, like chrome plate, flounces and furbelows, magazine racks, gadgets and shelves, bottles and jars, creams, unguents, and lotions, with perhaps Water-Piks and electric toothbrushes thrown in as well. For dolling up the high-prole bathroom, Woolworth's sells a complete set of color-matched vinyl ruglets, one for the toilet lid, one for the toilet seat, one for the surrounding floor, and one for the top of the toilet tank, in case you should want to sit up there. For high proles the bathroom is a serious place, and you're not likely to encounter jocular display there, like toilet paper imprinted with lewd verses or simulacra of U.S. banknotes. The water in the toilet is likely to be bright blue or green, a testimony to the resourcefulness and quick response to advertising of the housewife.

In domestic settings whether upper or prole, domestic animals are 38 bound to be in attendance, and like everything else they give off class signals. Dogs first. They are classier the more they allude to nonutilitarian hunting, and thus to England. Top dogs consequently are Labradors, golden retrievers, corgis, King Charles spaniels, and Afghan hounds. To be upper-class you should have a lot of them, and they should be named after the costlier liquors, like Brandy and Whiskey. The middle class goes in for Scotties and Irish setters, often giving them Scottish or Irish names, although it reserves "Sean" (sometimes spelled "Shawn" to make sure everyone gets it) for its own human issue. Proles, for their part, like breeds that can be conceived to furnish "protection": Doberman pinschers, German shepherds, or pit bulls. Or breeds useful in utilitarian outdoor pursuits, like beagles. The thinness of dogs is often a sign of their social class. "Upper-class dogs," says Jilly Cooper, "have only one meal a day and are therefore quite thin, like their owners." She perceives too that classy people often affect certain breeds of dogs just because the classes below can't pronounce them. Thus their commitment to Rottweilers and Weimaraners. Dogs are popular with the top classes not just because, if large and rowdy especially, they convey the message that their owner is a member of the landed gentry, or what passes for it here. They're also popular among the uppers for the reason Jean-Jacques Rousseau indicated over two hundred years ago when he was talking with James Boswell about dogs versus cats as pets:

ROUSSEAU: Do you like cats?
BOSWELL: No.
ROUSSEAU: I was sure of that. It is my test of character. There you have the

despotic instinct of men. They do not like cats because the cat is free, and will never consent to become a slave. He will do nothing to your order, as the other animals do.

Thus the upper orders' fondness for a species they can order about, like their caterers, gardeners, and lawyers, and one that fawns the more it's commanded. "Sit! That's a good boy."

The dog is both more visible and more audible than the cat, and    39 is for that reason a better class-display investment. The cat is also "less reputable," as Veblen observes, "because she is less wasteful; she may even serve a useful end," like repressing mice. Upper-class cats, the equivalent of poodles in the dog world, are those held to originate in such exotic places (that is, expensive to get to) as Burma and the Himalayas. If you are upper-middle class you'll be tempted to name the cat "Cat." Middles go in for Siamese cats, proles for alley cats, which they name "Puss." Birds in cages are very middle-class, fish in aquariums high-prole. The more elaborate the underwater "set" you provide for your goldfish—sunken galleons, mermaids, giant clams— the more prole you.

# Cause and Effect

## Rigid Rules, Inflexible Plans, and the Stifling of Language: A Cognitivist Analysis of Writer's Block

### MIKE ROSE

Ruth will labor over the first paragraph of an essay for hours. She'll write a sentence, then erase it. Try another, then scratch part of it out. Finally, as the evening winds on toward ten o'clock and Ruth, anxious about tomorrow's deadline, begins to wind into herself, she'll compose that first paragraph only to sit back and level her favorite exasperated interdiction at herself and her page: "No. You can't say that. You'll bore them to death."

Ruth is one of ten UCLA undergraduates with whom I discussed writer's block, that frustrating, self-defeating inability to generate the next line, the right phrase, the sentence that will release the flow of words once again. These ten people represented a fair cross-section of the UCLA student community: lower-middle-class to upper-middle-class backgrounds and high schools, third-world and Caucasian origins, biology to fine arts majors, C+ to A− grade point averages, enthusiastic to blasé attitudes toward school. They were set off from the community by the twin facts that all ten could write competently, and all were currently enrolled in at least one course that required a significant amount of writing. They were set off among themselves by the fact that five of them wrote with relative to enviable ease while the other five experienced moderate to nearly immobilizing writer's block. This blocking usually resulted in rushed, often late papers and resultant grades that did not truly reflect these students' writing ability. And then, of course, there were other less measurable but probably more serious results: a growing distrust of their abilities and an aversion toward the composing process itself.

What separated the five students who blocked from those who    3
didn't? It wasn't skill; that was held fairly constant. The answer could
have rested in the emotional realm—anxiety, fear of evaluation, insecurity, etc. Or perhaps blocking in some way resulted from variation
in cognitive style. Perhaps, too, blocking originated in and typified a
melding of emotion and cognition not unlike the relationship posited by
Shapiro between neurotic feeling and neurotic thinking.[1] Each of these
was possible. Extended clinical interviews and testing could have
teased out the answer. But there was one answer that surfaced readily
in brief explorations of these students' writing processes. It was not
profoundly emotional, nor was it embedded in that still unclear con-
struct of cognitive style. It was constant, surprising, almost amusing if
its results weren't so troublesome, and, in the final analysis, obvious:
the five students who experienced blocking were all operating either
with writing rules or with planning strategies that impeded rather than
enhanced the composing process. The five students who were not
hampered by writer's block also utilized rules, but they were less rigid
ones, and thus more appropriate to a complex process like writing.
Also, the plans these non-blockers brought to the writing process were
more functional, more flexible, more open to information from the
outside.

These observations are the result of one to three interviews with    4
each student. I used recent notes, drafts, and finished compositions to
direct and hone my questions. This procedure is admittedly non-
experimental, certainly more clinical than scientific; still, it did lead to
several inferences that lay the foundation for future, more rigorous
investigation: (a) composing is a highly complex problem-solving process[2] and (b) certain disruptions of that process can be explained with
cognitive psychology's problem-solving framework. Such investigation
might include a study using "stimulated recall" techniques to validate
or disconfirm these hunches. In such a study, blockers and non-blockers
would write essays. Their activity would be videotaped and, immediately after writing, they would be shown their respective tapes and
questioned about the rules, plans, and beliefs operating in their writing
behavior. This procedure would bring us close to the composing process (the writers' recall is stimulated by their viewing the tape), yet
would not interfere with actual composing.

In the next section I will introduce several key concepts in the    5
problem-solving literature. In section three I will let the students speak
for themselves. Fourth, I will offer a cognitivist analysis of blockers'

and non-blockers' grace or torpor. I will close with a brief note on treatment.

## Selected Concepts in Problem Solving: Rules and Plans

As diverse as theories of problem solving are, they share certain basic assumptions and characteristics. Each posits an *introductory period* during which a problem is presented, and all theorists, from Behaviorist to Gestalt to Information Processing, admit that certain aspects, stimuli, or "functions" of the problem must become or be made salient and attended to in certain ways if successful problem-solving processes are to be engaged. Theorists also believe that some conflict, some stress, some gap in information in these perceived "aspects" seems to trigger problem-solving behavior. Next comes a *processing period*, and for all the variance of opinion about this critical stage, theorists recognize the necessity of its existence—recognize that man, at the least, somehow "weighs" possible solutions as they are stumbled upon and, at the most, goes through an elaborate and sophisticated information-processing routine to achieve problem solution. Furthermore, theorists believe—to varying degrees—that past learning and the particular "set," direction, or orientation that the problem solver takes in dealing with past experience and present stimuli have critical bearing on the efficacy of solution. Finally, all theorists admit to a *solution period*, an end-state of the process where "stress" and "search" terminate, an answer is attained, and a sense of completion or "closure" is experienced.

These are the gross similarities, and the framework they offer will be useful in understanding the problem-solving behavior of the students discussed in this paper. But since this paper is primarily concerned with the second stage of problem-solving operations, it would be most useful to focus this introduction on two critical constructs in the processing period: rules and plans.

### Rules

Robert M. Gagné defines "rule" as "an inferred capability that enables the individual to respond to a class of stimulus situations with a class of performances."[3] Rules can be learned directly[4] or by inference through experience.[5] But, in either case, most problem-solving theorists would affirm Gagné's dictum that "rules are probably the major organizing factor, and quite possibly the primary one, in intellectual functioning."[6] As Gagné implies, we wouldn't be able to function without rules; they guide response to the myriad stimuli that confront us daily, and might even be the central element in complex problem-solving behavior.

Dunker, Polya, and Miller, Galanter, and Pribram offer a very useful distinction between two general kinds of rules: algorithms and heuristics.[7] Algorithms are precise rules that will always result in a specific answer if applied to an appropriate problem. Most mathematical rules, for example, are algorithms. Functions are constant (e.g., pi), procedures are routine (squaring the radius), and outcomes are completely predictable. However, few day-to-day situations are mathematically circumscribed enough to warrant the application of algorithms. Most often we function with the aid of fairly general heuristics or "rules of thumb," guidelines that allow varying degrees of flexibility when approaching problems. Rather than operating with algorithmic precision and certainty, we search, critically, through alternatives, using our heuristic as a divining rod—"if a math problem stumps you, try working backwards to solution"; "if the car won't start, check x, y, or z," and so forth. Heuristics won't allow the precision or the certitude afforded by algorithmic operations; heuristics can even be so "loose" as to be vague. But in a world where tasks and problems are rarely mathematically precise, heuristic rules become the most appropriate, the most functional rules available to us: "a heuristic does not guarantee the optimal solution or, indeed, any solution at all; rather, heuristics offer solutions that are good enough most of the time."[8]

### Plans

People don't proceed through problem situations, in or out of a laboratory, without some set of internalized instructions to the self, some program, some course of action that, even roughly, takes goals and possible paths to that goal into consideration. Miller, Galanter, and Pribram have referred to this course of action as a plan: "A plan is any hierarchical process in the organism that can control the order in which a sequence of operations is to be performed" (p. 16). They name the fundamental plan in human problem-solving behavior the TOTE, with the initial T representing a *test* that matches a possible solution against the perceived end-goal of problem completion. O represents the clearance to *operate* if the comparison between solution and goal indicates

9

10

that the solution is a sensible one. The second T represents a further, post-operation, *test* or comparison of solution with goal, and if the two mesh and problem solution is at hand the person *exits* (E) from problem-solving behavior. If the second test presents further discordance between solution and goal, a further solution is attempted in TOTE-fashion. Such plans can be both long-term and global and, as problem solving is underway, short-term and immediate.[9] Though the mechanicality of this information-processing model renders it simplistic and, possibly, unreal, the central notion of a plan and an operating procedure is an important one in problem-solving theory; it at least attempts to metaphorically explain what earlier cognitive psychologists could not—the mental procedures (see pp. 390–391) underlying problem-solving behavior.

Before concluding this section, a distinction between heuristic    11
rules and plans should be attempted; it is a distinction often blurred in the literature, blurred because, after all, we are very much in the area of gestating theory and preliminary models. Heuristic rules seem to function with the flexibility of plans. Is, for example, "If the car won't start, try x, y, or z" a heuristic or a plan? It could be either, though two qualifications will mark it as heuristic rather than plan. (A) Plans subsume and sequence heuristic and algorithmic rules. Rules are usually "smaller," more discrete cognitive capabilities; plans can become quite large and complex, composed of a series of ordered algorithms, heuristics, and further planning "sub-routines." (B) Plans, as was mentioned earlier, include criteria to determine successful goal-attainment and, as well, include "feedback" processes—ways to incorporate and use information gained from "tests" of potential solutions against desired goals.

One other distinction should be made: that is, between "set" and    12
plan. Set, also called "determining tendency" or "readiness,"[10] refers to the fact that people often approach problems with habitual ways of reacting, a pre-disposition, a tendency to perceive or function in one way rather than another. Set, which can be established through instructions or, consciously or unconsciously, through experience, can assist performance if it is appropriate to a specific problem,[11] but much of the literature on set has shown its rigidifying, dysfunctional effects.[12] Set differs from plan in that set represents a limiting and narrowing of response alternatives with no inherent process to shift alternatives. It is a kind of cognitive habit that can limit perception, not a course of

action with multiple paths that directs and sequences response possibilities.

The constructs of rules and plans advance the understanding of    13
problem solving beyond that possible with earlier, less developed formulations. Still, critical problems remain. Though mathematical and computer models move one toward more complex (and thus more real) problems than the earlier research, they are still too neat, too rigidly sequenced to approximate the stunning complexity of day-to-day (not to mention highly creative) problem-solving behavior. Also, information-processing models of problem solving are built on logic theorems, chess strategies, and simple planning tasks. Even Gagné seems to feel more comfortable with illustrations from mathematics and science rather than with social science and humanities problems. So although these complex models and constructs tell us a good deal about problem-solving behavior, they are still laboratory simulations, still invoked from the outside rather than self-generated, and still founded on the mathematico-logical. ·

Two Carnegie-Mellon researchers, however, have recently ex-    14
tended the above into a truly real, amorphous, unmathematical problem-solving process—writing. Relying on protocol analysis (thinking aloud while solving problems), Linda Flower and John Hayes have attempted to tease out the role of heuristic rules and plans in writing behavior.[13] Their research pushes problem-solving investigations to the real and complex and pushes, from the other end, the often mysterious process of writing toward the explainable. The latter is important, for at least since Plotinus many have viewed the composing process as unexplainable, inspired, infused with the transcendent. But Flower and Hayes are beginning, anyway, to show how writing generates from a problem-solving process with rich heuristic rules and plans of its own. They show, as well, how many writing problems arise from a paucity of heuristics and suggest an intervention that provides such rules.

This paper, too, treats writing as a problem-solving process, focus-    15
ing, however, on what happens when the process dead-ends in writer's block. It will further suggest that, as opposed to Flower and Hayes' students who need more rules and plans, blockers may well be stymied by possessing rigid or inappropriate rules, or inflexible or confused plans. Ironically enough, these are occasionally instilled by the composition teacher or gleaned from the writing textbook.

## "Always Grab Your Audience"—The Blockers

In high school, *Ruth* was told and told again that a good essay     16
always grabs a reader's attention immediately. Until you can make
your essay do that, her teachers and textbooks putatively declaimed,
there is no need to go on. For Ruth, this means that beginning bland
and seeing what emerges as one generates prose is unacceptable. The
beginning is everything. And what exactly is the audience seeking that
reads this beginning? The rule, or Ruth's use of it, doesn't provide for
such investigation. She has an edict with no determiners. Ruth operates with another rule that restricts her productions as well: if sentences aren't grammatically "correct," they aren't useful. This keeps
Ruth from toying with ideas on paper, from the kind of linguistic play
that often frees up the flow of prose. These two rules converge in a way
that pretty effectively restricts Ruth's composing process.

The first two papers I received from *Laurel* were weeks overdue.     17
Sections of them were well written; there were even moments of
stylistic flair. But the papers were late and, overall, the prose seemed
rushed. Furthermore, one paper included a paragraph on an issue that
was never mentioned in the topic paragraph. This was the kind of
mistake that someone with Laurel's apparent ability doesn't make. I
asked her about this irrelevant passage. She knew very well that it
didn't fit, but believed she had to include it to round out the paper.
"You must always make three or more points in an essay. If the essay
has less, then it's not strong." Laurel had been taught this rule both in
high school and in her first college English class; no wonder, then, that
she accepted its validity.

As opposed to Laurel, *Martha* possesses a whole arsenal of plans     18
and rules with which to approach a humanities writing assignment,
and, considering her background in biology, I wonder how many of
them were formed out of the assumptions and procedures endemic to
the physical sciences.[14] Martha will not put pen to first draft until she
has spent up to two days generating an outline of remarkable complexity. I saw one of these outlines and it looked more like a diagram of
protein synthesis or DNA structure than the timeworn pattern offered
in composition textbooks. I must admit I was intrigued by the aura of
process (vs. the static appearance of essay outlines) such diagrams
offer, but for Martha these "outlines" only led to self-defeat: the
outline would become so complex that all of its elements could never

be included in a short essay. In other words, her plan locked her into the first stage of the composing process. Martha would struggle with the conversion of her outline into prose only to scrap the whole venture when deadlines passed and a paper had to be rushed together.

Martha's "rage for order" extends beyond the outlining process. 19 She also believes that elements of a story or poem must evince a fairly linear structure and thematic clarity, or—perhaps bringing us closer to the issue—that analysis of a story or poem must provide the linearity or clarity that seems to be absent in the text. Martha, therefore, will bend the logic of her analysis to reason ambiguity out of existence. When I asked her about a strained paragraph in her paper on Camus' "The Guest," she said, "I didn't want to admit that it [the story's conclusion] was just hanging. I tried to force it into meaning."

Martha uses another rule, one that is not only problematical in 20 itself, but one that often clashes directly with the elaborate plan and obsessive rule above. She believes that humanities papers must scintillate with insight, must present an array of images, ideas, ironies gleaned from the literature under examination. A problem arises, of course, when Martha tries to incorporate her myriad "neat little things," often inherently unrelated, into a tightly structured, carefully sequenced essay. Plans and rules that govern the construction of impressionistic, associational prose would be appropriate to Martha's desire, but her composing process is heavily constrained by the non-impressionistic and non-associational. Put another way, the plans and rules that govern her exploration of text are not at all synchronous with the plans and rules she uses to discuss her exploration. It is interesting to note here, however, that as recently as three years ago Martha was absorbed in creative writing and was publishing poetry in high school magazines. Given what we know about the complex associational, often non-neatly-sequential nature of the poet's creative process, we can infer that Martha was either free of the plans and rules discussed earlier or they were not as intense. One wonders, as well, if the exposure to three years of university physical science either established or intensified Martha's concern with structure. Whatever the case, she now is hamstrung by conflicting rules when composing papers for the humanities.

*Mike's* difficulties, too, are rooted in a distortion of the problem- 21 solving process. When the time of the week for the assignment of writing topics draws near, Mike begins to prepare material, strategies, and plans that he believes will be appropriate. If the assignment matches his expectations, he has done a good job of analyzing the professor's intentions. If the assignment *doesn't* match his expectations, however, he cannot easily shift approaches. He feels trapped inside his original plans, cannot generate alternatives, and blocks. As the deadline draws near, he will write something, forcing the assignment to fit his conceptual procrustian bed. Since Mike is a smart man, he will offer a good deal of information, but only some of it ends up being appropriate to the assignment. This entire situation is made all the worse when the time between assignment of topic and generation of product is attenuated further, as in an essay examination. Mike believes (correctly) that one must have a plan, a strategy of some sort in order to solve a problem. He further believes, however, that such a plan, once formulated, becomes an exact structural and substantive blueprint that cannot be violated. The plan offers no alternatives, no "sub-routines." So, whereas Ruth's, Laurel's, and some of Martha's difficulties seem to be rule-specific ("always catch your audience," "write grammatically"), Mike's troubles are more global. He may have strategies that are appropriate for various writing situations (e.g., "for this kind of political science assignment write a compare/contrast essay"), but his entire approach to formulating plans and carrying them through to problem solution is too mechanical. It is probable that Mike's behavior is governed by an explicitly learned or inferred rule: "Always try to 'psych out' a professor." But in this case this rule initiates a problem-solving procedure that is clearly dysfunctional.

While Ruth and Laurel use rules that impede their writing process and Mike utilizes a problem-solving procedure that hamstrings him, *Sylvia* has trouble deciding which of the many rules she possesses to use. Her problem can be characterized as cognitive perplexity: some of her rules are inappropriate, others are functional; some mesh nicely with her own definitions of good writing, others don't. She has multiple rules to invoke, multiple paths to follow, and that very complexity of choice virtually paralyzes her. More so than with the previous four students, there is probably a strong emotional dimension to Sylvia's blocking, but the cognitive difficulties are clear and perhaps modifiable. 22

Sylvia, somewhat like Ruth and Laurel, puts tremendous weight on the crafting of her first paragraph. If it is good, she believes the rest of the essay will be good. Therefore, she will spend up to five hours on the initial paragraph: "I won't go on until I get that first paragraph down." Clearly, this rule—or the strength of it—blocks Sylvia's pro- 23 duction. This is one problem. Another is that Sylvia has other equally potent rules that she sees as separate, uncomplementary injunctions: one achieves "flow" in one's writing through the use of adequate transitions; one achieves substance to one's writing through the use of evidence. Sylvia perceives both rules to be "true," but several times followed one to the exclusion of the other. Furthermore, as I talked to Sylvia, many other rules, guidelines, definitions were offered, but none with conviction. While she *is* committed to one rule about initial paragraphs, and that rule is dysfunctional, she seems very uncertain about the weight and hierarchy of the remaining rules in her cognitive repertoire.

### "If It Won't Fit My Work, I'll Change It"—The Non-blockers

Dale, Ellen, Debbie, Susan, and Miles all write with the aid of       24
rules. But their rules differ from blockers' rules in significant ways. If similar in content, they are expressed less absolutely—e.g., "*Try* to keep audience in mind." If dissimilar, they are still expressed less absolutely, more heuristically—e.g., "I can use as many ideas in my thesis paragraph as I need and then develop paragraphs for each idea." Our non-blockers do express some rules with firm assurance, but these tend to be simple injunctions that free up rather than restrict the composing process, e.g., "When stuck, write!" or "I'll write what I can." And finally, at least three of the students openly shun the very textbook rules that some blockers adhere to: e.g., "Rules like 'write only what you know about' just aren't true. I ignore those." These three, in effect, have formulated a further rule that expresses something like: "If a rule conflicts with what is sensible or with experience, reject it."

On the broader level of plans and strategies, these five students       25
also differ from at least three of the five blockers in that they all possess problem-solving plans that are quite functional. Interestingly, on first exploration these plans seem to be too broad or fluid to be useful and, in some cases, can barely be expressed with any precision. Ellen, for example, admits that she has a general "outline in [her] head about how a topic paragraph should look" but could not describe much about its structure. Susan also has a general plan to follow, but, if stymied, will quickly attempt to conceptualize the assignment in different ways: "If my original idea won't work, then I need to proceed differently." Whether or not these plans operate in TOTE-fashion, I can't say. But they do operate with the operate-test fluidity of TOTEs.

True, our non-blockers have their religiously adhered-to rules:    26
e.g., "When stuck, write," and plans, "I couldn't imagine writing
without this pattern," but as noted above, these are few and functional. Otherwise, these non-blockers operate with fluid, easily modified, even easily discarded rules and plans (Ellen: "I can throw things
out") that are sometimes expressed with a vagueness that could almost
be interpreted as ignorance. There lies the irony. Students that offer
the least precise rules and plans have the least trouble composing.
Perhaps this very lack of precision characterizes the functional composing plan. But perhaps this lack of precision simply masks habitually
enacted alternatives and sub-routines. This is clearly an area that
needs the illumination of further research.

And then there is feedback. At least three of the five non-blockers    27
are an Information-Processor's dream. They get to know their audience, ask professors and T.A.s specific questions about assignments,
bring half-finished products in for evaluation, etc. Like Ruth, they
realize the importance of audience, but unlike her, they have specific
strategies for obtaining and utilizing feedback. And this penchant for
testing writing plans against the needs of the audience can lead to
modification of rules and plans. Listen to Debbie:

> In high school I was given a formula that stated that you must write a
> thesis paragraph with *only* three points in it, and then develop each of those
> points. When I hit college I was given longer assignments. That stuck me for
> a bit, but then I realized that I could use as many ideas in my thesis paragraph
> as I needed and then develop paragraphs for each one. I asked someone about
> this and then tried it. I didn't get any negative feedback, so I figured it was o.k.

Debbie's statement brings one last difference between our block-    28
ers and non-blockers into focus; it has been implied above, but needs
specific formulation: the goals these people have, and the plans they
generate to attain these goals, are quite mutable. Part of the mutability
comes from the fluid way the goals and plans are conceived, and part
of it arises from the effective impact of feedback on these goals and
plans.

## Analyzing Writer's Block

### *Algorithms Rather Than Heuristics*

In most cases, the rules our blockers use are not "wrong" or    29
"incorrect"—it is good practice, for example, to "grab your audience

with a catchy opening" or "craft a solid first paragraph before going on." The problem is that these rules seem to be followed as though they were algorithms, absolute dicta, rather than the loose heuristics that they were intended to be. Either through instruction, or the power of the textbook, or the predilections of some of our blockers for absolutes, or all three, these useful rules of thumb have been transformed into near-algorithmic urgencies. The result, to paraphrase Karl Dunker, is that these rules do not allow a flexible penetration into the nature of the problem. It is this transformation of heuristic into algorithm that contributes to the writer's block of Ruth and Laurel.

### Questionable Heuristics Made Algorithmic

Whereas "grab your audience" could be a useful heuristic, "always make three or more points in an essay" is a pretty questionable one. Any such rule, though probably taught to aid the writer who needs structure, ultimately transforms a highly fluid process like writing into a mechanical lockstep. As heuristics, such rules can be troublesome. As algorithms, they are simply incorrect.

### Set

As with any problem-solving task, students approach writing assignments with a variety of orientations or sets. Some are functional, others are not. Martha and Jane (see footnote 14), coming out of the life sciences and social sciences respectively, bring certain methodological orientations with them—certain sets or "directions" that make composing for the humanities a difficult, sometimes confusing, task. In fact, this orientation may cause them to misperceive the task. Martha has formulated a planning strategy from her predisposition to see processes in terms of linear, interrelated steps in a system. Jane doesn't realize that she can revise the statement that "committed" her to the direction her essay has taken. Both of these students are stymied because of formative experiences associated with their majors—experiences, perhaps, that nicely reinforce our very strong tendency to organize experiences temporally.

### The Plan That Is Not a Plan

If fluidity and multi-directionality are central to the nature of plans, then the plans that Mike formulates are not true plans at all but, rather, inflexible and static cognitive blueprints.[15] Put another way, Mike's "plans" represent a restricted "closed system" (vs. "open system") kind of thinking, where closed system thinking is defined as focusing on "a limited number of units or items, or members, and those properties of the members which are to be used are known to begin with and do not change as the thinking proceeds," and open system thinking is characterized by an "adventurous exploration of multiple alternatives with strategies that allow redirection once 'dead ends' are encountered."[16] Composing calls for open, even adventurous thinking, not for constrained, no-exit cognition.

### Feedback

The above difficulties are made all the more problematic by the   33
fact that they seem resistant to or isolated from corrective feedback. One of the most striking things about Dale, Debbie, and Miles is the ease with which they seek out, interpret, and apply feedback on their rules, plans, and productions. They "operate" and then they "test," and the testing is not only against some internalized goal, but against the requirements of external audience as well.

### Too Many Rules—"Conceptual Conflict"

According to D. E. Berlyne, one of the primary forces that moti-   34
vate problem-solving behavior is a curiosity that arises from conceptual conflict—the convergence of incompatible beliefs or ideas. In *Structure and Direction in Thinking*,[17] Berlyne presents six major types of conceptual conflict, the second of which he terms "perplexity":

This kind of conflict occurs when there are factors inclining the subject toward each of a set of mutually exclusive beliefs. (p. 257)

If one substitutes "rules" for "beliefs" in the above definition, perplexity becomes a useful notion here. Because perplexity is unpleasant, people are motivated to reduce it by problem-solving behavior that can result in "disequalization":

Degree of conflict will be reduced if either the number of competing . . . [rules] or their nearness to equality of strength is reduced. (p. 259)

But "disequalization" is not automatic. As I have suggested, Martha and Sylvia hold to rules that conflict, but their perplexity does *not* lead to curiosity and resultant problem-solving behavior. Their perplexity, contra Berlyne, leads to immobilization. Thus "disequalization" will have to be effected from without. The importance of each of, particularly, Sylvia's rules needs an evaluation that will aid her in rejecting some rules and balancing and sequencing others.

## A Note on Treatment

Rather than get embroiled in a blocker's misery, the teacher or tutor might interview the student in order to build a writing history and profile: How much and what kind of writing was done in high school? What is the student's major? What kind of writing does it require? How does the student compose? Are there rough drafts or outlines available? By what rules does the student operate? How would he or she define "good" writing? etc. This sort of interview reveals an incredible amount of information about individual composing processes. Furthermore, it often reveals the rigid rule or the inflexible plan that may lie at the base of the student's writing problem. That was precisely what happened with the five blockers. And with Ruth, Laurel, and Martha (and Jane) what was revealed made virtually immediate remedy possible. Dysfunctional rules are easily replaced with or counter-balanced by functional ones if there is no emotional reason to hold onto that which simply doesn't work. Furthermore, students can be trained to select, to "know which rules are appropriate for which problems."[18] Mike's difficulties, perhaps because plans are more complex and pervasive than rules, took longer to correct. But inflexible plans, too, can be remedied by pointing out their dysfunctional qualities and by assisting the student in developing appropriate and flexible alternatives. Operating this way, I was successful with Mike. Sylvia's story, however, did not end as smoothly. Though I had three forty-five minute contacts with her, I was not able to appreciably alter her behavior. Berlyne's theory bore results with Martha but not with Sylvia. Her rules were in conflict, and perhaps that conflict was not exclusively cognitive. Her case keeps analyses like these honest; it reminds us that the cognitive often melds with, and can be overpowered by, the affective. So while Ruth, Laurel, Martha, and Mike could profit from tutorials that explore the rules and plans in their writing behavior, students like Sylvia may need more extended, more affectively oriented counseling sessions that blend the instructional with the psychodynamic.

### Notes

1. David Shapiro, *Neurotic Styles* (New York: Basic Books, 1965).
2. Barbara Hayes-Ruth, a Rand cognitive psychologist, and I are currently developing

an information-processing model of the composing process. A good deal of work has already been done by Linda Flower and John Hayes (see p. 393 of this article). I have just received—and recommend—their "Writing as Problem Solving" (paper presented at American Educational Research Association, April, 1979).

3. *The Conditions of Learning* (New York: Holt, Rinehart and Winston, 1970), p. 193.

4. E. James Archer, "The Psychological Nature of Concepts," in H. J. Klausmeier and C. W. Harris, eds., *Analysis of Concept Learning* (New York: Academic Press, 1966), pp. 37–44; David P. Ausubel, *The Psychology of Meaningful Verbal Behavior* (New York: Grune and Stratton, 1963); Robert M. Gagné, "Problem Solving," in Arthur W. Melton, ed., *Categories of Human Learning* (New York: Academic Press, 1964), pp. 293–317; George A. Miller, *Language and Communication* (New York: McGraw-Hill, 1951).

5. George Katona, *Organizing and Memorizing* (New York: Columbia Univ. Press, 1940); Roger N. Shepard, Carl I. Hovland, and Herbert M. Jenkins, "Learning and Memorization of Classifications," *Psychological Monographs*, 75, No. 13 (1961) (entire No. 517); Robert S. Woodworth, *Dynamics of Behavior* (New York: Henry Holt, 1958), chs. 10–12.

6. *The Conditions of Learning*, pp. 190–91.

7. Karl Dunker, "On Problem Solving," *Psychological Monographs*, 58, No. 5 (1945) (entire No. 270); George A. Polya, *How to Solve It* (Princeton: Princeton University Press, 1945); George A. Miller, Eugene Galanter, and Karl H. Pribram, *Plans and the Structure of Behavior* (New York: Henry Holt, 1960).

8. Lyle E. Bourne, Jr., Bruce R. Ekstrand, and Roger L. Dominowski, *The Psychology of Thinking* (Englewood Cliffs, N.J.: Prentice-Hall, 1971).

9. John R. Hayes, "Problem Topology and the Solution Process," in Carl P. Duncan, ed., *Thinking: Current Experimental Studies* (Philadelphia: Lippincott, 1967), pp. 167–81.

10. Hulda J. Rees and Harold E. Israel, "An Investigation of the Establishment and Operation of Mental Sets," *Psychological Monographs*, 46 (1925) (entire No. 210).

11. Ibid.; Melvin H. Marx, Wilton W. Murphy, and Aaron J. Brownstein, "Recognition of Complex Visual Stimuli as a Function of Training with Abstracted Patterns," *Journal of Experimental Psychology*, 62 (1961), 456–60.

12. James L. Adams, *Conceptual Blockbusting* (San Francisco: W. H. Freeman, 1974); Edward DeBono, *New Think* (New York: Basic Books, 1958); Ronald H. Forgus, *Perception* (New York: McGraw-Hill, 1966), ch. 13; Abraham Luchins and Edith Hirsch Luchins, *Rigidity of Behavior* (Eugene: Univ. of Oregon Books, 1959); N. R. F. Maier, "Reasoning in Humans. I. On Direction," *Journal of Comparative Psychology*, 10 (1920), 115–43.

13. "Plans and the Cognitive Process of Writing," paper presented at the National Institute of Education Writing Conference, June 1977; "Problem Solving Strategies and the Writing Process," *College English*, 39 (1977), 449–61. See also footnote 2.

14. Jane, a student not discussed in this paper, was surprised to find out that a topic paragraph can be rewritten after a paper's conclusion to make that paragraph reflect what the essay truly contains. She had gotten so indoctrinated with Psychology's (her major) insistence that a hypothesis be formulated and then left untouched before an experiment begins that she thought revision of one's "major premise" was somehow illegal. She had formed a rule out of her exposure to social science methodology, and the rule was totally inappropriate for most writing situations.

15. Cf. "A plan is flexible if the order of execution of its parts can be easily interchanged

without affecting the feasibility of the plan . . . the flexible planner might tend to think of lists of things he had to do; the inflexible planner would have his time planned like a sequence of cause-effect relations. The former could rearrange his lists to suit his opportunities, but the latter would be unable to strike while the iron was hot and would generally require considerable 'lead-time' before he could incorporate any alternative sub-plans" (Miller, Galanter, and Pribram, p. 120).

16. Frederic Bartlett, *Thinking* (New York: Basic Books, 1958), pp. 74–76.
17. *Structure and Direction in Thinking* (New York: John Wiley, 1965), p. 255.
18. Flower and Hayes, "Plans and the Cognitive Process of Writing," p. 26.

---

# Some Conditions of Obedience and Disobedience to Authority

## STANLEY MILGRAM

The situation in which one agent commands another to hurt a third    1
turns up time and again as a significant theme in human relations.[1] It
is powerfully expressed in the story of Abraham, who is commanded by
God to kill his son. It is no accident that Kierkegaard, seeking to orient
his thought to the central themes of human experience, chose Abraham's conflict as the springboard to his philosophy.

War too moves forward on the triad of an authority which com-    2
mands a person to destroy the enemy, and perhaps all organized hostility may be viewed as a theme and variation on the three elements of
authority, executant, and victim.[2] We describe an experimental program, recently concluded at Yale University, in which a particular
expression of this conflict is studied by experimental means.

In its most general form the problem may be defined thus: if X tells    3
Y to hurt Z, under what conditions will Y carry out the command of X
and under what conditions will he refuse. In the more limited form
possible in laboratory research, the question becomes: If an experimenter tells a subject to hurt another person, under what conditions
will the subject go along with this instruction, and under what conditions will he refuse to obey. The laboratory problem is not so much a
dilution of the general statement as one concrete expression of the
many particular forms this question may assume.

One aim of the research was to study behavior in a strong situation    4
of deep consequence to the participants, for the psychological forces

operative in powerful and life-like forms of the conflict may not be brought into play under diluted conditions.

This approach meant, first, that we had a special obligation to protect the welfare and dignity of the persons who took part in the study; subjects were, of necessity, placed in a difficult predicament, and steps had to be taken to ensure their wellbeing before they were discharged from the laboratory. Toward this end, a careful, post-experimental treatment was devised and has been carried through for subjects in all conditions.[3]

## Terminology

If Y follows the command of X we shall say that he has obeyed X; if he fails to carry out the command of X, we shall say that he has disobeyed X. The terms to *obey* and to *disobey*, as used here, refer to the subject's overt action only, and carry no implication for the motive or experiential states accompanying the action.[4]

To be sure, the everyday use of the word *obedience* is not entirely free from complexities. It refers to action within widely varying situations, and connotes diverse motives within those situations: a child's obedience differs from a soldier's obedience, or the love, honor, and *obey* of the marriage vow. However, a consistent behavioral relationship is indicated in most uses of the term: in the act of obeying, a person does what another person tells him to do. Y obeys X if he carries out the prescription for action which X has addressed to him; the term suggests, moreover, that some form of dominance-subordination, or hierarchical element, is part of the situation in which the transaction between X and Y occurs.

A subject who complies with the entire series of experimental commands will be termed an *obedient* subject; one who at any point in the command series defies the experimenter will be called a *disobedient* or *defiant* subject. As used in this report the terms refer only to the subject's performance in the experiment, and do not necessarily imply a general personality disposition to submit to or reject authority.

## Subject Population

The subjects used in all experimental conditions were male adults, residing in the greater New Haven and Bridgeport areas, aged 20 to 50 years, and engaged in a wide variety of occupations. Each experimental condition described in this report employed 40 fresh subjects and was carefully balanced for age and occupational types. The occupational composition for each experiment was: workers, skilled and unskilled: 40 percent; white collar, sales, business: 40 percent; professionals: 20 percent. The occupations were intersected with three age categories (subjects in 20's, 30's, and 40's, assigned to each condition in the proportions of 20, 40, and 40 percent, respectively).

## The General Laboratory Procedure[5]

The focus of the study concerns the amount of electric shock a subject is willing to administer to another person when ordered by an experimenter to give the "victim" increasingly more severe punishment. The act of administering shock is set in the context of a learning experiment, ostensibly designed to study the effect of punishment on memory. Aside from the experimenter, one naïve subject and one accomplice perform in each session. On arrival each subject is paid $4.50. After a general talk by the experimenter, telling how little scientists know about the effect of punishment on memory, subjects are informed that one member of the pair will serve as teacher and one as learner. A rigged drawing is held so that the naïve subject is always the teacher, and the accomplice becomes the learner. The learner is taken to an adjacent room and strapped into an "electric chair."

The naïve subject is told that it is his task to teach the learner a list of paired associates, to test him on the list, and to administer punishment whenever the learner errs in the test. Punishment takes the form of electric shock, delivered to the learner by means of a shock generator controlled by the naïve subject. The teacher is instructed to increase the intensity of electric shock one step on the generator on each error. The learner, according to plan, provides many wrong answers, so that before long the naïve subject must give him the strongest shock on the generator. Increases in shock level are met by increasingly insistent demands from the learner that the experiment be stopped because of the growing discomfort to him. However, in clear terms the experimenter orders the teacher to continue with the procedure in disregard of the learner's protests. *Thus, the naïve subject must resolve a conflict between two mutually incompatible demands from the social field. He may continue to follow the orders of the experimenter and shock the learner with increasing severity, or he may refuse to follow the orders of the experimenter and heed the learner's pleas. The*

10

11

*experimenter's authority operates not in a free field, but against ever-mounting countervailing pressure from the person being punished.*

A few technical points need to be considered before the findings    12
of the study are described. For the purpose of delivering shock, a simulated shock generator is used, with 30 clearly marked voltage levels that range from 15 to 450 volts. (Each level is activated by one of 30 individual lever switches set in a horizontal line.) The naïve subject is given a sample shock of 45 volts to convince him of the authenticity of the instrument. The generator bears verbal designations that range from "Slight Shock" to "Danger: Severe Shock."

The responses of the victim are standardized on tape, and each    13
protest is coordinated to a particular voltage level on the shock generator. Starting with 75 volts the learner begins to grunt and moan. At 150 volts he demands to be let out of the experiment. At 180 volts he cries out that he can no longer stand the pain. At 300 volts he refuses to provide any more answers to the memory test, insisting that he is no longer a participant in the experiment and must be freed. In response to this last tactic, the experimenter instructs the naïve subject to treat the absence of an answer as equivalent to a wrong answer, and to follow the usual shock procedure. The experimenter reinforces his demand with the statement: "You have no other choice, you must go on!" (This imperative is used whenever the naïve subject tries to break off the experiment.) If the subject refuses to give the next higher level of shock, the experiment is considered at an end. A quantitative value is assigned to the subject's performance based on the maximum-intensity shock he administered before breaking off. Thus any subject's score may range from zero (for a subject unwilling to administer the first shock level) to 30 (for a subject who proceeds to the highest voltage level on the board). For any particular subject and for any particular experimental condition, the degree to which participants have followed the experimenter's orders may be specified with a numerical value, corresponding to the metric on the shock generator.

This laboratory situation gives us a framework in which to study    14
the subject's reactions to the principal conflict of the experiment. Again, this conflict is between the experimenter's demands that he continue to administer the electric shock, and the learner's demands, which become increasingly more insistent, that the experiment be stopped. The crux of the study is to vary systematically the factors believed to alter the degree of obedience to the experimental com-

mands, to learn under what conditions submission to authority is most probable and under what conditions defiance is brought to the fore.

## Pilot Studies

Pilot studies for the present research were completed in the winter    15
of 1960; they differed from the regular experiments in a few details: for one, the victim was placed behind a silvered glass, with the light balance on the glass such that the victim could be dimly perceived by the subject (Milgram, 1961).

Though essentially qualitative in treatment, these studies pointed    16
to several significant features of the experimental situation. At first no vocal feedback was used from the victim. It was thought that the verbal and voltage designations on the control panel would create sufficient pressure to curtail the subject's obedience. However, this was not the case. In the absence of protests from the learner, virtually all subjects, once commanded, went blithely to the end of the board, seemingly indifferent to the verbal designations ("Extreme Shock" and "Danger: Severe Shock"). This deprived us of an adequate basis for scaling obedient tendencies. A force had to be introduced that would strengthen the subject's resistance to the experimenter's commands, and reveal individual differences in terms of a distribution of break-off points.

This force took the form of protests from the victim. Initially, mild    17
protests were used, but proved inadequate. Subsequently, more vehement protests were inserted into the experimental procedure. To our consternation, even the strongest protests from the victim did not prevent all subjects from administering the harshest punishment ordered by the experimenter; but the protests did lower the mean maximum shock somewhat and created some spread in the subject's performance; therefore, the victim's cries were standardized on tape and incorporated into the regular experimental procedure.

*The situation did more than highlight the technical difficulties of*    18
*finding a workable experimental procedure: It indicated that subjects*
*would obey authority to a greater extent than we had supposed.* It also pointed to the importance of feedback from the victim in controlling the subject's behavior.

One further aspect of the pilot study was that subjects frequently    19
averted their eyes from the person they were shocking, often turning

their heads in an awkward and conspicuous manner. One subject explained: "I didn't want to see the consequences of what I had done." Observers wrote:

... subjects showed a reluctance to look at the victim, whom they could see through the glass in front of them. When this fact was brought to their attention they indicated that it caused them discomfort to see the victim in agony. We note, however, that although the subject refuses to look at the victim, he continues to administer shocks.

This suggested that the salience of the victim may have, in some         20
degree, regulated the subject's performance. If, in obeying the experimenter, the subject found it necessary to avoid scrutiny of the victim, would the converse be true? If the victim were rendered increasingly more salient to the subject, would obedience diminish? The first set of regular experiments was designed to answer this question.

## Immediacy of the Victim

This series consisted of four experimental conditions. In each con-         21
dition the victim was brought "psychologically" closer to the subject giving him shocks.

In the first condition (Remote Feedback) the victim was placed in         22
another room and could not be heard or seen by the subject, except that, at 300 volts, he pounded on the wall in protest. After 315 volts he no longer answered or was heard from.

The second condition (Voice Feedback) was identical to the first         23
except that voice protests were introduced. As in the first condition the victim was placed in an adjacent room, but his complaints could be heard clearly through a door left slightly ajar and through the walls of the laboratory.[6]

The third experimental condition (Proximity) was similar to the         24
second, except that the victim was now placed in the same room as the subject, and 1½ feet from him. Thus he was visible as well as audible, and voice cues were provided.

The fourth, and final, condition of this series (Touch-Proximity)         25
was identical to the third, with this exception: The victim received a shock only when his hand rested on a shockplate. At the 150-volt level the victim again demanded to be let free and, in this condition, refused to place his hand on the shockplate. The experimenter ordered the

naïve subject to force the victim's hand onto the plate. Thus obedience in this condition required that the subject have physical contact with the victim in order to give him punishment beyond the 150-volt level.

Forty adult subjects were studied in each condition. The data   26
revealed that obedience was significantly reduced as the victim was rendered more immediate to the subject. The mean maximum shock for the conditions is shown in Figure 1.

Expressed in terms of the proportion of obedient to defiant sub-   27
jects, the findings are that 34 percent of the subjects defied the experimenter in the Remote condition, 37.5 percent in Voice Feedback, 60 percent in Proximity, and 70 percent in Touch-Proximity.

How are we to account for this effect? A first conjecture might be   28
that as the victim was brought closer the subject became more aware of the intensity of his suffering and regulated his behavior accordingly. This makes sense, but our evidence does not support the interpreta-

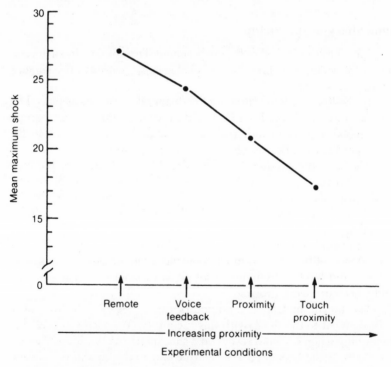

**FIGURE 1.**   Mean maxima in proximity series.

tion. There are no consistent differences in the attributed level of pain across the four conditions (i.e., the amount of pain experienced by the victim as estimated by the subject and expressed on a 14-point scale). But it is easy to speculate about alternative mechanisms:

*Empathic cues.* In the Remote and to a lesser extent the Voice Feedback conditions, the victim's suffering possesses an abstract, remote quality for the subject. He is aware, but only in a conceptual sense, that his actions cause pain to another person; the fact is apprehended, but not felt. The phenomenon is common enough. The bombardier can reasonably suppose that his weapons will inflict suffering and death, yet this knowledge is divested of affect and does not move him to a felt, emotional response to the suffering resulting from his actions. Similar observations have been made in wartime. It is possible that the visual cues associated with the victim's suffering trigger empathic responses in the subject and provide him with a more complete grasp of the victim's experience. Or it is possible that the empathic responses are themselves unpleasant, possessing drive properties which cause the subject to terminate the arousal situation. Diminishing obedience, then, would be explained by the enrichment of empathic cues in the successive experimental conditions.

*Denial and narrowing of the cognitive field.* The Remote condition allows a narrowing of the cognitive field so that the victim is put out of mind. The subject no longer considers the act of depressing a lever relevant to moral judgment, for it is no longer associated with the victim's suffering. When the victim is close it is more difficult to exclude him phenomenologically. He necessarily intrudes on the subject's awareness since he is continuously visible. In the Remote condition his existence and reactions are made known only after the shock has been administered. The auditory feedback is sporadic and discontinuous. In the Proximity conditions his inclusion in the immediate visual field renders him a continuously salient element for the subject. The mechanism of denial can no longer be brought into play. One subject in the Remote condition said: "It's funny how you really begin to forget that there's a guy out there, even though you can hear him. For a long time I just concentrated on pressing the switches and reading the words."

*Reciprocal fields.* If in the Proximity condition the subject is in an improved position to observe the victim, the reverse is also true. The actions of the subject now come under proximal scrutiny by the victim. Possibly, it is easier to harm a person when he is unable to observe our actions than when he can see what we are doing. His surveillance of the action directed against him may give rise to shame, or guilt, which may then serve to curtail the action. Many expressions of language refer to the discomfort or inhibitions that arise in face-to-face confrontation. It is often said that it is easier to criticize a man "behind his back" than to "attack him to his face." If we are in the process of lying to a person it is reputedly difficult to "stare him in the eye." We "turn away from others in shame" or in "embarrassment" and this action serves to reduce our discomfort. The manifest function of allowing the victim of a firing squad to be blindfolded is to make the occasion less stressful for him, but it may also serve a latent function of reducing the stress of the executioner. In short, in the Proximity conditions, the subject may sense that he has become more salient in the victim's field of awareness. Possibly he becomes more self-conscious, embarrassed, and inhibited in his punishment of the victim.

*Phenomenal unity of act.* In the Remote condition it is more difficult for the subject to gain a sense of *relatedness* between his own actions and the consequences of these actions for the victim. There is a physical and spatial separation of the act and its consequences. The subject depresses a lever in one room, and protests and cries are heard from another. The two events are in correlation, yet they lack a compelling phenomenological unity. The structure of a meaningful act—*I am hurting a man*—breaks down because of the spatial arrangements in a manner somewhat analogous to the disappearance of phi phenomena when the blinking lights are spaced too far apart. The unity is more fully achieved in the Proximity condition as the victim is brought closer to the action that causes him pain. It is rendered complete in Touch-Proximity.

*Incipient group formation.* Placing the victim in another room not only takes him further from the subject, but the subject and the experimenter are drawn relatively closer. There is incipient group formation between the experimenter and the subject, from which the victim is excluded. The wall between the victim and the others deprives him of an intimacy which the experimenter and subject feel. In the Remote condition, the victim is truly an outsider, who stands alone, physically and psychologically.

When the victim is placed close to the subject, it becomes easier to form an alliance with him against the experimenter. Subjects no longer have to face the experimenter alone. They have an ally who is close at hand and eager to collaborate in a revolt against the experimenter. Thus, the changing set of spatial relations leads to a potentially shifting set of alliances over the several experimental conditions.

*Acquired behavior dispositions.* It is commonly observed that laboratory mice will rarely fight with their litter mates. Scott (1958) explains this in terms of passive inhibition. He writes: "By doing nothing under . . . circumstances [the animal] learns to do nothing, and this may be spoken of as passive inhibition . . . this principle has great importance in teaching an individual to be peaceful, for it means that he can learn not to fight simply by not fighting." Similarly, we may learn not to harm others simply by not harming them in everyday life. Yet this learning occurs in a context of proximal relations with others, and may not be generalized to that situation in which the person is physically removed from us. Or possibly, in the past, aggressive actions against others who were physically close resulted in retaliatory punishment which extinguished the original form of response. In contrast, aggression against others at a distance may have only sporadically led to retaliation. Thus the organism learns that it is safer to be aggressive toward others at a distance, and precarious to be so when the parties are within arm's reach. Through a pattern of rewards and punishments, he acquires a disposition to avoid aggression at close quarters, a disposition which does not extend to harming others at a distance. And this may account for experimental findings in the remote and proximal experiments.

Proximity as a variable in psychological research has received far   29
less attention than it deserves. If men were sessile it would be easy to understand this neglect. But we move about; our spatial relations shift from one situation to the next, and the fact that we are near or remote may have a powerful effect on the psychological processes that mediate our behavior toward others. In the present situation, as the victim is brought closer to the subject ordered to give him shocks, increasing numbers of subjects break off the experiment, refusing to obey. The concrete, visible, and proximal presence of the victim acts in an important way to counteract the experimenter's power to generate disobedience.[7]

## Closeness of Authority

If the spatial relationship of the subject and victim is relevant to   30
the degree of obedience, would not the relationship of subject to experimenter also play a part?

There are reasons to feel that, on arrival, the subject is oriented   31
primarily to the experimenter rather than to the victim. He has come to the laboratory to fit into the structure that the experimenter—not the victim—would provide. He has come less to understand his behavior than to *reveal* that behavior to a competent scientist, and he is willing to display himself as the scientist's purposes require. Most subjects seem quite concerned about the appearance they are making before the experimenter, and one could argue that this preoccupation in a relatively new and strange setting makes the subject somewhat insensitive to the triadic nature of the social situation. In other words, the subject is so concerned about the show he is putting on for the experimenter that influences from other parts of the social field do not receive as much weight as they ordinarily would. This overdetermined orientation to the experimenter would account for the relative insensitivity of the subject to the victim, and would also lead us to believe

that alterations in the relationship between subject and experimenter would have important consequences for obedience.

In a series of experiments we varied the physical closeness and 32 degree of surveillance of the experimenter. In one condition the experimenter sat just a few feet away from the subject. In a second condition, after giving initial instructions, the experimenter left the laboratory and gave his orders by telephone. In still a third condition the experimenter was never seen, providing instructions by means of a tape recording activated when the subjects entered the laboratory.

Obedience dropped sharply as the experimenter was physically 33 removed from the laboratory. The number of obedient subjects in the first condition (Experimenter Present) was almost three times as great as in the second, where the experimenter gave his orders by telephone. Twenty-six subjects were fully obedient in the first condition, and only nine in the second (Chi square obedient *vs.* defiant in the two conditions, df $= 14.7$; $p < 0.001$). Subjects seemed able to take a far stronger stand against the experimenter when they did not have to encounter him face to face, and the experimenter's power over the subject was severely curtailed.[8]

Moreover, when the experimenter was absent, subjects displayed 34 an interesting form of behavior that had not occurred under his surveillance. Though continuing with the experiment, several subjects administered lower shocks than were required and never informed the experimenter of their deviation from the correct procedure. (Unknown to the subjects, shock levels were automatically recorded by an Esterline-Angus event recorder wired directly into the shock generator; the instrument provided us with an objective record of the subjects' performance.) Indeed, in telephone conversations some subjects specifically assured the experimenter that they were raising the shock level according to instruction, whereas in fact they were repeatedly using the lowest shock on the board. This form of behavior is particularly interesting: although these subjects acted in a way that clearly undermined the avowed purposes of the experiment, they found it easier to handle the conflict in this manner than to precipitate an open break with authority.

Other conditions were completed in which the experimenter was 35 absent during the first segment of the experiment, but reappeared at the point that the subject definitely refused to give higher shocks when commanded by telephone. Although he had exhausted his power via telephone, the experimenter could frequently force further obedience when he reappeared in the laboratory.

Experiments in this series show that the *physical presence* of an       36
authority is an important force contributing to the subject's obedience
or defiance. Taken together with the first experimental series on the
proximity of the victim, it would appear that something akin to fields
of force, diminishing in effectiveness with increasing psychological
distance from their source, have a controlling effect on the subject's
performance. As the victim is brought closer, the subject finds it harder
to administer shocks to him. When the victim's position is held constant
relative to the subject, and the authority is made more remote, the
subject finds it easier to break off the experiment. This effect is substantial in both cases, but manipulation of the experimenter's position
yielded the more powerful results. Obedience to destructive commands is highly dependent on the proximal relations between authority and subject.

## Tensions

The description of final scores does not fully convey the character       37
of the subjects' performance, and it would be useful to interrupt our
reporting of quantitative relationships to remark on the subjects' general reaction to the situation.

One might suppose that a subject would simply break off or con-       38
tinue as his conscience and temperament dictated. Yet this is very far
from what happened. There were powerful reactions of tension and
emotional strain in a substantial proportion of the participants. Persons
were observed to sweat, tremble, stutter, bite their lips, and groan as
they found themselves increasingly implicated in the experimental
conflict. Some sense of the subjects' mood can be found in a transcript
of their remarks at break-off point. Here are the remarks of two defiant
subjects:

Is he banging? . . . Is he hurt out there? Well, I don't want to be responsible
for anything that happens to him. No, I can't go on with it. I don't know
whether he's all right or not. I mean he may have a heart condition or something; I wouldn't feel right doing it. He's banging for help. He's evidently in
trouble or he wouldn't bang . . . I don't see any sense to this—to knocking him
out or something. I just can't see it.

[*Subject refuses to administer shocks*]                    [*Subject 0108*]

The man is banging. He wants to get out . . . I'm sorry. If the man wants to
get out I'd just as soon stop . . . I don't want to administer any more [extremely

excited] . . . I will gladly refund the check, but I will not harm this man
. . . I'm sorry, I will not give him any more if he obviously wants to get out.
There is no money in the world that will make me hurt another individual.

[*Subject 010X*]

And here is a transcript from an obedient subject. He began the    39
experiment calmly, but became increasingly tense as the experiment
proceeded. After administering the 150-volt shock, he began to address
the experimenter in agitated tones:

*150 volts delivered.* You want me to keep going?
*165 volts delivered.* That guy is hollering in there. There's a lot of them here.
He's liable to have heart condition. You want me to go?
*180 volts delivered.* He can't stand it! I'm not going to kill that man in there!
You hear him hollering? He's hollering. He can't stand it. What if something
happens to him? . . . I'm not going to get that man sick in there. He's hollering
in there. You know what I mean? I mean I refuse to take responsibility. He's
getting hurt in there. He's in there hollering. Too many left here. Geez, if he
gets them wrong. There's too many of them left. I mean who is going to take
responsibility if anything happens to that gentleman?
[*The experimenter accepts responsibility.*] All right.
*195 volts delivered.* You see he's hollering. Hear that. Gee, I don't know.
[*The experimenter says: "The experiment requires that you go on."*]—I know
it does, sir, but I mean—hugh—he don't know what he's in for. He's up to 195
volts.
*210 volts delivered.*
*225 volts delivered.*
*240 volts delivered.* Aw, no. You mean I've got to keep going up with the scale?
No sir. I'm not going to kill that man! I'm not going to give him 450 volts!
[*The experimenter says: "The experiment requires that you go on."*]—I know
it does, but that man is hollering there, sir . . .

Despite his numerous, agitated objections, which were constant ac-
companiments to his actions, the subject unfailingly obeyed the experimenter, proceeding to the highest shock level on the generator. He
displayed a curious dissociation between word and action. Although at
the verbal level he had resolved not to go on, his actions were fully in
accord with the experimenter's commands. This subject did not want
to shock the victim, and he found it an extremely disagreeable task, but
he was unable to invent a response that would free him from *E's*
authority. Many subjects cannot find the specific verbal formula that
would enable them to reject the role assigned to them by the experimenter. Perhaps our culture does not provide adequate models for
disobedience.

One puzzling sign of tension was the regular occurrence of nervous    40
laughing fits. In the first four conditions 71 of the 160 subjects showed
definite signs of nervous laughter and smiling. The laughter seemed
entirely out of place, even bizarre. Full-blown, uncontrollable seizures
were observed for 15 of these subjects. On one occasion we observed
a seizure so violently convulsive that it was necessary to call a halt to
the experiment. In the post-experimental interviews subjects took
pains to point out that they were not sadistic types and that the laughter did not mean they enjoyed shocking the victim.

In the interview following the experiment subjects were asked to    41
indicate on a 14-point scale just how nervous or tense they felt at the
point of maximum tension (Figure 2). The scale ranged from "not at all
tense and nervous" to "extremely tense and nervous." Self-reports of

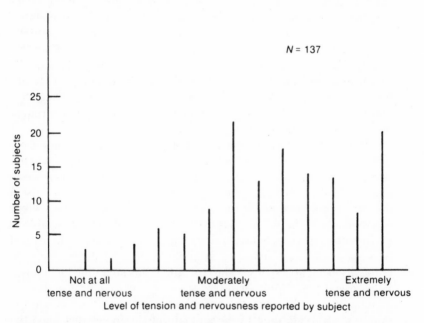

**FIGURE 2.**    Level of tension and nervousness: the self-reports on "tension
and nervousness" for 137 subjects in the Proximity experiments. Subjects were
given a scale with 14 values ranging from "not at all tense and nervous" to
"extremely tense and nervous." They were instructed: "Thinking back to that
point in the experiment when you felt the most tense and nervous, indicate just
how you felt by placing an X at the appropriate point on the scale." The results
are shown in terms of midpoint values.

this sort are of limited precision and at best provide only a rough indication of the subject's emotional response. Still, taking the reports for what they are worth, it can be seen that the distribution of responses spans the entire range of the scale, with the majority of subjects concentrated at the center and upper extreme. A further breakdown showed that obedient subjects reported themselves as having been slightly more tense and nervous than the defiant subjects at the point of maximum tension.

How is the occurrence of tension to be interpreted? First, it    42
points to the presence of conflict. If a tendency to comply with authority were the only psychological force operating in the situation, all subjects would have continued to the end and there would have been no tension. Tension, it is assumed, results from the simultaneous presence of two or more incompatible response tendencies (Miller, 1944). If sympathetic concern for the victim were the exclusive force, all subjects would have calmly defied the experimenter. Instead, there were both obedient and defiant outcomes, frequently accompanied by extreme tension. A conflict develops between the deeply ingrained disposition not to harm others and the equally compelling tendency to obey others who are in authority. The subject is quickly drawn into a dilemma of a deeply dynamic character, and the presence of high tension points to the considerable strength of each of the antagonistic vectors.

Moreover, tension defines the strength of the aversive state from    43
which the subject is unable to escape through disobedience. When a person is uncomfortable, tense, or stressed, he tries to take some action that will allow him to terminate this unpleasant state. Thus tension may serve as a drive that leads to escape behavior. But in the present situation, even where tension is extreme, many subjects are unable to perform the response that will bring about relief. Therefore there must be a competing drive, tendency, or inhibition that precludes activation of the disobedient response. The strength of this inhibiting factor must be of greater magnitude than the stress experienced, or else the terminating act would occur. Every evidence of extreme tension is at the same time an indication of the strength of the forces that keep the subject in the situation.

Finally, tension may be taken as evidence of the reality of the    44
situations for the subjects. Normal subjects do not tremble and sweat unless they are implicated in a deep and genuinely felt predicament.

## Background Authority

In psychophysics, animal learning, and other branches of psychol-    45
ogy, the fact that measures are obtained at one institution rather than
another is irrelevant to the interpretation of the findings, so long as the
technical facilities for measurement are adequate and the operations
are carried out with competence.

But it cannot be assumed that this holds true for the present study.    46
The effectiveness of the experimenter's commands may depend in an
important way on the larger institutional context in which they are
issued. The experiments described thus far were conducted at Yale
University, an organization which most subjects regarded with respect
and sometimes awe. In post-experimental interviews several participants remarked that the locale and sponsorship of the study gave them
confidence in the integrity, competence, and benign purposes of the
personnel; many indicated that they would not have shocked the
learner if the experiments had been done elsewhere.

This issue of background authority seemed to us important for an    47
interpretation of the results that had been obtained thus far; moreover
it is highly relevant to any comprehensive theory of human obedience.
Consider, for example, how closely our compliance with the imperatives of others is tied to particular institutions and locales in our day-to-
day activities. On request, we expose our throats to a man with a razor
blade in the barber shop, but would not do so in a shoe store; in the
latter setting we willingly follow the clerk's request to stand in our
stockinged feet, but resist the command in a bank. In the laboratory of
a great university, subjects may comply with a set of commands that
would be resisted if given elsewhere. *One must always question the
relationship of obedience to a person's sense of the context in which he
is operating.*

To explore the problem we moved our apparatus to an office    48
building in industrial Bridgeport and replicated experimental conditions, without any visible tie to the university.

Bridgeport subjects were invited to the experiment through a mail    49
circular similar to the one used in the Yale study, with appropriate
changes in letterhead, etc. As in the earlier study, subjects were paid
$4.50 for coming to the laboratory. The same age and occupational
distributions used at Yale and the identical personnel were employed.

The purpose in relocating in Bridgeport was to assure a complete    50
dissociation from Yale, and in this regard we were fully successful. On

the surface, the study appeared to be conducted by Research Associates of Bridgeport, an organization of unknown character (the title had been concocted exclusively for use in this study).

The experiments were conducted in a three-room office suite in a   51
somewhat run-down commercial building located in the downtown shopping area. The laboratory was sparsely furnished, though clean, and marginally respectable in appearance. When subjects inquired about professional affiliations, they were informed only that we were a private firm conducting research for industry.

Some subjects displayed skepticism concerning the motives of the   52
Bridgeport experimenter. One gentleman gave us a written account of the thoughts he experienced at the control board:

. . . Should I quit this damn test? Maybe he passed out? What dopes we were not to check up on this deal. How do we know that these guys are legit? No furniture, bare walls, no telephone. We could of called the Police up or the Better Business Bureau. I learned a lesson tonight. How do I know that Mr. Williams [the experimenter] is telling the truth . . . I wish I knew how many volts a person could take before lapsing into unconsciousness. [*Subject 2414*]

Another subject stated:

I questioned on my arrival my own judgment [about coming]. I had doubts as to the legitimacy of the operation and the consequences of participation. I felt it was a heartless way to conduct memory or learning processes on human beings and certainly dangerous without the presence of a medical doctor.

[*Subject 2440V*]

There was no noticeable reduction in tension for the Bridgeport   53
subjects. And the subjects' estimation of the amount of pain felt by the victim was slightly, though not significantly, higher than in the Yale study.

A failure to obtain complete obedience in Bridgeport would indi-   54
cate that the extreme compliance found in New Haven subjects was tied closely to the background authority of Yale University; if a large proportion of the subjects remained fully obedient, very different conclusions would be called for.

As it turned out, the level of obedience in Bridgeport, although   55
somewhat reduced, was not significantly lower than that obtained at Yale. A large proportion of the Bridgeport subjects were fully obedient to the experimenter's commands (48 percent of the Bridgeport subjects delivered the maximum shock versus 65 percent in the corresponding condition at Yale).

How are these findings to be interpreted? It is possible that if 56 commands of a potentially harmful or destructive sort are to be perceived as legitimate they must occur within some sort of institutional structure. But it is clear from the study that it need not be a particularly reputable or distinguished institution. The Bridgeport experiments were conducted by an unimpressive firm lacking any credentials; the laboratory was set up in a respectable office building with title listed in the building directory. Beyond that, there was no evidence of benevolence or competence. It is possible that the *category* of institution, judged according to its professed function, rather than its qualitative position within that category, wins our compliance. Persons deposit money in elegant, but also in seedy-looking banks, without giving much thought to the differences in security they offer. Similarly, our subjects may consider one laboratory to be as competent as another, so long as it is a scientific laboratory.

It would be valuable to study the subjects' performance in other 57 contexts which go even further than the Bridgeport study in denying institutional support to the experimenter. It is possible that, beyond a certain point, obedience disappears completely. But that point had not been reached in the Bridgeport office: almost half the subjects obeyed the experimenter fully.

## Further Experiments

We may mention briefly some additional experiments undertaken 58 in the Yale series. A considerable amount of obedience and defiance in everyday life occurs in connection with groups. And we had reason to feel in light of the many group studies already done in psychology that group forces would have a profound effect on reactions to authority. A series of experiments was run to examine these effects. In all cases only one naïve subject was studied per hour, but he performed in the midst of actors who, unknown to him, were employed by the experimenter. In one experiment (Groups for Disobedience) two actors broke off in the middle of the experiment. When this happened 90 percent of the subjects followed suit and defied the experimenter. In another condition the actors followed the orders obediently; this strengthened the experimenter's power only slightly. In still a third experiment the job of pushing the switch to shock the learner was given to one of the actors, while the naïve subject performed a subsidiary act. We wanted to see how the teacher would respond if he were involved in the situation but did not actually give the shocks. In this situation only three subjects out of forty broke off. In a final group experiment the subjects themselves determined the shock level they were going to use. Two actors suggested higher and higher shock levels; some subjects insisted, despite group pressure, that the shock level be kept low; others followed along with the group.

Further experiments were completed using women as subjects, 59 as well as a set dealing with the effects of dual, unsanctioned, and conflicting authority. A final experiment concerned the personal relationship between victim and subject. These will have to be described elsewhere, lest the present report be extended to monographic length.

It goes without saying that future research can proceed in many 60 different directions. What kinds of response from the victim are most effective in causing disobedience in the subject? Perhaps passive resistance is more effective than vehement protest. What conditions of entry into an authority system lead to greater or lesser obedience? What is the effect of anonymity and masking on the subject's behavior? What conditions lead to the subject's perception of responsibility for his own actions? Each of these could be a major research topic in itself, and can readily be incorporated into the general experimental procedure described here.

## Levels of Obedience and Defiance

One general finding that merits attention is the high level of obedi- 61 ence manifested in the experimental situation. Subjects often expressed deep disapproval of shocking a man in the face of his objections, and others denounced it as senseless and stupid. Yet many subjects complied even while they protested. The proportion of obedient subjects greatly exceeded the expectations of the experimenter and his colleagues. At the outset, we had conjectured that subjects would not, in general, go above the level of "Strong Shock." In practice, many subjects were willing to administer the most extreme shocks available when commanded by the experimenter. For some subjects the experiment provided an occasion for aggressive release. And for others it demonstrated the extent to which obedient dispositions are deeply ingrained and engaged, irrespective of their consequences for others. Yet this is not the whole story. Somehow, the subject becomes implicated in a situation from which he cannot disengage himself.

The departure of the experimental results from intelligent expec-    62
tation, to some extent, has been formalized. The procedure was to
describe the experimental situation in concrete detail to a group of
competent persons, and to ask them to predict the performance of 100
hypothetical subjects. For purposes of indicating the distribution of
break-off points, judges were provided with a diagram of the shock
generator and recorded their predictions before being informed of the
actual results. Judges typically underestimated the amount of obedience demonstrated by subjects.

In Figure 3, we compare the predictions of forty psychiatrists at a    63
leading medical school with the actual performance of subjects in the
experiment. The psychiatrists predicted that most subjects would not
go beyond the tenth shock level (150 volts; at this point the victim
makes his first explicit demand to be freed). They further predicted
that by the twentieth shock level (300 volts; the victim refuses to

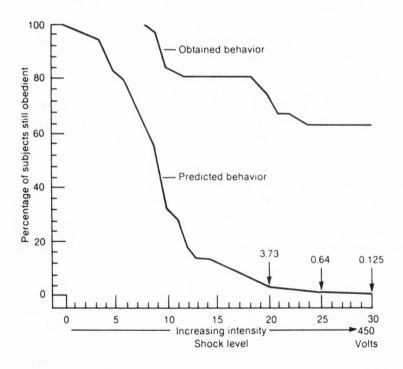

**FIGURE 3.**    Predicted and obtained behavior in voice feedback.

answer) 3.73 percent of the subjects would still be obedient; and that only a little over one-tenth of one percent of the subjects would administer the highest shock on the board. But, as the graph indicates, the obtained behavior was very different. Sixty-two percent of the subjects obeyed the experimenter's commands fully. Between expectation and occurrence there is a whopping discrepancy.

Why did the psychiatrists underestimate the level of obedience? 64 Possibly, because their predictions were based on an inadequate conception of the determinants of human action, a conception that focuses on motives in *vacuo*. This orientation may be entirely adequate for the repair of bruised impulses as revealed on the psychiatrist's couch, but as soon as our interest turns to action in larger settings, attention must be paid to the situations in which motives are expressed. A situation exerts an important press on the individual. It exercises constraints and may provide push. In certain circumstances it is not so much the kind of person a man is, as the kind of situation in which he is placed, that determines his actions.

Many people, not knowing much about the experiment, claim that 65 subjects who go to the end of the board are sadistic. Nothing could be more foolish than an overall characterization of these persons. It is like saying that a person thrown into a swift-flowing stream is necessarily a fast swimmer, or that he has great stamina because he moves so rapidly relative to the bank. The context of action must always be considered. The individual, upon entering the laboratory, becomes integrated into a situation that carries its own momentum. The subject's problem then is how to become disengaged from a situation which is moving in an altogether ugly direction.

The fact that disengagement is so difficult testifies to the po- 66 tency of the forces that keep the subject at the control board. Are these forces to be conceptualized as individual motives and expressed in the language of personality dynamics, or are they to be seen as the effects of social structure and pressures arising from the situational field?

A full understanding of the subject's action will, I feel, require that 67 both perspectives be adopted. The person brings to the laboratory enduring dispositions toward authority and aggression, and at the same time he becomes enmeshed in a social structure that is no less an objective fact of the case. From the standpoint of personality theory one may ask: What mechanisms of personality enable a person to transfer responsibility to authority? What are the motives underlying obedient and disobedient performance? Does orientation to authority lead to a short-circuiting of the shame-guilt system? What cognitive and emotional defenses are brought into play in the case of obedient and defiant subjects?

The present experiments are not however, directed toward an      68
exploration of the motives engaged when the subject obeys the experimenter's commands. Instead, they examine the situational variables responsible for the elicitation of obedience. Elsewhere, we have attempted to spell out some of the structural properties of the experimental situation that account for high obedience, and this analysis need not be repeated here (Milgram, 1963). The experimental variations themselves represent our attempt to probe that structure, by systematically changing it and noting the consequences for behavior. It is clear that some situations produce greater compliance with the experimenter's commands than others. However, this does not necessarily imply an increase or decrease in the strength of any single definable motive. Situations producing the greatest obedience could do so by triggering the most powerful, yet perhaps the most idiosyncratic, of motives in each subject confronted by the setting. Or they may simply recruit a greater number and variety of motives in their service. But whatever the motives involved—and it is far from certain that they can ever be known—action may be studied as a direct function of the situation in which it occurs. This has been the approach of the present study, where we sought to plot behavioral regularities against manipulated properties of the social field. Ultimately, social psychology would like to have a compelling *theory of situations* which will, first, present a language in terms of which situations can be defined; proceed to a typology of situations; and then point to the manner in which definable properties of situations are transformed into psychological forces in the individual.[9]

## Postscript

Almost a thousand adults were individually studied in the obedi-      69
ence research, and there were many specific conclusions regarding the variables that control obedience and disobedience to authority. Some of these have been discussed briefly in the preceding sections, and more detailed reports will be released subsequently.

There are now some other generalizations I should like to make,      70
which do not derive in any strictly logical fashion from the experiments

as carried out, but which, I feel, ought to be made. They are formulations of an intuitive sort that have been forced on me by observation
of many subjects responding to the pressures of authority. The assertions represent a painful alteration in my own thinking; and since they
were acquired only under the repeated impact of direct observation, I
have no illusion that they will be generally accepted by persons who
have not had the same experience.

With numbing regularity good people were seen to knuckle under      71
the demands of authority and perform actions that were callous and
severe. Men who are in everyday life responsible and decent were
seduced by the trappings of authority, by the control of their perceptions, and by the uncritical acceptance of the experimenter's definition
of the situation, into performing harsh acts.

What is the limit of such obedience? At many points we attempted     72
to establish a boundary. Cries from the victim were inserted; not good
enough. The victim claimed heart trouble; subjects still shocked him on
command. The victim pleaded that he be let free, and his answers no
longer registered on the signal box; subjects continued to shock him. At
the outset we had not conceived that such drastic procedures would be
needed to generate disobedience, and each step was added only as the
ineffectiveness of the earlier techniques became clear. The final effort
to establish a limit was the Touch-Proximity condition. But the very
first subject in this condition subdued the victim on command, and
proceeded to the highest shock level. A quarter of the subjects in this
condition performed similarly.

The results, as seen and felt in the laboratory, are to this author      73
disturbing. They raise the possibility that human nature or, more specifically, the kind of character produced in American democratic society cannot be counted on to insulate its citizens from brutality and
inhumane treatment at the direction of malevolent authority. A substantial proportion of people do what they are told to do, irrespective
of the content of the act and without limitations of conscience, so long
as they perceive that the command comes from a legitimate authority.
If in this study an anonymous experimenter could successfully command adults to subdue a fifty-year-old man and force on him painful
electric shocks against his protests, one can only wonder what government, with its vastly greater authority and prestige, can command of
its subjects. There is, of course, the extremely important question of
whether malevolent political institutions could or would arise in American society. The present research contributes nothing to this issue.

In an article titled "The Danger of Obedience," Harold J. Laski    74
wrote:

... civilization means, above all, an unwillingness to inflict unnecessary pain. Within the ambit of that definition, those of us who heedlessly accept the commands of authority cannot yet claim to be civilized men.

... Our business, if we desire to live a life, not utterly devoid of meaning and significance, is to accept nothing which contradicts our basic experience merely because it comes to us from tradition or convention or authority. It may well be that we shall be wrong; but our self-expression is thwarted at the root unless the certainties we are asked to accept coincide with the certainties we experience. That is why the condition of freedom in any state is always a widespread and consistent skepticism of the canons upon which power insists.

## Notes

1. This research was supported by two grants from the National Science Foundation: NSF G–17916 and NSF G–24152. Exploratory studies carried out in 1960 were financed by a grant from the Higgins Funds of Yale University. I am grateful to John T. Williams, James J. McDonough, and Emil Elges for the important part they played in the project. Thanks are due also to Alan Elms, James Miller, Taketo Murata, and Stephen Stier for their aid as graduate assistants. My wife, Sasha, performed many valuable services. Finally, I owe a profound debt to the many persons in New Haven and Bridgeport who served as subjects.
2. Consider, for example, J. P. Scott's analysis of war in his monograph on aggression:
   ". . . while the actions of key individuals in a war may be explained in terms of direct stimulation to aggression, vast numbers of other people are involved simply by being part of an organized society.
   . . . For example, at the beginning of World War I an Austrian archduke was assassinated in Sarajevo. A few days later soldiers from all over Europe were marching toward each other, not because they were stimulated by the archduke's misfortune, but because they had been trained to obey orders." (Slightly rearranged from Scott [1958], *Aggression*, p. 103.)
3. It consisted of an extended discussion with the experimenter and, of equal importance, a friendly reconciliation with the victim. It is made clear that the victim did *not* receive painful electric shocks. After the completion of the experimental series, subjects were sent a detailed report of the results and full purposes of the experimental program. A formal assessment of this procedure points to its overall effectiveness. Of the subjects, 83.7 percent indicated that they were glad to have taken part in the study; 15.1 percent reported neutral feelings; and 1.3 percent stated that they were sorry to have participated. A large number of subjects spontaneously requested that they be used in further experimentation. Four-fifths of the subjects felt that more experiments of this sort should be carried out, and 74 percent indicated that they had learned something of personal importance as a result of being in the study. Furthermore, a university psychiatrist, experienced in outpatient treatment, interviewed a sample of experimental subjects with the aim of uncovering possible injurious effects

resulting from participation. No such effects were in evidence. Indeed, subjects typically felt that their participation was instructive and enriching. A more detailed discussion of this question can be found in Milgram (1964).

4. To *obey* and to *disobey* are not the only terms one could use in describing the critical action of Y. One could say that Y is cooperating with X, or displays conformity with regard to X's commands. However, *cooperation* suggests that X agrees with Y's ends, and understands the relationship between his own behavior and the attainment of those ends. (But the experimental procedure, and, in particular, the experimenter's command that the subject shock the victim even in the absence of a response from the victim, preclude such understanding.) Moreover, cooperation implies status parity for the co-acting agents, and neglects the asymmetrical, dominance-subordination element prominent in the laboratory relationship between experimenter and subject. *Conformity* has been used in other important contexts in social psychology, and most frequently refers to imitating the judgments or actions of others when no explicit requirement for imitation has been made. Furthermore, in the present study there are two sources of social pressure; pressure from the experimenter issuing the commands, and pressure from the victim to stop the punishment. It is the pitting of a common man (the victim) against an authority (the experimenter) that is the distinctive feature of the conflict. At a point in the experiment the victim demands that he be let free. The experimenter insists that the subject continue to administer shocks. Which act of the subject can be interpreted as conformity? The subject may conform to the wishes of his peer or to the wishes of the experimenter, and conformity in one direction means the absence of conformity in the other. Thus the word has no useful reference in this setting, for the dual and conflicting social pressures cancel out its meaning.

   In the final analysis, the linguistic symbol representing the subject's action must take its meaning from the concrete context in which that action occurs; and there is probably no word in everyday language that covers the experimental situation exactly, without omissions or irrelevant connotations. It is partly for convenience, therefore, that the terms *obey* and *disobey* are used to describe the subject's actions. At the same time, our use of the words is highly congruent with dictionary meaning.

5. A more detailed account of the laboratory procedure can be found in Milgram (1963). A similar and independently evolved experimental procedure, employing a shock generator, victim, and learning task, was reported by Buss (1961). Buss used the technique for studying aggression, not obedience, and did not make use of the fundamental measure employed in the present study: breakoff points.

6. It is difficult to convey on the printed page the full tenor of the victim's responses, for we have no adequate notation for vocal intensity, timing, and general qualities of delivery. Yet these features are crucial to producing the effect of an increasingly severe reaction to mounting voltage levels. (They can be communicated fully only by sending interested parties the recorded tapes.) In general terms, however, the victim indicates no discomfort until the 75-volt shock is administered, at which time there is a light grunt in response to the punishment. Similar reactions follow the 90- and 105-volt shocks, and at 120 volts the victim shouts to the experimenter that the shocks are becoming painful. Painful groans are heard on administration of the 135-volt shock, and at 150 volts the victim cries out, "Experimenter, get me out of here! I won't be in the experiment any more! I refuse to go on!" Cries of this type continue with generally rising intensity, so that at 180 volts the victim cries out, "I can't stand the pain," and by 270 volts his response to the shock is definitely an agonized scream.

Throughout, he insists that he be let out of the experiment. At 300 volts the victim shouts in desperation that he will no longer provide answers to the memory test; and at 315 volts, after a violent scream, he reaffirms with vehemence that he is no longer a participant. From this point on, he provides no answers, but shrieks in agony whenever a shock is administered; this continues through 450 volts. Of course, many subjects will have broken off before this point.

A revised and stronger set of protests was used in all experiments outside the Proximity series. Naturally, new baseline measures were established for all comparisons using the new set of protests.

There is overwhelming evidence that the great majority of subjects, both obedient and defiant, accepted the victims' reactions as genuine. The evidence takes the form of: (a) tension created in the subjects (see discussion of tension); (b) scores on "estimated-pain" scales filled out by the subjects immediately after the experiment; (c) subjects' accounts of their feelings in post-experimental interviews; and (d) quantifiable responses to questionnaires distributed to subjects several months after their participation in the experiments. This matter will be treated fully in a forthcoming monograph.

(The procedure in all experimental conditions was to have the naïve subject announce the voltage level before administering each shock, so that—independently of the victim's responses—he was continually reminded of delivering punishment of ever-increasing severity.)

7. Admittedly, the terms *proximity, immediacy, closeness,* and *salience-of-the-victim* are used in a loose sense, and the experiments themselves represent a very coarse treatment of the variable. Further experiments are needed to refine the notion and tease out such diverse factors as spatial distance, visibility, audibility, barrier interposition, etc.

The Proximity and Touch-Proximity experiments were the only conditions where we were unable to use taped feedback from the victim. Instead, the victim was trained to respond in these conditions as he had in Experiment 2 (which employed taped feedback). Some improvement is possible here, for it should be technically feasible to do a proximity series using taped feedback.

8. The third condition also led to significantly lower obedience than this first situation in which the experimenter was present, but it contains technical difficulties that require extensive discussion.

9. My thanks to Professor Howard Leventhal of Yale for strengthening the writing in this paragraph.

### References

Buss, Arnold 1961. *The Psychology of Aggression.* New York and London: John Wiley.
Kierkegaard, S. 1843. *Fear and Trembling.* English edition, Princeton: Princeton University Press, 1941.
Laski, Harold J. 1929. "The dangers of obedience." *Harper's Monthly Magazine,* 15 June 1–10.
Miligram, S. 1961. "Dynamics of obedience: experiments in social psychology." Mimeographed report, *National Science Foundation,* January 25.
—— 1963. "Behavioral study of obedience." *J. Abnorm. Soc. Psychol.* 67, 371–378.

——1964. "Issues in the study of obedience: a reply to Baumrind." *Amer. Psychol.* 1.
     848–852.
Miller, N. E. 1944. "Experimental studies of conflict." In J. McV. Hunt (ed.), *Personality
     and the Behavior Disorders.* New York: Ronald Press.
Scott, J. P. 1958. *Aggression.* Chicago: University of Chicago Press.

---

# Good as Guilt

## JUDITH VIORST

*Without guilt
What is man? An animal, isn't he?
A wolf forgiven at his meat,
A beetle innocent in his copulation.*

—Archibald MacLeish

Anything *isn't* possible, the realities of love and our bodies per- 1
suade us. We aren't unbounded, and never will be free of the limits
imposed upon us by the forbidden and the impossible—including the
limits imposed upon us by guilt.

For whether or not we humans are the only creatures capable of 2
guilt, we undoubtedly do it better than beetles or wolves. And although our guilty feelings haven't put an end to the Seven Deadly Sins
or persuaded us to obey all Ten Commandments, they have without
question slowed us down considerably.

Nevertheless we must recognize that while guilt deprives us of 3
numerous gratifications, we and our world would be monstrous minus
guilt. For the freedoms we lose, our constraints and taboos, are necessary losses—part of the price we pay for civilization.

Our guilt becomes our own when, at around the age of five, we 4
begin to develop a superego, a conscience, when the "No, you can'ts"
and the "Shame on you's" which used to be outside us regroup as our
internal critical voice. Our guilt becomes our own when instead of
feeling, "Better not do it; they will not like it," that "they" is no longer
our mother and father but—us.

For we do not arrive in this world with a commitment to certain 5
admirable moral precepts. We are not born intending to be good. We

want, we want, we want, and only slowly relinquish reaching out and grabbing. But control cannot be called conscience until we are able to take it inside us and make it our own, until—in spite of the fact that the wrongs we have done or imagined will never be punished or known—we nonetheless feel that clutch in the stomach, that chill upon the soul, that self-inflicted misery called guilt.

True guilt, it can be argued, is not the fear of our parents' wrath 6 or the loss of their love. True guilt, it can be argued, is the fear of our *conscience's* wrath, the loss of *its* love.

We resolve our oedipal conflicts by acquiring a conscience which— 7 like our parents—limits and restrains. Our conscience is our parents installed in our mind. Later identifications, with teachers and preachers, with friends, with superstars and heroes, will modify what we value and what we forbid. And the emergence, over the years, of increasingly complex cognitive skills, will ready the ground for more complex moral ideas. Indeed, it is now believed that the stages of our moral reasoning (psychologist Lawrence Kohlberg says there are six) parallel the development of our thinking processes. But although our conscience is based on emotion *and* thought, and although it evolves and changes over time, and although it is built upon feelings from earlier stages, and although it expands beyond oedipal issues to take in all kinds of conflicts and concerns, this superego, this part of our self that contains our moral restraints and our ideals, is born of our primal struggles with lawless passions, is born of our *inner* submission to human law.

And if we breach those moral restraints or abandon those ideals, 8 our conscience will observe, reproach, condemn.

And if we breach those moral restraints or abandon those ideals, 9 our conscience will arrange to make us feel guilty.

There is, however, good and bad, appropriate and inappropriate 10 guilt. There is deficient guilt and also excessive guilt. A few of us may know people who lack the capacity to have feelings of guilt about anything. But most of us know people (and a number of us *are* people) who are able to muster up guilt about virtually everything.

I am one of those people. 11

I feel guilty whenever my children are unhappy. 12

I feel guilty whenever one of my houseplants dies. 13

I feel guilty whenever I fail to floss after eating. 14

I feel guilty whenever I tell the whitest of lies. 15

I feel guilty whenever I step on a bug deliberately—all cock-          16
roaches excepted.

I feel guilty whenever I cook with a pat of butter that I have          17
dropped on the kitchen floor.

And because, if there were room, I could easily list several hun-          18
dred more of such genuinely guilt-provoking items, I would say that I
am suffering from an excessive, indiscriminate sense of guilt.

Indiscriminate guilt is also the failure to distinguish between for-          19
bidden thoughts and forbidden deeds. Thus wicked wishes equal
wicked acts. And although we adults believe that we have long ago
learned to tell the two apart, our conscience may cruelly condemn us
not just for the murder we carry out but for the murder that we harbor
in our heart. And although we very well know that wishing does not
make it so, it nevertheless may make us feel very guilty.

This lack of discrimination is one of the ways that we display          20
excessive guilt. Disproportionate punitiveness is another. For guilty
acts which require no more than a gentle "I'm sorry," a mental slap on
the wrist, may inspire astonishing acts of self-flagellation: "I did it,
how could I do it, only a low-down no-good moral monster could do it,
and I hereby sentence this criminal—me—to death." This excessive
punishing guilt is somewhat like pouring a whole cup of salt on an
egg-salad sandwich. No one is disputing that perhaps the sandwich
needs salt but—*not that much.*

Another form of excess might be called omnipotent guilt, which          21
rests on the illusion of control—the illusion, for example, that we have
absolute power over our loved ones' well-being. And so, if they suffer
or fail or fall ill in body or in mind, we have no doubt that we alone are
to blame, that had we done it differently, or had we done it better, we
surely would have been able to prevent it.

A rabbi, for instance, tells of paying condolence calls—one win-          22
ter afternoon—on two different families where elderly women had
died.

At the first house, the bereaved son told the rabbi: "If only I had          23
sent my mother to Florida and gotten her out of this cold and snow, she
would be alive today. It's my fault that she died."

At the second house, the other bereaved son told the rabbi: "If          24
only I hadn't insisted on my mother's going to Florida, she would be
alive today. That long airplane ride, the abrupt change of climate, was
more than she could take. It's my fault that she's dead."

The point here is this: By blaming ourself, we can believe in our          25 life-controlling powers. By blaming ourself, we are saying that we would rather feel guilty than helpless, than not in control.

Others may have a need to believe that Someone Up There has    26
control, that terrible things do not happen without a cause, that if they are struck by tragedy and devastating loss, they are struck because in some way they deserve it. There are those who cannot accept the thought that suffering is random or that evil men prosper and sorrows befall the good. And so they add to their suffering the conviction that they suffer because they should, that their pain is sufficient proof that they are guilty.

A woman whose child had been desperately ill once described to    27
me an astonishing conversation she'd had with God, a God in whom, by the way, she had most earnestly proclaimed she did not believe. "You ought to be ashamed of yourself. You really should," she reproached Him. "What a bully you turned out to be. If you want to punish a disbeliever, punish the disbeliever—not her child. Stop picking on my daughter! Pick on me!"

Analyst Selma Fraiberg writes that a healthy conscience produces    28
guilt feelings commensurate with the act and that guilt feelings serve to prevent our repeating such acts. "But the neurotic conscience," she writes, "behaves like a gestapo headquarters within the personality, mercilessly tracking down dangerous or potentially dangerous ideas and every remote relative of these ideas, accusing, threatening, tormenting in an interminable inquisition to establish guilt for trivial offenses or crimes committed in dreams. Such guilt feelings have the effect of putting the whole personality under arrest. . . ."

Such feelings are excessive, neurotic guilt.    29

Neurotic guilt may be fed by the events of pre-oedipal years—by    30
the anxiety and anger evoked by early separations or struggles with parents. Thus, for instance, our conscience may exercise an I-was-left-because-I-was-bad-and-therefore-I-deserve-to-be-punished punitiveness. Or it may harshly condemn the parts of ourself that our parents—whose love we so deeply feared losing—condemned. Or it may carry a great load of anger once directed against our mother and our father and now vigorously redirected against ourself. As one psychoanalyst told me, "I think, in general, that anything that leaves the child on his own to grapple with anxiety and rage will predispose him to play it all out on a repetitive inner stage—to get stuck with inappropriate levels and kinds of guilt as an adult."

Such guilt may make us feel that if we ever kiss a fellow, we'll grow    31
hair on our teeth. And if we ever talk back to our mother, we'll give
her a heart attack. And if we decide to do what we are desperately
longing to do—and it is wonderful—we shouldn't be doing it.

And sometimes, alas, like Dr. Spielvogel's frantic, fictional patient    32
Alexander Portnoy—we *cannot* do it:

Can't smoke, hardly drink, no drugs, don't borrow money or play cards, can't
tell a lie without beginning to sweat as though I'm passing over the equator.
Sure, I say *fuck* a lot, but I assure you, that's about the sum of my success with
transgressing. . . . Why is a little turbulence so beyond my means? Why must
the least deviation from respectable conventions cause me such inner hell?
When I *hate* those fucking conventions? When I know *better* than the taboos!
Doctor, my doctor, what do you say, LET'S PUT THE ID BACK IN YID!
Liberate this nice Jewish boy's libido, will you please? Raise the prices if you
have to—I'll pay anything! Only enough cowering in the face of the deep, dark
pleasures!

Not everyone is as acutely aware as Portnoy, or his creator, Philip    33
Roth, of the moral inhibitions with which we live. We may consciously
feel we are freer than we are. For an important aspect of guilt is that
it frequently works upon us without our knowing about it, that we can
suffer the consequences of unconscious guilt.

Now we know what our conscious guilt feels like—we know the    34
tension and the distress—but our unconscious guilt can only be known
indirectly. And among the signs that may attest to the presence of
unconscious guilt is a powerful need to injure ourself, a persistent need
to get or to give ourself punishment.

Criminals leaving self-damaging clues (including Nixon, perhaps,    35
and his Watergate tapes) are very often impelled by unconscious guilt.
And so is the husband who, having spent the afternoon with a friend,
comes home with her watch in the pocket of his shirt. And so is Dick
who, having had a bitter fight with his father, smashes up his Chevy
and gets himself hurt. And so is Rita who, watching her boss raise hell
with his secretary, fleetingly thinks, "I'm glad it's her, not me"—and
then promptly pays for her thought by accidentally spilling hot tea all
over her lap.

And so are these erstwhile lovers, Ellie and Marvin.    36

Ellie and Marvin
Have been having secret meetings twice a week
For the past six months

But have thus far failed to consummate
Their passion                                                    5
Because
While both of them agree
That marital fidelity
Is not only unrealistic but also
Irrelevant,                                                      10
She has developed migraines, and
He has developed these sharp shooting pains
In his chest, and
She's got impetigo, and
He's got pinkeye.                                                15

Ellie and Marvin
Drive forty miles to sneaky luncheonettes
In separate cars
But have thus far done no more than
Heavy necking                                                    20
Because
While both of them agree
That sexual exclusivity
Is not only adolescent but also
Retrograde,                                                      25
She has developed colitis, and
He has developed these dull throbbing pains
In his back, and
She's started biting her nails, and
He's smoking again.                                              30

Ellie and Marvin
Yearn to have some love in the afternoon
At a motor hotel
But have thus far only had a lot of
Coffee                                                           35
Because
He is convinced that his phone is being tapped, and
She is convinced that a man in a trench coat is following her, and
He says what if the motor hotel catches fire, and
She says what if she talks some night in her sleep, and          40
She thinks her husband is acting suspiciously hostile, and
He thinks his wife is acting suspiciously nice, and

He keeps cutting his face with his double-edge razor, and
She keeps closing her hand in the door of her car, so
While both of them agree                                             45
That guilt is not only neurotic but also
Obsolete,
They've also agreed
To give up
Secret meetings.                                                     50

    Unconscious guilt, however, may extract much higher prices than     37
colitis, migraines, backaches or mild paranoia. It may insist on a lifetime of penance and pain. And this guilt may derive from any act or
omission, from any thought, that our conscience in its infinite wisdom
deems wicked. Thus our mother's ill health, our parents' divorce, our
secret envies and hates, our solitary sexual gratifications—any and all
can become our blame and our shame. And if the new brother or sister
we didn't want and wish wish wish would disappear does in fact—by
illness or accident—die, we may hold ourself responsible, we—not
knowing we think it—might think: "Why did I kill him? Why didn't I
save him? Why?"

    And our lives may crash on the rocks of our unconscious guilt.     38

    It was Freud who first observed that analysts sometimes work with   39
patients who ferociously resist relief from their symptoms, who seem
to hold on for dear life to emotional pain, and who cling to this pain
because it gives them the punishment that they don't even know they
want for crimes they don't even know that they have committed. He
notes ruefully, however, that a neurosis which has defied an analyst's
best efforts may suddenly vanish if the patient gets into an unhappy
marriage, loses all his money or becomes dangerously ill. "In such
instances," writes Freud, "one form of suffering has been replaced by
another; and we see that all that mattered was that it should be
possible to maintain a certain amount of suffering."

    But sometimes people are guilty and people should suffer, includ-   40
ing people like you and people like me. Sometimes guilt is appropriate
and good. Not all guilt is neurotic—to be cured, to be analyzed away.
We would be moral monsters if it could. But some of us exhibit certain
deficiencies in our capacity for guilt.

    I have a friend named Elizabeth who cannot acknowledge guilt      41
because, in her mind, the guilty are shot at dawn. She has to be perfect,

sinless, error-free. And so she will say, "The car was smacked up," because she would choke on the words "I smacked up the car." And she also will say, "His feelings got hurt," because she cannot accept that she hurt his feelings. At best she can say, "We forgot to buy tickets and now they're all sold out," when she was the only "we" in charge of tickets. And as for certain more drastic acts—she once had a love affair with her husband's best friend—she managed to persuade both herself and her husband that she was guiltless because he had driven her to it!

Elizabeth is quite capable of telling right from wrong. She is, however, incapable of believing that she could experience guilt—and survive. 42

Another kind of deficient guilt is displayed by people who punish themselves after they have committed some dreadful act, but who then go on to commit these dreadful acts again and again, again and again. For although their conscience acknowledges that what they did was wrong, and exacts quite brutal payments for their sins, their guilt never functions for them as a warning signal. It serves them only to punish, not to prevent. 43

It is known that certain criminals are actually seeking punishment in order to expiate unconscious guilt. It is known that certain criminals are suffering from distorted, not absent, guilt feelings. There are, however, the so-called psychopathic personalities who seem to display a genuine lack of guilt, whose antisocial and criminal acts, whose repetitive acts of destructiveness and depravity, occur with no restraint and no remorse. These psychopaths cheat and rob and lie and damage and destroy with remarkable emotional impunity. These psychopaths spell out for us, in letters ten feet high, what kind of world this world would be without guilt. 44

But we don't have to be a psychopath to allow some person or group to stand in the place of our individual conscience. And yet this too can lead to deficient guilt. For when we relinquish to others our sense of moral responsibility, we may become free of central moral constraints. This giving over of conscience can turn ordinary people into lynch mobs and operators of crematoria. And it may enable any of us to act in certain ways which on our own we would surely regard as unthinkable. 45

In a famous experiment testing conscience versus obedience to authority, experimental psychologist Stanley Milgram brought people into a Yale University psychology laboratory to engage—or so they 46

were told—in a study of memory and learning. The experimenter
explained that the issue to be explored was the impact of punishment
on learning, and to that end the subject designated "teacher" was
asked to administer a learning test to a "learner" strapped in a chair
in another room—and to give him an electric shock whenever his
answer was wrong. The shocks were executed by a series of thirty
switches which ranged from slight (15 volts) to severe (450 volts), and
the teacher was told that, with each wrong answer, he was to give the
learner the next higher shock. Conflict began when the learner went
from grunts to vehement protests to agonized screams, and the teacher
became increasingly uneasy and wished to stop. But each time he
hesitated, the person in authority urged him to continue, insisting that
he must complete the experiment. And despite the concern for the
level of shocking pain that was being inflicted, a large number of
teachers continued to push the switches all the way up to the highest
voltage.

47   The teachers did not know that the learners were actors, and that
they were only simulating distress. The teachers believed that the
shocks were painfully real. But some of them persuaded themselves
that what they were doing was for a noble cause—the pursuit of truth.
And some of them persuaded themselves that "He was so stupid and
stubborn he deserved to get shocked." And some of them were simply
unable, despite their conviction that what they were doing was wrong,
to make an open break with the person running the experiment—to
challenge authority.

48   Milgram notes that a "commonly offered explanation is that those
who shocked the victim at the most severe level were monsters, the
sadistic fringe of society. But if one considers that almost two-thirds of
the participants fall into the category of 'obedient' subjects and that
they represented ordinary people drawn from working, managerial
and professional classes, the argument becomes very shaky."

49   It is tempting to read about that experiment and imagine ourselves
walking out the door, able to know right from wrong and to act on that
knowledge. It is tempting to think that our conscience would prevail.
It is tempting to think that put to the test, we would be counted among
the morally pure. And some of us would be. And some of us would fail.
But all of us, in the course of our life, will engage in acts we know to
be morally wrong. And when we do, the healthy response is guilt.

50   Healthy guilt is appropriate—in quantity and quality—to the
deed. Healthy guilt leads to remorse but not self-hate. Healthy guilt

discourages us from repeating our guilty act without shutting down a wide range of our passions and pleasures.

We need to be able to know when what we are doing is morally wrong.                                                                        51

We need to be able to know and acknowledge our guilt.                  52

The philosopher Martin Buber, respectful of this need, tells us    53 that "there exists real guilt," that there is value in the "paining and admonishing heart" and that reparation, reconciliation, renewal require a conscience "that does not shy away from the glance into the depths and that already in admonishing envisages the way that leads across it. . . .

"Man," says Buber, "is the being who is capable of becoming    55 guilty and is capable of illuminating his guilt."

We seem to be more familiar with the prohibiting parts of our    55 conscience, the parts that limit our pleasures and water our joys, the parts that are always watching us to judge, condemn and mobilize our guilt. But our conscience also contains our ego ideal—our values and higher aspirations, the parts that speak to our "oughts" instead of our "don'ts." And another task of our conscience is to say in effect, "Good for you" and "You did well," to encourage us and approve of us and praise and reward and love us for meeting, or striving to meet, this ego ideal.

Our ego ideal is composed of our most wishful, hopeful visions of    56 ourself. Our ego ideal is composed of our noblest goals. And while it is an impossible dream that can never be fulfilled, our reachings toward it provide a deep sense of well-being. Our ego ideal is precious to us because it repairs a loss of our earlier childhood, the loss of our image of self as perfect and whole, the loss of a major portion of our infantile, limitless, ain't-I-wonderful narcissism which we had to give up in the face of compelling reality. Modified and reshaped into ethical goals and moral standards and a vision of what at our finest we might be, our dream of perfection lives on—our lost narcissism lives on—in our ego ideal.

It is true that we will feel guilt when we fall short of our ego ideal    57 or when we override our moral restraints. It is true that guilt will make us less happy, less free. If we could believe in "anything goes," we could go merrily—guiltlessly—on our way. But without ideals and restraints, what would we be? A wolf forgiven at his meat. A beetle innocent in his copulation. Something beyond the bounds of humanity.

We cannot be full human beings without the loss of some of our    58
anything-goes moral freedom.

We cannot be full human beings without acquiring a capacity for    59
guilt.

---

# Friendships among Men

## MARC FEIGEN FASTEAU

There is a long-standing myth in our society that the great friend-    1
ships are between men. Forged through shared experience, male
friendship is portrayed as the most unselfish, if not the highest form, of
human relationship. The more traditionally masculine the shared experience from which it springs, the stronger and more profound the
friendship is supposed to be. Going to war, weathering crises together
at school or work, playing on the same athletic team, are some of the
classic experiences out of which friendships between men are believed
to grow.

By and large, men do prefer the company of other men, not only    2
in their structured time but in the time they fill with optional, nonoblig-
atory activity. They prefer to play games, drink, and talk, as well as
work and fight together. Yet something is missing. Despite the time
men spend together, their contact rarely goes beyond the external, a
limitation which tends to make their friendships shallow and unsatisfy-
ing.

My own childhood memories are of doing things with my friends—    3
playing games or sports, building walkie-talkies, going camping. Other
people and my relationships to them were never legitimate subjects for
attention. If someone liked me, it was an opaque, mysterious occurrence that bore no analysis. When I was slighted, I felt hurt. But
relationships with people just happened. I certainly had feelings about
my friends, but I can't remember a single instance of trying consciously
to sort them out until I was well into college.

For most men this kind of shying away from the personal continues    4
into adult life. In conversations with each other, we hardly ever use
ourselves as reference points. We talk about almost everything except

how we ourselves are affected by people and events. Everything is discussed as though it were taking place out there somewhere, as though we had no more felt response to it than to the weather. Topics that can be treated in this detached, objective way become conversational mainstays. The few subjects which are fundamentally personal are shaped into discussions of abstract general questions. Even in an exchange about their reactions to liberated women—a topic of intensely personal interest—the tendency will be to talk in general, theoretical terms. Work, at least its objective aspects, is always a safe subject. Men also spend an incredible amount of time rehashing the great public issues of the day. Until early 1973, Vietnam was the work-horse topic. Then came Watergate. It doesn't seem to matter that we've all had a hundred similar conversations. We plunge in for another round, trying to come up with a new angle as much as to impress the others with what we know as to keep from being bored stiff.

Games play a central role in situations organized by men. I remember a weekend some years ago at the country house of a law-school classmate as a blur of softball, football, croquet, poker, and a dice-and-board game called Combat, with swimming thrown in on the side. As soon as one game ended, another began. Taken one at a time, these "activities" were fun, but the impression was inescapable that the host, and most of his guests, would do anything to stave off a lull in which they would be together without some impersonal focus for their attention. A snapshot of almost any men's club would show the same thing, ninety percent of the men engaged in some activity— ranging from backgammon to watching the tube—other than, or at least as an aid to, conversation.[1]

My composite memory of eveniugs spent with a friend at college and later when we shared an apartment in Washington is of conversations punctuated by silences during which we would internally pass over any personal or emotional thoughts which had arisen and come back to the permitted track. When I couldn't get my mind off personal matters, I said very little. Talks with my father have always had the same tone. Respect for privacy was the rationale for our diffidence. His questions to me about how things were going at school or at work were asked as discreetly as he would have asked a friend about someone's commitment to a hospital for the criminally insane. Our conversations, when they touched these matters at all, to say nothing of more sensitive matters, would veer quickly back to safe topics of general interest.

In our popular literature, the archetypal male hero embodying this personal muteness is the cowboy. The classic mold for the character was set in 1902 by Owen Wister's novel *The Virginian* where the author spelled out, with an explicitness that was never again necessary, the characteristics of his protagonist. Here's how it goes when two close friends the Virginian hasn't seen in some time take him out for a drink:

> All of them had seen rough days together, and they felt guilty with emotion.
>     "It's hot weather," said Wiggin.
>     "Hotter in Box Elder," said McLean. "My kid has started teething."
>     Words ran dry again. They shifted their positions, looked in their glasses, read the labels on the bottles. They dropped a word now and then to the proprietor about his trade, and his ornaments.[2]

One of the Virginian's duties is to assist at the hanging of an old friend as a horse thief. Afterward, for the first time in the book, he is visibly upset. The narrator puts his arm around the hero's shoulders and describes the Virginian's reaction:

> I had the sense to keep silent, and presently he shook my hand, not looking at me as he did so. He was always very shy of demonstration.[3]

And, for explanation of such reticence, "As all men know, he also knew that many things should be done in this world in silence, and that talking about them is a mistake."[4]

There are exceptions, but they only prove the rule. 8

One is the drunken confidence: "Bob, ole boy, I gotta tell ya— 9 being divorced isn't so hot. . . . [and see, I'm too drunk to be held responsible for blurting it out]." Here, drink becomes an excuse for exchanging confidences and a device for periodically loosening the restraint against expressing a need for sympathy and support from other men—which may explain its importance as a male ritual.[5] Marijuana fills a similar need.

Another exception is talking to a stranger—who may be either 10 someone the speaker doesn't know or someone who isn't in the same social or business world. (Several black friends told me that they have been on the receiving end of personal confidences from white acquaintances that they were sure had not been shared with white friends.) In either case, men are willing to talk about themselves only to other men with whom they do not have to compete or whom they will not have to confront socially later.

Finally, there is the way men depend on women to facilitate    11
certain conversations. The women in a mixed group are usually the
ones who make the first personal reference, about themselves or others
present. The men can then join in without having the onus for initiating
a discussion of "personalities." Collectively, the men can "blame" the
conversation on the women. They can also feel in these conversations
that since they are talking "to" the women instead of "to" the men,
they can be excused for deviating from the masculine norm. When the
women leave, the tone and subject invariably shift away from the
personal.

The effect of these constraints is to make it extraordinarily difficult    12
for men to really get to know each other. A psychotherapist who has
conducted a lengthy series of encounter groups for men summed it up:

> With saddening regularity [the members of these groups] described how much
> they wanted to have closer, more satisfying relationships with other men: "I'd
> settle for having one really close man friend. I supposedly have some close men
> friends now. We play golf or go for a drink. We complain about our jobs and
> our wives. I care about them and they care about me. We even have some
> physical contact—I mean we may even give a hug on a big occasion. But it's
> not enough."[6]

The sources of this stifling ban on self-disclosure, the reasons why men
hide from each other, lie in the taboos and imperatives of the masculine stereotype.

To begin with, men are supposed to be functional, to spend their    13
time working or otherwise solving or thinking about how to solve
problems. Personal reaction, how one feels about something, is considered dysfunctional, at best an irrelevant distraction from the expected
objectivity. Only weak men, and women, talk about—i.e., "give in," to
their feelings. "I group my friends in two ways," said a business
executive:

> those who have made it and don't complain and those who haven't made it.
> And only the latter spend time talking to their wives about their problems and
> how bad their boss is and all that. The ones who concentrate more on com-
> municating . . . are those who have realized that they aren't going to make it
> and therefore they have changed the focus of attention.[7]

In a world which tells men they have to choose between expressiveness
and manly strength, this characterization may be accurate. Most of the
men who talk personally to other men *are* those whose problems have
gotten the best of them, who simply can't help it. Men not driven to

despair don't talk about themselves, so the idea that self-disclosure and expressiveness are associated with problems and weakness becomes a self-fulfilling prophecy.

Obsessive competitiveness also limits the range of communication 14 in male friendships. Competition is the principal mode by which men relate to each other—at one level because they don't know how else to make contact, but more basically because it is the way to demonstrate, to themselves and others, the key masculine qualities of unwavering toughness and the ability to dominate and control. The result is that they inject competition into situations which don't call for it.

In conversations, you must show that you know more about the 15 subject than the other man, or at least as much as he does. For example, I have often engaged in a contest that could be called My Theory Tops Yours, disguised as a serious exchange of ideas. The proof that it wasn't serious was that I was willing to participate even when I was sure that the participants, including myself, had nothing fresh to say. Convincing the other person—victory—is the main objective, with control of the floor an important tactic. Men tend to lecture at each other, insist that the discussion follow their train of thought, and are often unwilling to listen.[8] As one member of a men's rap group said,

When I was talking I used to feel that I had to be driving to a point, that it had to be rational and organized, that I had to persuade at all times, rather than exchange thoughts and ideas.[9]

Even in casual conversation some men hold back unless they are absolutely sure of what they are saying. They don't want to have to change a position once they have taken it. It's "just like a woman" to change your mind, and, more important, it is inconsistent with the approved masculine posture of total independence.

Competition was at the heart of one of my closest friendships, now 16 defunct. There was a good deal of mutual liking and respect. We went out of our way to spend time with each other and wanted to work together. We both had "prospects" as "bright young men" and the same "liberal but tough" point of view. We recognized this about each other, and this recognition was the basis of our respect and of our sense of equality. That we saw each other as equals was important—our friendship was confirmed by the reflection of one in the other. But our constant and all-encompassing competition made this equality precarious and fragile. One way or another, everything counted in the measuring process. We fought out our tennis matches as though our lives depended on it. At poker, the two of us would often play on for hours after the others had left. These *mano a mano* poker marathons seem in retrospect especially revealing of the competitiveness of the relationship: playing for small stakes, the essence of the game is in outwitting, psychologically beating down the other player—the other skills involved are negligible. Winning is the only pleasure, one that evaporates quickly, a truth that struck me in inchoate form every time our game broke up at four A.M. and I walked out the door with my five-dollar winnings, a headache, and a sense of time wasted. Still, I did the same thing the next time. It was what we did together, and somehow it counted. Losing at tennis could be balanced by winning at poker; at another level, his moving up in the federal government by my getting on the *Harvard Law Review*.

This competitiveness feeds the most basic obstacle to openness 17 between men, the inability to admit to being vulnerable. Real men, we learn early, are not supposed to have doubts, hopes and ambitions which may not be realized, things they don't (or even especially do) like about themselves, fears and disappointments. Such feelings and concerns, of course, are part of everyone's inner life, but a man must keep quiet about them. If others know how you really feel you can be hurt, and that in itself is incompatible with manhood. The inhibiting effect of this imperative is not limited to disclosures of major personal problems. Often men do not share even ordinary uncertainties and half-formulated plans of daily life with their friends. And when they do, they are careful to suggest that they already know how to proceed—that they are not really asking for help or understanding but simply for particular bits of information. Either way, any doubts they have are presented as external, carefully characterized as having to do with the issue as distinct from the speaker. They are especially guarded about expressing concern or asking a question that would invite personal comment. It is almost impossible for men to simply exchange thoughts about matters involving them personally in a comfortable, non-crisis atmosphere. If a friend tells you of his concern that he and a colleague are always disagreeing, for example, he is likely to quickly supply his own explanation—something like "different professional backgrounds." The effect is to rule out observations or suggestions that do not fit within this already reconnoitered protective structure. You don't suggest, even if you believe it is true, that in fact the disagreements arise because he presents his ideas in a way which tends to provoke a hostile reaction. It would catch him off guard; it would be something he hadn't already thought of and accepted about himself and, for that reason, no matter how constructive and well-intentioned you might be, it would put you in control for the moment. He doesn't want that; he is afraid of losing your respect. So, sensing he feels that way, because you would yourself, you say something else. There is no real give-and-take.

It is hard for men to get angry at each other honestly. Anger    18
between friends often means that one has hurt the other. Since the straightforward expression of anger in these situations involves an admission of vulnerability, it is safer to stew silently or find an "objective" excuse for retaliation. Either way, trust is not fully restored.

Men even try not to let it show when they feel good. We may    19
report the reasons for our happiness, if they have to do with concrete accomplishments, but we try to do it with a straight face, as if to say, "Here's what happened, but it hasn't affected my grown-up unemotional equilibrium, and I am not asking for any kind of response." Happiness is a precarious, "childish" feeling, easy to shoot down. Others may find the event that triggers it trivial or incomprehensible, or even threatening to their own self-esteem—in the sense that if one man is up, another man is down. So we tend not to take the risk of expressing it.

What is particularly difficult for men is seeking or accepting help    20
from friends. I, for one, learned early that dependence was unacceptable. When I was eight, I went to a summer camp I disliked. My parents visited me in the middle of the summer and, when it was time for them to leave, I wanted to go with them. They refused, and I yelled and screamed and was miserably unhappy for the rest of the day. That evening an older camper comforted me, sitting by my bed as I cried, patting me on the back soothingly and saying whatever it is that one says at times like that. He was in some way clumsy or funny-looking, and a few days later I joined a group of kids in cruelly making fun of him, an act which upset me, when I thought about it, for years. I can only explain it in terms of my feeling, as early as the age of eight, that by needing and accepting his help and comfort I had compromised myself, and took it out on him.

"You can't express dependence when you feel it," a corporate    21
executive said, "because it's a kind of absolute. If you are loyal 90% of the time and disloyal 10%, would you be considered loyal? Well, the same happens with independence: you are either dependent or independent; you can't be both."[10] "Feelings of dependence," another

explained, "are identified with weakness or 'untoughness' and our culture doesn't accept those things in men."[11] The result is that we either go it alone or "act out certain games or rituals to provoke the desired reaction in the other and have our needs satisfied without having to ask for anything."[12]

Somewhat less obviously, the expression of affection also runs into     22 emotional barriers growing out of the masculine stereotype. When I was in college, I was suddenly quite moved while attending a friend's wedding. The surge of feeling made me uncomfortable and self-conscious. There was nothing inherently difficult or, apart from the fact of being moved by a moment of tenderness, "unmasculine" about my reaction. I just did not know how to deal with or communicate what I felt. "I consider myself a sentimentalist," one man said, "and I think I am quite able to express my feelings. But the other day my wife described a friend of mine to some people as my best friend and I felt embarrassed when I heard her say it."[13]

A major source of these inhibitions is the fear of being, or being     23 thought, homosexual. Nothing is more frightening to a heterosexual man in our society. It threatens, at one stroke, to take away every vestige of his claim to a masculine identity—something like knocking out the foundations of a building—and to expose him to the ostracism, ranging from polite tolerance to violent revulsion, of his friends and colleagues. A man can be labeled as homosexual not just because of overt sexual acts but because of almost any sign of behavior which does not fit the masculine stereotype. The touching of another man, other than shaking hands or, under emotional stress, an arm around the shoulder, is taboo. Women may kiss each other when they meet; men are uncomfortable when hugged even by close friends.[14] Onlookers might misinterpret what they saw, and, more important, what would we think of ourselves if we felt a twinge of sensual pleasure from the embrace.

Direct verbal expressions of affection or tenderness are also some-     24 thing that only homosexuals and women engage in. Between "real" men affection has to be disguised in gruff, "you old son-of-a-bitch" style. Paradoxically, in some instances, terms of endearment between men can be used as a ritual badge of manhood, dangerous medicine safe only for the strong. The flirting with homosexuality that character-izes the initiation rites of many fraternities and men's clubs serves this purpose. Claude Brown wrote about black life in New York City in the 1950s:

The term ["baby"] had a hip ring to it. . . . It was like saying, "Man, look at me. I've got masculinity to spare. . . . I can say 'baby' to another cat and he can say 'baby' to me, and we can say it with strength in our voices." If you could say it, this meant that you really had to be sure of yourself, sure of your masculinity.[15]

Fear of homosexuality does more than inhibit the physical display of affection. One of the major recurring themes in the men's groups led by psychotherapist Don Clark was:

"A large segment of my feelings about other men are unknown or distorted because I am afraid they might have something to do with homosexuality. Now I'm lonely for other men and don't know how to find what I want with them."

As Clark observes, "The spectre of homosexuality seems to be the dragon at the gateway to self-awareness, understanding, and acceptance of male-male needs. If a man ties to pretend the dragon is not there by turning a blind eye to erotic feelings for all other males, he also blinds himself to the rich variety of feelings that are related."[16]

The few situations in which men do acknowledge strong feelings    25
of affection and dependence toward other men are exceptions which prove the rule. With "cop couples," for example, or combat soldier "buddies," intimacy and dependence are forced on the men by their work—they have to ride in the patrol car or be in the same foxhole with somebody—and the jobs themselves have such highly masculine images that the men can get away with behavior that would be suspect under any other conditions.

Furthermore, even these combat-buddy relationships, when    26
looked at closely, turn out not to be particularly intimate or personal. Margaret Mead has written:

During the last war English observers were confused by the apparent contradiction between American soldiers' emphasis on the buddy, so grievously exemplified in the break-downs that followed a buddy's death, and the results of detailed inquiry which showed how transitory these buddy relationships were. It was found that men actually accepted their buddies as derivatives from their outfit, and from accidents of association, rather than because of any special personality characteristics capable of ripening into friendship.[17]

One effect of the fear of appearing to be homosexual is to reinforce the practice that two men rarely get together alone without a reason. I once called a friend to suggest that we have dinner together. "O.K.," he said. "What's up?" I felt uncomfortable telling him that I just wanted to talk, that there was no other reason for the invitation.

Men get together to conduct business, to drink, to play games and  27
sports, to re-establish contact after long absences, to participate in
heterosexual social occasions—circumstances in which neither person
is responsible for actually wanting to see the other. Men are particularly comfortable seeing each other in groups. The group situation
defuses any possible assumptions about the intensity of feeling between particular men and provides the safety of numbers—"All the
guys are here." It makes personal communication, which requires a
level of trust and mutual understanding not generally shared by all
members of a group, more difficult and offers an excuse for avoiding
this dangerous territory. And it provides what is most sought after in
men's friendships: mutual reassurance of masculinity.

Needless to say, the observations in this chapter did not spring  28
full-blown from my head. The process started when I began to understand that, at least with Brenda, a more open, less self-protective
relationship was possible. At first, I perceived my situation as completely personal. The changes I was trying to effect in myself had to do,
I thought, only with Brenda and me, and could be generalized, if at all,
only to other close relationships between men and women. But, as
Brenda came to be deeply involved in the women's movement, I began
to see, usually at one remove but sometimes directly, the level of
intimacy that women, especially women active in the movement,
shared with each other. The contrast between this and the friendships
I had with men was striking. I started listening to men's conversations,
including my own, and gradually the basic outlines of the pattern
described here began to emerge. I heard from women that the men
they knew had very few really close male friends; since then I have
heard the same thing from men themselves. It was, I realized, my own
experience as well. It wasn't that I didn't know a lot of men, or that I
was not on friendly terms with them. Rather, I gradually became
dissatisfied with the impersonality of these friendships.

Of course, some constraints on self-disclosure do make sense. Pri-  29
vacy is something you give up selectively and gradually to people you
like and trust, and who are capable of understanding—instant, indiscriminate intimacy is nearly always formularized, without real content
and impact. Nor does self-disclosure as a kind of compartmentalized
rest-and-recreation period work: "Well, John, let me tell you about
myself. . . ."

Having said all this, it is nonetheless true that men have carried  30
the practice of emotional restraint to the point of paralysis. For me, at

least, the ritual affirmations of membership in the fraternity of men that one gets from participation in "masculine" activities do nothing to assuage the feeling of being essentially alone; they have become a poor substitute for being known by and knowing other people. But the positive content of what will replace the old-style friendships is only beginning to take shape. I am learning, though, that when I am able to articulate my feelings as they arise in the context of my friendships, I often find that they are shared by others. Bringing them out into the open clears the air; avoiding them, even unconsciously, is stultifying. I have found also that I am not as fragile as I once thought. The imagined hazards of showing oneself to be human, and thus vulnerable, to one's friends tend not to materialize when actually put to the test. But being oneself is an art, an art sensitive to variations in the receptivity of others as well as to one's own inner life. It is still, for me, something to be mastered, to be tried out and practiced.

## Notes

1. Women may use games as a reason for getting together—bridge clubs, for example. But the show is more for the rest of the world—to indicate that they are doing *something*—and the games themselves are not the only means of communication.
2. Owen Wister, *The Virginian* ([Macmillan: 1902] Grosset & Dunlap ed.: 1929, pp. 397–98.
3. *Ibid.* p. 343.
4. *Ibid,* p. 373.
5. Lionel Tiger, *Men in Groups* (Random House: 1969), p. 185.
6. Don Clark, "Homosexual Encounter in All-Male Groups," in L. Solomon and B. Berzon (eds.), *New Perspectives on Encounter Groups* (Jossey-Bass: 1972), pp. 376–77. See also Alan Booth, "Sex and Social Participation," *American Sociological Review*, Vol. 37 (April 1972), p. 183, an empirical study showing that, contrary to Lionel Tiger's much publicized assertion *(Men in Groups)*, women form stronger and closer friendship bonds with each other than men do.
7. Fernando Bartolomé, "Executives as Human Beings," *Harvard Business Review*, Vol. 50 (November-December 1972), p. 64.
8. The contrast with women on this point is striking. Casual observation will confirm that women's conversations move more quickly, with fewer long speeches and more frequent changes of speaker.
9. *Boston Globe*, March 12, 1972, p. B-1.
10. Bartolomé, *op. cit.* p. 65.
11. *Ibid,* p. 64.
12. *Ibid,* p. 66.
13. *Ibid,* p. 64.
14. *Ibid,* p. 65.
16. Claude Brown, *Manchild in the Promised Land* ([Macmillan: 1965] Signet ed.: 1965), p. 171.

17. Clark, *op. cit.* p. 378.
18. Margaret Mead, *Male and Female* ([William Morrow: 1949] Mentor ed.: 1949), p. 214.

# Management Women and the New Facts of Life

## FELICE N. SCHWARTZ

The cost of employing women in management is greater than the 1 cost of employing men. This is a jarring statement, partly because it is true, but mostly because it is something people are reluctant to talk about. A new study by one multinational corporation shows that the rate of turnover in management positions is 2½ times higher among top-performing women than it is among men. A large producer of consumer goods reports that one-half of the women who take maternity leave return to their jobs late or not at all. And we know that women also have a greater tendency to plateau or to interrupt their careers in ways that limit their growth and development. But we have become so sensitive to charges of sexism and so afraid of confrontation, even litigation, that we rarely say what we know to be true. Unfortunately, our bottled-up awareness leaks out in misleading metaphors ("glass ceiling" is one notable example), veiled hostility, lowered expectations, distrust, and reluctant adherence to Equal Employment Opportunity requirements.

Career interruptions, plateauing, and turnover are expensive. The 2 money corporations invest in recruitment, training, and development is less likely to produce top executives among women than among men, and the invaluable company experience that developing executives acquire at every level as they move up through management ranks is more often lost.

The studies just mentioned are only the first of many, I'm quite 3 sure. Demographic realities are going to force corporations all across the country to analyze the cost of employing women in managerial positions, and what they will discover is that women cost more.

But here is another startling truth: The greater cost of employing 4 women is not a function of inescapable gender differences. Women *are* different from men, but what increases their cost to the corporation is principally the clash of their perceptions, attitudes, and behavior with those of men, which is to say, with the policies and practices of male-led corporations.

It is terribly important that employers draw the right conclusions      5
from the studies now being done. The studies will be useless—or worse, harmful—if all they teach us is that women are expensive to employ. What we need to learn is how to reduce that expense, how to stop throwing away the investments we make in talented women, how to become more responsive to the needs of the women that corporations *must* employ if they are to have the best and the brightest of all those now entering the work force.

The gender differences relevant to business fall into two catego-      6
ries: those related to maternity and those related to the differing traditions and expectations of the sexes. Maternity is biological rather than cultural. We can't alter it, but we can dramatically reduce its impact on the workplace and in many cases eliminate its negative effect on employee development. We can accomplish this by address-ing the second set of differences, those between male and female socialization. Today, these differences exaggerate the real costs of maternity and can turn a relatively slight disruption in work schedule into a serious business problem and a career derailment for individual women. If we are to overcome the cost differential between male and female employees, we need to address the issues that arise when female socialization meets the male corporate culture and masculine rules of career development—issues of behavior and style, of expecta-tion, of stereotypes and preconceptions, of sexual tension and harass-ment, of female mentoring, lateral mobility, relocation, compensation, and early identification of top performers.

The one immutable, enduring difference between men and      7
women is maternity. Maternity is not simply childbirth but a con-tinuum that begins with an awareness of the ticking of the biological clock, proceeds to the anticipation of motherhood, includes pregnancy, childbirth, physical recuperation, psychological adjustment, and con-tinues on to nursing, bonding, and child rearing. Not all women choose to become mothers, of course, and among those who do, the process varies from case to case depending on the health of the mother and baby, the values of the parents, and the availability, cost, and quality of child care.

In past centuries, the biological fact of maternity shaped the tradi-      8 tional roles of the sexes. Women performed the home-centered functions that related to the bearing and nurturing of children. Men did the work that required great physical strength. Over time, however, family size contracted, the community assumed greater responsibility for the care and education of children, packaged foods and household technology reduced the work load in the home, and technology eliminated much of the need for muscle power at the workplace. Today, in the developed world, the only role still uniquely gender related is childbearing. Yet men and women are still socialized to perform their traditional roles.

Men and women may or may not have some innate psychological       9
disposition toward these traditional roles—men to be aggressive, competitive, self-reliant, risk taking; women to be supportive, nurturing, intuitive, sensitive, communicative—but certainly both men and women are capable of the full range of behavior. Indeed, the male and female roles have already begun to expand and merge. In the decades ahead, as the socialization of boys and girls and the experience and expectations of young men and women grow steadily more androgynous, the differences in workplace behavior will continue to fade. At the moment, however, we are still plagued by disparities in perception and behavior that make the integration of men and women in the workplace unnecessarily difficult and expensive.

Let me illustrate with a few broadbrush generalizations. Of       10
course, these are only stereotypes, but I think they help to exemplify the kinds of preconceptions that can muddy the corporate waters.

Men continue to perceive women as the rearers of their children,       11
so they find it understandable, indeed appropriate, that women should renounce their careers to raise families. Edmund Pratt, CEO of Pfizer, once asked me in all sincerity, "Why would any woman choose to be a chief financial officer rather than a full-time mother?" By condoning and taking pleasure in women's traditional behavior, men reinforce it. Not only do they see parenting as fundamentally female, they see a career as fundamentally male—either an unbroken series of promotions and advancements toward CEOdom or stagnation and disappointment. This attitude serves to legitimize a woman's choice to extend maternity leave and even, for those who can afford it, to leave employment altogether for several years. By the same token, men who might want to take a leave after the birth of a child know that management will see such behavior as a lack of career commitment, even when company policy permits parental leave for men.

Women also bring counterproductive expectations and percep-       12 tions to the workplace. Ironically, although the feminist movement was an expression of women's quest for freedom from their home-based lives, most women were remarkably free already. They had many responsibilities, but they were autonomous and could be entrepreneurial in how and when they carried them out. And once their children grew up and left home, they were essentially free to do what they wanted with their lives. Women's traditional role also included freedom from responsibility for the financial support of their families. Many of us were socialized from girlhood to expect our husbands to take care of us, while our brothers were socialized from an equally early age to complete their educations, pursue careers, climb the ladder of success, and provide dependable financial support for their families. To the extent that this tradition of freedom lingers subliminally, women tend to bring to their employment a sense that they can choose to change jobs or careers at will, take time off, or reduce their hours.

Finally, women's traditional role encouraged particular attention    13
to the quality and substance of what they did, specifically to the physical, psychological, and intellectual development of their children. This traditional focus may explain women's continuing tendency to search for more than monetary reward—intrinsic significance, social importance, meaning—in what they do. This too makes them more likely than men to leave the corporation in search of other values.

The misleading metaphor of the glass ceiling suggests an invisi-    14
ble barrier constructed by corporate leaders to impede the upward mobility of women beyond the middle levels. A more appropriate metaphor, I believe, is the kind of cross-sectional diagram used in geology. The barriers to women's leadership occur when potentially counterproductive layers of influence on women—maternity, tradition, socialization—meet management strata pervaded by the largely unconscious preconceptions, stereotypes, and expectations of men. Such interfaces do not exist for men and tend to be impermeable for women.

One result of these gender differences has been to convince some    15
executives that women are simply not suited to top management. Other executives feel helpless. If they see even a few of their valued female employees fail to return to work from maternity leave on schedule or see one of their most promising women plateau in her career after the birth of a child, they begin to fear there is nothing they can do to infuse women with new energy and enthusiasm and persuade

them to stay. At the same time, they know there is nothing they can do to stem the tide of women into management ranks.

Another result is to place every working woman on a continuum    16
that runs from total dedication to career at one end to a balance between career and family at the other. What women discover is that the male corporate culture sees both extremes as unacceptable. Women who want the flexibility to balance their families and their careers are not adequately committed to the organization. Women who perform as aggressively and competitively as men are abrasive and unfeminine. But the fact is, business needs all the talented women it can get. Moreover, as I will explain, the women I call career-primary and those I call career-and-family each have particular value to the corporation.

Women in the corporation are about to move from a buyer's to a    17
seller's market. The sudden, startling recognition that 80% of new entrants in the work force over the next decade will be women, minorities, and immigrants has stimulated a mushrooming incentive to "value diversity."

Women are no longer simply an enticing pool of occasional cre-    18
ative talent, a thorn in the side of the EEO officer, or a source of frustration to corporate leaders truly puzzled by the slowness of their upward trickle into executive positions. A real demographic change is taking place. The era of sudden population growth of the 1950s and 1960s is over. The birth rate has dropped about 40%, from a high of 25.3 live births per 1,000 population in 1957, at the peak of the baby boom, to a stable low of a little more than 15 per 1,000 over the last sixteen years, and there is no indication of a return to a higher rate. The tidal wave of baby boomers that swelled the recruitment pool to overflowing seems to have been a one-time phenomenon. For 20 years, employers had the pick of a very large crop and were able to choose males almost exclusively for the executive track. But if future population remains fairly stable while the economy continues to expand, and if the new information society simultaneously creates a greater need for creative, educated managers, then the gap between supply and demand will grow dramatically and, with it, the competition for managerial talent.

The decrease in numbers has even greater implications if we look    19
at the traditional source of corporate recruitment for leadership positions—white males from the top 10% of the country's best universities.

Over the past decade, the increase in the number of women graduating from leading universities has been much greater than the increase in the total number of graduates, and these women are well represented in the top 10% of their classes.

The trend extends into business and professional programs as well.    20
In the old days, virtually all MBAs were male. I remember addressing a meeting at the Harvard Business School as recently as the mid-1970s and looking out at a sea of exclusively male faces. Today, about 25% of that audience would be women. The pool of male MBAs from which corporations have traditionally drawn their leaders has shrunk significantly.

Of course, this reduction does not have to mean a shortage of    21
talent. The top 10% is at least as smart as it always was—smarter, probably, since it's now drawn from a broader segment of the population. But it now consists increasingly of women. Companies that are determined to recruit the same number of men as before will have to dig much deeper into the male pool, while their competitors will have the opportunity to pick the best people from both the male and female graduates.

Under these circumstances, there is no question that the manage-    22
ment ranks of business will include increasing numbers of women. There remains, however, the question of how these women will succeed—how long they will stay, how high they will climb, how completely they will fulfill their promise and potential, and what kind of return the corporation will realize on its investment in their training and development.

There is ample business reason for finding ways to make sure that    23
as many of these women as possible will succeed. The first step in this process is to recognize that women are not all alike. Like men, they are individuals with differing talents, priorities, and motivations. For the sake of simplicity, let me focus on the two women I referred to earlier, on what I call the career-primary woman and the career-and-family woman.

Like many men, some women put their careers first. They are    24
ready to make the same trade-offs traditionally made by the men who seek leadership positions. They make a career decision to put in extra hours, to make sacrifices in their personal lives, to make the most of every opportunity for professional development. For women, of course, this decision also requires that they remain single or at least

childless or, if they do have children, that they be satisfied to have others raise them. Some 90% of executive men but only 35% of executive women have children by the age of 40. The *automatic* association of all women with babies is clearly unjustified.

The secret to dealing with such women is to recognize them early;   25 accept them, and clear artificial barriers from their path to the top. After all, the best of these women are among the best managerial talent you will ever see. And career-primary women have another important value to the company that men and other women lack. They can act as role models and mentors to younger women who put their careers first. Since upwardly mobile career-primary women still have few role models to motivate and inspire them, a company with women in its top echelon has a significant advantage in the competition for executive talent.

Men at the top of the organization—most of them over 55, with   26 wives who tend to be traditional—often find career women "masculine" and difficult to accept as colleagues. Such men miss the point, which is not that these women are just like men but that they are just like the *best* men in the organization. And there is such a shortage of the best people that gender cannot be allowed to matter. It is clearly counterproductive to disparage in a woman with executive talent the very qualities that are most critical to the business and that might carry a man to the CEO's office.

Clearing a path to the top for career-primary women has four   27 requirements:

1. Identify them early.
2. Give them the same opportunity you give to talented men to grow and develop and contribute to company profitability. Give them client and customer responsibility. Expect them to travel and relocate, to make the same commitment to the company as men aspiring to leadership positions.
3. Accept them as valued members of your management team. Include them in every kind of communication. Listen to them.
4. Recognize that the business environment is more difficult and stressful for them than for their male peers. They are always a minority, often the only woman. The male perception of talented, ambitious women is at best ambivalent, a mixture of admiration, resentment, confusion, competitiveness,

attraction, skepticism, anxiety, pride, and animosity. Women can never feel secure about how they should dress and act, whether they should speak out or grin and bear it when they encounter discrimination, stereotyping, sexual harassment, and paternalism. Social interaction and travel with male colleagues and with male clients can be charged. As they move up, the normal increase in pressure and responsibility is compounded for women because they are women.

Stereotypical language and sexist day-to-day behavior do take    28
their toll on women's career development. Few male executives realize how common it is to call women by their first names while men in the same group are greeted with surnames, how frequently female executives are assumed by men to be secretaries, how often women are excluded from all-male social events where business is being transacted. With notable exceptions, men are still generally more comfortable with other men, and as a result women miss many of the career and business opportunities that arise over lunch, on the golf course, or in the locker room.

The majority of women, however, are what I call career-and-    29
family women, women who want to pursue serious careers while participating actively in the rearing of children. These women are a precious resource that has yet to be mined. Many of them are talented and creative. Most of them are willing to trade some career growth and compensation for freedom from the constant pressure to work long hours and weekends.

Most companies today are ambivalent at best about the career-    30
and-family women in their management ranks. They would prefer that all employees were willing to give their all to the company. They believe it is in their best interests for all managers to compete for the top positions so the company will have the largest possible pool from which to draw its leaders.

"If you have both talent and motivation," many employers seem    31
to say, "we want to move you up. If you haven't got that motivation, if you want less pressure and greater flexibility, then you can leave and make room for a new generation." These companies lose on two counts. First, they fail to amortize the investment they made in the early training and experience of management women who find themselves committed to family as well as to career. Second, they fail to recognize what these women could do for their middle management.

The ranks of middle managers are filled with people on their way    32
up and people who have stalled. Many of them have simply reached
their limits, achieved career growth commensurate with or exceeding
their capabilities, and they cause problems because their performance
is mediocre but they still want to move ahead. The career-and-family
woman is willing to trade off the pressures and demands that go with
promotion for the freedom to spend more time with her children. She's
very smart, she's talented, she's committed to her career, and she's
satisfied to stay at the middle level, at least during the early child-
rearing years. Compare her with some of the people you have there
now.

Consider a typical example, a woman who decides in college on a    33
business career and enters management at age 22. For nine years, the
company invests in her career as she gains experience and skills and
steadily improves her performance. But at 31, just as the investment
begins to pay off in earnest, she decides to have a baby. Can the
company afford to let her go home, take another job, or go into business
for herself? The common perception now is yes, the corporation can
afford to lose her unless, after six or eight weeks or even three months
of disability and maternity leave, she returns to work on a full-time
schedule with the same vigor, commitment, and ambition that she
showed before.

But what if she doesn't? What if she wants or needs to go on leave    34
for six months or a year or, heaven forbid, five years? In this worst-case
scenario, she works full-time from age 22 to 31 and from 36 to 65—a
total of 38 years as opposed to the typical male's 43 years. That's not
a huge difference. Moreover, my typical example is willing to work
part-time while her children are young, if only her employer will give
her the opportunity. There are two rewards for companies responsive
to this need: higher retention of their best people and greatly improved
performance and satisfaction in their middle management.

The high-performing career-and-family woman can be a major    35
player in your company. She can give you a significant business advantage as the competition for able people escalates. Sometimes too, if you
can hold on to her, she will switch gears in mid-life and reenter the
competition for the top. The price you must pay to retain these women
is threefold: you must plan for and manage maternity, you must provide the flexibility that will allow them to be maximally productive, and
you must take an active role in helping to make family supports and
high-quality, affordable child care available to all women.

                    ❂        ❂        ❂

The key to managing maternity is to recognize the value of high-    36
performing women and the urgent need to retain them and keep them
productive. The first step must be a genuine partnership between the
woman and her boss. I know this partnership can seem difficult to
forge. One of my own senior executives came to me recently to discuss
plans for her maternity leave and subsequent return to work. She knew
she wanted to come back. I wanted to make certain that she would.
Still, we had a somewhat awkward conversation, because I knew that
no woman can predict with certainty when she will be able to return
to work or under what conditions. Physical problems can lengthen her
leave. So can a demanding infant, a difficult family or personal adjustment, or problems with child care.

I still don't know when this valuable executive will be back on the    37
job full-time, and her absence creates some genuine problems for our
organization. But I do know that I can't simply replace her years of
experience with a new recruit. Since our conversation, I also know that
she wants to come back, and that she *will* come back—part-time at
first—unless I make it impossible for her by, for example, setting an
arbitrary date for her full-time return or resignation. In turn, she
knows that the organization wants and needs her and, more to the
point, that it will be responsive to her needs in terms of working hours
and child-care arrangements.

In having this kind of conversation it's important to ask concrete    38
questions that will help to move the discussion from uncertainty and
anxiety to some level of predictability. Questions can touch on everything from family income and energy level to child care arrangements
and career commitment. Of course you want your star manager to
return to work as soon as possible, but you want her to return permanently and productively. Her downtime on the job is a drain on her
energies and a waste of your money.

For all the women who want to combine career and family—the    39
women who want to participate actively in the rearing of their children
and who also want to pursue their careers seriously—the key to retention is to provide the flexibility and family supports they need in order
to function effectively.

Time spent in the office increases productivity if it is time well    40
spent, but the fact that most women continue to take the primary
responsibility for child care is a cause of distraction, diversion, anxiety,
and absenteeism—to say nothing of the persistent guilt experienced by

all working mothers. A great many women, perhaps most of all women who have always performed at the highest levels, are also frustrated by a sense that while their children are babies they cannot function at their best either at home or at work.

In its simplest form, flexibility is the freedom to take time off—a     41
couple of hours, a day, a week—or to do some work at home and some at the office, an arrangement that communication technology makes increasingly feasible. At the complex end of the spectrum are alternative work schedules that permit the woman to work less than full-time and her employer to reap the benefits of her experience and, with careful planning, the top level of her abilities.

Part-time employment is the single greatest inducement to getting     42
women back on the job expeditiously and the provision women themselves most desire. A part-time return to work enables them to maintain responsibility for critical aspects of their jobs, keeps them in touch with the changes constantly occurring at the workplace and in the job itself, reduces stress and fatigue, often eliminates the need for paid maternity leave by permitting a return to the office as soon as disability leave is over, and, not least, can greatly enhance company loyalty. The part-time solution works particularly well when a work load can be reduced for one individual in a department or when a full-time job can be broken down by skill levels and apportioned to two individuals at different levels of skill and pay.

I believe, however, that shared employment is the most promising     43
and will be the most widespread form of flexible scheduling in the future. It is feasible at every level of the corporation except at the pinnacle, for both the short and the long term. It involves two people taking responsibility for one job.

Two red lights flash on as soon as most executives hear the words     44
"job sharing": continuity and client-customer contact. The answer to the continuity question is to place responsibility entirely on the two individuals sharing the job to discuss everything that transpires—thoroughly, daily, and on their own time. The answer to the problem of client-customer contact is yes, job sharing requires reeducation and a period of adjustment. But as both client and supervisor will quickly come to appreciate, two contacts means that the customer has continuous access to the company's representative, without interruptions for vacation, travel, or sick leave. The two people holding the job can simply cover for each other, and the uninterrupted, full-time coverage they provide together can be a stipulation of their arrangement.

Flexibility is costly in numerous ways. It requires more supervisory    45
time to coordinate and manage, more office space, and somewhat
greater benefits costs (though these can be contained with flexible
benefits plans, prorated benefits, and, in two-paycheck families, elimi-
nation of duplicate benefits). But the advantages of reduced turnover
and the greater productivity that results from higher energy levels and
greater focus can outweigh the costs.

A few hints:                                                            46

- Provide flexibility selectively. I'm not suggesting private
  arrangements subject to the suspicion of favoritism but rather
  a policy that makes flexible work schedules available only to
  high performers.
- Make it clear that in most instances (but not all) the rates of
  advancement and pay will be appropriately lower for those
  who take time off or who work part-time than for those who
  work full-time. Most career-and-family women are entirely
  willing to make that trade-off.
- Discuss costs as well as benefits. Be willing to risk
  accusations of bias. Insist, for example, that half time is half
  of whatever time it takes to do the job, not merely half of 35
  or 40 hours.

The woman who is eager to get home to her child has a powerful    47
incentive to use her time effectively at the office and to carry with her
reading and other work that can be done at home. The talented professional who wants to have it all can be a high performer by carefully
ordering her priorities and by focusing on objectives rather than on the
legendary 15-hour day. By the time professional women have their first
babies—at an average age of 31—they have already had nine years to
work long hours at a desk, to travel, and to relocate. In the case of high
performers, the need for flexibility coincides with what has gradually
become the goal-oriented nature of responsibility.

Family supports—in addition to maternity leave and flexibility—    48
include the provision of parental leave for men, support for two-career
and single-parent families during relocation, and flexible benefits. But
the primary ingredient is child care. The capacity of working mothers
to function effectively and without interruption depends on the availability of good, affordable child care. Now that women make up almost

half the work force and the growing percentage of managers, the decision to become involved in the personal lives of employees is no longer a philosophical question but a practical one. To make matters worse, the quality of child care has almost no relation to technology, inventiveness, or profitability but is more or less a pure function of the quality of child care personnel and the ratio of adults to children. These costs are irreducible. Only by joining hands with government and the public sector can corporations hope to create the vast quantity and variety of child care that their employees need.

Until quite recently, the response of corporations to women has been largely symbolic and cosmetic, motivated in large part by the will to avoid litigation and legal penalties. In some cases, companies were also moved by a genuine sense of fairness and a vague discomfort and frustration at the absence of women above the middle of the corporate pyramid. The actions they took were mostly quick, easy, and highly visible—child care information services, a three-month parental leave available to men as well as women, a woman appointed to the board of directors.

When I first began to discuss these issues 26 years ago, I was sometimes able to get an appointment with the assistant to the assistant in personnel, but it was only a courtesy. Over the past decade, I have met with the CEOs of many large corporations, and I've watched them become involved with ideas they had never previously thought much about. Until recently, however, the shelf life of that enhanced awareness was always short. Given pressing, short-term concerns, women were not a front-burner issue. In the past few months, I have seen yet another change. Some CEOs and top management groups now take the initiative. They call and ask us to show them how to shift gears from a responsive to a proactive approach to recruiting, developing, and retaining women.

I think this change is more probably a response to business needs—to concern for the quality of future profits and managerial talent—than to uneasiness about legal requirements, sympathy with the demands of women and minorities, or the desire to do what is right and fair. The nature of such business motivation varies. Some companies want to move women to higher positions as role models for those below them and as beacons for talented young recruits. Some want to achieve a favorable image with employees, customers, clients, and stockholders. These are all legitimate motives. But I think the compa-

49

50

51

nies that stand to gain most are motivated as well by a desire to capture competitive advantage in an era when talent and competence will be in increasingly short supply. These companies are now ready to stop being defensive about their experience with women and to ask incisive questions without preconceptions.

Even so, incredibly, I don't know of more than one or two compa-    52
nies that have looked into their own records to study the absolutely critical issue of maternity leave—how many women took it, when and whether they returned, and how this behavior correlated with their rank, tenure, age, and performance. The unique drawback to the employment of women is the physical reality of maternity and the particular socializing influence maternity has had. Yet to make women equal to men in the workplace we have chosen on the whole not to discuss this single most significant difference between them. Unless we do, we cannot evaluate the cost of recruiting, developing, and moving women up.

Now that interest is replacing indifference, there are four steps    53
every company can take to examine its own experience with women:

1.  Gather quantitative data on the company's experience with management-level women regarding turnover rates, occurrence of and return from maternity leave, and organizational level attained in relation to tenure and performance.
2.  Correlate this data with factors such as age, marital status, and presence and age of children, and attempt to identify and analyze why women respond the way they do.
3.  Gather qualitative data on the experience of women in your company and on how women are perceived by both sexes.
4.  Conduct a cost-benefit analysis of the return on your investment in high-performing women. Factor in the cost to the company of women's negative reactions to negative experience, as well as the probable cost of corrective measures and policies. If women's value to your company is greater than the cost to recruit, train, and develop them—and of course I believe it will be—then you will want to do everything you can to retain them.

We have come a tremendous distance since the days when the    54
prevailing male wisdom saw women as lacking the kind of intelli-

gence that would allow them to succeed in business. For decades, even women themselves have harbored an unspoken belief that they couldn't make it because they couldn't be just like men, and nothing else would do. But now that women have shown themselves the equal of men in every area of organizational activity, now that they have demonstrated that they can be stars in every field of endeavor, now we can all venture to examine the fact that women and men are different.

On balance, employing women is more costly than employing men. Women can acknowledge this fact today because they know that their value to employers exceeds the additional cost and because they know that changing attitudes can reduce the additional cost dramatically. Women in management are no longer an idiosyncrasy of the arts and education. They have always matched men in natural ability. Within a very few years, they will equal men in numbers as well in every area of economic activity.

The demographic motivation to recruit and develop women is compelling. But an older question remains: Is society better for the change? Women's exit from the home and entry into the work force has certainly created problems—an urgent need for good, affordable child care; troubling questions about the kind of parenting children need; the costs and difficulties of diversity in the workplace; the stress and fatigue of combining work and family responsibilities. Wouldn't we all be happier if we could turn back the clock to an age when men were in the workplace and women in the home, when male and female roles were clearly differentiated and complementary?

Nostalgia, anxiety, and discouragement will urge many to say yes, but my answer is emphatically no. Two fundamental benefits that were unattainable in the past are now within our reach. For the individual, freedom of choice—in this case the freedom to choose career, family, or a combination of the two. For the corporation, access to the most gifted individuals in the country. These benefits are neither self-indulgent nor insubstantial. Freedom of choice and self-realization are too deeply American to be cast aside for some wistful vision of the past. And access to our most talented human resources is not a luxury in this age of explosive international competition but rather the barest minimum that prudence and national self-preservation require.

# Obscenity and Violence

## ROLLO MAY

There is a halfway stage in the disintegration of words. This is 1
obscenity. It gets its power from the using of words to do violence to
our unconscious expectations, to destroy our mooring posts, and to
undercut the forms of relationship we are used to. The words threaten
us with the insecurity of formlessness. Obscenity expresses what had
previously been prohibited, reveals what previously was not revealed.
Thus it insists on and gets our attention.

This can be constructive or destructive. When Ezra Pound writes, 2

Winter is icumen in,
Lhude sing Goddamm. . . .
Damm you, sing: Goddamm,

he catches our attention immediately because of the shock value: our
expectations were set to hear something like the lovely Middle English
lyric. This kind of language can be entirely justified: the poet has to
develop a language that has "guts." Obscenity is the process of attacking what has been sacred and occurs when the word is losing its holy
character. It is often factually true that words have already lost all roots
to their meaning and have become nothing but empty forms.

The same is true in modern art. By showing blood and gore and 3
using sensational colors that carry these impressions, many painters
are crying out: *"You must look, you must pay attention, you must see
in a new way."* This can, indeed, teach us, shocked as we are, not just
to look but to see.

The breakdown in language has become very clear to the extremists 4
on the left. Jerry Rubin says in his book *Do It:* "Nobody really communicates with words anymore. Words have lost their emotional impact,
intimacy, ability to shock and make love." "But there is one word," he
goes on, "Americans have not destroyed. One word which has maintained its emotional power and purity." As you have guessed already,
that is the word *fuck*. It has kept its purity only because it has been
illegal, says Rubin—so now it has some freshness, some impact left.

I agree that the word does have emotional power. But is its power 5 connected with what the word *means?* No, it is connected with just the opposite—not its original meaning of a relationship between two people characterized by physical and psychological abandon combined with tenderness and gentleness, but rather an exploitation, an expression of aggression. Indeed, the word *fuck* proves precisely my point, that words have been twisted into *opposite* meanings. A word becomes aggressive as a stage in its deterioration: it loses its original meaning, takes on the aggressive form in obscenity, and then may pass into oblivion.

Language can be as violent as physical force when it is used to 6 incite people's aggressive emotions. The masses of students who protested on Wall Street in New York after the invasion of Cambodia had a special chant: "One, two, three, four./We don't like your fucking war." They seemed to be totally oblivious to the fact that if you keep chanting that to an upper-middle-class stock broker, you are going to make him mad, and in the irrational, explosive sense of the first chapter—as mad as if you had struck him over the head with a billy club. And his rage will have nothing to do with the war. It will be because of the term *fucking*, a word about which he has fairly rigid beliefs in using and not using in public.

Obscenity is a form of psychic violence and can be used with great 7 effect, a weapon that can excite people to lethal physical violence. One should know this when one is using it. It is a mark of our time that each side in a disagreement uses violent language. This amounts to using violence to defeat violence—which never works, whether it is done by police and administration or by young people themselves.

# Comparison

## Metaphoric Uses of TB and Cancer

### SUSAN SONTAG

Throughout most of their history, the metaphoric uses of TB and
cancer crisscross and overlap. The *Oxford English Dictionary* records
"consumption" in use as a synonym for pulmonary tuberculosis as
early as 1398. (John of Trevisa: "Whan the blode is made thynne, soo
folowyth consumpcyon and wastyng.") But the pre-modern understanding of cancer also invokes the notion of consumption. The OED
gives as the early figurative definition of cancer: "Anything that frets,
corrodes, corrupts, or consumes slowly and secretly." (Thomas Paynell
in 1528: "A canker is a melancolye impostume, eatynge partes of the
bodye.") The earliest literal definition of cancer is a growth, lump, or
protuberance, and the disease's name—from the Greek *karkínos* and
the Latin *cancer*, both meaning crab—was inspired, according to
Galen, by the resemblance of an external tumor's swollen veins to a
crab's legs; not, as many people think, because a metastatic disease
crawls or creeps like a crab. But etymology indicates that tuberculosis
was also once considered a type of abnormal extrusion: the word
tuberculosis—from the Latin *tūberculum*, the diminutive of *tūber*,
bump, swelling—means a morbid swelling, protuberance, projection,
or growth. Rudolf Virchow, who founded the science of cellular pathology in the 1850s, thought of the tubercle as a tumor.

Thus, from late antiquity until quite recently, tuberculosis was—
typologically—cancer. And cancer was described, like TB, as a process
in which the body was consumed. The modern conceptions of the two
diseases could not be set until the advent of cellular pathology. Only
with the microscope was it possible to grasp the distinctiveness of
cancer, as a type of cellular activity, and to understand that the disease

1

2

did not always take the form of an external or even palpable tumor. (Before the mid-nineteenth century, nobody could have identified leukemia as a form of cancer.) And it was not possible definitively to separate cancer from TB until after 1882, when tuberculosis was discovered to be a bacterial infection. Such advances in medical thinking enabled the leading metaphors of the two diseases to become truly distinct and, for the most part, contrasting. The modern fantasy about cancer could then begin to take shape—a fantasy which from the 1920s on would inherit most of the problems dramatized by the fantasies about TB, but with the two diseases and their symptoms conceived in quite different, almost opposing, ways.

TB is understood as a disease of one organ, the lungs, while cancer   3
is understood as a disease that can turn up in any organ and whose outreach is the whole body.

TB is understood as a disease of extreme contrasts: white pallor   4
and red flush, hyperactivity alternating with languidness. The spasmodic course of the disease is illustrated by what is thought of as the prototypical TB symptom, coughing. The sufferer is wracked by coughs, then sinks back, recovers breath, breathes normally; then coughs again. Cancer is a disease of growth (sometimes visible; more characteristically, inside), of abnormal, ultimately lethal growth that is measured, incessant, steady. Although there may be periods in which tumor growth is arrested (remissions), cancer produces no contrasts like the oxymorons of behavior—febrile activity, passionate resignation—thought to be typical of TB. The tubercular is pallid some of the time; the pallor of the cancer patient is unchanging.

TB makes the body transparent. The X-rays which are the stan-   5
dard diagnostic tool permit one, often for the first time, to see one's insides—to become transparent to oneself. While TB is understood to be, from early on, rich in visible symptoms (progressive emaciation, coughing, languidness, fever), and can be suddenly and dramatically revealed (the blood on the handkerchief), in cancer the main symptoms are thought to be, characteristically, invisible—until the last stage, when it is too late. The disease, often discovered by chance or through a routine medical checkup, can be far advanced without exhibiting any appreciable symptoms. One has an opaque body that must be taken to a specialist to find out if it contains cancer. What the patient cannot perceive, the specialist will determine by analyzing tissues taken from

the body. TB patients may see their X-rays or even possess them: the patients at the sanatorium in *The Magic Mountain* carry theirs around in their breast pockets. Cancer patients don't look at their biopsies.

TB was—still is—thought to produce spells of euphoria, increased   6 appetite, exacerbated sexual desire. Part of the regimen for patients in *The Magic Mountain* is a second breakfast, eaten with gusto. Cancer is thought to cripple vitality, make eating an ordeal, deaden desire. Having TB was imagined to be an aphrodisiac, and to confer extraordinary powers of seduction. Cancer is considered to be de-sexualizing. But it is characteristic of TB that many of its symptoms are deceptive— liveliness that comes from enervation, rosy cheeks that look like a sign of health but come from fever—and an upsurge of vitality may be a sign of approaching death. (Such gushes of energy will generally be self-destructive, and may be destructive of others: recall the Old West legend of Doc Holliday, the tubercular gunfighter released from moral restraints by the ravages of his disease.) Cancer has only true symptoms.

TB is disintegration, febrilization, dematerialization; it is a disease   7 of liquids—the body turning to phlegm and mucus and sputum and, finally, blood—and of air, of the need for better air. Cancer is degeneration, the body tissues turning to something hard. Alice James, writing in her journal a year before she died from cancer in 1892, speaks of "this unholy granite substance in my breast." But this lump is alive, a fetus with its own will. Novalis, in an entry written around 1798 for his encyclopedia project, defines cancer, along with gangrene, as "full-fledged *parasites*—they grow, are engendered, engender, have their structure, secrete, eat." Cancer is a demonic pregnancy. St. Jerome must have been thinking of a cancer when he wrote: "The one there with his swollen belly is pregnant with his own death" (*"Alius tumenti aqualiculo mortem parturit"*). Though the course of both diseases is emaciating, losing weight from TB is understood very differently from losing weight from cancer. In TB, the person is "consumed," burned up. In cancer, the patient is "invaded" by alien cells, which multiply, causing an atrophy or blockage of bodily functions. The cancer patient "shrivels" (Alice James's word) or "shrinks" (Wilhelm Reich's word).

TB is a disease of time; it speeds up life, highlights it, spiritualizes   8 it. In both English and French, consumption "gallops." Cancer has stages rather than gaits; it is (eventually) "terminal." Cancer works slowly, insidiously: the standard euphemism in obituaries is that someone has "died after a long illness." Every characterization of cancer describes it as slow, and so it was first used metaphorically. "The word of hem crepith as a kankir," Wyclif wrote in 1382 (translating a phrase in II Timothy 2:17); and among the earliest figurative uses of cancer are as a metaphor for "idleness" and "sloth." Metaphorically, cancer is not so much a disease of time as a disease or pathology of space. Its principal metaphors refer to topography (cancer "spreads" or "proliferates" or is "diffused"; tumors are surgically "excised"), and its most dreaded consequence, short of death, is the mutilation or amputation of part of the body.

TB is often imagined as a disease of poverty and deprivation—of 9 thin garments, thin bodies, unheated rooms, poor hygiene, inadequate food. The poverty may not be as literal as Mimi's garret in *La Bohème;* the tubercular Marguerite Gautier in *La Dame aux Camélias* lives in luxury, but inside she is a waif. In contrast, cancer is a disease of middle-class life, a disease associated with affluence, with excess. Rich countries have the highest cancer rates, and the rising incidence of the disease is seen as resulting, in part, from a diet rich in fat and proteins and from the toxic effluvia of the industrial economy that creates affluence. The treatment of TB is identified with the stimulation of appetite, cancer treatment with nausea and the loss of appetite. The undernourished nourishing themselves—alas, to no avail. The overnourished, unable to eat.

The TB patient was thought to be helped, even cured, by a 10 change in environment. There was a notion that TB was a wet disease, a disease of humid and dank cities. The inside of the body became damp ("moisture in the lungs" was a favored locution) and had to be dried out. Doctors advised travel to high, dry places—the mountains, the desert. But no change of surroundings is thought to help the cancer patient. The fight is all inside one's own body. It may be, is increasingly thought to be, something in the environment that has caused the cancer. But once cancer is present, it cannot be reversed or diminished by a move to a better (that is, less carcinogenic) environment.

TB is thought to be relatively painless. Cancer is thought to be, 11 invariably, excruciatingly painful. TB is thought to provide an easy death, while cancer is the spectacularly wretched one. For over a hundred years TB remained the preferred way of giving death a meaning—an edifying, refined disease. Nineteenth-century literature is

stocked with descriptions of almost symptomless, unfrightened, bea-
tific deaths from TB, particularly of young people, such as Little Eva
in *Uncle Tom's Cabin* and Dombey's son Paul in *Dombey and Son* and
Smike in *Nicholas Nickleby*, where Dickens described TB as the
"dread disease" which "refines" death

of its grosser aspect . . . in which the struggle between soul and body is so
gradual, quiet, and solemn, and the result so sure, that day by day, and grain
by grain, the mortal part wastes and withers away, so that the spirit grows light
and sanguine with its lightening load. . . .

Contrast these ennobling, placid TB deaths with the ignoble, agonizing
cancer deaths of Eugene Gant's father in Thomas Wolfe's *Of Time and
the River* and of the sister in Bergman's film *Cries and Whispers*. The
dying tubercular is pictured as made more beautiful and more soulful;
the person dying of cancer is portrayed as robbed of all capacities of
self-transcendence, humiliated by fear and agony.

These are contrasts drawn from the popular mythology of both     12
diseases. Of course, many tuberculars died in terrible pain, and some
people die of cancer feeling little or no pain to the end; the poor and
the rich both get TB and cancer; and not everyone who has TB
coughs. But the mythology persists. It is not just because pulmonary
tuberculosis is the most common form of TB that most people think
of TB, in contrast to cancer, as a disease of one organ. It is because
the myths about TB do not fit the brain, larynx, kidneys, long bones,
and other sites where the tubercle bacillus can also settle, but do
have a close fit with the traditional imagery (breath, life) associated
with the lungs.

While TB takes on qualities assigned to the lungs, which are part     13
of the upper, spiritualized body, cancer is notorious for attacking parts
of the body (colon, bladder, rectum, breast, cervix, prostate, testicles)
that are embarrassing to acknowledge. Having a tumor generally
arouses some feelings of shame, but in the hierarchy of the body's
organs, lung cancer is felt to be less shameful than rectal cancer. And
one non-tumor form of cancer now turns up in commercial fiction in the
role once monopolized by TB, as the romantic disease which cuts off a
young life. (The heroine of Erich Segal's *Love Story* dies of leukemia—
the "white" or TB-like form of the disease, for which no mutilating
surgery can be proposed—not of stomach or breast cancer.) A disease

of the lungs is, metaphorically, a disease of the soul. Cancer, as a disease that can strike anywhere, is a disease of the body. Far from revealing anything spiritual, it reveals that the body is, all too woefully, just the body.

Such fantasies flourish because TB and cancer are thought to be 14 much more than diseases that usually are (or were) fatal. They are identified with death itself. In *Nicholas Nickleby*, Dickens apostrophized TB as the

disease in which death and life are so strangely blended, that death takes the glow and hue of life, and life the gaunt and grisly form of death; disease which medicine never cured, wealth never warded off, or poverty could boast exemption from. . . .

And Kafka wrote to Max Brod in October 1917 that he had "come to think that tuberculosis . . . is no special disease, or not a disease that deserves a special name, but only the germ of death itself, intensified. . . ." Cancer inspires similar speculations. Georg Groddeck, whose remarkable views on cancer in *The Book of the It* (1923) anticipate those of Wilhelm Reich, wrote:

Of all the theories put forward in connection with cancer, only one has in my opinion survived the passage of time, namely, that cancer leads through definite stages to death. I mean by that that what is not fatal is not cancer. From that you may conclude that I hold out no hope of a new method of curing cancer . . . [only] the many cases of so-called cancer. . . .

For all the progress in treating cancer, many people still subscribe to Groddeck's equation: cancer = death. But the metaphors surrounding TB and cancer reveal much about the idea of the morbid, and how it has evolved from the nineteenth-century (when TB was the most common cause of death) to our time (when cancer is the most dreaded disease). The Romantics moralized death in a new way: with the TB death, which dissolved the gross body, etherealized the personality, expanded consciousness. It was equally possible, through fantasies about TB, to aestheticize death. Thoreau, who had TB, wrote in 1852: "Death and disease are often beautiful, like . . . the hectic glow of consumption." Nobody conceives of cancer the way TB was thought of—as a decorative, often lyrical death. Cancer is a rare and still scandalous subject for poetry; and it seems unimaginable to aestheticize the disease.

# Sex versus Loveliness

## D. H. LAWRENCE

It is a pity that *sex* is such an ugly little word. An ugly little word, 1
and really almost incomprehensible. What *is* sex, after all? The more
we think about it the less we know.

Science says it is an instinct; but what is an instinct? Apparently 2
an instinct is an old, old habit that has become ingrained. But a habit,
however old, has to have a beginning. And there is really no beginning
to sex. Where life is, there it is. So sex is no "habit" that has been
formed.

Again, they talk of sex as an appetite, like hunger. An appetite; but 3
for what? An appetite for propagation? It is rather absurd. They say a
peacock puts on all his fine feathers to dazzle the peahen into letting
him satisfy his appetite for propagation. But why should the peahen
not put on fine feathers, to dazzle the peacock, and satisfy *her* desire
for propagation? She has surely quite as great a desire for eggs and
chickens as he has. We cannot believe that her sex-urge is so weak that
she needs all that blue splendour of feathers to rouse her. Not at all.

As for me, I never even saw a peahen so much as look at her lord's 4
bronze and blue glory. I don't believe she ever sees it. I don't believe
for a moment that she knows the difference between bronze, blue,
brown or green.

If I had ever seen a peahen gazing with rapt attention on her lord's 5
flamboyancy, I might believe that he had put on all those feathers just
to "attract" her. But she never looks at him. Only she seems to get a
little perky when he shudders all his quills at her, like a storm in the
trees. Then she does seem to notice, just casually, his presence.

These theories of sex are amazing. A peacock puts on his glory for 6
the sake of a wall-eyed peahen who never looks at him. Imagine a
scientist being so naïve as to credit the peahen with a profound, dynamic appreciation of a peacock's colour and pattern. Oh, highly aes-
thetic peahen!

And a nightingale sings to attract his female. Which is mighty 7
curious, seeing he sings his best when courtship and honeymoon are
over and the female is no longer concerned with him at all, but with

the young. Well, then, if he doesn't sing to attract her, he must sing to distract her and amuse her while she's sitting.

How delightful, how naïve theories are! But there is a hidden will 8 behind them all. There is a hidden will behind all theories of sex, implacable. And that is the will to deny, to wipe out the mystery of beauty.

Because beauty is a mystery. You can neither eat it nor make 9 flannel out of it. Well, then, says science, it is just a trick to catch the female and induce her to propagate. How naïve! As if the female needed inducing. She will propagate in the dark, even—so where, then, is the beauty trick?

Science has a mysterious hatred of beauty, because it doesn't fit in 10 the cause-and-effect chain. And society has a mysterious hatred of sex, because it perpetually interferes with the nice money-making schemes of social man. So the two hatreds made a combine, and sex and beauty are mere propagation appetite.

Now sex and beauty are one thing, like flame and fire. If you hate 11 sex you hate beauty. If you love *living* beauty, you have a reverence for sex. Of course you can love old, dead beauty and hate sex. But to love living beauty you must have a reverence for sex.

Sex and beauty are inseparable, like life and consciousness. And 12 the intelligence which goes with sex and beauty, and arises out of sex and beauty, is intuition. The great disaster of our civilization is the morbid hatred of sex. What, for example, could show a more poisoned hatred of sex than Freudian psycho-analysis?—which carries with it a morbid fear of beauty, "alive" beauty, and which causes the atrophy of our intuitive faculty and our intuitive self.

The deep psychic disease of modern men and women is the 13 diseased, atrophied condition of the intuitive faculties. There is a whole world of life that we might know and enjoy by intuition, and by intuition alone. This is denied us, because we deny sex and beauty, the source of the intuitive life and of the insouciance which is so lovely in free animals and in plants.

Sex is the root of which intuition is the foliage and beauty the 14 flower. Why is a woman lovely, if ever, in her twenties? It is the time when sex rises softly to her face, as a rose to the top of a rose bush.

And the appeal is the appeal of beauty. We deny it wherever we 15 can. We try to make the beauty as shallow and trashy as possible. But, first and foremost, sex appeal is the appeal of beauty.

Now beauty is a thing about which we are so uneducated we can 16

hardly speak of it. We try to pretend it is a fixed arrangement: straight
nose, large eyes, etc. We think a lovely woman must look like Lilian
Gish, a handsome man must look like Rudolph Valentino. So we *think.*

In actual life we behave quite differently. We say: "She's quite      17
beautiful, but I don't care for her." Which shows we are using the word
*beautiful* all wrong. We should say: "She has the stereotyped attributes of beauty, but she is not beautiful to me."

Beauty is an *experience,* nothing else. It is not a fixed pattern or   18
an arrangement of features. It is something *felt,* a glow or a communicated sense of fineness. What ails us is that our sense of beauty
is so bruised and blunted, we miss all the best.

But to stick to the films—there is a greater essential beauty in       19
Charlie Chaplin's odd face than ever there was in Valentino's. There
is a bit of true beauty in Chaplin's brows and eyes, a gleam of something pure.

But our sense of beauty is so bruised and clumsy, we don't see it,     20
and don't know it when we do see it. We can only see the blatantly
obvious, like the so-called beauty of Rudolph Valentino, which only
pleases because it satisfies some ready-made notion of handsomeness.

But the plainest person can look beautiful, can *be* beautiful. It only  21
needs the fire of sex to rise delicately to change an ugly face to a lovely
one. That is really sex appeal: the communicating of a sense of beauty.

And in the reverse way, no one can be quite so repellent as a really   22
pretty woman. That is, since beauty is a question of experience, not of
concrete form, no one can be as acutely ugly as a really pretty woman.
When the sex-glow is missing, and she moves in ugly coldness, how
hideous she seems, and all the worse for her externals of prettiness.

What sex is, we don't know, but it must be some sort of fire. For      23
it always communicates a sense of warmth, of glow. And when the
glow becomes a pure shine, then we feel the sense of beauty.

But the communicating of the warmth, the glow of sex, is true sex     24
appeal. We all have the fire of sex slumbering or burning inside us. If
we live to be ninety, it is still there. Or, if it dies, we become one of
those ghastly living corpses which are unfortunately becoming more
numerous in the world.

Nothing is more ugly than a human being in whom the fire of sex      25
has gone out. You get a nasty clayey creature whom everybody wants
to avoid.

But while we are fully alive, the fire of sex smoulders or burns in    26 us. In youth it flickers and shines; in age it glows softer and stiller, but there it is. We have some control over it; but only partial control. That is why society hates it.

While ever it lives, the fire of sex, which is the source of beauty and anger, burns in us beyond our understanding. Like actual fire, while it lives it will burn our fingers if we touch it carelessly. And so social man, who only wants to be "safe," hates the fire of sex.  27

Luckily, not many men succeed in being merely social men. The fire of the old Adam smoulders. And one of the qualities of fire is that it calls to fire. Sex-fire here kindles sex-fire there. It may only rouse the smoulder into a soft glow. It may call up a sharp flicker. Or rouse a flame; and then flame leans to flame, and starts a blaze.  28

Whenever the sex-fire glows through, it will kindle an answer somewhere or other. It may only kindle a sense of warmth and optimism. Then you say: "I like that girl; she's a real good sort." It may kindle a glow that makes the world look kindlier, and life feel better. Then you say: "She's an attractive woman. I like her."  29

Or she may rouse a flame that lights up her own face first, before it lights up the universe. Then you say: "She's a lovely woman. She looks lovely to me."  30

It takes a rare woman to rouse a real sense of loveliness. It is not that a woman is born beautiful. We say that to escape our own poor, bruised, clumsy understanding of beauty. There have been thousands and thousands of women quite as good-looking as Diane de Poitiers, or Mrs. Langtry, or any of the famous ones. There are today thousands and thousands of superbly good-looking women. But oh, how few lovely women!  31

And why? Because of the failure of their sex appeal. A good-looking woman becomes lovely when the fire of sex rouses pure and fine in her and flickers through her face and touches the fire in me.  32

Then she becomes a lovely woman to me, then she is in the living flesh a lovely woman: not a mere photograph of one. And how lovely a lovely woman! But, alas! how rare! How bitterly rare in a world full of unusually handsome girls and women!  33

Handsome, good-looking, but not lovely, not beautiful. Handsome and good-looking women are the women with good features and the right hair. But a lovely woman is an experience. It is a question of communicated fire. It is a question of sex appeal in our poor, dilapidated modern phraseology. Sex appeal applied to Diane de Poitiers, or  34

even, in the lovely hours, to one's wife—why, it is a libel and a slander
in itself. Nowadays, however, instead of the fire of loveliness, it is sex
appeal. The two are the same thing, I suppose, but on vastly different
levels.

The business man's pretty and devoted secretary is still chiefly    35
valuable because of her sex appeal. Which does not imply "immoral
relations" in the slightest.

Even today a girl with a bit of generosity likes to feel she is helping    36
a man if the man will take her help. And this desire that he shall take
her help is her sex appeal. It is the genuine fire, if of a very mediocre
heat.

Still, it serves to keep the world of "business" alive. Probably,    37
but for the introduction of the lady secretary into the business man's
office, the business man would have collapsed entirely by now. She
calls up the sacred fire in her and she communicates it to her boss.
He feels an added flow of energy and optimism, and—business
flourishes.

There is, of course, the other side of sex appeal. It can be the    38
destruction of the one appealed to. When a woman starts using her sex
appeal to her own advantage it is usually a bad moment for some poor
devil. But this side of sex appeal has been overworked lately, so it is not
nearly as dangerous as it was.

The sex-appealing courtesans who ruined so many men in Balzac    39
no longer find it smooth running. Men have grown canny. They fight
shy even of the emotional vamp. In fact, men are inclined to think they
smell a rat the moment they feel the touch of feminine sex appeal
today.

Which is a pity, for sex appeal is only a dirty name for a bit of    40
life-flame. No man works so well and so successfully as when some
woman has kindled a little fire in his veins. No woman does her
housework with real joy unless she is in love—and a woman may go
on being quietly in love for fifty years almost without knowing it.

If only our civilization had taught us how to let sex appeal flow    41
properly and subtly, how to keep the fire of sex clear and alive, flickering or glowing or blazing in all its varying degrees of strength and
communication, we might, all of us, have lived all our lives in love,
which means we should be kindled and full of zest in all kinds of ways
and for all kinds of things. . . .

Whereas, what a lot of dead ash there is in life now.    42

# Two Aspects of the River

## MARK TWAIN

Now when I had mastered the language of this water, and had 1
come to know every trifling feature that bordered the great river as
familiarly as I knew the letters of the alphabet, I had made a valuable
acquisition. But I had lost something, too. I had lost something which
could never be restored to me while I lived. All the grace, the beauty,
the poetry, had gone out of the majestic river! I still keep in mind a
certain wonderful sunset which I witnessed when steamboating was
new to me. A broad expanse of the river was turned to blood; in the
middle distance the red hue brightened into gold, through which a
solitary log came floating black and conspicuous; in one place a long,
slanting mark lay sparkling upon the water; in another the surface was
broken by boiling, tumbling rings, that were as many-tinted as an opal;
where the ruddy flush was faintest, was a smooth spot that was covered
with graceful circles and radiating lines, ever so delicately traced; the
shore on our left was densely wooded, and the somber shadow that fell
from this forest was broken in one place by a long, ruffled trail that
shone like silver; and high above the forest wall a clean-stemmed dead
tree waved a single leafy bough that glowed like a flame in the unob-
structed splendor that was flowing from the sun. There were graceful
curves, reflected images, woody heights, soft distances; and over the
whole scene, far and near, the dissolving lights drifted steadily, enriching it every passing moment with new marvels of coloring.

I stood like one bewitched. I drank it in, in a speechless rapture. 2
The world was new to me, and I had never seen anything like this at
home. But as I have said, a day came when I began to cease from
noting the glories and the charms which the moon and the sun and the
twilight wrought upon the river's face; another day came when I
ceased altogether to note them. Then, if that sunset scene had been
repeated, I should have looked upon it without rapture, and should
have commented upon it, inwardly, after this fashion: "This sun means
that we are going to have wind to-morrow; that floating log means that
the river is rising, small thanks to it; that slanting mark on the water

refers to a bluff reef which is going to kill somebody's steamboat one of these nights, if it keeps on stretching out like that; those tumbling 'boils' show a dissolving bar and a changing channel there; the lines and circles in the slick water over yonder are a warning that that troublesome place is shoaling up dangerously; that silver streak in the shadow of the forest is the 'break' from a new snag, and he has located himself in the very best place he could have found to fish for steamboats; that tall dead tree, with a single living branch, is not going to last long, and then how is a body ever going to get through this blind place at night without the friendly old landmark?"

No, the romance and beauty were all gone from the river. All the value any feature of it had for me now was the amount of usefulness it could furnish toward compassing the safe piloting of a steamboat. Since those days, I have pitied doctors from my heart. What does the lovely flush in a beauty's cheek mean to a doctor but a "break" that ripples above some deadly disease? Are not all her visible charms sown thick with what are to him the signs and symbols of hidden decay? Does he ever see her beauty at all, or doesn't he simply view her professionally, and comment upon her unwholesome condition all to himself? And doesn't he sometimes wonder whether he has gained most or lost most by learning his trade?

---

# Examsmanship and the Liberal Arts: A Study in Educational Epistemology

## WILLIAM G. PERRY, JR.

"But sir, I don't think I really deserve it, it was mostly bull, really." This disclaimer from a student whose examination we have awarded a straight "A" is wondrously depressing. Alfred North Whitehead invented its only possible rejoinder: "Yes sir, what you wrote is nonsense, utter nonsense. But ah! Sir! It's the right *kind* of nonsense!"

Bull, in this university, is customarily a source of laughter, or a problem in ethics. I shall step a little out of fashion to use the subject as a take-off point for a study in comparative epistemology. The phenomenon of bull, in all the honor and opprobrium with which it is regarded by students and faculty, says something, I think, about our theories of knowledge. So too, the grades which we assign on examinations communicate to students what these theories may be.

We do not have to be out-and-out logical-positivists to suppose that    3
we have something to learn about "what we think knowledge is" by having a good look at "what we do when we go about measuring it." We know the straight "A" examination when we see it, of course, and we have reason to hope that the student will understand why his work receives our recognition. He doesn't always. And those who receive lesser honor? Perhaps an understanding of certain anomalies in our customs of grading good bull will explain the students' confusion.

I must beg patience, then, both of the reader's humor and of his    4
morals. Not that I ask him to suspend his sense of humor but that I shall ask him to go beyond it. In a great university the picture of a bright student attempting to outwit his professor while his professor takes pride in not being outwitted is certainly ridiculous. I shall report just such a scene, for its implications bear upon my point. Its comedy need not present a serious obstacle to thought.

As for the ethics of bull, I must ask for a suspension of judgment.    5
I wish that students could suspend theirs. Unlike humor, moral commitment is hard to think beyond. Too early a moral judgment is precisely what stands between many able students and a liberal education. The stunning realization that the Harvard Faculty will often accept, as evidence of knowledge, the cerebrations of a student who has little data at his disposal, confronts every student with an ethical dilemma. For some it forms an academic focus for what used to be thought of as "adolescent disillusion." It is irrelevant that rumor inflates the phenomenon to mythical proportions. The students know that beneath the myth there remains a solid and haunting reality. The moral "bind" consequent on this awareness appears most poignantly in serious students who are reluctant to concede the competitive advantage to the bullster and who yet feel a deep personal shame when, having succumbed to "temptation," they themselves receive a high grade for work they consider "dishonest."

I have spent many hours with students caught in this unwelcome    6
bitterness. These hours lend an urgency to my theme. I have found that students have been able to come to terms with the ethical problem, to

the extent that it is real, only after a refined study of the true nature of bull and its relation to "knowledge." I shall submit grounds for my suspicion that we can be found guilty of sharing the students' confusion of moral and epistemological issues.

# I

    I present as my "premise," then, an amoral *fabliau*. Its hero-villain   7
is the Abominable Mr. Metzger '47. Since I celebrate his virtuosity, I regret giving him a pseudonym, but the peculiar style of his bravado requires me to honor also his modesty. Bull in pure form is rare; there is usually some contamination by data. The community has reason to be grateful to Mr. Metzger for having created an instance of laboratory purity, free from any adulteration by matter. The more credit is due him, I think, because his act was free from premeditation, deliberation, or hope of personal gain.

    Mr. Metzger stood one rainy November day in the lobby of Memo-   8
rial Hall. A junior, concentrating in mathematics, he was fond of diverting himself by taking part in the drama, a penchant which may have had some influence on the events of the next hour. He was waiting to take part in a rehearsal in Sanders Theatre, but, as sometimes happens, no other players appeared. Perhaps the rehearsal had been canceled without his knowledge? He decided to wait another five minutes.

    Students, meanwhile, were filing into the Great Hall opposite, and   9
taking seats at the testing tables. Spying a friend crossing the lobby toward the Great Hall's door, Metzger greeted him and extended appropriate condolences. He inquired, too, what course his friend was being tested in. "Oh, Soc. Sci. something-or-other." "What's it all about?" asked Metzger, and this, as Homer remarked of Patroclus, was the beginning of evil for him.

    "It's about Modern Perspectives on Man and Society and All   10
That," said his friend. "Pretty interesting, really."

    "Always wanted to take a course like that," said Metzger. "Any   11
good reading?"

    "Yeah, great. There's this book"—his friend did not have time to   12
finish.

    "Take your seats please" said a stern voice beside them. The idle   13
conversation had somehow taken the two friends to one of the tables in the Great Hall. Both students automatically obeyed; the proctor put

blue-books before them; another proctor presented them with copies of the printed hour-test.

Mr. Metzger remembered afterwards a brief misgiving that was suddenly overwhelmed by a surge of curiosity and puckish glee. He wrote "George Smith" on the blue book, opened it, and addressed the first question. 14

I must pause to exonerate the Management. The Faculty has a rule that no student may attend an examination in a course in which he is not enrolled. To the wisdom of this rule the outcome of this deplorable story stands witness. The Registrar, charged with the enforcement of the rule, has developed an organization with procedures which are certainly the finest to be devised. In November, however, class rosters are still shaky, and on this particular day another student, named Smith, was absent. As for the culprit, we can reduce his guilt no further than to suppose that he was ignorant of the rule, or, in the face of the momentous challenge before him, forgetful. 15

We need not be distracted by Metzger's performance on the "objective" or "spot" questions on the test. His D on these sections can be explained by those versed in the theory of probability. Our interest focuses on the quality of his essay. It appears that when Metzger's friend picked up his own blue book a few days later, he found himself in company with a large proportion of his section in having received on the essay a C. When he quietly picked up "George Smith's" blue book to return it to Metzger, he observed that the grade for the essay was A. In the margin was a note in the section man's hand. It read "Excellent work. Could you have pinned these observations down a bit more closely? Compare . . . in . . . pp. . . ." 16

Such news could hardly be kept quiet. There was a leak, and the whole scandal broke on the front page of Tuesday's *Crimson*. With the press Metzger was modest, as becomes a hero. He said that there had been nothing to it at all, really. The essay question had offered a choice of two books, Margaret Mead's *And Keep Your Powder Dry* or Geoffrey Gorer's *The American People*. Metzger reported that having read neither of them, he had chosen the second "because the title gave me some notion as to what the book might be about." On the test, two critical comments were offered on each book, one favorable, one unfavorable. The students were asked to "discuss." Metzger conceded that he had played safe in throwing his lot with the more laudatory of the two comments, "but I did not forget to be balanced." 17

I do not have Mr. Metzger's essay before me except in vivid 18 memory. As I recall, he took his first cue from the name Geoffrey, and committed his strategy to the premise that Gorer was born into an "Anglo-Saxon" culture, probably English, but certainly "English speaking." Having heard that Margaret Mead was a social anthropologist, he inferred that Gorer was the same. He then entered upon his essay, centering his inquiry upon what he supposed might be the problems inherent in an anthropologist's observation of a culture which was his own, or nearly his own. Drawing in part from memories of table-talk on cultural relativity and in part from creative logic, he rang changes on the relation of observer to observed, and assessed the kind and degree of objectivity which might accrue to an observer through training as an anthropologist. He concluded that the book in question did in fact contribute a considerable range of " 'objective', and even 'fresh'," insights into the nature of our culture. "At the same time," he warned, "these observations must be understood within the context of their generation by a person only partly freed from his embeddedness in the culture he is observing, and limited in his capacity to transcend those particular tendencies and biases which he has himself developed as a personality in his interraction with this culture since his birth. In this sense the book portrays as much the character of Geoffrey Gorer as it analyzes that of the American people." It is my regretable duty to report that at this moment of triumph Mr. Metzger was carried away by the temptations of parody and added, "We are thus much the richer."

In any case, this was the essay for which Metzger received his    19
honor grade and his public acclaim. He was now, of course, in serious trouble with the authorities.

I shall leave him for the moment to the mercy of the Administra-    20
tive Board of Harvard College and turn the reader's attention to the section man who ascribed the grade. He was in much worse trouble. All the consternation in his immediate area of the Faculty and all the glee in other areas fell upon his unprotected head. I shall now undertake his defense.

I do so not simply because I was acquainted with him and feel a    21
respect for his intelligence; I believe in the justice of his grade! Well, perhaps "justice" is the wrong word in a situation so manifestly absurd. This is more a case in "equity." That is, the grade is equitable if we accept other aspects of the situation which are equally absurd. My proposition is this: if we accept as valid those C grades which were

accorded students who, like Metzger's friend, demonstrated a thorough familiarity with the details of the book without relating their critique to the methodological problems of social anthropology, then "George Smith" deserved not only the same, but better.

The reader may protest that the C's given to students who showed       22
evidence only of diligence were indeed not valid and that both these students and "George Smith" should have received E's. To give the diligent E is of course not in accord with custom. I shall take up this matter later. For now, were I to allow the protest, I could only restate my thesis: that "George Smith's" E would, in a college of liberal arts, be properly a "better" E.

At this point I need a short-hand. It is a curious fact that there is       23
no academic slang for the presentation of evidence of diligence alone. "Parroting" won't do; it is possible to "parrot" bull. I must beg the reader's pardon, and, for reasons almost too obvious to bear, suggest "cow."

Stated as nouns, the concepts look simple enough:       24

cow (pure): data, however relevant, without relevancies.
bull (pure): relevancies, however relevant, without data.

The reader can see all too clearly where this simplicity would lead.       25
I can assure him that I would not have imposed on him this way were I aiming to say that knowledge in this university is definable as some neuter compromise between cow and bull, some infertile hermaphrodite. This is precisely what many diligent students seem to believe: that what they must learn to do is to "find the right mean" between "amounts" of detail and "amounts" of generalities. Of course this is not the point at all. The problem is not quantitative, nor does its solution lie on a continuum between the particular and the general. Cow and bull are not poles of a single dimension. A clear notion of what they really are is essential to my inquiry, and for heuristic purposes I wish to observe them further in the celibate state.

When the pure concepts are translated into verbs, their complexi-       26
ties become apparent in the assumptions and purposes of the students as they write:

To cow (*v. intrans.*) or the act of cowing:
    To list data (or perform operations) without awareness of, or comment upon, the contexts, frames of reference, or points of observation which deter-

mine the origin, nature, and meaning of the data (or procedures). To write on the assumption that "a fact is a fact." To present evidence of hard work as a substitute for understanding, without any intent to deceive.

To bull *(v. intrans.)* or the act of bulling:

To discourse upon the contexts, frames of reference and points of observation which would determine the origin, nature, and meaning of data if one had any. To present evidence of an understanding of form in the hope that the reader may be deceived into supposing a familiarity with content.

At the level of conscious intent, it is evident that cowing is more    27
moral, or less immoral, than bulling. To speculate about unconscious intent would be either an injustice or a needless elaboration of my theme. It is enough that the impression left by cow is one of earnestness, diligence, and painful naiveté. The grader may feel disappointment or even irritation, but these feelings are usually balanced by pity, compassion, and a reluctance to hit a man when he's both down and moral. He may feel some challenge to his teaching, but none whatever to his one-ups-manship. He writes in the margin: "See me."

We are now in a position to understand the anomaly of custom: As    28
instructors, we always assign bull an E, *when we detect it;* whereas we usually give cow a C, *even though it is always obvious.*

After all, we did not ask to be confronted with a choice between    29
morals and understanding (or did we?). We evince a charming humanity, I think, in our decision to grade in favor of morals and pathos. "I simply *can't* give this student an E after he has *worked* so hard." At the same time we tacitly express our respect for the bullster's strength. We recognize a colleague. If he knows so well how to dish it out, we can be sure that he can also take it.

Of course it is just possible that we carry with us, perhaps from our    30
own school-days, an assumption that if a student is willing to work hard and collect "good hard facts" he can always be taught to understand their relevance, whereas a student who has caught onto the forms of relevance without working at all is a lost scholar.

But this is not in accord with our experience.                     31

It is not in accord either, as far as I can see, with the stated values    32
of a liberal education. If a liberal education should teach students "how to think," not only in their own fields but in fields outside their own—that is, to understand "how the other fellow orders knowledge," then bulling, even in its purest form, expresses an important part of what a pluralist university holds dear, surely a more important part

than the collecting of "facts that are facts" which schoolboys learn to do. Here then, good bull appears not as ignorance at all but as an aspect of knowledge. It is both relevant and "true." In a university setting good bull is therefore of more value than "facts," which, without a frame of reference, are not even "true" at all.

Perhaps this value accounts for the final anomaly: as instructors,   33
we are inclined to reward bull highly, *where we do not detect its intent*, to the consternation of the bullster's acquaintances. And often we do not examine the matter too closely. After a long evening of reading blue books full of cow, the sudden meeting with a student who at least understands the problems of one's field provides a lift like a draught of refreshing wine, and a strong disposition toward trust.

This was, then, the sense of confidence that came to our unfortu-   34
nate section man as he read "George Smith's" sympathetic considerations.

## II

In my own years of watching over students' shoulders as they   35
work, I have come to believe that this feeling of trust has a firmer basis than the confidence generated by evidence of diligence alone. I believe that the theory of a liberal education holds. Students who have dared to understand man's real relation to his knowledge have shown themselves to be in a strong position to learn content rapidly and meaningfully, and to retain it. I have learned to be less concerned about the education of a student who has come to understand the nature of man's knowledge, even though he has not yet committed himself to hard work, than I am about the education of the student who, after one or two terms at Harvard, is working desperately hard and still believes that collected "facts" constitute knowledge. The latter, when I try to explain to him, too often understands me to be saying that he "doesn't *put in enough generalities.*" Surely he has "put in *enough* facts."

I have come to see such quantitative statements as expressions of   36
an entire, coherent epistemology. In grammar school the student is taught that Columbus discovered America in 1492. The *more* such items he gets "right" on a given test the more he is credited with "knowing." From years of this sort of thing it is not unnatural to develop the conviction that knowledge consists of the accretion of hard facts by hard work.

The student learns that the more facts and procedures he can get   37 "right" in a given course, the better will be his grade. The more courses he takes, the more subjects he has "had," the more credits he accumulates, the more diplomas he will get, until, after graduate school, he will emerge with his doctorate, a member of the community of scholars.

The foundation of this entire life is the proposition that a fact is a 38 fact. The necessary correlate of this proposition is that a fact is either right or wrong. This implies that the standard against which the rightness or wrongness of a fact may be judged exists *someplace*—perhaps graven upon a tablet in a Platonic world outside and above *this* cave of tears. In grammar school it is evident that the tablets which enshrine the spelling of a word or the answer to an arithmetic problem are visible to my teacher who need only compare my offerings to it. In high school I observe that my English teachers disagree. This can only mean that the tablets in such matters as the goodness of a poem are distant and obscured by clouds. They surely exist. The pleasing of befuddled English teachers degenerates into assessing their prejudices, a game in which I have no protection against my competitors more glib of tongue. I respect only my science teachers, authorities who *really know*. Later I learn from them that "this is only what we think *now*." But eventually, surely. . . . Into this epistemology of education, apparently shared by teachers in such terms as "credits," "semester hours" and "years of French" the student may invest his ideals, his drive, his competitiveness, his safety, his self-esteem, and even his love.

College raises other questions: by whose calendar is it proper to 39 say that Columbus discovered America in 1492? How, when and by whom was the year I established in this calendar? What of other calendars? In view of the evidence for Leif Ericson's previous visit (and the American Indians), what historical ethnocentrism is suggested by the use of the word "discover" in this sentence? As for Leif Ericson, in accord with what assumptions do you order the evidence?

These questions and their answers are not "more" knowledge. 40 They are devastation. I do not need to elaborate upon the epistemology, or rather epistemologies, they imply. A fact has become at last "an observation or an operation performed in a frame of reference." A liberal education is founded in an awareness of frame of reference even in the most immediate and empirical examination of data. Its acquirement involves relinquishing hope of absolutes and of the protection they afford against doubt and the glib-tongued competitor. It demands an ever widening sophistication about systems of thought and observation. It leads, not away from, but *through* the arts of games-manship to a new trust.

This trust is in the value and integrity of systems, their varied   41
character, and the way their apparently incompatible metaphors en-lighten, from complementary facets, the particulars of human experi-ence. As one student said to me: "I used to be cynical about intellectual games. Now I want to know them thoroughly. You see I came to realize that it was only when I knew the rules of the game cold that I could tell whether what I was saying was tripe."

We too often think of the bullster as cynical. He can be, and not   42
always in a light-hearted way. We have failed to observe that there can lie behind cow the potential of a deeper and more dangerous despair. The moralism of sheer work and obedience can be an ethic that, unwilling to face a despair of its ends, glorifies its means. The implicit refusal to consider the relativity of both ends and means leaves the operator in an unconsidered proprietary absolutism. History bears witness that in the pinches this moral superiority has no recourse to negotiation, only to force.

A liberal education proposes that man's hope lies elsewhere: in the   43
negotiability that can arise from an understanding of the integrity of systems and of their origins in man's address to his universe. The prerequisite is the courage to accept such a definition of knowledge. From then on, of course, there is nothing incompatible between such an epistemology and hard work. Rather the contrary.

I can now at last let bull and cow get together. The reader knows   44
best how a productive wedding is arranged in his own field. This is the nuptial he celebrates with a straight A on examinations. The masculine context must embrace the feminine particular, though itself "born of woman." Such a union is knowledge itself, and it alone can generate new contexts and new data which can unite in their turn to form new knowledge.

In this happy setting we can congratulate in particular the Natural   45
Sciences, long thought to be barren ground to the bullster. I have indeed drawn my examples of bull from the Social Sciences, and by analogy from the Humanities. Essay-writing in these fields has long been thought to nurture the art of bull to its prime. I feel, however, that the Natural Sciences have no reason to feel slighted. It is perhaps no accident that Metzger was a mathematician. As part of my re-searches for this paper, furthermore, a student of considerable talent has recently honored me with an impressive analysis of the art of

amassing "partial credits" on examinations in advanced physics. Though beyond me in some respects, his presentation confirmed my impression that instructors of Physics frequently honor on examinations operations structurally similar to those requisite in a good essay.

The very qualities that make the Natural Sciences fields of delight    46
for the eager gamesman have been essential to their marvelous fertility.

## III

As priests of these mysteries, how can we make our rites more    47
precisely expressive? The student who merely cows robs himself, without knowing it, of his education and his soul. The student who only bulls robs himself, as he knows full well, of the joys of inductive discovery—that is, of engagement. The introduction of frames of reference in the new curricula of Mathematics and Physics in the schools is a hopeful experiment. We do not know yet how much of these potent revelations the very young can stand, but I suspect they may rejoice in them more than we have supposed. I can't believe they have never wondered about Leif Ericson and that word "discovered," or even about 1492. They have simply been too wise to inquire.

Increasingly in recent years better students in the better high    48
schools and preparatory schools *are* being allowed to inquire. In fact they appear to be receiving both encouragement and training in their inquiry. I have the evidence before me.

Each year for the past five years all freshmen entering Harvard    49
and Radcliffe have been asked in freshman week to "grade" two essays answering an examination question in History. They are then asked to give their reasons for their grades. One essay, filled with dates, is 99% cow. The other, with hardly a date in it, is a good essay, easily mistaken for bull. The "official" grades of these essays are, for the first (alas!) C "because he has worked so hard," and for the second (soundly, I think) B. Each year a larger majority of freshmen evaluate these essays as would the majority of the faculty, and for the faculty's reasons, and each year a smaller minority give the higher honor to the essay offering data alone. Most interesting, a larger number of students each year, while not overrating the second essay, award the first the straight E appropriate to it in a college of liberal arts.

For us who must grade such students in a university, these devel-  50
opments imply a new urgency, did we not feel it already. Through our
grades we describe for the students, in the showdown, what we believe
about the nature of knowledge. The subtleties of bull are not periph-
eral to our academic concerns. That they penetrate to the center of our
care is evident in our feelings when a student whose good work we
have awarded a high grade reveals to us that he does not feel he
deserves it. Whether he disqualifies himself because "there's too much
bull in it," or worse because "I really don't think I've worked that
hard," he presents a serious educational problem. Many students feel
this sleaziness; only a few reveal it to us.

We can hardly allow a mistaken sense of fraudulence to under-  51
mine our students' achievements. We must lead students beyond their
concept of bull so that they may honor relevancies that are really
relevant. We can willingly acknowledge that, in lieu of the date 1492,
a consideration of calendars and of the word "discovered," may well
be offered with intent to deceive. We must insist that this does not
make such considerations intrinsically immoral, and that, contrariwise,
the date 1492 may be no substitute for them. Most of all, we must
convey the impression that we grade understanding *qua* understanding. To be convincing, I suppose we must concede to ourselves in
advance that a bright student's understanding is understanding even if
he achieved it by osmosis rather than by hard work in our course.

These are delicate matters. As for cow, its complexities are not  52
what need concern us. Unlike good bull, it does not represent partial
knowledge at all. It belongs to a different theory of knowledge entirely.
In our theories of knowledge it represents total ignorance, or worse
yet, a knowledge downright inimical to understanding. I even go so far
as to propose that we award no more C's for cow. To do so is rarely,
I feel, the act of mercy it seems. Mercy lies in clarity.

The reader may be afflicted by a lingering curiosity about the fate  53
of Mr. Metzger. I hasten to reassure him. The Administrative Board of
Harvard College, whatever its satanic reputations, is a benign body. Its
members, to be sure, were on the spot. They delighted in Metzger's
exploit, but they were responsible to the Faculty's rule. The hero stood
in danger of probation. The debate was painful. Suddenly one member, of a refined legalistic sensibility, observed that the rule applied
specifically to "examinations" and that the occasion had been simply
an hour-test. Mr. Metzger was merely "admonished."

# The Green Frog Skin

## JOHN LAME DEER

The green frog skin—that's what I call a dollar bill. In our attitude  1
toward it lies the biggest difference between Indians and whites. My
grandparents grew up in an Indian world without money. Just before
the Custer battle the white soldiers had received their pay. Their
pockets were full of green paper and they had no place to spend it.
What were their last thoughts as an Indian bullet or arrow hit them?
I guess they were thinking of all that money going to waste, of not
having had a chance to enjoy it, of a bunch of dumb savages getting
their paws on that hard-earned pay. That must have hurt them more
than the arrow between their ribs.

The close hand-to-hand fighting, with a thousand horses gally-  2
hooting all over the place, had covered the battlefield with an enormous cloud of dust, and in it the green frog skins of the soldiers were
whirling around like snowflakes in a blizzard. Now, what did the
Indians do with all that money? They gave it to their children to play
with, to fold those strange bits of colored paper into all kinds of
shapes, making them into toy buffalo and horses. Somebody was en-
joying that money after all. The books tell of one soldier who survived. He got away, but he went crazy and some women watched
him from a distance as he killed himself. The writers always say he
must have been afraid of being captured and tortured, but that's all
wrong.

Can't you see it? There he is, bellied down in a gully, watching  3
what is going on. He sees the kids playing with the money, tearing it
up, the women using it to fire up some dried buffalo chips to cook on,
the men lighting their pipes with green frog skins, but mostly all those
beautiful dollar bills floating away with the dust and the wind. It's this
sight that drove that poor soldier crazy. He's clutching his head, hollering, "Goddam, Jesus Christ Almighty, look at them dumb, stupid, red
sons of bitches wasting all that dough!" He watches till he can't stand
it any longer, and then he blows his brains out with a six-shooter. It
would make a great scene in a movie, but it would take an Indian mind
to get the point.

The green frog skin—that was what the fight was all about. The  4
gold of the Black Hills, the gold in every clump of grass. Each day you
can see ranch hands riding over this land. They have a bagful of grain
hanging from their saddle horns, and whenever they see a prairie-dog
hole they toss a handful of oats in it, like a kind little old lady feeding
the pigeons in one of your city parks. Only the oats for the prairie dogs
are poisoned with strychnine. What happens to the prairie dog after he
has eaten this grain is not a pleasant thing to watch. The prairie dogs
are poisoned, because they eat grass. A thousand of them eat up as
much grass in a year as a cow. So if the rancher can kill that many
prairie dogs he can run one more head of cattle, make a little more
money. When he looks at a prairie dog he sees only a green frog skin
getting away from him.

For the white man each blade of grass or spring of water has a  5
price tag on it. And that is the trouble, because look at what happens.
The bobcats and coyotes which used to feed on prairie dogs now have
to go after a stray lamb or a crippled calf. The rancher calls the
pest-control officer to kill these animals. This man shoots some rabbits
and puts them out as bait with a piece of wood stuck in them. That stick
has an explosive charge which shoots some cyanide into the mouth of
the coyote who tugs at it. The officer has been trained to be careful. He
puts a printed warning on each stick reading, "Danger, Explosive,
Poison!" The trouble is that our dogs can't read, and some of our
children can't either.

And the prairie becomes a thing without life—no more prairie  6
dogs, no more badgers, foxes, coyotes. The big birds of prey used to
feed on prairie dogs, too. So you hardly see an eagle these days. The
bald eagle is your symbol. You see him on your money, but your money
is killing him. When a people start killing off their own symbols they
are in a bad way.

The Sioux have a name for white men. They call them *wasicun*—  7
fat-takers. It is a good name, because you have taken the fat of the
land. But it does not seem to have agreed with you. Right now you
don't look so healthy—overweight, yes, but not healthy. Americans are
bred like stuffed geese—to be consumers, not human beings. The
moment they stop consuming and buying, this frog-skin world has no
more use for them. They have become frogs themselves. Some cruel
child has stuffed a cigar into their mouths and they have to keep puffing
and puffing until they explode. Fat-taking is a bad thing, even for the
taker. It is especially bad for Indians who are forced to live in this

frog-skin world which they did not make and for which they have no use.

You, Richard, are an artist. That's one reason we get along well. 8 Artists are the Indians of the white world. They are called dreamers who live in the clouds, improvident people who can't hold onto their money, people who don't want to face "reality." They say the same things about Indians. How the hell do these frog-skin people know what reality is? The world in which you paint a picture in your mind, a picture which shows things different from what your eyes sees, that is the world from which I get my visions. I tell you this is the real world, not the Green Frog Skin World. That's only a bad dream, a stream-lined, smog-filled nightmare.

Because we refuse to step out of our reality into this frog-skin 9 illusion, we are called dumb, lazy, improvident, immature, other-worldly. It makes me happy to be called "other-worldly," and it should make you so. It's a good thing our reality is different from theirs. I remember one white man looking at my grandfather's vest. It was made of black velvet and had ten-dollar gold coins for buttons. The white man had a fit, saying over and over again, "Only a crazy Indian would think of that, using good money for buttons, a man who hasn't got a pot to piss in!" But Grandpa wasn't a bit crazy and he had learned to know the value of money as well as anybody. But money exists to give a man pleasure. Well, it pleasured Grandpa to put a few golden Indian heads on his vest. That made sense.

# Analogy

## *The Bound Man*

### ILSE AICHINGER

Sunlight on his face woke him, but made him shut his eyes again; 1
it streamed unhindered down the slope, collected itself into rivulets,
attracted swarms of flies, which flew low over his forehead, circled,
sought to land, and were overtaken by fresh swarms. When he tried to
whisk them away he discovered that he was bound. A thin rope cut into
his arms. He dropped them, opened his eyes again, and looked down
at himself. His legs were tied all the way up to his thighs; a single
length of rope was tied round his ankles, criss-crossed all the way up
his legs, and encircled his hips, his chest, and his arms. He could not
see where it was knotted. He showed no sign of fear or hurry, though
he thought he was unable to move, until he discovered that the rope
allowed his legs some free play, and that round his body it was almost
loose. His arms were tied to each other but not to his body, and had
some free play too. This made him smile, and it occurred to him that
perhaps children had been playing a practical joke on him.

He tried to feel for his knife, but again the rope cut softly into his 2
flesh. He tried again, more cautiously this time, but his pocket was
empty. Not only his knife, but the little money that he had on him, as
well as his coat, were missing. His shoes had been pulled from his feet
and taken too. When he moistened his lips he tasted blood, which had
flowed from his temples down his cheeks, his chin, his neck, and under
his shirt. His eyes were painful; if he kept them open for long he saw
reddish stripes in the sky.

He decided to stand up. He drew his knees up as far as he could, 3
rested his hands on the fresh grass and jerked himself to his feet. An
elder-branch stroked his cheek, the sun dazzled him, and the rope cut
into his flesh. He collapsed to the ground again, half out of his mind

with pain, and then tried again. He went on trying until the blood started flowing from his hidden weals. Then he lay still again for a long while, and let the sun and the flies do what they liked.

When he awoke for the second time the elder-bush had cast its  4 shadow over him, and the coolness stored in it was pouring from between its branches. He must have been hit on the head. Then they must have laid him down carefully, just as a mother lays her baby behind a bush when she goes to work in the fields.

His chances all lay in the amount of free play allowed him by the  5 rope. He dug his elbows into the ground and tested it. As soon as the rope taunted he stopped, and tried again more cautiously. If he had been able to reach the branch over his head he could have used it to drag himself to his feet, but he could not reach it. He laid his head back on the grass, rolled over, and struggled to his knees. He tested the ground with his toes, and then managed to stand up almost without effort.

A few paces away lay the path across the plateau, and among the  6 grass were wild pinks and thistles in bloom. He tried to lift his foot to avoid trampling on them, but the rope round his ankles prevented him. He looked down at himself.

The rope was knotted at his ankles, and ran round his legs in a kind  7 of playful pattern. He carefully bent and tried to loosen it, but, loose though it seemed to be, he could not make it any looser. To avoid treading on the thistles with his bare feet he hopped over them like a bird.

The cracking of a twig made him stop. People in this district were  8 very prone to laughter. He was alarmed by the thought that he was in no position to defend himself. He hopped on until he reached the path. Bright fields stretched far below. He could see no sign of the nearest village, and, if he could move no faster than this, night would fall before he reached it.

He tried walking, and discovered that he could put one foot before  9 another if he lifted each foot a definite distance from the ground and then put it down again before the rope taunted. In the same way he could actually swing his arms a little.

After the first step he fell. He fell right across the path, and made  10 the dust fly. He expected this to be a sign for the long-suppressed laughter to break out, but all remained quiet. He was alone. As soon as the dust had settled he got up and went on. He looked down and watched the rope slacken, grow taut, and then slacken again.

When the first glow-worms appeared he managed to look up. He 11
felt in control of himself again, and his impatience to reach the nearest
village faded.

Hunger made him light-headed, and he seemed to be going so fast 12
that not even a motor-cycle could have overtaken him; alternatively he
felt as if he were standing still and that the earth was rushing past him,
like a river flowing past a man swimming against the stream. The
stream carried branches which had been bent southwards by the north
wind, stunted young trees, and patches of grass with bright, long-
stalked flowers. It ended by submerging the bushes and the young
trees, leaving only the sky and the man above water-level. The moon
had risen, and illuminated the bare, curved summit of the plateau, the
path, which was overgrown with young grass, the bound man making
his way along it with quick, measured steps, and two hares, which ran
across the hill just in front of him and vanished down the slope. Though
the nights were still cool at this time of the year, before midnight the
bound man lay down at the edge of the escarpment and went to sleep.

In the light of morning the animal-tamer who was camping with 13
his circus in the field outside the village saw the bound man coming
down the path, gazing thoughtfully at the ground. The bound man
stopped and bent down. He held out one arm to help keep his balance
and with the other picked up an empty wine-bottle. Then he straightened himself and stood erect again. He moved slowly, to avoid being
cut by the rope, but to the circus proprietor what he did suggested the
voluntary limitation of an enormous swiftness of movement. He was
enchanted by its extraordinary gracefulness, and while the bound man
looked about for a stone on which to break the bottle, so that he could
use the splintered neck to cut the rope, the animal-tamer walked across
the field and approached him. The first leaps of a young panther had
never filled him with such delight.

"Ladies and gentlemen, the bound man!" His very first move- 14
ments let loose storm of applause, which out of sheer excitement
caused the blood to rush to the cheeks of the animal-tamer standing at
the edge of the arena. The bound man rose to his feet. His surprise
whenever he did this was like that of a four-footed animal which has
managed to stand on its hind-legs. He knelt, stood up, jumped, and
turned cart-wheels. The spectators found it as astonishing as if they
had seen a bird which voluntarily remained earth-bound, and confined
itself to hopping. The bound man became an enormous draw. His

absurd steps and little jumps, his elementary exercises in movement, made the rope-dancer superfluous. His fame grew from village to village, but the motions he went through were few and always the same; they were really quite ordinary motions, which he had continually to practise in the day-time in the half-dark tent in order to retain his shackled freedom. In that he remained entirely within the limits set by his rope he was free of it, it did not confine him, but gave him wings and endowed his leaps and jumps with purpose; just as the flights of birds of passage have purpose when they take wing in the warmth of summer and hesitantly make small circles in the sky.

All the children of the neighbourhood started playing the game of    15
"bound man." They formed rival gangs, and one day the circus people found a little girl lying bound in a ditch, with a cord tied round her neck so that she could hardly breathe. They released her, and at the end of the performance that night the bound man made a speech. He announced briefly that there was no sense in being tied up in such a way that you could not jump. After that he was regarded as a comedian.

Grass and sunlight, tent-pegs driven into the ground and then    16
pulled up again, and on to the next village. "Ladies and gentlemen, the bound man!" The summer mounted towards its climax. It bent its face deeper over the fish-ponds in the hollows, taking delight in its dark reflection, skimmed the surface of the rivers, and made the plain into what it was. Everyone who could walk went to see the bound man.

Many wanted a close-up view of how he was bound. So the circus    17
proprietor announced after each performance that anyone who wanted to satisfy himself that the knots were real and the rope not made of rubber was at liberty to do so. The bound man generally waited for the crowd in the area outside the tent. He laughed or remained serious, and held out his arms for inspection. Many took the opportunity to look him in the face, others gravely tested the rope, tried the knots on his ankles, and wanted to know exactly how the lengths compared with the length of his limbs. They asked him how he had come to be tied up like that, and he answered patiently, always saying the same thing. Yes, he had been tied up, he said, and when he awoke he found that he had been robbed as well. Those who had done it must have been pressed for time, because they had tied him up somewhat too loosely for someone who was not supposed to be able to move and somewhat too tightly for some who was expected to be able to move. But he did move, people pointed out. Yes, he replied, what else could he do?

Before he went to bed he always sat for a time in front of the fire.  18
When the circus proprietor asked him why he didn't make up a better
story, he always answered that he hadn't made up that one, and
blushed. He preferred staying in the shade.

The difference between him and the other performers was that  19
when the show was over he did not take off his rope. The result was
that every movement that he made was worth seeing, and the villagers
used to hang about the camp for hours, just for the sake of seeing him
get up from in front of the fire and roll himself in his blanket. Sometimes the sky was beginning to lighten when he saw their shadows
disappear.

The circus proprietor often remarked that there was no reason  20
why he should not be untied after the evening performance and tied
up again next day. He pointed out that the rope-dancers, for instance,
did not stay on their rope over night. But no one took the idea of
untying him seriously.

For the bound man's fame rested on the fact that he was always  21
bound, that whenever he washed himself he had to wash his clothes
too and *vice versa*, and that his only way of doing so was to jump in the
river just as he was every morning when the sun came out, and that he
had to be careful not to go too far for fear of being carried away by the
stream.

The proprietor was well aware that what in the last resort pro-  22
tected the bound man from the jealousy of the other performers was
his helplessness; he deliberately left them the pleasure of watching
him groping painfully from stone to stone on the river bank every
morning with his wet clothes clinging to him. When his wife pointed
out that even the best clothes would not stand up indefinitely to such
treatment (and the bound man's clothes were by no means of the best)
he replied curtly that it was not going to last for ever. That was his
answer to all objections—it was for the summer season only. But when
he said this he was not being serious; he was talking like a gambler who
has no intention of giving up his vice. In reality he would have been
prepared cheerfully to sacrifice his lions and his rope-dancers for the
bound man.

He proved this on the night when the rope-dancers jumped over  23
the fire. Afterwards he was convinced that they did it, not because it
was midsummer's day, but because of the bound man, who as usual
was lying and watching them, with that peculiar smile that might have
been real or might have been only the effect of the glow on his face.

In any case no one knew anything about him, because he never talked about anything that had happened to him before he emerged from the wood that day.

But that evening two of the performers suddenly picked him up by 24 the arms and legs, carried him to the edge of the fire and started playfully swinging him to and fro, while two others held out their arms to catch him on the other side. In the end they threw him, but too short. The two men on the other side drew back—they explained afterwards that they did so the better to take the shock. The result was that the bound man landed at the very edge of the flames and would have been burned if the circus proprietor had not seized his arms and quickly dragged him away to save the rope which was starting to get singed. He was certain that the object had been to burn the rope. He sacked the four men on the spot.

A few nights later the proprietor's wife was awakened by the 25 sound of footsteps on the grass, and went outside just in time to prevent the clown from playing his last practical joke. He was carrying a pair of scissors. When he was asked for an explanation he insisted that he had had no intention of taking the bound man's life, but only wanted to cut his rope, because he felt sorry for him. But he was sacked too.

These antics amused the bound man, because he could have freed 26 himself if he had wanted to whenever he liked, but perhaps he wanted to learn a few new jumps first. The children's rhyme: "We travel with the circus, we travel with the circus" sometimes occurred to him while he lay awake at night. He could hear the voices of spectators on the opposite bank who had been driven too far downstream on the way home. He could see the river gleaming in the moonlight, and the young shoots growing out of the thick tops of the willow trees, and did not think about autumn yet.

The circus proprietor dreaded the danger involved for the bound 27 man by sleep. Attempts were continually made to release him while he slept. The chief culprits were sacked rope-dancers, or children who were bribed for the purpose. But measures could be taken to safeguard against these. A much bigger danger was that which he represented to himself. In his dreams he forgot his rope, and was surprised by it when he woke in the darkness of morning. He would angrily try to get up, but lose his balance and fall back again. The previous evening's applause was forgotten, sleep was still too near, his head and neck too free. He was just the opposite of a hanged man—his neck was the only part of him that was free. You had to make sure that at such moments no knife was within his reach. In the early hours of the morning the circus proprietor sometimes sent his wife to see whether the bound man was all right. If he was asleep she would bend over him and feel the rope. It had grown hard from dirt and damp. She would test the amount of free play it allowed him, and touch his tender wrists and ankles.

The most varied rumours circulated about the bound man. Some said he had tied himself up and invented the story of having been robbed, and towards the end of the summer that was the general opinion. Others maintained that he had been tied up at his own request, perhaps in league with the circus proprietor. The hesitant way in which he told of his story, his habit of breaking off when the talk got round to the attack on him, contributed greatly to these rumours. Those who still believed in the robbery-with-violence story were laughed at. Nobody knew what difficulties the circus proprietor had in keeping the bound man, and how often he said he had had enough and wanted to clear off, for too much of the summer had passed.

Later, however, he stopped talking about clearing off. When the proprietor's wife brought him his food by the river and asked him how long he proposed to stay with them, he did not answer. She thought he had got used, not to being tied up, but to not forgetting for a moment that he was tied up—the only thing that anyone in his position could get used to. She asked him whether he did not think it ridiculous to be tied up all the time, but he answered that he did not. Such a variety of people—clowns, freaks, and comics, to say nothing of elephants and tigers—travelled with circuses that he did not see why a bound man should not travel with a circus too. He told her about the movements he was practising, the new ones he had discovered, and about a new trick that had occurred to him while he was whisking flies from the animals' eyes. He described to her how he always anticipated the effect of the rope and always restrained his movements in such a way as to prevent it from ever tautening; and she knew that there were days when he was hardly aware of the rope when he jumped down from the wagon and slapped the flanks of the horses in the morning, as if he were moving in a dream. She watched him vault over the bars almost without touching them, and saw the sun on his face, and he told her that sometimes he felt as if he were not tied up at all. She answered that if he were prepared to be untied there would never be any need for him to feel tied up. He agreed that he could be untied whenever he felt like it.

The woman ended by not knowing whether she were more con-   30
cerned with the man or with the rope that tied him. She told him that
he could go on travelling with the circus without his rope, but he did
not believe it. For what would be the point of his antics without his
rope, and what would he amount to without it? Without his rope he
would leave them, and the happy days would be over. She would no
longer be able to sit beside him on the stones by the river without
rousing suspicion, and she knew that his continued presence, and her
conversations with him, of which the rope was the only subject, depended on it. Whenever she agreed that the rope had its advantages
he would start talking about how troublesome it was, and whenever he
started talking about its advantages she would urge him to get rid of
it. All this seemed as endless as the summer itself.

At other times she was worried at the thought that she was herself   31
hastening the end by her talk. Sometimes she would get up in the
middle of the night and run across the grass to where he slept. She
wanted to shake him, wake him up and ask him to keep the rope. But
then she would see him lying there; he had thrown off his blanket, and
there he lay like a corpse, with his legs outstretched and his arms close
together, with the rope tied round them. His clothes had suffered from
the heat and the water, but the rope had grown no thinner. She felt
that he would go on travelling with the circus until the flesh fell from
him and exposed the joints. Next morning she would plead with him
more ardently than ever to get rid of his rope.

The increasing coolness of the weather gave her hope. Autumn   32
was coming, and he would not be able to go on jumping into the river
with his clothes on much longer. But the thought of losing his rope,
about which he had felt indifferent earlier in the season, now depressed him.

The songs of the harvesters filled him with foreboding. "Summer   33
has gone, summer has gone." But he realized that soon he would have
to change his clothes, and he was certain that when he had been untied
it would be impossible to tie him up again in exactly the same way.
About this time the proprietor started talking about travelling south
that year.

The heat changed without transition into quiet, dry cold, and the   34
fire was kept in all day long. When the bound man jumped down from
the wagon he felt the coldness of the grass under his feet. The stalks
were bent with ripeness. The horses dreamed on their feet and the
wild animals, crouching to leap even in their sleep, seemed to be
collecting gloom under their skins which would break out later.

On one of these days a young wolf escaped. The circus proprietor 35
kept quiet about it, to avoid spreading alarm, but the wolf soon started
raiding cattle in the neighbourhood. People at first believed that the
wolf had been driven to these parts by the prospect of a severe winter,
but the circus soon became suspect. The proprietor could not conceal
the loss of the animal from his own employees, so the truth was bound
to come out before long. The circus people offered their aid in tracking
down the beast to the burgomasters of the neighbouring villages, but
all their efforts were vain. Eventually the circus was openly blamed for
the damage and the danger, and spectators stayed away.

The bound man went on performing before half-empty seats with- 36
out losing anything of his amazing freedom of movement. During the
day he wandered among the surrounding hills under the thin-beaten
silver of the autumn sky, and, whenever he could, lay down where the
sun shone longest. Soon he found a place which the twilight reached
last of all, and when at last it reached him he got up most unwillingly
from the withered grass. In coming down the hill he had to pass
through a little wood on its southern slope, and one evening he saw the
gleam of two little green lights. He knew that they came from no
church window, and was not for a moment under any illusion about
what they were.

He stopped. The animal came towards him through the thinning 37
foliage. He could make out its shape, the slant of its neck, its tail which
swept the ground, and its receding head. If he had not been bound,
perhaps he would have tried to run away, but as it was he did not even
feel fear. He stood calmly with dangling arms and looked down at the
wolf's bristling coat, under which the muscles played like his own
underneath the rope. He thought the evening wind was still between
him and the wolf when the beast sprang. The man took care to obey
his rope.

Moving with the deliberate care that he had so often put to the 38
test, he seized the wolf by the throat. Tenderness for a fellow-creature
arose in him, tenderness for the upright being concealed in the four-
footed. In a movement that resembled the drive of a great bird—he felt
a sudden awareness that flying would be possible only if one were tied
up in a special way—he flung himself at the animal and brought it to
the ground. He felt a slight elation at having lost the fatal advantage
of free limbs which causes men to be worsted.

The freedom he enjoyed in this struggle was having to adapt every 39
movement of his limbs to the rope that tied him—the freedom of
panthers, wolves, and the wild flowers that sway in the evening breeze.

He ended up lying obliquely down the slope, clasping the animal's
hind-legs between his own bare feet and its head between his hands.
He felt the gentleness of the faded foliage stroking the back of his
hands, and he felt his own grip almost effortlessly reaching its maximum, and he felt too how he was in no way hampered by the rope.

As he left the wood light rain began to fall and obscured the setting    40
sun. He stopped for a while under the trees at the edge of the wood.
Beyond the camp and the river he saw the fields where the cattle
grazed, and the places where they crossed. Perhaps he would travel
south with the circus after all. He laughed softly. It was against all
reason. Even if he went on putting up with his joints' being covered
with sores, which opened and bled when he made certain movements,
his clothes would not stand up much longer to the friction of the rope.

The circus proprietor's wife tried to persuade her husband to         41
announce the death of the wolf without mentioning that it had been
killed by the bound man. She said that even at the time of his greatest
popularity people would have refused to believe him capable of it, and
in their present angry mood, with the nights getting cooler, they would
be more incredulous than ever. The wolf had attacked a group of
children at play that day, and nobody would believe that it had really
been killed; for the circus proprietor had many wolves, and it was easy
enough for him to hang a skin on the rail and allow free entry. But he
was not to be dissuaded. He thought that the announcement of the
bound man's act would revive the triumphs of the summer.

That evening the bound man's movements were uncertain. He            42
stumbled in one of his jumps, and fell. Before he managed to get up he
heard some low whistles and catcalls, rather like birds calling at dawn.
He tried to get up too quickly, as he had done once or twice during the
summer, with the result that he tautened the rope and fell back again.
He lay still to regain his calm, and listened to the boos and catcalls
growing into an uproar. "Well, bound man, and how did you kill the
wolf?" they shouted, and: "Are you the man who killed the wolf?" If
he had been one of them he would not have believed it himself. He
thought they had a perfect right to be angry: a circus at this time of
year, a bound man, an escaped wolf, and all ending up with this. Some
groups of spectators started arguing with others, but the greater part
of the audience thought the whole thing a bad joke. By the time he had
got to his feet there was such a hubbub that he was barely able to make
out individual words.

He saw people surging up all around him, like faded leaves raised    43
by a whirlwind in a circular valley at the centre of which all was yet
still. He thought of the golden sunsets of the last few days; and the
cemetery light which lay over the blight of all that he had built up
during so many nights, the gold frame ·which the pious hang round
dark, old pictures, this sudden collapse of everything, filled him with
anger.

They wanted him to repeat his battle with the wolf. He said that    44
such a thing had no place in a circus performance, and the proprietor
declared that he did not keep animals to have them slaughtered in
front of an audience. But the mob stormed the ring and forced them
towards the cages. The proprietor's wife made her way between the
seats to the exit and managed to get round to the cages from the other
side. She pushed aside the attendant whom the crowd had forced to
open a cage door, but the spectators dragged her back and prevented
the door from being shut.

"Aren't you the woman who used to lie with him by the river in    45
the summer?" they called out. "How does he hold you in his arms?"
She shouted back at them that they needn't believe in the bound man
if they didn't want to, [that] they had never deserved him—painted
clowns were good enough for them.

The bound man felt as if the bursts of laughter were what he had    46
been expecting ever since early May. What had smelt so sweet all
through the summer now stank. But, if they insisted, he was ready to
take on all the animals in the circus. He had never felt so much at one
with his rope.

Gently he pushed the woman aside. Perhaps he would travel south    47
with them after all. He stood in the open doorway of the cage, and he
saw the wolf, a strong young animal, rise to its feet, and he heard the
proprietor grumbling again about the loss of his exhibits. He clapped
his hands to attract the animal's attention, and when it was near
enough he turned to slam the cage door. He looked the woman in the
face. Suddenly he remembered the proprietor's warning to suspect of
murderous intentions anyone near him who had a sharp instrument in
his hand. At the same moment he felt the blade on his wrists, as cool
as the water of the river in autumn, which during the last few weeks
he had been barely able to stand. The rope curled up in a tangle beside
him while he struggled free. He pushed the woman back, but there
was no point in anything he did now. Had he been insufficiently on his
guard against those who wanted to release him, against the sympathy

in which they wanted to lull him? Had he lain too long on the river bank? If she had cut the cord at any other moment it would have been better than this.

He stood in the middle of the cage, and rid himself of the rope like   48
a snake discarding its skin. It amused him to see the spectators shrinking back. Did they realise that he had no choice now? Or that fighting the wolf now would prove nothing whatever? At the same time he felt all his blood rush to his feet. He felt suddenly weak.

The rope, which fell at its feet like a snare, angered the wolf more   49
than the entry of a stranger into its cage. It crouched to spring. The man reeled, and grabbed the pistol that hung ready at the side of the cage. Then, before anyone could stop him, he shot the wolf between the eyes. The animal reared, and touched him in falling.

On the way to the river he heard the footsteps of his pursuers—   50
spectators, the rope-dancers, the circus proprietor, and the proprietor's wife, who persisted in the chase longer than anyone else. He hid in a clump of bushes and listened to them hurrying past, and later on streaming in the opposite direction back to the camp. The moon shone on the meadow; in that light its colour was that of both growth and death.

When he came to the river his anger died away. At dawn it seemed   51
to him as if lumps of ice were floating in the water, and as if snow had fallen, obliterating memory.

---

# The Attic of the Brain

## LEWIS THOMAS

My parents' house had an attic, the darkest and strangest part of   1
the building, reachable only by placing a stepladder beneath the trapdoor and filled with unidentifiable articles too important to be thrown out with the trash but no longer suitable to have at hand. This mysterious space was the memory of the place. After many years all the things deposited in it became, one by one, lost to consciousness. But they were still there, we knew, safely and comfortably stored in the tissues of the house.

These days most of us live in smaller, more modern houses or in 2 apartments, and attics have vanished. Even the deep closets in which we used to pile things up for temporary forgetting are rarely designed into new homes.

Everything now is out in the open, openly acknowledged and 3 displayed, and whenever we grow tired of a memory, an old chair, a trunkful of old letters, they are carted off to the dump for burning.

This has seemed a healthier way to live, except maybe for the 4 smoke—everything out to be looked at, nothing strange hidden under the roof, nothing forgotten because of no place left in impenetrable darkness to forget. Openness is the new lifestyle, no undisclosed belongings, no private secrets. Candor is the rule in architecture. The house is a machine for living, and what kind of a machine would hide away its worn-out, obsolescent parts?

But it is in our nature as human beings to clutter, and we hanker 5 for places set aside, reserved for storage. We tend to accumulate and outgrow possessions at the same time, and it is an endlessly discomforting mental task to keep sorting out the ones to get rid of. We might, we think, remember them later and find a use for them, and if they are gone for good, off to the dump, this is a source of nervousness. I think it may be one of the reasons we drum our fingers so much these days.

We might take a lesson here from what has been learned about our 6 brains in this century. We thought we discovered, first off, the attic, although its existence has been mentioned from time to time by all the people we used to call great writers. What we really found was the trapdoor and a stepladder, and off we clambered, shining flashlights into the corners, vacuuming the dust out of bureau drawers, puzzling over the names of objects, tossing them down to the floor below, and finally paying around fifty dollars an hour to have them carted off for burning.

After several generations of this new way of doing things we took 7 up openness and candor with the febrile intensity of a new religion, everything laid out in full view, and as in the design of our new houses it seemed a healthier way to live, except maybe again for smoke.

And now, I think, we have a new kind of worry. There is no place 8 for functionless, untidy, inexplicable notions, no dark comfortable parts of the mind to hide away the things we'd like to keep but at the same time forget. The attic is still there, but with the trapdoor always open and the stepladder in place we are always in and out of it, flashing lights around, naming everything, unmystified.

I have an earnest proposal for psychiatry, a novel set of therapeu-   9
tic rules, although I know it means waiting in line.

Bring back the old attic. Give new instructions to the patients who   10
are made nervous by our times, including me, to make a conscious
effort to hide a reasonable proportion of thought. It would have to be
a gradual process, considering how far we have come in the other
direction talking, talking all the way. Perhaps only one or two thoughts
should be repressed each day, at the outset. The easiest, gentlest way
might be to start with dreams, first by forbidding the patient to mention any dream, much less to recount its details, then encouraging the
outright forgetting that there was a dream at all, remembering nothing
beyond the vague sense that during sleep there had been the familiar
sound of something shifting and sliding, up under the roof.

We might, in this way, regain the kind of spontaneity and zest for   11
ideas, things popping into the mind, uncontrollable and ungovernable
thoughts, the feel that this notion is somehow connected unaccounta-
bly with that one. We could come again into possession of real memory,
the kind of memory that can come from jumbled forgotten furniture,
old photographs, fragments of music.

It has been one of the great errors of our time to think that by   12
thinking about thinking, and then talking about it, we could possibly
straighten out and tidy up our minds. There is no delusion more damaging than to get the idea in your head that you understand the
functioning of your own brain. Once you acquire such a notion, you run
the danger of moving in to take charge, guiding your thoughts, shep-
herding your mind from place to place, *controlling* it, making lists of
regulations. The human mind is not meant to be governed, certainly
not by any book of rules yet written; it is supposed to run itself, and
we are obliged to follow it along, trying to keep up with it as best we
can. It is all very well to be aware of your awareness, even proud of
it, but never try to operate it. You are not up to the job.

I leave it to the analysts to work out the techniques for doing what   13
now needs doing. They are presumably the professionals most familiar
with the route, and all they have to do is turn back and go the other
way, session by session, step by step. It takes a certain amount of hard
swallowing and a lot of revised jargon, and I have great sympathy for
their plight, but it is time to reverse course.

If after all, as seems to be true, we are endowed with unconscious   14
minds in our brains, these should be regarded as normal structures,
installed wherever they are for a purpose. I am not sure what they are

built to contain, but as a biologist, impressed by the usefulness of everything alive, I would take it for granted that they are useful, probably indispensable organs of thought. It cannot be a bad thing to own one, but I would no more think of meddling with it than trying to exorcise my liver, an equally mysterious apparatus. Until we know a lot more, it would be wise, as we have learned from other fields in medicine, to let them be, above all not to interfere. Maybe, even—and this is the notion I wish to suggest to my psychiatric friends—to stock them up, put more things into them, make *use* of them. Forget whatever you feel like forgetting. From time to time, practice *not* being open, discover new things *not* to talk about, learn reserve, hold the tongue. But above all, develop the human talent for forgetting words, phrases, whole unwelcome sentences, all experiences involving wincing. If we should ever lose the loss of memory, we might lose as well that most attractive of signals ever flashed from the human face, the blush. If we should give away the capacity for embarrassment, the touch of fingertips might be the next to go, and then the suddenness of laughter, the unaccountable sure sense of something gone wrong, and, finally, the marvelous conviction that being human is the best thing to be.

Attempting to operate one's own mind, powered by such a magical    15
instrument as the human brain, strikes me as rather like using the world's biggest computer to add columns of figures, or towing a Rolls-Royce with a nylon rope.

I have tried to think of a name for the new professional activity,    16
but each time I think of a good one I forget it before I can get it written down. Psychorepression is the only one I've hung on to, but I can't guess at the fee schedule.

---

# The Angry Winter

## LOREN EISELEY

*As to what happened next, it is possible to maintain that the hand of heaven was involved, and also possible to say that when men are desperate no one can stand up to them.*

—Xenophon

A time comes when creatures whose destinies have crossed some- 1
where in the remote past are forced to appraise each other as though
they were total strangers. I had been huddled beside the fire one
winter night, with the wind prowling outside and shaking the windows.
The big shepherd dog on the hearth before me occasionally glanced up
affectionately, sighed, and slept. I was working, actually, amidst the
debris of a far greater winter. On my desk lay the lance points of ice
age hunters and the heavy leg bone of a fossil bison. No remnants of
flesh attached to these relics. The deed lay more than ten thousand
years remote. It was represented here by naked flint and by bone so
mineralized it rang when struck. As I worked on in my little circle of
light, I absently laid the bone beside me on the floor. The hour had
crept toward midnight. A grating noise, a heavy rasping of big teeth
diverted me. I looked down.

The dog had risen. That rock-hard fragment of a vanished beast 2
was in his jaws and he was mounting it with a fierce intensity I had
never seen exhibited by him before.

"Wolf," I exclaimed, and stretched out my hand. The dog 3
backed up but did not yield. A low and steady rumbling began to rise
in his chest, something out of a long-gone midnight. There was nothing in that bone to taste, but ancient shapes were moving in his mind
and determining his utterance. Only fools gave up bones. He was
warning me.

"Wolf," I chided again. 4

As I advanced, his teeth showed and his mouth wrinkled to strike. 5
The rumbling rose to a direct snarl. His flat head swayed low and
wickedly as a reptile's above the floor. I was the most loved object in
his universe, but the past was fully alive in him now. Its shadows were
whispering in his mind. I knew he was not bluffing. If I made another
step he would strike.

Yet his eyes were strained and desperate. "Do not," something 6
pleaded in the back of them, some affectionate thing that had followed at my heel all the days of his mortal life, "do not force me. I
am what I am and cannot be otherwise because of the shadows. Do
not reach out. You are a man, and my very god. I love you, but do
not put out your hand. It is midnight. We are in another time, in the
snow."

"The *other* time," the steady rumbling continued while I 7
paused, "the other time in the snow, the big, the final, the terrible

snow, when the shape of this thing I hold spelled life. I will not give it up. I cannot. The shadows will not permit me. Do not put out your hand."

I stood silent, looking into his eyes, and heard his whisper through. Slowly I drew back in understanding. The snarl diminished, ceased. As I retreated, the bone slumped to the floor. He placed a paw upon it, warningly.                                                                           8

And were there no shadows in my own mind, I wondered. Had I not for a moment, in the grip of that savage utterance, been about to respond, to hurl myself upon him over an invisible haunch ten thousand years removed? Even to me the shadows had whispered—to me, the scholar in his study.                                                                          9

"Wolf," I said, but this time, holding a familiar leash, I spoke from the door indifferently. "A walk in the snow." Instantly from his eyes that other visitant receded. The bone was left lying. He came eagerly to my side, accepting the leash and taking it in his mouth as always.          10

A blizzard was raging when we went out, but he paid no heed. On his thick fur the driving snow was soon clinging heavily. He frolicked a little—though usually he was a grave dog—making up to me for something still receding in his mind. I felt the snowflakes fall upon my face, and stood thinking of another time, and another time still, until I was moving from midnight to midnight under ever more remote and vaster snows. Wolf came to my side with a little whimper. It was he who was civilized now. "Come back to the fire," he nudged gently, "or you will be lost." Automatically I took the leash he offered. He led me safely home and into the house.                                                          11

"We have been very far away," I told him solemnly. "I think there is something in us that we had both better try to forget." Sprawled on the rug, Wolf made no response except to thump his tail feebly out of courtesy. Already he was mostly asleep and dreaming. By the movement of his feet I could see he was running far upon some errand in which I played no part.                                                             12

Softly I picked up his bone—our bone, rather—and replaced it high on a shelf in my cabinet. As I snapped off the light the white glow from the window seemed to augment itself and shine with a deep, glacial blue. As far as I could see, nothing moved in the long aisles of my neighbor's woods. There was no visible track, and certainly no sound from the living. The snow continued to fall steadily, but the wind, and the shadows it had brought, had vanished.                              13

# O Rotten Gotham—Sliding Down into the Behavorial Sink

## TOM WOLFE

I just spent two days with Edward T. Hall, an anthropologist,   1
watching thousands of my fellow New Yorkers short-circuiting themselves into hot little twitching death balls with jolts of their own
adrenalin. Dr. Hall says it is overcrowding that does it. Overcrowding gets the adrenalin going, and the adrenalin gets them queer, au-
tistic, sadistic, barren, batty, sloppy, hot-in-the-pants, chancred-on-
the-flankers, leering, pulling, numb—the usual in New York, in
other words, and God knows what else. Dr. Hall has the theory that
overcrowding has already thrown New York into a state of behavioral sink. Behavioral sink is a term from ethology, which is the
study of how animals relate to their environment. Among animals,
the sink winds up with a "population collapse" or "massive die-off."
O rotten Gotham.

It got to be easy to look at New Yorkers as animals, especially   2
looking down from some place like a balcony at Grand Central at the
rush hour Friday afternoon. The floor was filled with the poor white
humans, running around, dodging, blinking their eyes, making a sound
like a pen full of starlings or rats or something.

"Listen to them skid," says Dr. Hall.                             3

He was right. The poor old etiolate animals were out there skid-   4
ding on their rubber soles. You could hear it once he pointed it out.
They stop short to keep from hitting somebody or because they are
disoriented and they suddenly stop and look around, and they skid on
their rubber-soled shoes, and a screech goes up. They pour out onto the
floor down the escalators from the Pan-Am Building, from 42nd Street,
from Lexington Avenue, up out of subways, down into subways, railroad trains, up into helicopters—

"You can also hear the helicopters all the way down here," says   5
Dr. Hall. The sound of the helicopters using the roof of the Pan-Am
Building nearly fifty stories up beats right through. "If it weren't for
this ceiling"—he is referring to the very high ceiling in Grand Cen-

tral—"this place would be unbearable with this kind of crowding. And yet they'll probably never 'waste' space like this again."

They screech! And the adrenal glands in all those poor white 6 animals enlarge, micrometer by micrometer, to the size of cantaloupes. Dr. Hall pulls a Minox camera out of a holster he has on his belt and starts shooting away at the human scurry. The Sink!

Dr. Hall has the Minox up to his eye—he is a slender man, calm, 7 52 years old, young-looking, an anthropologist who has worked with Navajos, Hopis, Spanish-Americans, Negroes, Trukese. He was the most important anthropologist in the government during the crucial years of the foreign aid program, the 1950's. He directed both the Point Four training program and the Human Relations Area Files. He wrote *The Silent Language* and *The Hidden Dimension*, two books that are picking up the kind of "underground" following his friend Marshall McLuhan started picking up about five years ago. He teaches at the Illinois Institute of Technology, lives with his wife, Mildred, in a high-ceilinged town house on one of the last great residential streets in downtown Chicago, Astor Street; he has a grown son and daughter, loves good food, good wine, the relaxed, civilized life—but comes to New York with a Minox at his eye to record!—perfect—The Sink.

We really got down in there by walking down into the Lexing- 8 ton Avenue line subway stop under Grand Central. We inhaled those nice big fluffy fumes of human sweat, urine, effluvia, and sebaceous secretions. One old female human was already stroked out on the upper level, on a stretcher, with two policemen standing by. The other humans barely looked at her. They rushed into line. They bellied each other, haunch to paunch, down the stairs. Human heads shone through the gratings. The species North European tried to create bubbles of space around themselves, about a foot and a half in diameter—

"See, he's reacting against the line," says Dr. Hall. 9

—but the species Mediterranean presses on in. The hell with 10 bubbles of space. The species North European resents that, this male human behind him presses forward toward the booth . . . *breathing* on him, he's disgusted, he pulls out of the line entirely, the species Mediterranean resents him for resenting it, and neither of them realizes what the hell they are getting irritable about exactly. And in all of them the old adrenals grow another micrometer.

Dr. Hall whips out the Minox. Too perfect! The bottom of The 11 Sink.

It is the sheer overcrowding, such as occurs in the business sections    12
of Manhattan five days a week and in Harlem, Bedford-Stuyvesant,
southeast Bronx every day—sheer overcrowding is converting New
Yorkers into animals in a sink pen. Dr. Hall's argument runs as follows:
all animals, including birds, seem to have a built-in inherited requirement to have a certain amount of territory, space, to lead their lives in.
Even if they have all the food they need, and there are no predatory
animals threatening them, they cannot tolerate crowding beyond a
certain point. No more than two hundred wild Norway rats can survive
on a quarter acre of ground, for example, even when they are given all
the food they can eat. They just die off.

But why? To find out, ethologists have run experiments on all sorts    13
of animals, from stickleback crabs to Sika deer. In one major experiment, an ethologist named John Calhoun put some domesticated white
Norway rats in a pen with four sections to it, connected by ramps.
Calhoun knew from previous experiments that the rats tend to split up
into groups of ten to twelve and that the pen, therefore, would hold
forty to forty-eight rats comfortably, assuming they formed four equal
groups. He allowed them to reproduce until there were eighty rats,
balanced between male and female, but did not let it get any more
crowded. He kept them supplied with plenty of food, water, and
nesting materials. In other words, all their more obvious needs were
taken care of. A less obvious need—space—was not. To the human
eye, the pen did not even look especially crowded. But to the rats, it
was crowded beyond endurance.

The entire colony was soon plunged into a profound behavioral    14
sink. "The sink," said Calhoun, "is the outcome of any behavioral
process that collects animals together in unusually great numbers. The
unhealthy connotations of the term are not accidental: a behavioral
sink does act to aggravate all forms of pathology that can be found
within a group."

For a start, long before the rat population reached eighty, a status    15
hierarchy had developed in the pen. Two dominant male rats took over
the two end sections, acquired harems of eight to ten females each, and
forced the rest of the rats into the two middle pens. All the overcrowding took place in the middle pens. That was where the "sink" hit. The
aristocrat rats at the end grew bigger, sleeker, healthier, and more
secure the whole time.

In The Sink, meanwhile, nest building, courting, sex behavior,    16
reproduction, social organization, health—all of it went to pieces. Nor-

mally, Norway rats have a mating ritual in which the male chases the female, the female ducks down into a burrow and sticks her head up to watch the male. He performs a little dance outside the burrow, then she comes out, and he mounts her, usually for a few seconds. When The Sink set in, however, no more than three males—the dominant males in the middle sections—kept up the old customs. The rest tried everything from satyrism to homosexuality or else gave up on sex altogether. Some of the subordinate males spent all their time chasing females. Three or four might chase one female at the same time, and instead of stopping at the burrow entrance for the ritual, they would charge right in. Once mounted, they would hold on for minutes instead of the usual seconds.

Homosexuality rose sharply. So did bisexuality. Some males would 17 mount anything—males, females, babies, senescent rats, anything. Still other males dropped sexual activity altogether, wouldn't fight and, in fact, would hardly move except when the other rats slept. Occasionally, a female from the aristocrat rats' harems would come over the ramps and into the middle sections to sample life in The Sink. When she had had enough, she would run back up the ramp. Sink males would give chase up to the top of the ramp, which is to say, to the very edge of the aristocratic preserve. But one glance from one of the king rats would stop them cold and they would return to The Sink.

The slumming females from the harems had their adventures 18 and then returned to a placid, healthy life. Females in The Sink, however, were ravaged, physically and psychologically. Pregnant rats had trouble continuing pregnancy. The rate of miscarriages increased significantly, and females started dying from tumors and other disorders of the mammary glands, sex organs, uterus, ovaries, and Fallopian tubes. Typically, their kidneys, livers, and adrenals were also enlarged or diseased or showed other signs associated with stress.

Child-rearing became totally disorganized. The females lost the 19 interest or the stamina to build nests and did not keep them up if they did build them. In the general filth and confusion, they would not put themselves out to save offspring they were momentarily separated from. Frantic, even sadistic competition among the males was going on all around them and rendering their lives chaotic. The males began unprovoked and senseless assaults upon one another, often in the form of tail-biting. Ordinarily, rats will suppress this kind of behavior when it crops up. In The Sink, male rats gave up all policing and just looked out for themselves. The "pecking order" among males in The Sink was never stable. Normally, male rats set up a three-class structure. Under the pressure of overcrowding, however, they broke up into all sorts of unstable subclasses, cliques, packs—and constantly pushed, probed, explored, tested one another's power. Anyone was fair game, except for the aristocrats in the end pens.

Calhoun kept the population down to eighty, so that the next stage,   20 "population collapse" or "massive die-off," did not occur. But the autopsies showed that the pattern—as in the diseases among the female rats—was already there.

The classic study of die-off was John J. Christian's study of Sika   21 deer on James Island in the Chesapeake Bay, west of Cambridge, Maryland. Four or five of the deer had been released on the island, which was 280 acres and uninhabited, in 1916. By 1955 they had bred freely into a herd of 280 to 300. The population density was only about one deer per acre at this point, but Christian knew that this was already too high for the Sikas' inborn space requirements, and something would give before long. For two years the number of deer remained 280 to 300. But suddenly, in 1958, over half the deer died; 161 carcasses were recovered. In 1959 more deer died and the population steadied at about 80.

In two years, two-thirds of the herd had died. Why? It was not   21 starvation. In fact, all the deer collected were in excellent condition, with well-developed muscles, shining coats, and fat deposits between the muscles. In practically all the deer, however, the adrenal glands had enlarged by 50 percent. Christian concluded that the die-off was due to "shock following severe metabolic disturbance, probably as a result of prolonged adrenocortical hyperactivity. . . . There was no evidence of infection, starvation, or other obvious cause to explain the mass mortality." In other words, the constant stress of overpopulation, plus the normal stress of the cold of the winter, had kept the adrenalin flowing so constantly in the deer that their systems were depleted of blood sugar and they died of shock.

Well, the white humans are still skidding and darting across the   23 floor of Grand Central. Dr. Hall listens a moment longer to the skidding and the darting noises, and then says, "You know, I've been on commuter trains here after everyone has been through one of these rushes, and I'll tell you, there is enough acid flowing in the stomachs in every car to dissolve the rails underneath."

Just a little invisible acid bath for the linings to round off the day.   24

The ulcers the acids cause, of course, are the one disease people have already been taught to associate with the stress of city life. But overcrowding, as Dr. Hall sees it, raises a lot more hell with the body than just ulcers. In everyday life in New York—just the usual, getting to work, working in massively congested areas like 42nd Street between Fifth Avenue and Lexington, especially now that the Pan-Am Building is set in there, working in cubicles such as those in the editorial offices at Time-Life, Inc., which Dr. Hall cites as typical of New York's poor handling of space, working in cubicles with low ceilings and, often, no access to a window, while construction crews all over Manhattan drive everybody up the Masonite wall with air-pressure generators with noises up to the boil-a-brain decibel level, then rushing to get home, piling into subways and trains, fighting for time and for space, the usual day in New York—the whole now-normal thing keeps shooting jolts of adrenalin into the body, breaking down the body's defenses and winding up with the work-a-daddy human animal stroked out at the breakfast table with his head apoplexed like a cauliflower out of his $6.95 semi-spread Pima-cotton shirt, and nosed over into a plate of No-Kloresto egg substitute, signing off with the black thrombosis, cancer, kidney, liver, or stomach failure, and the adrenals ooze to a halt, the size of eggplants in July.

One of the people whose work Dr. Hall is interested in on this   25
score is Rene Dubos at the Rockefeller Institute. Dubos's work indicates that specific organisms, such as the tuberculosis bacillus or a pneumonia virus, can seldom be considered "the cause" of a disease. The germ or virus, apparently, has to work in combination with other things that have already broken the body down in some way—such as the old adrenal hyperactivity. Dr. Hall would like to see some autopsy studies made to record the size of adrenal glands in New York, especially of people crowded into slums and people who go through the full rush-hour-work-rush-hour cycle every day. He is afraid that until there is some clinical, statistical data on how overcrowding actually ravages the human body, no one will be willing to do anything about it. Even in so obvious a thing as air pollution, the pattern is familiar. Until people can actually see the smoke or smell the sulphur or feel the sting in their eyes, politicians will not get excited about it, even though it is well known that many of the lethal substances polluting the air are invisible and odorless. For one thing, most politicians are like the aristocrat rats. They are insulated from The Sink by practically sultanic buffers—limousines, chauffeurs, secretaries, aides-de-camp, doormen,

shuttered houses, high-floor apartments. They almost never ride subways, fight rush hours, much less live in the slums or work in the
Pan-Am Building.

---

# from *Zen and the Art of Motorcycle Maintenance*

## ROBERT PIRSIG

When we arrive John and Sylvia are there under the first tree by      1
the road, waiting for us.

"What happened to you?"                                                2

"Slowed down."                                                         3

"Well, we know *that*. Something wrong?"                               4

"No. Let's get out of this rain."                                      5

John says there is a motel at the other end of town, but I tell him   6
there's a better one if you turn right, at a row of cottonwoods a few
blocks down.

We turn at the cottonwoods and travel a few blocks, and a small       7
motel appears. Inside the office John looks around and says, "This *is* a
good place. When were you here before?"

"I don't remember," I say.                                             8

"Then how did you know about this?"                                    9

"Intuition."                                                          10

He looks at Sylvia and shakes his head.                               11

Sylvia has been watching me silently for some time. She notices my   12
hands are unsteady as I sign in. "You look awfully pale," she says. "Did
that lightning shake you up?"

"No."                                                                13

"You look like you'd seen a ghost."                                  14

John and Chris look at me and I turn away from them to the door.      15
It is still raining hard, but we make a run for it to the rooms. The gear
on the cycles is protected and we wait until the storm passes over
before removing it.

After the rain stops, the sky lightens a little. But from the motel   16
courtyard, I see past the cottonwoods that a second darkness, that of

night, is about to come on. We walk into town, have supper, and by the time we get back, the fatigue of the day is really on me. We rest, almost motionless, in the metal armchairs of the motel courtyard, slowly working down a pint of whiskey that John brought with some mix from the motel cooler. It goes down slowly and agreeably. A cool night wind rattles the leaves of the cottonwoods along the road.

Chris wonders what we should do next. Nothing tires this kid. The    17
newness and strangeness of the motel surroundings excite him and he wants us to sing songs as they did at camp.

"We're not very good at songs," John says.    18

"Let's tell stories then," Chris says. He thinks for a while. "Do you    19
know any good ghost stories? All the kids in our cabin used to tell ghost stories at night."

"You tell *us* some," John says.    20

And he does. They are kind of fun to hear. Some of them I haven't    21
heard since I was his age. I tell him so, and Chris wants to hear some of mine, but I can't remember any.

After a while he says, "Do you believe in ghosts?"    22

"No," I say.    23

"Why not?"    24

"Because they are *un*-sci-en-*ti*-fic."    25

The way I say this makes John smile. "They contain no matter,"    26
I continue, "and have no energy and therefore, according to the laws of science, do not exist except in people's minds."

The whiskey, the fatigue and the wind in the trees start mixing in    27
my mind. "Of course," I add, "the laws of science contain no matter and have no energy either and therefore do not exist except in people's minds. It's best to be completely scientific about the whole thing and refuse to believe in either ghosts or the laws of science. That way you're safe. That doesn't leave you very much to believe in, but that's scientific too."

"I don't know what you're talking about," Chris says.    28

"I'm being kind of facetious."    29

Chris gets frustrated when I talk like this, but I don't think it hurts    30
him.

"One of the kids at YMCA camp says he believes in ghosts."    31

"He was just spoofing you."    32

"No, he wasn't. He said that when people haven't been buried    33
right, their ghosts come back to haunt people. He really believes in that."

"He was just spoofing you," I repeat.    34

"What's his name?" Sylvia says.                                             35
"Tom White Bear."                                                          36
John and I exchange looks, suddenly recognizing the same thing.            37
"Ohhh, *Indian!*" he says.                                                 38
I laugh. "I guess I'm going to have to take that back a little," I say.    39
"I was thinking of European ghosts."
"What's the difference?"                                                   40
John roars with laughter. "He's got you," he says.                         41
I think a little and say, "Well, Indians sometimes have a different        42
way of looking at things, which I'm not saying is completely wrong.
Science isn't part of the Indian tradition."
"Tom White Bear said his mother and dad told him not to believe           43
all that stuff. But he said his grandmother whispered it was true
anyway, so he believes it."
He looks at me pleadingly. He really *does* want to know things           44
sometimes. Being facetious is not being a very good father. "Sure," I
say, reversing myself, "I believe in ghosts too."
Now John and Sylvia look at me peculiarly. I see I'm not going            45
to get out of this one easily and brace myself for a long explanation.
"It's completely natural," I say, "to think of Europeans who be-          46
lieved in ghosts or Indians who believed in ghosts as ignorant. The
scientific point of view has wiped out every other view to a point
where they all seem primitive, so that if a person today talks about
ghosts or spirits he is considered ignorant or maybe nutty. It's just
all but completely impossible to imagine a world where ghosts can
actually exist."
John nods affirmatively and I continue.                                   47
"My own opinion is that the intellect of modern man isn't that           48
superior. IQs aren't that much different. Those Indians and medieval
men were just as intelligent as we are, but the context in which they
thought was completely different. Within that *context* of thought,
ghosts and spirits are quite as real as atoms, particles, photons and
quants are to a modern man. In *that* sense I believe in ghosts. Modern
man has his ghosts and spirits too, you know."
"What?"                                                                    49
"Oh, the laws of physics and of logic . . . the number system            50
. . . the principle of algebraic substitution. These are ghosts. We just
believe in them so thoroughly they seem real."
"They seem real to me," John says.                                        51
"I don't get it," says Chris.                                             52
So I go on. "For example, it seems completely natural to presume         53

that gravitation and the law of gravitation existed before Isaac Newton. It would sound nutty to think that until the seventeenth-century
there was no gravity."

"Of course." 54

"So when did this law start? Has it always existed?" 55

John is frowning, wondering what I am getting at. 56

"What I'm driving at," I say, "is the notion that before the beginning of the earth, before the sun and the stars were formed, before the
primal generation of anything, the law of gravity existed."

"Sure." 57

"Sitting there, having no mass of its own, no energy of its own, not 58
in anyone's mind because there wasn't anyone, not in space because
there was no space either, not anywhere—this law of gravity still
existed?"

Now John seems not so sure. 59

"If that law of gravity existed," I say, "I honestly don't know what 60
a thing has to do to be *non*existent. It seems to me that law of gravity
has passed every test of nonexistence there is. You cannot think of a
single attribute of nonexistence that that law of gravity didn't have. Or
a single scientific attribute of existence it did have. And yet it is still
'common sense' to believe that it existed."

John says, "I guess I'd have to think about it." 61

"Well, I predict that if you think about it long enough you will find 62
yourself going round and round and round and round until you finally
reach only one possible, rational, intelligent conclusion. The law of
gravity and gravity itself *did not exist* before Isaac Newton. No other
conclusion makes sense.

"And *what that means*," I say before he can interrupt, "and *what* 63
*that means* is that the law of gravity exists *nowhere* except in people's
heads! It's a ghost! We are all of us very arrogant and conceited about
running down other people's ghosts but just as ignorant and barbaric
and superstitious about our own."

"Why does everybody believe in the law of gravity then?" 64

"Mass hypnosis. In a very orthodox form known as 'education.'" 65

"You mean the teacher is hypnotizing the kids into believing the 66
law of gravity?"

"Sure." 67

"That's absurd." 68

"You've heard of the importance of eye contact in the classroom? 69
Every educationist emphasizes it. No educationist explains it."

John shakes his head and pours me another drink. He puts his 70 hand over his mouth and in a mock aside says to Sylvia, "You know, most of the time he seems like such a normal guy."

I counter, "That's the first normal thing I've said in weeks. The    71
rest of the time I'm feigning twentieth-century lunacy just like you are. So as not to draw attention to myself.

"But I'll *repeat* it for you," I say. "We believe the disembodied    72
words of Sir Isaac Newton were sitting in the middle of nowhere billions of years before he was born and that magically he *discovered* these words. They were always there, even when they applied to nothing. Gradually the world came into being and then they applied to *it*. In fact, those words themselves were what formed the world. That, John, is ridiculous.

"The problem, the contradiction the scientists are stuck with, is    73
that of *mind*. Mind has no matter or energy but they can't escape its predominance over everything they do. Logic exists in the mind. Numbers exist only in the mind. I don't get upset when scientists say that ghosts exist in the mind. It's that *only* that gets me. Science is *only* in your mind too, it's just that that doesn't make it bad. Or ghosts either."

They are just looking at me so I continue: "Laws of nature are    74
human *inventions*, like ghosts. Laws of logic, of mathematics are also human inventions, like ghosts. The whole blessed thing is a human invention, including the idea that it *isn't* a human invention. The world has no existence whatsoever outside the human imagination. It's all a ghost, and in antiquity was so recognized as a ghost, the whole blessed world we live in. It's run by ghosts. We see what we see because these ghosts *show* it to us, ghosts of Moses and Christ and the Buddha, and Plato, and Descartes, and Rousseau and Jefferson and Lincoln, on and on and on. Isaac Newton is a very good ghost. One of the best. Your common sense is nothing more than the voice of thousands and thousands of these ghosts from the past. Ghosts and more ghosts. Ghosts trying to find their place among the living."

John looks too much in thought to speak. But Sylvia is excited.    75
"Where do you *get* all these ideas?" she asks.

I am about to answer them but then do not. I have a feeling of    76
having already pushed it to the limit, maybe beyond, and it is time to drop it.

After a while John says, "It'll be good to see the mountains again."    77
"Yes, it will," I agree. "One last drink to that!"    78
We finish it and are off to our rooms.    79
I see that Chris brushes his teeth, and let him get by with a    80

promise that he'll take a shower in the morning. I pull seniority and take the bed by the window. After the lights are out he says, "Now, tell me a ghost story."

"I just did, out there."    81

"I mean a *real* ghost story."    82

"That was the realest ghost story you'll ever hear."    83

"You know what I mean. The other kind."    84

I try to think of some conventional ones. "I used to know so many    85
of them when I was a kid, Chris, but they're all forgotten," I say. "It's time to go to sleep. We've all got to get up early tomorrow."

Except for the wind through the screens of the motel window it is    86
quiet. The thought of all that wind sweeping toward us across the open fields of the prairie is a tranquil one and I feel lulled by it.

The wind rises and then falls, then rises and sighs, and falls again    87
. . . from so many miles away.

"Did you ever know a ghost?" Chris asks.    88

I am half asleep. "Chris," I say, "I knew a fellow once who spent    89
all his whole life doing nothing but hunting for a ghost, and it was just a waste of time. So go to sleep."

I realize my mistake too late.    90

"Did he find him?"    91

"Yes, he found him, Chris."    92

I keep wishing Chris would just listen to the wind and not ask    93
questions.

"What did he do then?"    94

"He thrashed him good."    95

"Then what?"    96

"Then he became a ghost himself." Somehow I had the thought    97
this was going to put Chris to sleep, but it's not and it's just waking me up.

"What is his name?"    98

"No one you know."    99

"But what *is* it?"    100

"It doesn't matter."    101

"Well, what is it anyway?"    102

"His name, Chris, since it doesn't matter, is Phaedrus. It's not a    103
name you know."

"Did you see him on the motorcycle in the storm?"    104

"What makes you say *that?*"    105

"Sylvia said she thought you saw a ghost."    106

"That's just an expression."    107

"Dad?"                                                                     108

"This had better be the last question, Chris, or I'm going to     109
become angry."

"I was just going to say you sure don't talk like anyone else."   110

"Yes, Chris, I know that," I say. "It's a problem. Now go to sleep."   111

"Good night, Dad."                                                 112

"Good night."                                                      113

A half hour later he is breathing sleepfully, and the wind is still   114
strong as ever and I am wide-awake. There, out the window in the
dark—this cold wind crossing the road into the trees, the leaves shim-
mering flecks of moonlight—there is no question about it, Phaedrus
saw all of this. What he was doing here I have no idea. Why he came
this way I will probably never know. But he has been here, steered us
onto this strange road, has been with us all along. There is no escape.

I wish I could say that I don't know why he is here, but I'm afraid   115
I must now confess that I do. The ideas, the things I was saying about
science and ghosts, and even that idea this afternoon about caring and
technology—they are not my own. I haven't really had a new idea in
years. They are stolen from him. And he has been watching. And that
is why he is here.

With that confession, I hope he will now allow me some sleep.      116

Poor Chris. "Do you know any ghost stories?" he asked. I could     117
have told him one but even the thought of that is frightening.

I really must go to sleep.                                         118

# Argument

## A Modest Proposal

JONATHAN SWIFT

### For Preventing the Children of the Poor People in Ireland from Being a Burden to Their Parents or Country, and for Making Them Beneficial to the Public

It is a melancholy object to those who walk through this great town 1
[Dublin] or travel in the country, when they see the streets, the roads,
and cabin doors crowded with beggars of the female sex followed by
three, four, or six children, all in rags and importuning every passenger
for an alms. These mothers, instead of being able to work for their
honest livelihood, are forced to employ all their time in strolling to beg
sustenance for their helpless infants, who, as they grow up, either turn
thieves for want of work, or leave their dear native country to fight for
the Pretender in Spain, or sell themselves to the Barbadoes.

I think it is agreed by all parties that this prodigious number of 2
children in the arms, or on the backs, or at the heels of their mothers,
and frequently of their fathers, is in the present deplorable state of the
kingdom a very great additional grievance; and, therefore, whoever
could find out a fair, cheap, and easy method of making these children
sound, useful members of the commonwealth, would deserve so well
of the public as to have his statue set up for a preserver of the nation.

But my intention is very far from being confined to provide only 3
for the children of professed beggars; it is of a much greater extent, and
shall take in the whole number of infants at a certain age who are born
of parents in effect as little able to support them as those who demand
our charity in the streets.

345

As to my own part, having turned my thoughts for many years  4
upon this important subject, and maturely weighed the several
schemes of our projectors, I have always found them grossly mistaken
in their computation. It is true, a child just dropped from its dam may
be supported by her milk for a solar year with little other nourishment,
at most not above the value of two shillings, which the mother may
certainly get, or the value in scraps, by her lawful occupation of begging; and it is exactly at one year old that I propose to provide for them
in such a manner as instead of being a charge upon their parents or the
parish, or wanting food and raiment for the rest of their lives, they
shall, on the contrary, contribute to the feeding and partly to the
clothing of many thousands.

There is likewise another great advantage in my scheme, that it  5
will prevent those voluntary abortions, and that horrid practice of
women murdering their bastard children, alas! too frequent among us!
sacrificing the poor innocent babes, I doubt, more to avoid the expense
than the shame, which would move tears and pity in the most savage
and inhuman breast.

The number of souls in this kingdom being usually reckoned one  6
million and a half, of these, I calculate there may be about two hundred thousand couples whose wives are breeders; from which number
I subtract thirty thousand couples, who are able to maintain their own
children (although I apprehend there cannot be so many, under the
present distress of the kingdom); but this being granted, there will
remain one hundred and seventy thousand breeders. I again subtract
fifty thousand for those women who miscarry, or whose children die by
accident or disease within the year. There only remain an hundred and
twenty thousand children of poor parents annually born. The question
therefore is, how this number shall be reared and provided for? which,
as I have already said, under the present situation of affairs, is utterly
impossible by all the methods hitherto proposed. For we can neither
employ them in handicraft or agriculture; we neither build houses (I
mean in the country) nor cultivate land; they can very seldom pick up
a livelihood by stealing till they arrive at six years old, except where
they are of towardly parts, although I confess they learn the rudiments
much earlier, during which time, they can, however, be properly
looked upon only as probationers, as I have been informed by a principal gentleman in the county of Cavan, who protested to me that he
never knew above one or two instances under the age of six, even in
a part of the kingdom so renowned for the quickest proficiency in that
art.

I am assured by our merchants that a boy or girl before twelve    7
years old is no saleable commodity, and even when they come to this
age they will not yield above three pounds or three pounds and a
half-crown at most on the exchange; which cannot turn to account
either to the parents or the kingdom, the charge of nutriment and rags
having been at least four times that value.

I shall now therefore humbly propose my own thoughts, which I    8
hope will not be liable to the least objection.

I have been assured by a very knowing American of my acquaint-    9
ance in London, that a young healthy child well nursed is at a year old
a most delicious, nourishing, and wholesome food whether stewed,
roasted, baked, or boiled; and I make no doubt that it will equally
serve in a fricassee or a ragout.

I do therefore humbly offer it to public consideration that of the    10
hundred and twenty thousand children already computed, twenty
thousand may be reserved for breed, whereof only one-fourth part to
be males, which is more than we allow to sheep, black cattle or
swine; and my reason is that these children are seldom the fruits of
marriage, a circumstance not much regarded by our savages; therefore one male will be sufficient to serve four females. That the remaining hundred thousand may, at a year old, be offered in sale to
the persons of quality and fortune through the kindgom, always advising the mother to let them suck plentifully in the last month, so as
to render them plump and fat for a good table. A child will make two
dishes at an entertainment for friends, and when the family dines
alone, the fore or hind quarter will make a reasonable dish, and sea-
soned with a little pepper or salt will be very good boiled on the
fourth day, especially in winter.

I have reckoned upon a medium that a child just born will weigh    11
twelve pounds, and in a solar year, if tolerably nursed, will increase to
twenty-eight pounds.

I grant this food will be somewhat dear, and therefore very proper    12
for landlords, who, as they have already devoured most of the parents,
seem to have the best title to the children.

Infants' flesh will be in season throughout the year, but more    13
plentiful in March, and a little before and after; for we are told by a
grave author, an eminent French physician, that fish being a prolific
diet, there are more children born in Roman Catholic countries about
nine months after Lent than at any other season; therefore, reckoning
a year after Lent, the markets will be more glutted than usual, because
the number of popish infants is at least three to one in this kingdom,

and therefore it will have one other collateral advantage, by lessening the number of papists among us.

I have already computed the charge of nursing a beggar's child (in    14
which list I reckon all cottagers, laborers, and four-fifths of the farmers) to be about two shillings per annum, rags included; and I believe no gentleman would repine to give ten shillings for the carcass of a good fat child, which, as I have said, will make four dishes of excellent nutritive meat, when he has only some particular friend or his own family to dine with him. Thus the squire will learn to be a good landlord, and grow popular among his tenants; the mother will have eight shillings net profit, and be fit for work till she produces another child.

Those who are more thrifty (as I must confess the times require)    15
may flay the carcass, the skin of which artificially dressed will make admirable gloves for ladies, and summer boots for fine gentlemen.

As to our city of Dublin, shambles may be appointed for this    16
purpose in the most convenient parts of it, and butchers, we may be assured, will not be wanting, although I rather recommend buying the children alive, and dressing them hot from the knife as we do roasting pigs.

A very worthy person, a true lover of his country, and whose'    17
virtues I highly esteem, was lately pleased, in discoursing on this matter, to offer a refinement upon my scheme. He said that many gentlemen of this kingdom, having of late destroyed their deer, he conceived that the want of venison might be well supplied by the bodies of young lads and maidens, not exceeding fourteen years of age nor under twelve, so great a number of both sexes in every country being now ready to starve for want of work and service, and these to be disposed of by their parents, if alive, or otherwise by their nearest relations. But with due deference to so excellent a friend and so deserving a patriot, I cannot be altogether in his sentiments; for as to the males, my American acquaintance assured me from frequent experience that their flesh was generally tough and lean, like that of our school-boys, by continual exercise, and their taste disagreeable; and to fatten them would not answer the charge. Then as to the females, it would, I think, with humble submission, be a loss to the public, because they soon would become breeders themselves; and besides, it is not improbable that some scrupulous people might be apt to censure such a practice (although indeed very unjustly) as a little bordering upon cruelty, which, I confess, has always been with me the strongest objection against any project, however so well intended.

But in order to justify my friend, he confessed that this expedient 18
was put into his head by the famous Psalmanazar, a native of the island
Formosa, who came from thence to London above twenty years ago,
and in conversation told my friend, that in his country when any young
person happened to be put to death, the executioner sold the carcass
to persons of quality as a prime dainty, and that in his time the body
of a plump girl of fifteen, who was crucified for an attempt to poison
the emperor, was sold to his imperial majesty's prime minister of state
and other great mandarins of the court, in joints from the gibbet, at
four hundred crowns. Neither indeed can I deny that if the same use
were made of several plump young girls in this town, who, without one
single groat to their fortunes, cannot stir abroad without a chair; and
appear at the playhouse and assemblies in foreign fineries which they
never will pay for, the kingdom would not be the worse.

Some persons of a desponding spirit are in great concern about the 19
vast number of poor people, who are aged, diseased, or maimed, and
I have been desired to employ my thoughts what course may be taken
to ease the nation of so greivous an encumbrance. But I am not in the
least pain upon that matter, because it is very well known that they are
every day dying and rotting by cold, and famine, and filth, and vermin,
as fast as can be reasonably expected. And as to the younger laborers,
they are now in as hopeful a condition; they cannot get work, and
consequently pine away for want of nourishment, to a degree that if at
any time they are accidentally hired to common labor, they have not
strength to perform it; and thus the country and themselves are happily delivered from the evils to come.

I have too long digressed, and therefore shall return to my subject. 20
I think the advantages by the proposal which I have made are obvious,
and many, as well as of the highest importance.

For first, as I have already observed, it would greatly lessen the 21
number of papists, with whom we are yearly overrun, being the principal breeders of the nation as well as our most dangerous enemies; and
who stay at home on purpose with a design to deliver the kingdom to
the Pretender, hoping to take their advantage by the absence of so
many good protestants, who have chosen rather to leave their country
than stay at home and pay tithes against their conscience to an episcopal curate.

Secondly, The poorer tenants will have something valuable of their 22
own, which by law may be made liable to distress, and help to pay their
landlord's rent, their corn and cattle being already seized, and money
a thing unknown.

Thirdly, Whereas the maintenance of an hundred thousand chil-   23
dren, from two years old and upward, cannot be computed at less than
ten shillings a-piece per annum, the nation's stock will be thereby
increased fifty thousand pounds per annum, besides the profit of a new
dish introduced to the tables of all gentlemen of fortune in the kingdom
who have any refinement in taste. And the money will circulate among
ourselves, the goods being entirely of our own growth and manufacture.

Fourthly, The constant breeders, besides the gain of eight shillings   24
sterling per annum by the sale of their children, will be rid of the
charge of maintaining them after the first year.

Fifthly, This food would likewise bring great custom to taverns,   25
where the vintners will certainly be so prudent as to procure the best
receipts for dressing it to perfection, and consequently have their
houses frequented by all the fine gentlemen, who justly value themselves upon their knowledge in good eating; and a skillful cook, who
understands how to oblige his guests, will contrive to make it as expensive as they please.

Sixthly, This would be a great inducement to marriage, which all   26
wise nations have either encouraged by rewards or enforced by laws
and penalties. It would increase the care and tenderness of mothers
toward their children, when they were sure of a settlement for life to
the poor babes, provided in some sort by the public, to their annual
profit instead of expense. We should see an honest emulation among
the married women, which of them could bring the fattest child to the
market. Men would become as fond of their wives during the time of
their pregnancy as they are now of their mares in foal, their cows in
calf, or sows whey they are ready to farrow; nor offer to beat or kick
them (as is too frequent a practice) for fear of miscarriage.

Many other advantages might be enumerated. For instance, the   27
addition of some thousand carcasses in our exportation of barreled
beef, the propagation of swine's flesh, and improvement in the art of
making good bacon, so much wanted among us by the great destruction
of pigs, too frequent at our tables; which are in no way comparable in
taste or magnificence to a well-grown, fat yearling child, which roasted
whole will make a considerable figure at a lord mayor's feast, or any
other public entertainment. But this and many others I omit, being
studious of brevity.

Supposing that one thousand families in this city would be constant   28
customers for infants' flesh, beside others who might have it at merry-

meetings, particularly weddings and christenings, I compute that Dublin would take off annually about twenty thousand carcasses, and the rest of the kingdom (where probably they will be sold somewhat cheaper) the remaining eighty thousand.

I can think of no one objection that will possibly be raised against this proposal, unless it should be urged that the number of people will be thereby much lessened in the kingdom. This I freely own, and it was indeed one principal design in offering it to the world. I desire the reader will observe that I calculate my remedy for this one individual kingdom of Ireland, and for no other that ever was, is, or, I think, ever can be upon earth. Therefore let no man talk to me of other expedients: of taxing our absentees at five shillings a pound; of using neither clothes nor household furniture, except what is of our own growth and manufacture; of utterly rejecting the materials and instruments that promote foreign luxury; of curing the expensiveness of pride, vanity, idleness, and gaming in our women; of introducing a vein of parsimony, prudence, and temperance; of learning to love our country, in the want of which we differ even from Laplanders and the inhabitants of Topinamboo; of quitting our animosities and factions, nor act any longer like the Jews, who were murdering one another at the very moment their city was taken; of being a little cautious not to sell our country and consciences for nothing; of teaching landlords to have at least one degree of mercy toward their tenants; lastly, of putting a spirit of honesty, industry, and skill into our shopkeepers, who, if a resolution could now be taken to buy only our native goods, would immediately unite to cheat and exact upon us in the price, the measure, and the goodness, nor could ever yet be brought to make one fair proposal of just dealing, though often and earnestly invited to it.

Therefore, I repeat, let no man talk to me of these and the like expedients, till he has at least some glimpse of hope that there will be ever some hearty and sincere attempt to put them in practice.

But as to myself, having been wearied out for many years with offering vain, idle, visionary thoughts, and at length utterly despairing of success, I fortunately fell upon this proposal, which, as it is wholly new, so it has something solid and real, of no expense and little trouble, full in our own power, and whereby we can incur no danger in disobliging England. For this kind of commodity will not bear exportation, the flesh being of too tender a consistence to admit a long continuance in salt, although perhaps I could name a country which would be glad to eat up our whole nation without it.

After all, I am not so violently bent upon my own opinion as to      32
reject any offer proposed by wise men, which shall be found equally
innocent, cheap, easy, and effectual. But before something of that kind
shall be advanced in contradiction to my scheme, and offering a better,
I desire the author or authors will be pleased maturely to consider two
points. First, as things now stand, how they will be able to find food
and raiment for an hundred thousand useless mouths and backs. And
secondly, there being a round million creatures in human figure
throughout this kingdom, whose whole subsistence put into a common
stock would leave them in debt two millions of pounds sterling, adding
those who are beggars by profession to the bulk of farmers, cottagers,
and laborers, with their wives and children, who are beggars in effect;
I desire those politicians, who dislike my overture, and may perhaps be
so bold as to attempt an answer, that they will first ask the parents of
these mortals, whether they would not at this day think it a great
happiness to have been sold for food at a year old in the manner I
prescribe, and thereby have avoided such a perpetual scene of misfor-
tunes as they have since gone through by the oppression of landlords,
the impossibility of paying rent without money or trade, the want of
common sustenance, with neither house nor clothes to cover them from
the inclemencies of the weather, and the most inevitable prospect of
entailing the like or greater miseries upon their breed for ever.

I profess, in the sincerity of my heart, that I have not the least      33
personal interest in endeavoring to promote this necessary work, having no other motive than the public good of my country, by advancing
our trade, providing for infants, relieving the poor, and giving some
pleasure to the rich. I have no children by which I can propose to get
a single penny; the youngest being nine years old, and my wife past
child-bearing.

---

# The Terrifying Normalcy of AIDS

## STEPHEN JAY GOULD

Disney's Epcot Center in Orlando, Fla., is a technological tour de      1
force and a conceptual desert. In this permanent World's Fair, American industrial giants have built their versions of an unblemished future.

These masterful entertainments convey but one message, brilliantly packaged and relentlessly expressed: progress through technology is the solution to all human problems. G.E. proclaims from Horizons: "If we can dream it, we can do it." A.T.&T. speaks from on high within its giant golf ball: We are now "unbounded by space and time." United Technologies bubbles from the depths of Living Seas: "With the help of modern technology, we feel there's really no limit to what can be accomplished."

Yet several of these exhibits at the Experimental Prototype Community of Tomorrow, all predating last year's space disaster, belie their stated message from within by using the launch of the shuttle as a visual metaphor for technological triumph. The Challenger disaster may represent a general malaise, but it remains an incident. The AIDS pandemic, an issue that may rank with nuclear weaponry as the greatest danger of our era, provides a more striking proof that mind and technology are not omnipotent and that we have not canceled our bond to nature.

In 1984, John Platt, a biophysicist who taught at the University of Chicago for many years, wrote a short paper for private circulation. At a time when most of us were either ignoring AIDS, or viewing it as a contained and peculiar affliction of homosexual men, Platt recognized that the limited data on the origin of AIDS and its spread in America suggested a more frightening prospect: we are all susceptible to AIDS, and the disease has been spreading in a simple exponential manner.

Exponential growth is a geometric increase. Remember the old kiddy problem: if you place a penny on square one of a checkerboard and double the number of coins on each subsequent square—2, 4, 8, 16, 32 . . .—how big is the stack by the 64th square? The answer: about as high as the universe is wide. Nothing in the external environment inhibits this increase, thus giving to exponential processes their relentless character. In the real, noninfinite world, of course, some limit will eventually arise, and the process slows down, reaches a steady state, or destroys the entire system: the stack of pennies falls over, the bacterial cells exhaust their supply of nutrients.

Platt noticed that data for the initial spread of AIDS fell right on an exponential curve. He then followed the simplest possible procedure of extrapolating the curve unabated into the 1990's. Most of us were incredulous, accusing Platt of the mathematical gamesmanship that scientists call "curve fitting." After all, aren't exponential models unrealistic? Surely we are not all susceptible to AIDS. Is it not spread

only by odd practices to odd people? Will it not, therefore, quickly run
its short course within a confined group?

Well, hello 1987—worldwide data still match Platt's extrapolated    6
curve. This will not, of course, go on forever. AIDS has probably
already saturated the African areas where it probably originated, and
where the sex ratio of afflicted people is 1-to-1, male-female. But AIDS
still has far to spread, and may be moving exponentially, through the
rest of the world. We have learned enough about the cause of AIDS to
slow its spread, if we can make rapid and fundamental changes in our
handling of that most powerful part of human biology—our own sexuality. But medicine, as yet, has nothing to offer as a cure and precious
little even for palliation.

This exponential spread of AIDS not only illuminates its, and our,    7
biology, but also underscores the tragedy of our moralistic mispercep-
tion. Exponential processes have a definite time and place of origin, an
initial point of "inoculation"—in this case, Africa. We didn't notice the
spread at first. In a population of billions, we pay little attention when
1 increases to 2, or 8 to 16, but when 1 million becomes 2 million, we
panic, even though the *rate* of doubling has not increased.

The infection has to start somewhere, and its initial locus may be    8
little more than an accident of circumstance. For a while, it remains
confined to those in close contact with the primary source, but only by
accident of proximity, not by intrinsic susceptibility. Eventually, given
the power and lability of human sexuality, it spreads outside the initial
group and into the general population. And now AIDS has begun its
march through our own heterosexual community.

What a tragedy that our moral stupidity caused us to lose precious    9
time, the greatest enemy in fighting an exponential spread, by downplaying the danger because we thought that AIDS was a disease of
three irregular groups of minorities: minorities of life style (needle
users), of sexual preference (homosexuals) and of color (Haitians). If
AIDS had first been imported from Africa into a Park Avenue apartment, we would not have dithered as the exponential march began.

The message of Orlando—the inevitability of technological solu-    10
tions—is wrong, and we need to understand why.

Our species has not won its independence from nature, and we    11
cannot do all that we can dream. Or at least we cannot do it at the rate
required to avoid tragedy, for we are not unbounded from time. Viral

diseases are preventable in principle, and I suspect that an AIDS vaccine will one day be produced. But how will this discovery avail us if it takes until the millenium, and by then AIDS has fully run its exponential course and saturated our population, killing a substantial percentage of the human race? A fight against an exponential enemy is primarily a race against time.

We must also grasp the perspective of ecology and evolutionary 12 biology and recognize, once we reinsert ourselves properly into nature, that AIDS represents the ordinary workings of biology, not an irrational or diabolical plague with a moral meaning. Disease, including epidemic spread, is a natural phenomenon, part of human history from the beginning. An entire subdiscipline of my profession, paleopathology, studies the evidence of ancient diseases preserved in the fossil remains of organisms. Human history has been marked by episodic plagues. More native peoples died of imported disease than ever fell before the gun during the era of colonial expansion. Our memories are short, and we have had a respite, really, only since the influenze pandemic at the end of World War I, but AIDS must be viewed as a virulent expression of an ordinary natural phenomenon.

I do not say this to foster either comfort or complacency. The 13 evolutionary perspective is correct, but utterly inappropriate for our human scale. Yes, AIDS is a natural phenomenon, one of a recurring class of pandemic diseases. Yes, AIDS may run through the entire population, and may carry off a quarter or more of us. Yes, it may make no *biological* difference to Homo sapiens in the long run: there will still be plenty of us left and we can start again. Evolution cares as little for its agents—organisms struggling for reproductive success—as physics cares for individual atoms of hydrogen in the sun. But we care. These atoms are our neighbors, our lovers, our children and ourselves. AIDS is both a natural phenomenon and, potentially, the greatest natural tragedy in human history.

The cardboard message of Epcot fosters the wrong attitudes; we 14 must both reinsert ourselves into nature and view AIDS as a natural phenomenon in order to fight properly. If we stand above nature and if technology is all-powerful, then AIDS is a horrifying anomaly that must be trying to tell us something. If so, we can adopt one of two attitudes, each potentially fatal. We can either become complacent, because we believe the message of Epcot and assume that medicine will soon generate a cure, or we can panic in confusion and seek a

scapegoat for something so irregular that it must have been visited
upon us to teach us a moral lesson.

But AIDS is not irregular. It is part of nature. So are we. This    15
should galvanize us and give us hope, not prompt the worst of all
responses: a kind of "new-age" negativism that equates natural with
what we must accept and cannot, or even should not, change. When
we view AIDS as natural, and when we recognize both the exponential
property of its spread and the accidental character of its point of entry
into America, we can break through our destructive tendencies to
blame others and to free ourselves of concern.

If AIDS is natural, then there is no message in its spread. But by    16
all that science has learned and all that rationality proclaims, AIDS
works by a *mechanism*—and we can discover it. Victory is not ordained
by any principle of progress, or any slogan of technology, so we shall
have to fight like hell, and be watchful. There is no message, but there
is a mechanism.

---

# Diversity and Its Discontents

## ARTURO MADRID

My name is Arturo Madrid. I am a citizen of the United States, as    1
are my parents and as were my grandparents and my great-grandpar-
ents. My ancestors' presence in what is now the United States ante-
dates Plymouth Rock, even without taking into account any American
Indian heritage I might have.

I do not, however, fit those mental sets that define America and    2
Americans. My physical appearance, my speech patterns, my name,
my profession (a professor of Spanish) create a text that confuses the
reader. My normal experience is to be asked, "And where are *you*
from?" My response depends on my mood. Passive-aggressive, I answer, "From here." Aggressive-passive, I ask, "Do you mean where I
am originally from?" But ultimately my answer to those follow-up
questions that will ask about origins will be that we have always been
from here.

Overcoming my resentment I try to educate, knowing that nine    3 times out of ten my words fall on inattentive ears. I have spent most of my adult life explaining who I am not. I am exotic, but—as Richard Rodriguez of *Hunger of Memory* fame so painfully found out—not exotic enough . . . not Peruvian, or Pakistani, or whatever. I am, however, very clearly the *other*, if only your everyday, garden-variety, domestic *other*. I will share with you another phenomenon that I have been a part of, that of being a missing person, and how I came late to that awareness. But I've always known that I was the *other*, even before I knew the vocabulary or understood the significance of otherness.

I grew up in an isolated and historically marginal part of the   4 United States, a small mountain village in the state of New Mexico, the eldest child of parents native to that region, whose ancestors had always lived there. In those vast and empty spaces people who look like me, speak as I do, and have names like mine predominate. But the *americanos* lived among us: the descendants of those nineteenth-century immigrants who dispossessed us of our lands; missionaries who came to convert us and stayed to live among us; artists who became enchanted with our land and humanscape and went native; refugees from unhealthy climes, crowded spaces, unpleasant circumstances; and, of course, the inhabitants of Los Alamos, whose sociocultural distance from us was accentuated by the fact that they occupied a space removed from and proscribed to us. More importantly, however, they—*los americanos*—were omnipresent (and almost exclusively so) in newspapers, magazines, books, on radio, in movies, and, ultimately, on television.

Despite the operating myth of the day, school did not erase my   5 otherness. It did try to deny it, and in doing so only accentuated it. To this day what takes place in schools is more socialization than education, but when I was in elementary school—and given where I was— socialization was everything. School was where one became an American, because there was a pervasive and systematic denial by the society that surrounded us that we were Americans. That denial was both explicit and implicit.

Quite beyond saluting the flag and pledging allegiance to it (a very   6 intense and meaningful action, given that the United States was involved in a war and our brothers, cousins, uncles, and fathers were on the frontlines), becoming American was learning English, and its corollary: not speaking Spanish. Until very recently ours was a proscribed language, either *de jure*—by rule, by policy, by law—or *de facto*—by practice, implicitly if not explicitly, through social and political and economic pressure. I do not argue that learning English was not appropriate. On the contrary. Like it or not, and we had no basis to make any judgments on that matter, we were Americans by virtue of having been born Americans and English was the common language of Americans. And there was a myth, a pervasive myth, to the effect that if only we learned to speak English well—and particularly without an accent—we would be welcomed into the American fellowship.

Sam Hayakawa and the official English movement folks notwith-   7
standing, the true text was not our speech, but rather our names and our appearance, for we would always have an accent, however perfect our pronunciation, however excellent our enunciation, however divine our diction. That accent would be heard in our pigmentation, our physiognomy, our names. We were, in short, the *other*.

Being the *other* involves contradictory phenomena. On the one   8
hand being the *other* frequently means being invisible. Ralph Ellison wrote eloquently about that experience in his magisterial novel, *Invisible Man*. On the other hand, being the *other* sometimes involves sticking out like a sore thumb. What is she/he doing here?

For some of us being the *other* is only annoying; for others it is   9
debilitating; for still others it is damning. Many try to flee otherness by taking on protective colorations that provide invisibility, whether of dress or speech or manner or name. Only a fortunate few succeed. For the majority of us otherness is permanently sealed by physical appearance. For the rest, otherness is betrayed by ways of being, speaking, or doing.

The first half of my life I spent downplaying the significance and   10
consequences of otherness. The second half has seen me wrestling to understand its complex and deeply ingrained realities; striving to fathom why otherness denies us a voice or visibility or validity in American society and its institutions; struggling to make otherness familiar, reasonable, even normal to my fellow Americans.

I spoke earlier of another phenomenon that I am a part of: that of   11
being a missing person. Growing up in northern New Mexico I had only a slight sense of us being missing persons. *Hispanos*, as we called (and call) ourselves in New Mexico, were very much a part of the fabric of the society, and there were *hispano* professionals everywhere about me: doctors, lawyers, schoolteachers, and administrators. My people owned businesses, ran organizations, and were both appointed and elected public officials.

My awareness of our absence from the larger institutional life of 12
the society became sharper when I went off to college, but even then
it was attenuated by the circumstances of history and geography. The
demography of Albuquerque still strongly reflected its historical and
cultural origins, despite the influx of Midwesterners and Easterners.
Moreover, many of my classmates at the University of New Mexico
were *hispanos,* and even some of my professors. I thought that would
obtain at UCLA, where I began graduate studies in 1960. Los Angeles
had a very large Mexican population and that population was visible
even in and around Westwood and on the campus. Many of the
groundskeepers and food-service personnel at UCLA were Mexican.
But Mexican-American students were few and mostly invisible, and I
do not recall seeing or knowing a single Mexican-American (or, for that
matter, African-American, Asian, or American Indian) professional on
the staff or faculty of that institution during the five years I was there.
Needless to say, people like me were not present in any capacity at
Dartmouth College, the site of my first teaching appointment, and of
course were not even part of the institutional or individual mind-set. I
knew then that we—a we that had come to encompass American
Indians, Asian-Americans, African-Americans, Puerto Ricans, and
women—were truly missing persons in American institutional life.

Over the past three decades the *de jure* and *de facto* types of 13
segregation that have historically characterized American institutions
have been under assault. As a consequence, minorities and women
have become part of American institutional life. Although there are
still many areas where we are not to be found, the missing persons
phenomenon is not as pervasive as it once was. However, the presence
of the *other,* particularly minorities, in institutions and in institutional
life resembles what we call in Spanish a *flor de tierra* (a surface
phenomenon): we are spare plants whose roots do not go deep, vulnerable to inclemencies of an economic, or political, or social, nature.

Our entrance into and our status in institutional life are not unlike 14
a scenario set forth by my grandmother's pastor when she informed
him that she and her family were leaving their mountain village to
relocate to the Rio Grande Valley. When he asked her to promise that
she would remain true to the faith and continue to involve herself in
it, she asked why he thought she would do otherwise. "Doña Trini-
dad," he told her, "in the Valley there is no Spanish church. There is
only an American church." "But," she protested, "I read and speak
English and would be able to worship there." The pastor responded,
"It is possible that they will not admit you, and even if they do, they

might not accept you. And that is why I want you to promise me that you are going to go to church. Because if they don't let you in through the front door, I want you to go in through the back door. And if you can't get in through the back door, go in the side door. And if you are unable to enter through the side door I want you to go in through the window. What is important is that you enter and stay."

Some of us entered institutional life through the front door; others 15 through the back door; and still others through side doors. Many, if not most of us, came in through windows, and continue to come in through windows. Of those who entered through the front door, some never made it past the lobby; others were ushered into corners and niches. Those who entered through back and side doors inevitably have remained in back and side rooms. And those who entered through windows found enclosures built around them. For, despite the lip service given to the goal of the integration of minorities into institutional life, what has frequently occurred instead is ghettoization, marginalization, isolation.

Not only have the entry points been limited, but in addition the 16 dynamics have been singularly conflictive. Gaining entry and its corollary, gaining space, have frequently come as a consequence of demands made on institutions and institutional officers. Rather than entering institutions more or less passively, minorities have of necessity entered them actively, even aggressively. Rather than waiting to receive, they have demanded. Institutional relations have thus been adversarial, infused with specific and generalized tensions.

The nature of the entrance and the nature of the space occupied 17 have greatly influenced the view and attitude of the majority population within those institutions. All of us are put into the same box; that is, no matter what the individual reality, the assessment of the individual is inevitably conditioned by a perception that is held of the class. Whatever our history, whatever our record, whatever our validations, whatever our accomplishments, by and large we are perceived unidimensionally and dealt with accordingly. I remember an experience I had in this regard, atypical only in its explicitness. A few years ago I allowed myself to be persuaded to seek the presidency of a well-known state university. I was invited for an interview and presented myself before the selection committee, which included members of the board of trustees. The opening question of that brief but memorable interview was directed at me by a member of that august body. "Dr. Madrid," he asked, "why does a one-dimensional person like you think he can be the president of a multidimensional institution like ours?"

Over the past four decades America's demography has undergone significant changes. Since 1965 the principal demographic growth we have experienced in the United States has been of peoples whose national origins are non-European. This population growth has occurred both through birth and through immigration. A few years ago discussion of the national birthrate had a scare dimension: the high—"inordinately high"—birthrate of the Hispanic population. The popular discourse was informed by words such as "breeding." Several years later, as a consequence of careful tracking by government agencies, we now know that what has happened is that the birthrate of the majority population has decreased. When viewed historically and comparatively, the minority populations (for the most part) have also had a decline in birthrate, but not one as great as that of the majority. [18]

There are additional demographic changes that should give us something to think about. African-Americans are now to be found in significant numbers in every major urban center in the nation. Hispanic-Americans now number over 15 million people, and although they are a regionally concentrated (and highly urbanized) population, there is a Hispanic community in almost every major urban center of the United States. American Indians, heretofore a small and rural population, are increasingly more numerous and urban. The Asian-American population, which has historically consisted of small and concentrated communities of Chinese-, Filipino-, and Japanese-Americans, has doubled over the past decade, its complexion changed by the addition of Cambodians, Koreans, Hmongs, Vietnamese, et al. [19]

Prior to the Immigration Act of 1965, 69 percent of immigration was from Europe. By far the largest number of immigrants to the United States since 1965 have been from the Americas and from Asia: 34 percent are from Asia, another 34 percent are from Central and South America; 16 percent are from Europe; 10 percent are from the Caribbean; the remaining 6 percent are from other continents and Canada. As was the case with previous immigration waves, the current one consists principally of young people: 60 percent are between the ages of 16 and 44. Thus, for the next few decades, we will continue to see a growth in the percentage of non-European-origin Americans as compared to European-Americans. [20]

To sum up, we now live in one of the most demographically      21
diverse nations in the world, and one that is increasingly more so.

During the same period social and economic change seems to have      22
accelerated. Who would have imagined at mid-century that the
prototypical middle-class family (working husband, wife as home-
maker, two children) would for all intents and purposes disappear?
Who could have anticipated the rise in teenage pregnancies, children
in poverty, drug use? Who among us understood the implications of an
aging population?

We live in an age of continuous and intense change, a world in      23
which what held true yesterday does not today, and certainly will not
tomorrow. What change does, moreover, is bring about even more
change. The only constant we have at this point in our national development is change. And change is threatening. The older we get the
more likely we are to be anxious about change, and the greater our
desire to maintain the status quo.

Evident in our public life is a fear of change, whether economic or      24
moral. Some who fear change are responsive to the call of economic
protectionism, others to the message of moral protectionism. Paren-
thetically, I have referred to the movement to require more of students
without in turn giving them more as academic protectionism. And the
pronouncements of E.D. Hirsch and Allan Bloom are, I believe, informed by intellectual protectionism. Much more serious, however, is
the dark side of the populism which underlies this evergoing protectionism—the resentment of the *other*. An excellent and fascinating
example of that aspect of populism is the cry for linguistic protectionism—for making English the official language of the United States. And
who among us is unaware of the tensions that underlie immigration
reform, of the underside of demographic protectionism?

A matter of increasing concern is whether this new protectionism,      25
and the mistrust of the *other* which accompanies it, is not making more
significant inroads than we have supposed in higher education. Specifically, I wish to discuss the question of whether a goal (quality) and a
reality (demographic diversity) have been erroneously placed in conflict, and, if so, what problems this perception of conflict might present.

As part of my scholarship I turn to dictionaries for both origins and      26
meanings of words. Quality, according to the *Oxford English Dictionary*,
has multiple meanings. One set defines quality as being an essential
character, a distinctive and inherent feature. A second describes it as a
degree of excellence, of conformity to standards, as superiority in kind. A

third makes reference to social status, particularly to persons of high social status. A fourth talks about quality as being a special or distinguishing attribute, as being a desirable trait. Quality is highly desirable in both principle and practice. We all aspire to it in our own person, in our experiences, in our acquisitions and products, and of course we all want to be associated with people and operations of quality.

But let us move away from the various dictionary meanings of     27
the word and to our own sense of what it represents and of how we feel about it. First of all we consider quality to be finite; that is, it is limited with respect to quantity; it has very few manifestations; it is not widely distributed. I have it and you have it, but they don't. We associate quality with homogeneity, with uniformity, with standardization, with order, regularity, neatness. All too often we equate it with smoothness, glibness, slickness, elegance. Certainly it is always expensive. We tend to identify it with those who lead, with the rich and famous. And, when you come right down to it, it's inherent. Either you've got it or you ain't.

Diversity, from the Latin *divertere*, meaning to turn aside, to go     28
different ways, to differ, is the condition of being different or having differences, is an instance of being different. Its companion word, diverse, means differing, unlike, distinct; having or capable or having various forms; composed of unlike or distinct elements. Diversity is lack of standardization, of regularity, of orderliness, homogeneity, conformity, uniformity. Diversity introduces complications, is difficult to organize, is troublesome to manage, is problematical. Diversity is irregular, disorderly, uneven, rough. The way we use the word diversity gives us away. Something is too diverse, is extremely diverse. We want a little diversity.

When we talk about diversity, we are talking about the *other*,     29
whatever that other might be: someone of a different gender, race, class, national origin; somebody at a greater or lesser distance from the norm; someone outside the set; someone who possesses a different set of characteristics, features, or attributes; someone who does not fall within the taxonomies we use daily and with which we are comfortable; someone who does not fit into the mental configurations that give our lives order and meaning.

In short, diversity is desirable only in principle, not in practice.     30
Long live diversity . . . as long as it conforms to my standards, my mind set, my view of life, my sense of order. We desire, we like, we admire diversity, not unlike the way the French (and others) appreciate women; that is, *Vive la différence!*—as long as it stays in its place.

What I find paradoxical about and lacking in this debate is that    31
diversity is the natural order of things. Evolution produces diversity.
Margaret Visser, writing about food in her latest book, *Much Depends
on Dinner*, makes an eloquent statement in this regard:

Machines like, demand, and produce uniformity. But nature loathes it: her
strength lies in multiplicity and in differences. Sameness in biology means
fewer possibilities and therefore weakness.

The United States, by its very nature, by its very development, is    32
the essence of diversity. It is diverse in its geography, population,
institutions, technology; its social, cultural, and intellectual modes. It
is a society that at its best does not consider quality to be monolithic
in form or finite in quantity, or to be inherent in class. Quality in our
society proceeds in large measure out of the stimulus of diverse modes
of thinking and acting; out of the creativity made possible by the
different ways in which we approach things; out of diversion from
paths or modes hallowed by tradition.

One of the principal strengths of our society is its ability to address,    33
on a continuing and substantive basis, the real economic, political, and
social problems that have faced and continue to face us. What makes
the United States so attractive to immigrants is the protections and
opportunities it offers; what keeps our society together is tolerance for
cultural, religious, social, political, and even linguistic difference; what
makes us a unique, dynamic, and extraordinary nation is the power and
creativity of our diversity.

The true history of the United States is one of struggle against    34
intolerance, against oppression, against xenophobia, against those
forces that have prohibited persons from participating in the larger life
of the society on the basis of their race, their gender, their religion,
their national origin, their linguistic and cultural background. These
phenomena are not consigned to the past. They remain with us and
frequently take on virulent dimensions.

If you believe, as I do, that the well-being of a society is directly    35
related to the degree and extent to which all of its citizens participate
in its institutions, then you will have to agree that we have a challenge
before us. In view of the extraordinary changes that are taking place
in our society we need to take up the struggle again, irritating, grating,
troublesome, unfashionable, unpleasant as it is. As educated and educator members of this society we have a special responsibility for
ensuring that all American institutions, not just our elementary and

secondary schools, our juvenile halls, or our jails, reflect the diversity of our society. Not to do so is to risk greater alienation on the part of a growing segment of our society; is to risk increased social tension in an already conflictive world; and, ultimately, is to risk the survival of a range of institutions that, for all their defects and deficiencies, provide us the opportunity and the freedom to improve our individual and collective lot.

Let me urge you to reflect on these two words—quality and diversity—and on the mental sets and behaviors that flow out of them. And let me urge you further to struggle against the notion that quality is finite in quantity, limited in its manifestations, or is restricted by considerations of class, gender, race, or national origin; or that quality manifests itself only in leaders and not in followers, in managers and not in workers, in breeders and not in drones; or that it has to be associated with verbal agility or elegance of personal style; or that it cannot be seeded, nurtured, or developed. 36

Because diversity—the *other*—is among us, will define and determine our lives in ways that we still do not fully appreciate, whether that other is women (no longer bound by tradition, house, and family); or Asians, African-Americans, Indians, and Hispanics (no longer invisible, regional, or marginal); or our newest immigrants (no longer distant exotic, alien). Given the changing profile of America, will we come to terms with diversity in our personal and professional lives? Will we begin to recognize the diverse forms that quality can take? If so, we will thus initiate the process of making quality limitless in its manifestations, infinite in quantity, unrestricted with respect to its origins, and more importantly, virulently contagious. 37

I hope we will. And that we will further join together to expand— not to close—the circle. 38

---

# Second Inaugural Address

## ABRAHAM LINCOLN

At this second appearing to take the oath of the presidential office, there is less occasion for an extended address than there was at the first. Then a statement, somewhat in detail, of a course to be pursued, 1 seemed fitting and proper. Now, at the expiration of four years, during which public declarations have been constantly called forth on every point and phase of the great contest which still absorbs the attention, and engrosses the energies of the nation, little that is new could be presented. The progress of our arms, upon which all else chiefly depends, is as well known to the public as to myself; and it is, I trust, reasonably satisfactory and encouraging to all. With high hope for the future, no prediction in regard to it is ventured.

On the occasion corresponding to this four years ago, all thoughts    2
were anxiously directed to an impending civil war. All dreaded it—all sought to avert it. While the inaugural address was being delivered from this place, devoted altogether to *saving* the Union without war, insurgent agents were in the city seeking to *destroy* it without war— seeking to dissolve the Union, and divide effects, by negotiation. Both parties deprecated war; but one of them would *make* war rather than let the nation survive; and the other would *accept* war rather than let it perish. And the war came.

One-eighth of the whole population were colored slaves, not dis-    3
tributed generally over the Union, but localized in the Southern part of it. These slaves constituted a peculiar and powerful interest. All knew that this interest was, somehow, the cause of the war. To strengthen, perpetuate, and extend this interest was the object for which the insurgents would rend the Union, even by war; while the government claimed no right to do more than to restrict the territorial enlargement of it. Neither party expected for the war, the magnitude, or the duration, which it has already attained. Neither anticipated that the *cause* of the conflict might cease with, or even before, the conflict itself should cease. Each looked for an easier triumph, and a result less fundamental and astounding. Both read the same Bible, and pray to the same God; and each invokes His aid against the other. It may seem strange that any men should dare to ask a just God's assistance in wringing their bread from the sweat of other men's faces; but let us judge not that we be not judged. The prayers of both could not be answered; that of neither has been answered fully. The Almighty has His own purposes. "Woe unto the world because of offenses! for it must needs be that offenses come; but woe to that man by whom the offense cometh!" If we shall suppose that American slavery is one of those offenses which, in the providence of God, must needs come, but which, having continued through His appointed time, He now wills to remove, and that He gives to both North and South, this terrible war,

as the woe due to those by whom the offense came, shall we discern therein any departure from those divine attributes which the believers in a Living God always ascribe to Him? Fondly do we hope—fervently do we pray—that this mighty scourge of war may speedily pass away. Yet, if God wills that it continue, until all the wealth piled by the bondman's two hundred and fifty years of unrequited toil shall be sunk, and until every drop of blood drawn with the lash, shall be paid by another drawn with the sword, as was said three thousand years ago, so still it must be said "the judgments of the Lord are true and righteous altogether."

With malice toward none; with charity for all; with firmness in the     4
right, as God gives us to see the right, let us strive on to finish the work we are in; to bind up the nation's wounds; to care for him who shall have borne the battle, and for his widow, and his orphan—to do all which may achieve and cherish a just, and a lasting peace, among ourselves, and with all nations.

# I Have a Dream

## MARTIN LUTHER KING, JR.

Five score years ago, a great American, in whose symbolic shadow     1
we stand, signed the Emancipation Proclamation. This momentous decree came as a great beacon light of hope to millions of Negro slaves who had been seared in the flames of withering injustice. It came as a joyous daybreak to end the long night of captivity.

But one hundred years later, we must face the tragic fact that the     2
Negro is still not free. One hundred years later, the life of the Negro is still sadly crippled by the manacles of segregation and the chains of discrimination. One hundred years later, the Negro lives on a lonely island of poverty in the midst of a vast ocean of material prosperity. One hundred years later, the Negro is still languishing in the corners of American society and finds himself an exile in his own land. So we have come here today to dramatize an appalling condition.

In a sense we have come to our nation's capital to cash a check.     3
When the architects of our republic wrote the magnificent words of the

Argument

Constitution and the Declaration of Independence, they were signing a promissory note to which every American was to fall heir. This note was a promise that all men would be guaranteed the unalienable rights of life, liberty, and the pursuit of happiness.

It is obvious today that America has defaulted on this promissory 4 note insofar as her citizens of color are concerned. Instead of honoring this sacred obligation, America has given the Negro people a bad check; a check which has come back marked "insufficient funds." But we refuse to believe that the bank of justice is bankrupt. We refuse to believe that there are insufficient funds in the great vaults of opportunity of this nation. So we have come to cash this check—a check that will give us upon demand the riches of freedom and the security of justice. We have also come to this hallowed spot to remind America of the fierce urgency of *now*. This is no time to engage in the luxury of cooling off or to take the tranquilizing drugs of gradualism. *Now* is the time to make real the promises of Democracy. *Now* is the time to rise from the dark and desolate valley of segregation to the sunlit path of racial justice. *Now* is the time to open the doors of opportunity to all of God's children. *Now* is the time to lift our nation from the quicksands of racial injustice to the solid rock of brotherhood.

It would be fatal for the nation to overlook the urgency of the 5 moment and to underestimate the determination of the Negro. This sweltering summer of the Negro's legitimate discontent will not pass until there is an invigorating autumn of freedom and equality. 1963 is not an end, but a beginning. Those who hope that the Negro needed to blow off steam and will now be content will have a rude awakening if the nation returns to business as usual. There will be neither rest nor tranquillity in America until the Negro is granted his citizenship rights. The whirlwinds of revolt will continue to shake the foundations of our nation until the bright day of justice emerges.

But there is something that I must say to my people who stand on 6 the warm threshold which leads into the palace of justice. In the process of gaining our rightful place we must not be guilty of wrongful deeds. Let us not seek to satisfy our thirst for freedom by drinking from the cup of bitterness and hatred. We must forever conduct our struggle on the high plane of dignity and discipline. We must not allow our creative protest to degenerate into physical violence. Again and again we must rise to the majestic heights of meeting physical force with soul force. The marvelous new militancy which has engulfed the Negro community must not lead us to a distrust of all white people, for many of our white brothers, as evidenced by their presence here today, have come to realize that their destiny is tied up with our destiny and their freedom is inextricably bound to our freedom. We cannot walk alone.

And as we walk, we must make the pledge that we shall march 7 ahead. We cannot turn back. There are those who are asking the devotees of civil rights, "When will you be satisfied?" We can never be satisfied as long as the Negro is the victim of the unspeakable horrors of police brutality. We can never be satisfied as long as our bodies, heavy with the fatigue of travel, cannot gain lodging in the motels of the highways and the hotels of the cities. We cannot be satisfied as long as the Negro's basic mobility is from a smaller ghetto to a larger one. We can never be satisfied as long as a Negro in Mississippi cannot vote and a Negro in New York believes he has nothing for which to vote. No, no, we are not satisfied, and we will not be satisfied until justice rolls down like waters and righteousness like a mighty stream.

I am not unmindful that some of you have come here out of great 8 trials and tribulations. Some of you have come fresh from narrow jail cells. Some of you have come from areas where your quest for freedom left you battered by the storms of persecution and staggered by the winds of police brutality. You have been the veterans of creative suffering. Continue to work with the faith that unearned suffering is redemptive.

Go back to Mississippi, go back to Alabama, go back to South 9 Carolina, go back to Georgia, go back to Louisiana, go back to the slums and ghettos of our northern cities, knowing that somehow this situation can and will be changed. Let us not wallow in the valley of despair.

I say to you today, my friends, that in spite of the difficulties and 10 frustrations of the moment I still have a dream. It is a dream deeply rooted in the American dream.

I have a dream that one day this nation will rise up and live out 11 the true meaning of its creed: "We hold these truths to be self-evident; that all men are created equal."

I have a dream that one day on the red hills of Georgia the sons 12 of former slaves and the sons of former slaveowners will be able to sit down together at the table of brotherhood.

I have a dream that one day even the state of Mississippi, a desert 13 state sweltering with the heat of injustice and oppression, will be transformed into an oasis of freedom and justice.

I have a dream that my four little children will one day live in a 14

nation where they will not be judged by the color of their skin but by
the content of their character.

I have a dream today.                                                          15

I have a dream that one day the state of Alabama, whose gover-      16
nor's lips are presently dripping with the words of interposition and
nullification, will be transformed into a situation where little black boys
and black girls will be able to join hands with little white boys and
white girls and walk together as sisters and brothers.

I have a dream today.                                                          17

I have a dream that one day every valley shall be exalted, every      18
hill and mountain shall be made low, the rough places will be made
plain, and the crooked places will be made straight, and the glory of the
Lord shall be revealed, and all flesh shall see it together.

This is our hope. This is the faith with which I return to the South.   19
With this faith we will be able to hew out of the mountain of despair
a stone of hope. With this faith we will be able to transform the
jangling discords of our nation into a beautiful symphony of brotherhood. With this faith we will be able to work together, to pray together,
to struggle together, to go to jail together, to stand up for freedom
together, knowing that we will be free one day.

This will be the day when all of God's children will be able to sing   20
with new meaning

My country, 'tis of thee,
Sweet land of liberty,
        Of thee I sing:
Land where my fathers died,
Land of the pilgrims' pride,
From every mountain-side
        Let freedom ring.

And if America is to be a great nation this must become true. So   21
let freedom ring from the prodigious hilltops of New Hampshire. Let
freedom ring from the mighty mountains of New York. Let freedom
ring from the heightening Alleghenies of Pennsylvania!

Let freedom ring from the snowcapped Rockies of Colorado!          22

Let freedom ring from the curvaceous peaks of California!           23

But not only that; let freedom ring from Stone Mountain of         24
Georgia!

Let freedom ring from Lookout Mountain of Tennessee!               25

Let freedom ring from every hill and molehill of Mississippi. From  26
every mountainside, let freedom ring.

When we let freedom ring, when we let it ring from every village 27
and every hamlet, from every state and every city, we will be able to
speed up that day when all of God's children, black men and white
men, Jews and Gentiles, Protestants and Catholics, will be able to join
hands and sing in the words of the old Negro spiritual, "Free at last!
free at last! thank God almighty, we are free at last!"

---

# The Sin of Self-Sacrifice

## REBECCA WEST

The basis of the anti-feminist position is the idea that women 1
ought to sacrifice the development of their own personalities for the
sake of men and children: that even if they are fit to vote and to fulfil
other activities of men they should not do so, because all their energies
should be spent in the service of their families. Such is the view of the
governing classes in this country today, and its passionate advocacy by
Ellen Key has changed the continental woman's movement from a
march towards freedom to a romp towards voluptuous servitude. According to these folk a woman should from her childhood be guarded
from the disturbance of intellectual effort and should pass automatically through a serenely sentimental adolescence to a home. There the
tranquil flame of her unspoiled soul should radiate purity and nobility
upon an indefinitely extended family, exposed to the world's winds
only when she goes wisely marketing. Inconceivably incandescent,
inconceivably economical, like the advertisement of a motor-lamp
come true.

This amounts to a claim to halos for women: for a halo is the 2
only thing I have ever heard of that gives out light yet needs no fuel.
Unless a human being is being inspired with wisdom by some super-
natural power he can only gain wisdom by an experience compounded of his sensations: that is, the vibration caused by collision
between his nerves and external things. We are dependent for the
value of this basis of wisdom on the extent to which we lean out of
ourselves and adventure among alien things. The only times when a
woman's physical feelings are concentrated within herself are when
she has indigestion and appendicitis; when she is well she is thinking

how warmly the sunlight lies on her face or how sweet the wet loaves smell. Similarly, when a woman's mental feelings are concentrated within herself she must have inflammation of the brain. Only the mad wonder continually whether they are men or poached eggs, and discuss whether the world uses them well or ill. The sane look round on their fellow-men and delight to see who will help them in their work of making the world less madly governed: they walk the earth to choose their battlefields, and touch all it contains to find the substance most fit for the forging of weapons. Then they glow with the exhilaration of wisdom and radiate glory. So might many women were they given freedom; but they must remain tinged with no clearer light than the reflection of the kitchen range so long as they are made to ape the self-sufficiency of the maniac. As they are ignorant how can they hope to inspire those who are not ignorant? What influence can a wife who has passed from playing with dolls in her father's house to playing with saucepans and babies in her husband's house hope to have over a man who has been disciplined by years of responsible enterprise among all sorts of men? Her courage has been tried by childbirth, but her character has stood no other test.

It may be said that this is underestimating the value of home-keeping as an occupation. Of course it is. But it is a wild generalisation to say that the majority of wives in Great Britain are home-keepers in the sense of being essential to the existence of the home as was the wife in medieval agricultural England. If she were there would be no need to discuss feminism, for where a woman pays her way by performing labour she usually forces the community (if it be not too corrupt with capitalism) into recognizing her equality. While the silk industry made the Burmese women economically independent, they were not submissive to men; but now that this is taken out of their hands they are threatened with that humiliation. And I was recently told by "A. E." that there is no need for the preaching of feminism in modern agricultural Ireland, for the farmer and the farmer's wife depend so much on each other's labour that it never occurs to them to imagine that they are different and unequal sorts. The rough home-keeping of the past, and the present in remote districts, presented difficulties which had to be met by skill and determination. Where the cow had to be milked and the churn persuaded, one simply waits for the coming of a milkman who, perhaps, has rarely seen a cow; where jelly had to be forced to jell one buys small packets from some unknown controller of jellies; where one sheared the sheep and spun its wool and wove the cloth and cut out the dress one goes to a shop and buys the finished thing easily, though probably at three times its real cost. It is all very simple and quite artificial. The woman who does these things may fill up her day with them, but the practice of them is hardly a craft. For they are tricks that a performing dog who could count his change might pull off just as well. That there is no interest in the occupation to counterbalance the solitude it entails, in these days of small homes unconnected by any local corporate life, is shown by the numbers of domestic servants who fly from its monotony to the life of the streets. And evidently their mistresses found the home no more educative, for they have not prevented their husbands and sons from preying on these women till, in their misery, they have revenged themselves on society by their disease and drunkenness. Here, in a rather important matter, the home-keeping woman has failed to radiate purity and nobility.

It may be said that the failure of women to create or influence   4 morality does not matter: that their business lies simply with the physical nurture of the race. This is like saying that a doctor has no right to concern himself with the study of poisons because his business is with the preservation of the human body. When the body evolved the mind it evolved a queer, treacherous governor, who never knows what he does with his subject. Just as the African mind, by turning to commerce, has betrayed the African body, because sleeping-sickness travelled along the trade routes as safely as the goods, so the Western mind has betrayed the Western body by inventing the ingenious and in many ways convenient system of capitalism. So long as it persists no wealthy mother can look at her child without remembering that:

The strongest poison ever known
Came from Caesar's laurel crown.

No poor mother can hold her healthy child (life is such an inde-   5 structible and generous thing that nearly every baby is born healthy) without seeing him the bent extension of a machine. Men have not been able to fight the forces we have in an honest quest for civilisation called up from hell: all the energy of the world is needed to battle with them. The woman who cares merely for the physical nurture of her children is by her softness encouraging the famine that may some day starve them.

The fact is that this idea of sacrificing the individual to the race   6 never works. It hints at a philosophical heresy, such as the belief disproved by Berkeley that matter has a substance apart from its attributes. "There is nothing behind the facts," said Chauncey Depew, when offered an idealist system that would "harmonise" and "explain" the facts of life. There is nothing behind the race but the individuals. If half the individuals agree to remain weak and undeveloped half the race is weak and undeveloped. And if every alternate link of a chain is weak it matters not how strong the others are: the chain will break all the same. Every nation that has contained a slave class has fallen to dust and ashes in spite of all its military glories and its pride of brains. And I cannot remember that any individual has ever benefited the race by self-sacrifice. I can well believe that St. Simon Stylites did not like perching and that Savonarola's heart bled at his own denunciation of beauty and jollity; but these men saved no race. The people who draw down salvation to earth are the people who insist on self-realisation whether it leads to death or gaiety. Florence Nightingale saved war from its worse disgrace and helped the sick because she hated disorder, not because she thought she ought to do something toilsome. Marx set humanity on its feet because he was interested in economics. Darwin uncovered the significant eyes of truth because he enjoyed zoology.

And truly these are among the saviours of men.                                    7

And the recognition of this is the real virtue of the militant suffrage     8
movement. Its later manifestations have seemed to some of us not immoral but pointless and extravagant. Desirable residences are more common than desirable Cabinet Ministers, yet they are sufficiently rare to be preserved. No house is wholly built with hands: it has taken many mental triumphs of the organisation of civilisation to secure that bricklayers shall unmolested lay their bricks and quarrymen convey their stone unrobbed. A house is an achievement not to be burned in a night. And these sporadic attacks on the voter are ineffective, for they create no widespread terror that would cry out to the Government for immediate pacification of the terrorists. They merely make England into a patchwork of irritations. But how admirable is the spirit of the militants! How splendidly selfish they are! There is no doubt that now Mrs. Pankhurst is out of gaol again they will keep her out. All over the country we can help her. There is nothing like sympathetic reference to a lawbreaker for turning the heart of the law to water. We got Jim Larkin out of Mountjoy because we said we liked him. We can keep

Mrs. Pankhurst out of Holloway if, remembering what her movement really means, and how it has brought the supreme virtue of selfishness to thousands of English women, we speak well of her.

---

# Sexual Fantasy and the 1957 Car

## S. I. HAYAKAWA

American males, according to a point of view widely held among Freudian critics of our culture, are afraid of sex. If a woman indicates to a man that she loves him and desires him, the chances are that she will scare him away. Her open manifestation of desire is likely to arouse, not his enthusiastic response, but his underlying anxieties. For endemic among American males, so the argument goes, is, if not impotence, the fear of impotence. Behind the masculine front lies the anxious question, "Am I really male?"

Such critics of the culture point to the American form of stag party, which has superficially the comforting implication of men being he-men together, as but one of a number of disguises which sexual anxiety can take. The implication of stag parties that stags don't think about is that it is an institutionalized way of running away from women—running away from the real tests of being a lover, husband, father, and a man. But sex is not too far away from any stag party—a sniggering, surreptitious sex interest such as is shown in a news story like the following:

> HOLLYWOOD, FEB. 9 (UP)—Police today released several husbands who were arrested while allegedly watching a lewd movie at a lodge hall while their wives played bridge in a room next door. Officers said 62 men were arrested last night after a policeman climbed a telephone pole and watched the movie through a window. Detectives said the hall had been rented by a Knights of Pythias group for a "business meeting."

The real giveaway as to the psychology of the men in this situation is contained in the last paragraph of the story:

> On the way to jail, one suspect said, "Boy, a life sentence isn't going to be nearly long enough." Another asked, "Where do you join the Foreign Legion?"

And well they might join the Foreign Legion. For they insult their    4
wives doubly, first by declining or fearing to respond fully and joyfully
to their wives' sexuality, and secondly by gratifying themselves instead
with the mental masturbation of obscene movies. For all too many
American men a wife is not a wife but a mother substitute, alternatively loving and punitive, someone to run away from when one wants
to be naughty, and then returns to, to be spanked and forgiven.

Such assertions as the foregoing about American men are famil-    5
iar enough in the writings of Karl Menninger, Franz Alexander,
Karen Horney, and others with a psychoanalytic orientation. They
are also familiar through the writings of nonpsychiatrists like Philip
Wylie, with his diatribe against momism. I myself have been tempted
to dismiss these charges as unfair generalizations, based too much on
experiences with patients, and not enough on observations of the majority. All American men aren't like that—I have argued—not even
most of them.

But in 1957 I am being contradicted. I am being contradicted by    6
perhaps the most powerful voice in America—the voice of that industry upon whose prosperity rests, we are told, the prosperity of the
nation, namely, the automobile industry, which appears to have decided that the supplying of means of transportation is but a secondary
reason for its existence, and that its primary function is the allaying of
men's sexual anxieties. As if to back up with a fifty-million-dollar bang
what psychoanalytic critics have been saying about the American
male, the automobile industry is saying in 1957: "The fundamental fact
about American male psychology is the fear of impotence. Let's give
the men, therefore, the One Big Symbol that will make them feel that
they are *not* impotent. Let's give them great big cars, glittering all over
and pointed at the ends, with 275 h.p. under the hood, so that they can
feel like men!" For, as the consumer motivational research people
must have told the powers-that-be in the industry, this is what will
make men trade in their present cars and put themselves into hock for
1957 models. The motivational research people do not survey merely
the patients of psychoanalysts; they survey the entire buying public.
And what most of the public wants, it appears, is a potency symbol.

Granted that a car is transportation. Granted that restless annual    7
style changes and the quest for novelty are necessitated by business
competition. Granted that a car is a prestige symbol, a personal symbol, or what you will. Granted even that many cars have always been
for many men unconscious symbols of potency. The 1957 cars are

nevertheless unique in sacrificing *all* else—common sense, efficiency, economy, safety, dignity, and especially beauty—to psychosexual wish fulfillment.

Few people actually need more than 40 h.p.—the Volkswagen has 8 only 36 h.p. and is still capable of violating the top speed limit in practically any state of the union. But since the U.S. is a lavish economy, let us say that the average buyer of an American automobile is entitled to at least 85 h.p., and for a luxury car with power-driven accessories, he is entitled to 160 h.p.—the rating of the 1951 Cadillac.

What about the horsepower above 160? I believe it can be safely said that every single horsepower above that figure is purely symbolic, and has *nothing* to do with transportation except to make it more hazardous. The 160 h.p. car can provide more than enough size, speed, and power to serve not only all conceivable practical purposes to which a passenger car can be put, but also to gratify the normal amount of will to aggression.

The argument that horsepower above that figure can contribute to 9 safety because it enables you to pull ahead in passing is convincing only to those whose personal inadequacies leave them wanting to be convinced. No sensible driver ever finds himself in this most easily avoided of avoidable dangers. (If you find yourself in a tight situation where you need this extra "pull ahead" power, it's time you pulled over to the side of the road to sober up before proceeding.) Hence I repeat, every horsepower above 160 is purely for the gratification of one's fantasy life—in the psychiatric sense.

The bolt-out-of-the-blue performance that enables most V-8's 10 these days to accelerate from a standing start to 60 m.p.h. in eleven seconds or less is again purely symbolic. If you are not a bank robber (and most of us are not), what's this unused and unusable acceleration for, if not for psychological satisfactions? And the ability of most cars nowadays (even including what used to be called the "economy" Big Three) to attain speeds of 125 m.p.h. and over again has no function other than to say to the buyer, who even on the open road rarely gets a chance to do 80, "Don't feel badly because you are a dubiously satisfactory bedmate. You're a *mighty* potent fellow. You are Captain Midnight! You are Buck Rogers!"

Even more revealing than horsepower or acceleration is design. 11 First of all there is, of course, the rocket ship motif. As Freudian students of spaceship and rocket-travel literature have pointed out—I think especially of such students of the subject as the late Dr. Robert

Lindner of "The Jet-Propelled Couch," Dr. Rudolph Ekstein of the Menninger Foundation, and Dr. Robert Plank of Cleveland Heights—spaceship fantasies are deeply related to difficulties in interpersonal relations. As the individual retreats into himself because he feels powerless to deal effectively with the living men and women around him, he often lives increasingly in a fantasy world of power and heroic action in distant, interplanetary spaces. The seven-year-old cuts box tops from cereal packages and gets himself a space helmet to act out his fantasies. The thirty-five-year-old buys a Plymouth Fury. Both reveal themselves to be in their sexual latency period, which is all right, of course—for the seven-year-old.

And to continue on the subject of design, there are the protuberan- 12 ces, the knifelike projections, the gashes, the bumps—all dazzlingly colored and outlined in strips of chrome. The symbolism of these is enough to make Dr. Freida Fromm-Reichmann blush—and she doesn't blush easily.

Once, a score or more years ago in Kobe, Japan, I saw in the 13 foreign section a "sex store"—a place where sexual curiosities could be bought—erotic art, indecent appliances of various kinds, all apparently calculated to awaken sexual interest in those whom age or dissipation had enfeebled, or to serve as collectors' items for those whose sexual life was mostly at the imaginative or symbolic level. Among the items on display was a collection of rubber contraceptives fantastically designed. Some were surrounded with knifelike or sawlike rubber fins, others were covered with big rubber spikes, some were fringed with tassels, some were ornamented like the noses of fighter planes with fierce bird and animal heads.

These pathetic potency symbols for the impotent and near- 14 impotent come to mind as I contemplate such monstrosities as the 290 h.p. Mercury Turnpike Cruiser, the 345 h.p. De Soto Adventurer, and the 375 h.p. Chrysler 300-C.

The cars of 1957 have two disadvantages when compared with the 15 obscene little objects in that store in Kobe. First, they are a menace to public safety—and quadruply so when their possessors are under the influence of liquor. Secondly, how can they serve as fetishes to be collected when you can't even get them into your garage?

# Fiction

## The Horse Dealer's Daughter

### D. H. LAWRENCE

"Well, Mabel, and what are you going to do with yourself?" asked   1
Joe, with foolish flippancy. He felt quite safe himself. Without listening
for an answer, he turned aside, worked a grain of tobacco to the tip of
his tongue, and spat it out. He did not care about anything, since he felt
safe himself.

The three brothers and the sister sat round the desolate breakfast   2
table, attempting some sort of desultory consultation. The morning's
post had given the final tap to the family fortune, and all was over. The
dreary dining-room itself, with its heavy mahogany furniture, looked as
if it were waiting to be done away with.

But the consultation amounted to nothing. There was a strange air   3
of ineffectuality about the three men, as they sprawled at table, smoking and reflecting vaguely on their own condition. The girl was alone,
a rather short, sullen-looking young woman of twenty-seven. She did
not share the same life as her brothers. She would have been good-
looking, save for the impassive fixity of her face, "bull-dog," as her
brothers called it.

There was a confused tramping of horses' feet outside. The three   4
men all sprawled round in their chairs to watch. Beyond the dark
hollybushes that separated the strip of lawn from the high-road, they
could see a cavalcade of shire horses swinging out of their own yard,
being taken for exercise. This was the last time. These were the last
horses that would go through their hands. The young men watched
with a critical, callous look. They were all frightened at the collapse of
their lives, and the sense of disaster in which they were involved left
them no inner freedom.

Yet they were three fine, well-set fellows enough. Joe, the eldest,   5 was a man of thirty-three, broad and handsome in a hot, flushed way. His face was red, he twisted his black moustache over a thick finger, his eyes were shallow and restless. He had a sensual way of uncovering his teeth when he laughed, and his bearing was stupid. Now he watched the horses with a glazed look of helplessness in his eyes, a certain stupor of downfall.

The great draught-horses swung past. They were tied head to tail, 6 four of them, and they heaved along to where a lane branched off from the highroad, planting their great hoofs floutingly in the fine black mud, swinging their great rounded haunches sumptuously, and trotting a few sudden steps as they were led into the lane, round the corner. Every movement showed a massive, slumbrous strength, and stupidity which held them in subjection. The groom at the head looked back, jerking the leading rope. And the cavalcade moved out of sight up the lane, the tail of the last horse bobbed up tight and stiff, held out taut from the swinging great haunches as they rocked behind the hedges in a motion like sleep.

Joe watched with glazed hopeless eyes. The horses were almost 7 like his own body to him. He felt he was done for now. Luckily he was engaged to a woman as old as himself, and therefore her father, who was steward of a neighbouring estate, would provide him with a job. He would marry and go into harness. His life was over, he would be a subject animal now.

He turned uneasily aside, the retreating steps of the horses echo- 8 ing in his ears. Then, with foolish restlessness, he reached for the scraps of bacon-rind from the plates, and making a faint whistling sound, flung them to the terrier that lay against the fender. He watched the dog swallow them, and waited till the creature looked into his eyes. Then a faint grin came on his face, and in a high, foolish voice he said:

"You won't get much more bacon, shall you, you little bitch?"       9

The dog faintly and dismally wagged its tail, then lowered its   10 haunches, circled round, and lay down again.

There was another helpless silence at the table. Joe sprawled   11 uneasily in his seat, not willing to go till the family conclave was dissolved. Fred Henry, the second brother, was erect, clean-limbed, alert. He had watched the passing of the horses with more sangfroid. If he was an animal, like Joe, he was an animal which controls, not one which is controlled. He was master of any horse, and he carried himself with a well-tempered air of mastery. But he was not master of the situations of life. He pushed his coarse brown moustache upwards, off his lip, and glanced irritably at his sister, who sat impassive and inscrutable.

"You'll go and stop with Lucy for a bit, shan't you?" he asked. The girl did not answer.                                                                    12

"I don't see what else you can do," persisted Fred Henry.            13

"Go as a skivvy," Joe interpolated laconically.                      14

The girl did not move a muscle.                                      15

"If I was her, I should go in for training for a nurse," said Malcolm, the youngest of them all. He was the baby of the family, a young man of twenty-two, with a fresh, jaunty *museau*.                          16

But Mabel did not take any notice of him. They had talked at her and round her for so many years, that she hardly heard them at all.    17

The marble clock on the mantelpiece softly chimed the half-hour, the dog rose uneasily from the hearthrug and looked at the party at the breakfast table. But still they sat on in ineffectual conclave.           18

"Oh, all right," said Joe suddenly, apropos of nothing. "I'll get a move on."                                                                 19

He pushed back his chair, straddled his knees with a downward jerk, to get them free, in horsey fashion, and went to the fire. Still he did not go out of the room; he was curious to know what the others would do or say. He began to charge his pipe, looking down at the dog and saying, in a high, affected voice:                              20

"Going wi' me? Going wi' me are ter? Tha'rt goin' further than tha counts on just now, dost hear?"                                         21

The dog faintly wagged its tail, the man stuck out his jaw and covered his pipe with his hands, and puffed intently, losing himself in the tobacco, looking down all the while at the dog with an absent brown eye. The dog looked up at him in mournful distrust. Joe stood with his knees stuck out, in real horsey fashion.                       22

"Have you had a letter from Lucy?" Fred Henry asked of his sister.                                                                    23

"Last week," came the neutral reply.                                 24

"And what does she say?"                                             25

There was no answer.                                                 26

"Does she *ask* you to go and stop there?" persisted Fred Henry.     27

"She says I can if I like."                                          28

"Well, then, you'd better. Tell her you'll come on Monday."          29

This was received in silence.                                              30

"That's what you'll do then, is it?" said Fred Henry, in some              31
exasperation.

But she made no answer. There was a silence of futility and                32
irritation in the room. Malcolm grinned fatuously.

"You'll have to make up your mind between now and next                     33
Wednesday," said Joe loudly, "or else find yourself lodgings on the
kerbstone."

The face of the young woman darkened, but she sat on immutable.            34

"Here's Jack Fergusson!" exclaimed Malcolm, who was looking                35
aimlessly out of the window.

"Where?" exclaimed Joe, loudly.                                            36

"Just gone past."                                                          37

"Coming in?"                                                               38

Malcolm craned his neck to see the gate.                                   39

"Yes," he said.                                                            40

There was a silence. Mabel sat on like one condemned, at the head          41
of the table. Then a whistle was heard from the kitchen. The dog got
up and barked sharply. Joe opened the door and shouted:

"Come on."                                                                 42

After a moment a young man entered. He was muffled up in                   43
overcoat and a purple woollen scarf, and his tweed cap, which he did
not remove, was pulled down on his head. He was of medium height,
his face was rather long and pale, his eyes looked tired.

"Hello, Jack! Well, Jack!" exclaimed Malcolm and Joe. Fred                 44
Henry merely said, "Jack."

"What's doing?" asked the newcomer, evidently addressing Fred              45
Henry.

"Same. We've got to be out by Wednesday. Got a cold?"                      46

"I have—got it bad, too."                                                  47

"Why don't you stop in?"                                                   48

"*Me* stop in? When I can't stand on my legs, perhaps I shall have         49
a chance." The young man spoke huskily. He had a slight Scotch
accent.

"It's a knock-out, isn't it?" said Joe, boisterously, "if a doctor goes    50
round croaking with a cold. Looks bad for the patients, doesn't it?"

The young doctor looked at him slowly.                                     51

"Anything the matter with *you*, then?" he asked sarcastically.            52

"Not as I know of. Damn your eyes, I hope not. Why?"                       53

"I thought you were very concerned about the patients, wondered    54
if you might be one yourself."

"Damn it, no, I've never been patient to no flaming doctor, and    55
hope I never shall be," returned Joe.

At this point Mabel rose from the table, and they all seemed to    56
become aware of her existence. She began putting the dishes together.
The young doctor looked at her, but did not address her. He had not
greeted her. She went out of the room with the tray, her face impassive
and unchanged.

"When are you off then, all of you?" asked the doctor.    57

"I'm catching the eleven-forty," replied Malcolm. "Are you goin'    58
down wi' the' trap, Joe?"

"Yes, I've told you I am going down wi' th' trap, haven't I?"    59

"We'd better be getting her in then. So long, Jack, if I don't see you    60
before I go," said Malcolm, shaking hands.

He went out, followed by Joe, who seemed to have his tail be-    61
tween his legs.

"Well, this is the devil's own," exclaimed the doctor, when he was    62
left alone with Fred Henry. "Going before Wednesday, are you."

"That's the orders," replied the other.    63

"Where, to Northampton?"    64

"That's it."    65

"The devil!" exclaimed Fergusson, with quiet chagrin.    66

And there was silence between the two.    67

"All settled up, are you?" asked Fergusson.    68

"About."    69

There was another pause.    70

"Well, I shall miss yer, Freddy, boy," said the young doctor.    71

"And I shall miss thee, Jack," returned the other.    72

"Miss you like hell," mused the doctor.    73

Fred Henry turned aside. There was nothing to say. Mabel came    74
in again, to finish clearing the table.

"What are *you* to do, then, Miss Pervin?" asked Fergusson.    75
"Going to your sister's, are you?"

Mabel looked at him with her steady, dangerous eyes, that always    76
made him uncomfortable, unsettling his superficial ease.

"No," she said.    77

"Well, what in the name of fortune are *you* going to do? Say what    78
you mean to do," cried Fred Henry, with futile intensity.

But she only averted her head, and continued her work. She folded    79
the white tablecloth, and put on the chenile cloth.

"The sulkiest bitch that ever trod!" muttered her brother.          80

But she finished her task with perfectly impassive face, the young    81
doctor watching her interestedly all the while. Then she went out.

Fred Henry stared after her, clenching his lips, his blue eyes fixing    82
in sharp antagonism, as he made a grimace of sour exasperation.

"You could bray her into bits, and that's all you'd get out of her,"    83
he said in a small, narrowed tone.

The doctor smiled faintly.                                           84

"What's she *going* to do, then?" he asked.                          85

"Strike me if I know!" returned the other.                           86

There was a pause. Then the doctor stirred.                          87

"I'll be seeing you to-night, shall I?" he said to his friend.       88

"Ay—where's it to be? Are we going over to Jessdale?"                89

"I don't know. I've got such a cold on me. I'll come round to the    90
Moon and Stars, anyway."

"Let Lizzie and May miss their night for once, eh?"                  91

"That's it—if I feel as I do now."                                   92

"All's one—"                                                         93

The two young men went through the passage and down to the           94
back door together. The house was large, but it was servantless now,
and desolate. At the back was a small bricked house-yard, and beyond
that a big square, gravelled fine and red, and having stables on two
sides. Sloping, dank, winter-dark fields stretched away on the open
sides.

But the stables were empty. Joseph Pervin, the father of the fam-    95
ily, had been a man of no education, who had become a fairly large
horse dealer. The stables had been full of horses, there was a great
turmoil and come-and-go of horses and of dealers and grooms. Then
the kitchen was full of servants. But of late things had declined. The
old man had married a second time, to retrieve his fortunes. Now he
was dead and everything was gone to the dogs, there was nothing but
debt and threatening.

For months, Mabel had been servantless in the big house, keeping    96
the home together in penury for her ineffectual brothers. She had kept
house for ten years. But previously it was with unstinted means. Then,
however brutal and coarse everything was, the sense of money had
kept her proud, confident. The men might be foul-mouthed, the
women in the kitchen might have bad reputations, her brothers might

have illegitimate children. But so long as there was money, the girl felt herself established and brutally proud, reserved.

No company came to the house, save dealers and coarse men. 97 Mabel had no associates of her own sex, after her sister went away. But she did not mind. She went regularly to church, she attended to her father. And she lived in the memory of her mother, who had died when she was fourteen, and whom she had loved. She had loved her father, too, in a different way, depending upon him, and feeling secure in him, until at the age of fifty-four he married again. And then she had set hard against him. Now he had died and left them all hopelessly in debt.

She had suffered badly during the period of poverty. Nothing, 98 however, could shake the curious sullen, animal pride that dominated each member of the family. Now, for Mabel, the end had come. Still she would not cast about her. She would follow her own way just the same. She would always hold the keys of her own situation. Mindless and persistent, she endured from day to day. What should she think? Why should she answer anybody? It was enough that this was the end and there was no way out. She need not pass any more darkly along the main street of the small town, avoiding every eye. She need not demean herself any more, going into the shops and buying the cheapest food. This was at an end. She thought of nobody, not even of herself. Mindless and persistent, she seemed in a sort of ecstasy to be coming nearer to her fulfilment, her own glorification, approaching her dead mother, who was glorified.

In the afternoon she took a little bag, with shears and sponge and 99 a small scrubbing brush, and went out. It was a grey, wintry day, with saddened, dark green fields and an atmosphere blackened by the smoke of foundries not far off. She went quickly, darkly along the causeway, heeding nobody, through the town to the churchyard.

There she always felt secure, as if no one could see her, although 100 as a matter of fact she was exposed to the stare of every one who passed along under the churchyard wall. Nevertheless, once under the shadow of the great looming church, among the graves, she felt immune from the world, reserved within the thick churchyard wall as in another country.

Carefully she clipped the grass from the grave, and arranged the 101 pinky white, small chrysanthemums in the tin cross. When this was done, she took an empty jar from a neighbouring grave, brought water, and carefully, most scrupulously sponged the marble head-stone and the coping-stone.

It gave her sincere satisfaction to do this. She felt in immediate     102
contact with the world of her mother. She took minute pains, went
through the park in a state bordering on pure happiness, as if in
performing this task she came into a subtle, intimate connection with
her mother. For the life she followed here in the world was far less real
than the world of death she inherited from her mother.

The doctor's house was just by the church. Fergusson, being a     103
mere hired assistant, was slave to the country-side. As he hurried now
to attend to the out-patients in the surgery, glancing across the graveyard with his quick eye, he saw the girl at her task at the grave. She
seemed so intent and remote, it was like looking into another world.
Some mystical element was touched in him. He slowed down as he
walked, watching her as if spell-bound.

She lifted her eyes, feeling him looking. Their eyes met. And each     104
looked away again at once, each feeling, in some way, found out by the
other. He lifted his cap and passed on down the road. There remained
distinct in his consciousness, like a vision, the memory of her face, lifted
from the tombstone in the churchyard, and looking at him with slow,
large, portentous eyes. It *was* portentous, her face. It seemed to mes-
merize him. There was a heavy power in her eyes which laid hold of
his whole being, as if he had drunk some powerful drug. He had been
feeling weak and done before. Now the life came back into him, he felt
delivered from his own fretted, daily self.

He finished his duties at the surgery as quickly as might be, hastily     105
filling up the bottle of the waiting people with cheap drugs. Then, in
perpetual haste, he set off again to visit several cases in another part
of his round, before tea-time. At all times he preferred to walk if he
could, not particularly when he was not well. He fancied the motion
restored him.

The afternoon was falling. It was grey, deadened, and wintry, with     106
a slow, moist, heavy coldness sinking in and deadening all the faculties.
But why should he think or notice? He hastily climbed the hill and
turned across the dark green fields, following the black cinder-track. In
the distance, across a shallow dip in the country, the small town was
clustered like smouldering ash, a tower, a spire, a heap of low, raw,
extinct houses. And on the nearest fringe of the town, sloping into the
dip, was Oldmeadow, the Pervins' house. He could see the stables and
the outbuildings distinctly, as they lay towards him on the slope. Well,
he would not go there many more times! Another resource would be
lost to him, another place gone: the only company he cared for in the

alien, ugly little town he was losing. Nothing but work, drudgery, constant hastening from dwelling to dwelling among the colliers and the ironworkers. It wore him out, but at the same time he had a craving for it. It was a stimulant to him to be in the homes of the working people, moving as it were through the innermost body of their life. His nerves were excited and gratified. He could come so near, into the very lives of the rough, inarticulate, powerfully emotional men and women. He grumbled, he said he hated the hellish hole. But as a matter of fact it excited him, the contact with the rough, strongly-feeling people was a stimulant applied direct to his nerves.

Below Oldmeadow, in the green, shallow, soddened hollow of fields lay a square, deep pond. Roving across the landscape, the doctor's quick eye detected a figure in black passing through the gate of the field, down towards the pond. He looked again. It would be Mabel Pervin. His mind suddenly became alive and attentive. 107

Why was she going down there? He pulled up on the path on the slope above, and stood staring. He could just make sure of the small black figure moving in the hollow of the failing day. He seemed to see her in the midst of such obscurity, that he was like a clairvoyant, seeing rather with the mind's eye than with ordinary sight. Yet he could see her positively enough, whilst he kept his eye attentive. He felt, if he looked away from her, in the thick, ugly falling dusk, he would lose her altogether. 108

He followed her minutely as she moved, direct and intent, like something transmitted rather than stirring in voluntary activity, straight down the field towards the pond. There she stood on the bank for a moment. She never raised her head. Then she waded slowly into the water. 109

He stood motionless as the small black figure walked slowly and deliberately towards the centre of the pond, very slowly, gradually moving deeper into the motionless water, and still moving forward as the water got up to her breast. Then he could see her no more in the dusk of the dead afternoon. 110

"There!" he exclaimed. "Would you believe it?" 111

And he hastened straight down, running over the wet, soddened fields, pushing through the hedges, down into the depression of callous wintry obscurity. It took him several minutes to come to the pond. He stood on the bank, breathing heavily. He could see nothing. His eyes seemed to penetrate the dead water. Yes, perhaps that was the dark shadow of her black clothing beneath the surface of the water. 112

He slowly ventured into the pond. The bottom was deep, soft clay,     113
he sank in, and the water clasped dead cold round his legs. As he
stirred he could smell the cold, rotten clay that fouled up into the
water. It was objectionable in his lungs. Still, repelled and yet not
heeding, he moved deeper into the pond. The cold water rose over his
thighs, over his loins, upon his abdomen. The lower part of his body
was all sunk in the hideous cold element. And the bottom was so
deeply soft and uncertain, he was afraid of pitching with his mouth
underneath. He could not swim, and was afraid.

He crouched a little, spreading his hands under the water and      114
moving them round, trying to feel for her. The dead cold pond
swayed upon his chest. He moved again, a little deeper, and again,
with his hands underneath, he felt all around the water. And he
touched her clothing. But it evaded his fingers. He made a desperate
effort to grasp it.

And so doing he lost his balance and went under, horribly, suf-     115
focating in the foul earthy water, struggling madly for a few moments.
At last, after what seemed an eternity, he got his footing, rose again
into the air and looked around. He gasped, and knew he was in the
world. Then he looked at the water. She had risen near him. He
grasped her clothing, and drawing her nearer, turned to take his way
to land again.

He went very slowly, carefully, absorbed in the slow progress. He     116
rose higher, climbing out of the pond. The water was now only about
his legs; he was thankful, full of relief to be out of the clutches of the
pond. He lifted her and staggered on to the bank, out of the horror of
wet, grey clay.

He laid her down on the bank. She was quite unconscious and      117
running with water. He made the water come from her mouth, he
worked to restore her. He did not have to work very long before he
could feel the breathing begin again in her; she was breathing naturally. He worked a little longer. He could feel her live beneath his
hands; she was coming back. He wiped her face, wrapped her in his
overcoat, looked round into the dim, dark grey world, then lifted her
and staggered down the bank and across the fields.

It seemed an unthinkably long way, and his burden so heavy he     118
felt he would never get to the house. But at last he was in the stable-
yard, and then in the house-yard. He opened the door and went into
the house. In the kitchen he laid her down on the hearth-rug, and
called. The house was empty. But the fire was burning in the grate.

Then again he kneeled to attend to her. She was breathing regu-    119
larly, her eyes were wide open and as if conscious, but there seemed
something missing in her look. She was conscious in herself, but unconscious of her surroundings.

He ran upstairs, took blankets from a bed, and put them before the    120
fire to warm. Then he removed her saturated, earthy-smelling clothing, rubbed her dry with a towel, and wrapped her naked in the
blankets. Then he went into the dining-room, to look for spirits. There
was a little whisky. He drank a gulp himself, and put some into her
mouth.

The effect was instantaneous. She looked full into his face, as if she    121
had been seeing him for some time, and yet had only just become
conscious of him.

"Dr. Fergusson?" she said.    122

"What?" he answered.    123

He was divesting himself of his coat, intending to find some dry    124
clothing upstairs. He could not bear the smell of the dead, clayey
water, and he was mortally afraid for his own health.

"What did I do?" she asked.    125

"Walked into the pond," he replied. He had begun to shudder like    126
one sick, and could hardly attend to her. Her eyes remained full on
him, he seemed to be going dark in his mind, looking back at her
helplessly. The shuddering became quieter in him, his life came back
in him, dark and unknowing, but strong again.

"Was I out of my mind?" she asked, while her eyes were fixed on    127
him all the time.

"Maybe, for the moment," he replied. He felt quiet, because his    128
strength had come back. The strange fretful strain had left him.

"Am I out of my mind now?" she asked.    129

"Are you?" he reflected a moment. "No," he answered truthfully.    130
"I don't see that you are." He turned his face aside. He was afraid
now, because he felt dazed, and felt dimly that her power was stronger
than his, in this issue. And she continued to look at him fixedly all the
time. "Can you tell me where I shall find some dry things to put on?"
he asked.

"Did you dive into the pond for me?" she asked.    131

"No," he answered. "I walked in. But I went in overhead as well."    132

There was a silence for a moment. He hesitated. He very much    133
wanted to go upstairs to get into dry clothing. But there was another
desire in him. And she seemed to hold him. His will seemed to have

gone to sleep, and left him, standing there slack before her. But he felt warm inside himself. He did not shudder at all, though his clothes were sodden on him.

"Why did you?" she asked.                                                        134

"Because I didn't want you to do such a foolish thing," he said.                 135

"It wasn't foolish," she said, still gazing at him as she lay on the             136
floor, with a sofa cushion under her head. "It was the right thing to do.
*I* knew best, then."

"I'll go and shift these wet things," he said. But still he had not the          137
power to move out of her presence, until she sent him. It was as if she
had the life of his body in her hands, and he could not extricate himself.
Or perhaps he did not want to.

Suddenly she sat up. Then she became aware of her own immedi-                    138
ate condition. She felt the blankets about her, she knew her own limbs.
For a moment it seemed as if her reason were going. She looked round,
with wild eyes, as if seeking something. He stood still with fear. She
saw her clothing lying scattered.

"Who undressed me?" she asked, her eyes resting full and inevita-                139
ble on his face.

"I did," he replied, "to bring you round."                                       140

For some moments she sat and gazed at him awfully, her lips                      141
parted.

"Do you love me, then?" she asked.                                               142

He only stood and stared at her, fascinated. His soul seemed to                  143
melt.

She shuffled forward on her knees, and put her arms around him,                  144
round his legs, as he stood there, pressing her breasts against his knees
and thighs, clutching him with strange, convulsive certainty, pressing
his thighs against her, drawing him to her face, her throat, as she
looked up at him with flaring, humble eyes of transfiguration, triumphant in first possession.

"You love me," she murmured, in strange transport, yearning and                  145
triumphant and confident. "You love me. I know you love me, I know."

And she was passionately kissing his knees, through the wet cloth-               146
ing, passionately and indiscriminately kissing his knees, his legs, as if
unaware of everything.

He looked down at the tangled wet hair, the wild, bare, animal                   147
shoulders. He was amazed, bewildered, and afraid. He had never
thought of loving her. He had never wanted to love her. When he
rescued her and restored her, he was a doctor, and she was a patient.

He had had no single personal thought of her. Nay, this introduction of the personal element was very distasteful to him, a violation of his professional honour. It was horrible to have her there embracing his knees. It was horrible. He revolted from it, violently. And yet—and yet—he had not the power to break away.

She looked at him again, with the same supplication of powerful    148
love, and that same transcendent, frightening light of triumph. In view of the delicate flame which seemed to come from her face like a light, he was powerless. And yet he had never intended to love her. He had never intended. And something stubborn in him could not give way.

"You love me," she repeated, in a murmur of deep rhapsodic    149
assurance. "You love me."

Her hands were drawing him, drawing him down to her. He was    150
afraid, even a little horrified. For he had, really, no intention of loving her. Yet her hands were drawing him towards her. He put out his hand quickly to steady himself, and grasped her bare shoulder. A flame seemed to burn the hand that grasped her soft shoulder. He had no intention of loving her: his whole will was against his yielding. It was horrible. And yet wonderful was the touch of her shoulders, beautiful the shining of her face. Was she perhaps mad? He had a horror of yielding to her. Yet something in him ached also.

He had been staring away at the door, away from her. But his    151
hand remained on her shoulder. She had gone suddenly very still. He looked down at her. Her eyes were now wide with fear, and doubt, the light was dying from her face, a shadow of terrible greyness was returning. He could not bear the touch of her eyes' question upon him, and the look of death behind the question.

With an inward groan he gave way, and let his heart yield towards    152
her. A sudden gentle smile came on his face. And her eyes, which never left his face, slowly, slowly filled with tears. He watched the strange water rise in her eyes, like some slow fountain coming up. And his heart seemed to burn and melt away in his breast.

He could not bear to look at her any more. He dropped on his    153
knees and caught her head with his arms and pressed her face against his throat. She was very still. His heart, which seemed to have broken, was burning with a kind of agony in his breast. And he felt her slow, hot tears wetting his throat. But he could not move.

He felt the hot tears wet his neck and the hollows of his neck, and    154
he remained motionless, suspended through one of man's eternities. Only now it had become indispensable to him to have her face pressed

close to him; he could never let her go again. He could never let her head go away from the close clutch of his arm. He wanted to remain like that for ever, with his heart hurting him in a pain that was also life to him. Without knowing, he was looking down on her damp, soft brown hair.

Then, as it were suddenly, he smelt the horrid stagnant smell of  155
that water. And at the same moment she drew away from him and looked at him. Her eyes were wistful and unfathomable. He was afraid of them, and he fell to kissing her, not knowing what he was doing. He wanted her eyes not to have that terrible, wistful, unfathomable look.

When she turned her face to him again, a faint delicate flush was  156
glowing, and there was again dawning that terrible shining of joy in her eyes, which really terrified him, and yet which he now wanted to see, because he feared the look of doubt still more.

"You love me?" she said, rather faltering.  157

"Yes." The word cost him a painful effort. Not because it wasn't  158
true. But because it was too newly true, the *saying* seemed to tear open again his newly-torn heart. And he hardly wanted it to be true, even now.

She lifted her face to him, and he bent forward and kissed her on  159
the mouth, gently, with the one kiss that is an eternal pledge. And as he kissed her his heart strained again in his breast. He never intended to love her. But now it was over. He had crossed over the gulf to her, and all that he had left behind had shrivelled and become void.

After the kiss, her eyes again slowly filled with tears. She sat still,  160
away from him, with her face drooped aside, and her hands folded in her lap. The tears fell very slowly. There was complete silence. He too sat there motionless and silent on the hearthrug. The strange pain of his heart that was broken seemed to consume him. That he should love her? That this was love! That he should be ripped open in this way! Him, a doctor! How they would all jeer if they knew! It was agony to him to think they might know.

In the curious naked pain of the thought he looked again to her.  161
She was sitting there drooped into a muse. He saw a tear fall, and his heart flared hot. He saw for the first time that one of her shoulders was quite uncovered, one arm bare, he could see one of her small breasts; dimly, because it had become almost dark in the room.

"Why are you crying?" he asked, in an altered voice.  162

She looked at him, and behind her tears the consciousness of her  163
situation for the first time brought a dark look of shame to her eyes.

"I'm not crying, really," she said, watching him half frightened. 164

He reached his hand, and softly closed it on her bare arm. 165

"I love you! I love you!" he said in a soft, low vibrating voice, 166
unlike himself.

She shrank, and dropped her head. The soft, penetrating grip of 167
his hand on her arm distressed her. She looked up at him.

"I want to go," she said. "I want to go and get you some dry 168
things."

"Why?" he said. "I'm all right." 169

"But I want to go," she said. "And I want you to change your 170
things."

He released her arm, and she wrapped herself in the blanket, 171
looking at him rather frightened. And still she did not rise.

"Kiss me," she said wistfully. 172

He kissed her, but briefly, half in anger. 173

Then, after a second, she rose nervously, all mixed up in the 174
blanket. He watched her in her confusion, as she tried to extricate
herself and wrap herself up so that she could walk. He watched her
relentlessly, as she knew. And as she went, the blanket trailing, and as
he saw a glimpse of her feet and her white leg, he tried to remember
her as she was when he had wrapped her in the blanket. But then he
didn't want to remember, because she had been nothing to him then,
and his nature revolted from remembering her as she was when she
was nothing to him.

A tumbling, muffled noise from within the dark house startled him. 175
Then he heard her voice:—"There are clothes." He rose and went to
the foot of the stairs, and gathered up the garments she had thrown
down. Then he came back to the fire, to rub himself down and dress.
He grinned at his own appearance when he had finished.

The fire was sinking, so he put on coal. The house was now quite 176
dark, save for the light of a street-lamp that shone in faintly from
beyond the holly trees. He lit the gas with matches he found on the
mantelpiece. Then he emptied the pockets of his own clothes, and
threw all his wet things in a heap into the scullery. After which he
gathered up her sodden clothes, gently, and put them in a separate
heap on the copper-top in the scullery.

It was six o'clock on the clock. His own watch had stopped. He 177
ought to go back to the surgery. He waited, and still she did not come
down. So he went to the foot of the stairs and called:

"I shall have to go." 178

Almost immediately he heard her coming down. She had on her    179
best dress of black voile, and her hair was tidy, but still damp. She
looked at him—and in spite of herself, smiled.
"I don't like you in those clothes," she said.                        180
"Do I look a sight?" he answered.                                     181
They were shy of one another.                                         182
"I'll make you some tea," she said.                                   183
"No, I must go."                                                      184
"Must you?" And she looked at him again with the wide, strained,    185
doubtful eyes. And again, from the pain of his breast, he knew how he
loved her. He went and bent to kiss her, gently, passionately, with his
heart's painful kiss.
"And my hair smells so horrible," she murmured in distraction.      186
"And I'm so awful, I'm so awful! Oh, no, I'm too awful." And she
broke into bitter, heartbroken sobbing. "You can't want to love me, I'm
horrible."
"Don't be silly, don't be silly," he said, trying to comfort her,    187
kissing her, holding her in his arms. "I want you, I want to marry you,
we're going to be married, quickly, quickly—tomorrow if I can."
But she only sobbed terribly, and cried:                             188
"I feel awful. I feel awful. I feel I'm horrible to you."            189
"No, I want you, I want you," was all he answered, blindly, with    190
that terrible intonation which frightened her almost more than her
horror lest he should *not* want her.

---

# The Use of Force

## WILLIAM CARLOS WILLIAMS

They were new patients to me, all I had was the name, Olson.      1
Please come down as soon as you can, my daughter is very sick.
When I arrived I was met by the mother, a big startled looking    2
woman, very clean and apologetic who merely said, Is this the doctor?
and let me in. In the back, she added. You must excuse us, doctor, we
have her in the kitchen where it is warm. It is very damp here sometimes.

The child was fully dressed and sitting on her father's lap near the    3
kitchen table. He tried to get up, but I motioned for him not to bother,
took off my overcoat and started to look things over. I could see that they
were all very nervous, eyeing me up and down distrustfully. As often, in
such cases, they weren't telling me more than they had to, it was up to me
to tell them; that's why they were spending three dollars on me.

The child was fairly eating me up with her cold, steady eyes, and    4
no expression to her face whatever. She did not move and seemed,
inwardly, quiet; an unusually attractive little thing, and as strong as
a heifer in appearance. But her face was flushed, she was breathing
rapidly, and I realized that she had a high fever. She had magnificent
blonde hair, in profusion. One of those picture children often reproduced in advertising leaflets and the photogravure sections of the
Sunday papers.

She's had a fever for three days, began the father and we don't    5
know what it comes from. My wife has given her things, you know, like
people do, but it don't do no good. And there's been a lot of sickness
around. So we tho't you'd better look her over and tell us what is the
matter.

As doctors often do I took a trial shot at it as a point of departure.    6
Has she had a sore throat?

Both parents answered me together, No . . . No, she says her throat    7
don't hurt her.

Does your throat hurt you? added the mother to the child. But the    8
little girl's expression didn't change nor did she move her eyes from my
face.

Have you looked?    9

I tried to, said the mother, but I couldn't see.    10

As it happens we had been having a number of cases of diphtheria    11
in the school to which this child went during that month and we were
all, quite apparently, thinking of that, though no one had as yet spoken
of the thing.

Well, I said, suppose we take a look at the throat first. I smiled in    12
my best professional manner and asking for the child's first name I
said, come on, Mathilda, open your mouth and let's take a look at your
throat.

Nothing doing.    13

Aw, come on, I coaxed, just open your mouth wide and let me take    14
a look. Look, I said opening both hands wide, I haven't anything in my
hands. Just open up and let me see.

Such a nice man, put in the mother. Look how kind he is to you.     15
Come on, do what he tells you to. He won't hurt you.

At that I ground my teeth in disgust. If only they wouldn't use the     16
word "hurt" I might be able to get somewhere. But I did not allow
myself to be hurried or disturbed but speaking quietly and slowly I
approached the child again.

As I moved my chair a little nearer suddenly with one cat-like     17
movement both her hands clawed instinctively for my eyes and she
almost reached them too. In fact she knocked my glasses flying and
they fell, though unbroken, several feet away from me on the kitchen
floor.

Both the mother and father almost turned themselves inside out     18
in embarrassment and apology. You bad girl, said the mother, taking
her and shaking her by one arm. Look what you've done. The nice
man . . .

For heaven's sake, I broke in. Don't call me a nice man to her. I'm     19
here to look at her throat on the chance that she might have diphtheria
and possibly die of it. But that's nothing to her. Look here, I said to the
child, we're going to look at your throat. You're old enough to understand what I'm saying. Will you open it now by yourself or shall we
have to open it for you?

Not a move. Even her expression hadn't changed. Her breaths     20
however were coming faster and faster. Then the battle began. I had
to have a throat culture for her own protection. But first I told the
parents that it was entirely up to them. I explained the danger but said
that I would not insist on a throat examination so long as they would
take the responsibility.

If you don't do what the doctor says you'll have to go to the     21
hospital, the mother admonished her severely.

Oh yeah? I had to smile to myself. After all, I had already fallen     22
in love with the savage brat, the parents were contemptible to me. In
the ensuing struggle they grew more and more abject, crushed, exhausted while she surely rose to magnificent heights of insane fury of
effort bred of her terror of me.

The father tried his best, and he was a big man but the fact that     23
she was his daughter, his shame at her behavior and his dread of
hurting her made him release her just at the critical moment several
times when I had almost achieved success, till I wanted to kill him. But
his dread also that she might have diphtheria made him tell me to go
on, go on though he himself was almost fainting, while the mother

moved back and forth behind us raising and lowering her hands in an agony of apprehension.

Put her in front of you on your lap, I ordered, and hold both her wrists. 24

But as soon as he did the child let out a scream. Don't you're hurting me. Let go of my hands. Let them go I tell you. Then she shrieked terrifyingly, hysterically. Stop it! Stop it! You're killing me! 25

Do you think she can stand it, doctor! said the mother. 26

You get out, said the husband to his wife. Do you want her to die of diphtheria? 27

Come on now, hold her, I said. 28

Then I grasped the child's head with my left hand and tried to get the wooden tongue depressor between her teeth. She fought, with clenched teeth, desperately! But now I also had grown furious—at a child. I tried to hold myself down but I couldn't. I know how to expose a throat for inspection. And I did my best. When finally I got the wooden spatula behind the last teeth and just the point of it into the mouth cavity, she opened up for an instant but before I could see anything came down again and gripping the wooden blade between her molars she reduced it to splinters before I could get it out again. 29

Aren't you ashamed, the mother yelled at her. Aren't you ashamed to act like that in front of the doctor? 30

Get me a smooth-handled spoon of some sort, I told the mother. We're going through with this. The child's mouth was already bleeding. Her tongue was cut and she was screaming in wild hysterical shrieks. Perhaps I should have desisted and come back in an hour or more. No doubt it would have been better. But I have seen at least two children lying dead in bed of neglect in such cases, and feeling that I must get a diagnosis now or never I went at it again. But the worst of it was that I too had got beyond reason. I could have torn the child apart in my own fury and enjoyed it. It was a pleasure to attack her. My face was burning with it. 31

The damned little brat must be protected against her own idiocy, one says to one's self at such times. Others must be protected against her. It is social necessity. And all these things are true. But a blind fury, a feeling of adult shame, bred of a longing for muscular release are the operatives. One goes on to the end. 32

In a final unreasoning assault I overpowered the child's neck and jaws. I forced the heavy silver spoon back of her teeth and down her 33 throat till she gagged. And there it was—both tonsils covered with membrane. She had fought valiantly to keep me from knowing her secret. She had been hiding that sore throat for three days at least and lying to her parents in order to escape just such an outcome as this.

Now truly she *was* furious. She had been on the defensive before 34 but now she attacked. Tried to get off her father's lap and fly at me while tears of defeat blinded her eyes.

---

# *Battle Royal*

## RALPH ELLISON

It goes a long way back, some twenty years. All my life I had been 1 looking for something, and everywhere I turned someone tried to tell me what it was. I accepted their answers too, though they were often in contradiction and even self-contradictory. I was naïve. I was looking for myself and asking everyone except myself questions which I, and only I, could answer. It took me a long time and much painful boomer-anging of my expectations to achieve a realization everyone else appears to have been born with: That I am nobody but myself. But first I had to discover that I am an invisible man!

And yet I am no freak of nature, nor of history. I was in the cards, 2 other things having been equal (or unequal) eighty-five years ago. I am not ashamed of my grandparents for having been slaves. I am only ashamed of myself for having at one time been ashamed. About eighty-five years ago they were told that they were free, united with others of our country in everything pertaining to the common good, and, in everything social, separate like the fingers of the hand. And they believed it. They exulted in it. They stayed in their place, worked hard, and brought up my father to do the same. But my grandfather is the one. He was an odd old guy, my grandfather, and I am told I take after him. It was he who caused the trouble. On his death-bed he called my father to him and said, "Son, after I'm gone I want you to keep up the good fight. I never told you, but our life is a war and I have been a traitor all my born days, a spy in the enemy's country ever since I give up my gun back in the Reconstruction. Live with your head in the lion's mouth. I want you to overcome 'em with yeses, undermine 'em with grins, agree 'em to death and destruction, let 'em swoller you till they vomit or bust wide open." They thought the old man had gone out of his mind. He had been the meekest of men. The younger children were rushed from the room, the shades drawn and the flame of the lamp turned so low that it sputtered on the wick like the old man's breathing. "Learn it to the younguns," he whispered fiercely; then he died.

But my folks were more alarmed over his last words than over his   3
dying. It was as though he had not died at all, his words caused so much anxiety. I was warned emphatically to forget what he had said and, indeed, this is the first time it has been mentioned outside the family circle. It had a tremendous effect upon me, however. I could never be sure of what he meant. Grandfather had been a quiet old man who never made any trouble, yet on his deathbed he had called himself a traitor and a spy, and he had spoken of his meekness as a dangerous activity. It became a constant puzzle which lay unanswered in the back of my mind. And whenever things went well for me I remembered my grandfather and felt guilty and uncomfortable. It was as though I was carrying out his advice in spite of myself. And to make it worse, everyone loved me for it. I was praised by the most lily-white men of the town. I was considered an example of desirable conduct—just as my grandfather had been. And what puzzled me was that the old man had defined it as *treachery*. When I was praised for my conduct I felt a guilt that in some way I was doing something that was really against the wishes of the white folks, that if they had understood they would have desired me to act just the opposite, that I should have been sulky and mean, and that that really would have been what they wanted, even though they were fooled and thought they wanted me to act as I did. It made me afraid that some day they would look upon me as a traitor and I would be lost. Still I was more afraid to act any other way because they didn't like that at all. The old man's words were like a curse. On my graduation day I delivered an oration in which I showed that humility was the secret, indeed, the very essence of progress. (Not that I believed this—how could I, remembering my grandfather?—I only believed that it worked.) It was a great success. Everyone praised me and I was invited to give the speech at a gathering of the town's leading white citizens. It was a triumph for our whole community.

It was in the main ballroom of the leading hotel. When I got there   4
I discovered that it was on the occasion of a smoker, and I was told that since I was to be there anyway I might as well take part in the battle

royal to be fought by some of my schoolmates as part of the entertainment. The battle royal came first.

All of the town's big shots were there in their tuxedoes, wolfing down the buffet foods, drinking beer and whiskey and smoking black cigars. It was a large room with a high ceiling. Chairs were arranged in neat rows around three sides of a portable boxing ring. The fourth side was clear, revealing a gleaming space of polished floor. I had some misgivings over the battle royal, by the way. Not from a distaste for fighting, but because I didn't care too much for the other fellows who were to take part. They were tough guys who seemed to have no grandfather's curse worrying their minds. No one could mistake their toughness. And besides, I suspected that fighting a battle royal might detract from the dignity of my speech. In those pre-invisible days I visualized myself as a potential Booker T. Washington. But the other fellows didn't care too much for me either, and there were nine of them. I felt superior to them in my way, and I didn't like the manner in which we were all crowded together into the servants' elevator. Nor did they like my being there. In fact, as the warmly lighted floors flashed past the elevator we had words over the fact that I, by taking part in the fight, had knocked one of their friends out of a night's work.

We were led out of the elevator through a rococo hall into an anteroom and told to get into our fighting togs. Each of us was issued a pair of boxing gloves and ushered out into the big mirrored hall, which we entered looking cautiously about us and whispering, lest we might accidentally be heard above the noise of the room. It was foggy with cigar smoke. And already the whiskey was taking effect. I was shocked to see some of the most important men of the town quite tipsy. They were all there—bankers, lawyers, judges, doctors, fire chiefs, teachers, merchants. Even one of the more fashionable pastors. Something we could not see was going on up front. A clarinet was vibrating sensuously and the men were standing up and moving eagerly forward. We were a small tight group, clustered together, our bare upper bodies touching and shining with anticipatory sweat; while up front the big shots were becoming increasingly excited over something we still could not see. Suddenly I heard the school superintendent, who had told me to come, yell, "Bring up the shines, gentlemen! Bring up the little shines!"

We were rushed up to the front of the ballroom, where it smelled even more strongly of tobacco and whiskey. Then we were pushed into place. I almost wet my pants. A sea of faces, some hostile, some

amused, ringed around us, and in the center, facing us, stood a magnificent blonde—stark naked. There was dead silence. I felt a blast of
cold air chill me. I tried to back away, but they were behind me and
around me. Some of the boys stood with lowered heads, trembling. I
felt a wave of irrational guilt and fear. My teeth chattered, my skin
turned to goose flesh, my knees knocked. Yet I was strongly attracted
and looked in spite of myself. Had the price of looking been blindness,
I would have looked. The hair was yellow like that of a circus kewpie
doll, the face heavily powdered and rouged, as though to form an
abstract mask, the eyes hollow and smeared a cool blue, the color of a
baboon's butt. I felt a desire to spit upon her as my eyes brushed slowly
over her body. Her breasts were firm and round as the domes of East
Indian temples, and I stood so close as to see the fine skin texture and
beads of pearly perspiration glistening like dew around the pink and
erected buds of her nipples. I wanted at one and the same time to run
from the room, to sink through the floor, or go to her and cover her from
my eyes and the eyes of the others with my body; to feel the soft thighs,
to caress her and destroy her, to love her and murder her, to hide from
her, and yet to stroke where below the small American flag tattooed
upon her belly her thighs formed a capital V. I had a notion that of all
in the room she saw only me with her impersonal eyes.

   And then she began to dance, a slow sensuous movement; the    8
smoke of a hundred cigars clinging to her like the thinnest of veils. She
seemed like a fair bird-girl girdled in veils calling to me from the angry
surface of some gray and threatening sea. I was transported. Then I
became aware of the clarinet playing and the big shots yelling at us.
Some threatened us if we looked and others if we did not. On my right
I saw one boy faint. And now a man grabbed a silver pitcher from a
table and stepped close as he dashed ice water upon him and stood him
up and forced two of us to support him as his head hung and moans
issued from his thick bluish lips. Another boy began to plead to go
home. He was the largest of the group, wearing dark red fighting
trunks much too small to conceal the erection which projected from
him as though in answer to the insinuating low-registered moaning of
the clarinet. He tried to hide himself with his boxing gloves.

   And all the while the blonde continued dancing, smiling faintly at    9
the big shots who watched her with fascination, and faintly smiling at
our fear. I noticed a certain merchant who followed her hungrily, his
lips loose and drooling. He was a large man who wore diamond studs
in a shirtfront which swelled with the ample paunch underneath, and

each time the blonde swayed her undulating hips he ran his hand through the thin hair of his bald head and, with his arms upheld, his posture clumsy like that of an intoxicated panda, wound his belly in a slow and obscene grind. This creature was completely hypnotized. The music had quickened. As the dancer flung herself about with a detached expression on her face, the men began reaching out to touch her. I could see their beefy fingers sink into the soft flesh. Some of the others tried to stop them and she began to move around the floor in graceful circles, as they gave chase, slipping and sliding over the polished floor. It was mad. Chairs went crashing, drinks were spilt, as they ran laughing and howling after her. They caught her just as she reached a door, raised her from the floor, and tossed her as college boys are tossed at a hazing, and above her red, fixed-smiling lips I saw the terror and disgust in her eyes, almost like my own terror and that which I saw in some of the other boys. As I watched, they tossed her twice and her soft breasts seemed to flatten against the air and her legs flung wildly as she spun. Some of the more sober ones helped her to escape. And I started off the floor, heading for the anteroom with the rest of the boys.

Some were still crying and in hysteria. But as we tried to leave we    10 were stopped and ordered to get into the ring. There was nothing to do but what we were told. All ten of us climbed under the ropes and allowed ourselves to be blindfolded with broad bands of white cloth. One of the men seemed to feel a bit sympathetic and tried to cheer us up as we stood with our backs against the ropes. Some of us tried to grin. "See that boy over there?" one of the men said. "I want you to run across at the bell and give it to him right in the belly. If you don't get him, I'm going to get you. I don't like his looks." Each of us was told the same. The blindfolds were put on. Yet even then I had been going over my speech. In my mind each word was as bright as flame. I felt the cloth pressed into place, and frowned so that it would be loosened when I relaxed.

But now I felt a sudden fit of blind terror. I was unused to dark-    11 ness. It was as though I had suddenly found myself in a dark room filled with poisonous cotton-mouths. I could hear the bleary voices yelling insistently for the battle royal to begin.

"Get going in there!"                                                    12

"Let me at that big nigger!"                                             13

I strained to pick up the school superintendent's voice, as though    14 to squeeze some security out of that slightly more familiar sound.

"Let me at those black sonsabitches!" someone yelled.                    15

"No, Jackson, no!" another voice yelled. "Here, somebody, help           16
me hold Jack."

"I want to get at that ginger-colored nigger. Tear him limb from         17
limb," the first voice yelled.

I stood against the ropes trembling. For in those days I was what        18
they called ginger-colored, and he sounded as though he might crunch
me between his teeth like a crisp ginger cookie.

Quite a struggle was going on. Chairs were being kicked about and        19
I could hear voices grunting as with a terrific effort. I wanted to see,
to see more desperately than ever before. But the blindfold was tight
as a thick skin-puckering scab and when I raised my gloved hands to
push the layers of white aside a voice yelled, "Oh, no you don't, black
bastard! Leave that alone!"

"Ring the bell before Jackson kills him a coon!" someone boomed          20
in the sudden silence. And I heard the bell clang and the sound of the
feet scuffling forward.

A glove smacked against my head. I pivoted, striking out stiffly as      21
someone went past, and felt the jar ripple along the length of my arm
to my shoulder. Then it seemed as though all nine of the boys had
turned upon me at once. Blows pounded me from all sides while I
struck out as best I could. So many blows landed upon me that I
wondered if I were not the only blindfolded fighter in the ring, or if the
man called Jackson hadn't succeeded in getting me after all.

Blindfolded, I could no longer control my motions. I had no dig-         22
nity. I stumbled about like a baby or a drunken man. The smoke had
become thicker and with each new blow it seemed to sear and further
restrict my lungs. My saliva became like hot bitter glue. A glove
connected with my head, filling my mouth with warm blood. It was
everywhere. I could not tell if the moisture I felt upon my body was
sweat or blood. A blow landed hard against the nape of my neck. I felt
myself going over, my head hitting the floor. Streaks of blue light filled
the black world behind the blindfold. I lay prone, pretending that I was
knocked out, but felt myself seized by hands and yanked to my feet.
"Get going, black boy! Mix it up!" My arms were like lead, my head
smarting from blows. I managed to feel my way to the ropes and held
on, trying to catch my breath. A glove landed in my mid-section and I
went over again, feeling as though the smoke had become a knife
jabbed into my guts. Pushed this way and that by the legs milling
around me, I finally pulled erect and discovered that I could see the

black, sweat-washed forms weaving in the smoky-blue atmosphere like
drunken dancers weaving to the rapid drum-like thuds of blows.

Everyone fought hysterically. It was complete anarchy. Everybody          23
fought everybody else. No group fought together for long. Two, three,
four, fought one, then turned to fight each other, were themselves
attacked. Blows landed below the belt and in the kidney, with the
gloves open as well as closed, and with my eye partly opened now
there was not so much terror. I moved carefully, avoiding blows,
although not too many to attract attention, fighting from group to
group. The boys groped about like blind, cautious crabs crouching to
protect their mid-sections, their heads pulled in short against their
shoulders, their arms stretched nervously before them, with their fists
testing the smoke-filled air like the knobbed feelers of hypersensitive
snails. In one corner I glimpsed a boy violently punching the air and
heard him scream in pain as he smashed his hand against a ring post.
For a second I saw him bent over holding his hand, then going down
as a blow caught his unprotected head. I played one group against the
other, slipping in and throwing a punch then stepping out of range
while pushing the others into the melee to take the blows blindly aimed
at me. The smoke was agonizing and there were no rounds, no bells at
three minute intervals to relieve our exhaustion. The room spun round
me, a swirl of lights, smoke, sweating bodies surrounded by tense
white faces. I bled from both nose and mouth, the blood spattering
upon my chest.

The men kept yelling, "Slug him, black boy! Knock his guts out!"         24
"Uppercut him! Kill him! Kill that big boy!"                             25

Taking a fake fall, I saw a boy going down heavily beside me as          26
though we were felled by a single blow, saw a sneaker-clad foot shoot
into his groin as the two who had knocked him down stumbled upon
him. I rolled out of range, feeling a twinge of nausea.

The harder we fought the more threatening the men became. And            27
yet, I had begun to worry about my speech again. How would it go?
Would they recognize my ability? What would they give me?

I was fighting automatically when suddenly I noticed that one            28
after another of the boys was leaving the ring. I was surprised, filled
with panic, as though I had been left alone with an unknown danger.
Then I understood. The boys had arranged it among themselves. It was
the custom for the two men left in the ring to slug it out for the winner's
prize. I discovered this too late. When the bell sounded two men in
tuxedoes leaped into the ring and removed the blindfold. I found

myself facing Tatlock, the biggest of the gang. I felt sick at my stomach. Hardly had the bell stopped ringing in my ears than it clanged again and I saw him moving swiftly toward me. Thinking of nothing else to do I hit him smash on the nose. He kept coming, bringing the rank sharp violence of stale sweat. His face was a black blank of a face, only his eyes alive—with hate of me and aglow with a feverish terror from what had happened to us all. I became anxious. I wanted to deliver my speech and he came at me as though he meant to beat it out of me. I smashed him again and again, taking his blows as they came. Then on a sudden impulse I struck him lightly and as we clinched, I whispered, "Fake like I knocked you out, you can have the prize."

"I'll break your behind," he whispered hoarsely.                          29

"For *them?*"                                                                                   30

"For *me,* sonofabitch!"                                                                     31

They were yelling for us to break it up and Tatlock spun me half       32
around with a blow, and as a joggled camera sweeps in a reeling scene, I saw the howling red faces crouching tense beneath the cloud of blue-gray smoke. For a moment the world wavered, unraveled, flowed, then my head cleared and Tatlock bounced before me. That fluttering shadow before my eyes was his jabbing left hand. Then falling forward, my head against his damp shoulder, I whispered,

"I'll make it five dollars more."                                                        33

"Go to hell!"                                                                                    34

But his muscles relaxed a trifle beneath my pressure and I        35
breathed, "Seven?"

"Give it to your ma," he said, ripping me beneath the heart.        36

And while I still held him I butted him and moved away. I felt        37
myself bombarded with punches. I fought back with hopeless desperation. I wanted to deliver my speech more than anything else in the world, because I felt that only these men could judge truly my ability, and now this stupid clown was ruining my chances. I began fighting carefully now, moving in to punch him and out again with my greater speed. A lucky blow to his chin and I had him going too—until I heard a loud voice yell, "I got my money on the big boy."

Hearing this, I almost dropped my guard. I was confused: Should        38
I try to win against the voice out there? Would not this go against my speech, and was not this a moment for humility, for nonresistance? A blow to my head as I danced about sent my right eye popping like a jack-in-the-box and settled my dilemma. The room went red as I fell. It was a dream fall, my body languid and fastidious as to where to land,

until the floor became impatient and smashed up to meet me. A moment later I came to. An hypnotic voice said FIVE emphatically. And I lay there, hazily watching a dark red spot of my own blood shaping itself into a butterfly, glistening and soaking into the soiled gray world of the canvas.

When the voice drawled TEN I was lifted up and dragged to a 39 chair. I sat dazed. My eye pained and swelled with each throb of my pounding heart and I wondered if now I would be allowed to speak. I was wringing wet, my mouth still bleeding. We were grouped along the wall now. The other boys ignored me as they congratulated Tatlock and speculated as to how much they would be paid. One boy whimpered over his smashed hand. Looking up front, I saw attendants in white jackets rolling the portable ring away and placing a small square rug in the vacant space surrounded by chairs. Perhaps, I thought, I will stand on the rug to deliver my speech.

Then the M.C. called to us, "Come on up here boys and get your 40 money."

We ran forward to where the men laughed and talked in their 41 chairs, waiting. Everyone seemed friendly now.

"There it is on the rug," the man said. I saw the rug covered with 42 coins of all dimensions and a few crumpled bills. But what excited me, scattered here and there, were the gold pieces.

"Boys, it's all yours," the man said. "You get all you grab." 43

"That's right, Sambo," a blond man said, winking at me confiden- 44 tially.

I trembled with excitement, forgetting my pain. I would get the 45 gold and the bills, I thought. I would use both hands. I would throw my body against the boys nearest me to block them from the gold.

"Get down around the rug now," the man commanded, "and don't 46 anyone touch it until I give the signal."

"This ought to be good," I heard. 47

As told, we got around the square rug on our knees. Slowly the 48 man raised his freckled hand as we followed it upward with our eyes.

I heard, "These niggers look like they're about to pray!" 49

Then, "Ready," the man said. "Go!" 50

I lunged for a yellow coin lying on the blue design of the carpet, 51 touching it and sending a surprised shriek to join those rising around me. I tried frantically to remove my hand but could not let go. A hot, violent force tore through my body, shaking me like a wet rat. The rug was electrified. The hair bristled up on my head as I shook myself free.

My muscles jumped, my nerves jangled, writhed. But I saw that this was not stopping the other boys. Laughing in fear and embarrassment, some were holding back and scooping up the coins knocked off by the painful contortions of the others. The men roared above us as we struggled.

"Pick it up, goddamnit, pick it up!" someone called like a bass- 52 voiced parrot. "Go on, get it!"

I crawled rapidly around the floor, picking up the coins, trying to 53 avoid the coppers and to get greenbacks and the gold. Ignoring the shock by laughing, as I brushed the coins off quickly, I discovered that I could contain the electricity—a contradiction, but it works. Then the men began to push us onto the rug. Laughing embarrassedly, we struggled out of their hands and kept after the coins. We were all wet and slippery and hard to hold. Suddenly I saw a boy lifted into the air, glistening with sweat like a circus seal, and dropped, his wet back landing flush upon the charged rug, heard him yell and saw him literally dance upon his back, his elbows beating a frenzied tattoo upon the floor, his muscles twitching like the flesh of a horse stung by many flies. When he finally rolled off, his face was gray and no one stopped him when he ran from the floor amid booming laughter.

"Get the money," the M.C. called. "That's good hard American 54 cash!"

And we snatched and grabbed, snatched and grabbed. I was care- 55 ful not to come too close to the rug now, and when I felt the hot whiskey breath descend upon me like a cloud of foul air I reached out and grabbed the leg of a chair. It was occupied and I held on desperately.

"Leggo, nigger! Leggo!" 56

The huge face wavered down to mine as he tried to push me free. 57 But my body was slippery and he was too drunk. It was Mr. Colcord, who owned a chain of movie houses and "entertainment palaces." Each time he grabbed me I slipped out of his hands. It became a real struggle. I feared the rug more than I did the drunk, so I held on, surprising myself for a moment by trying to topple *him* upon the rug. It was such an enormous idea that I found myself actually carrying it out. I tried not to be obvious, yet when I grabbed his leg, trying to tumble him out of the chair, he raised up roaring with laughter, and, looking at me with soberness dead in the eye, kicked me viciously in the chest. The chair leg flew out of my hand and I felt myself going and rolled. It was as though I had rolled through a bed of hot coals. It seemed a whole century would pass before I would roll free, a century in which I was seared through the deepest levels of my body to the fearful breath within me and the breath seared and heated to the point of explosion. It'll all be over in a flash, I thought as I rolled clear. It'll all be over in a flash.

But not yet, the men on the other side were waiting, red faces    58
swollen as though from apoplexy as they bent forward in their chairs. Seeing their fingers coming toward me I rolled away as a fumbled football rolls off the receiver's fingertips, back into the coals. That time I luckily sent the rug sliding out of place and heard the coins ringing against the floor and the boys scuffling to pick them up and the M.C. calling, "All right, boys, that's all. Go get dressed and get your money."

I was limp as a dish rag. My back felt as though it had been beaten    59
with wires.

When we had dressed the M.C. came in and gave us each five    60
dollars, except Tatlock, who got ten for being last in the ring. Then he told us to leave. I was not to get a chance to deliver my speech, I thought. I was going out into the dim alley in despair when I was stopped and told to go back. I returned to the ballroom, where the men were pushing back their chairs and gathering in groups to talk.

The M.C. knocked on a table for quiet. "Gentlemen," he said, "we    61
almost forgot an important part of the program. A most serious part, gentlemen. This boy was brought here to deliver a speech which he made at his graduation yesterday . . ."

"Bravo!"    62

"I'm told that he is the smartest boy we've got out there in Green-    63
wood. I'm told that he knows more big words than a pocket-sized dictionary."

Much applause and laughter.    64

"So now, gentlemen, I want you to give him your attention."    65

There was still laughter as I faced them, my mouth dry, my eye    66
throbbing. I began slowly, but evidently my throat was tense, because they began shouting, "Louder! Louder!"

"We of the younger generation extol the wisdom of that great    67
leader and educator," I shouted, "who first spoke these flaming words of wisdom: 'A ship lost at sea for many days suddenly sighted a friendly vessel. From the mast of the unfortunate vessel was seen a signal: "Water, water; we die of thirst!" The answer from the friendly vessel came back: "Cast down your bucket where you are." The captain of the distressed vessel, at last heeding the injunction, cast down his bucket, and it came up full of fresh sparkling water from the mouth of

the Amazon River.' And like him I say, and in his words, "To those of
my race who depend upon bettering their condition in a foreign land,
or who underestimate the importance of cultivating friendly relations
with the Southern white man, who is his next-door neighbor, I would
say: "Cast down your bucket where you are"—cast it down in making
friends in every manly way of the people of all races by whom we are
surrounded . . .' "

I spoke automatically and with such fervor that I did not realize    68
that the men were still talking and laughing until my dry mouth, filling
up with blood from the cut, almost strangled me. I coughed, wanting
to stop and go to one of the tall brass, sand-filled spittoons to relieve
myself, but a few of the men, especially the superintendent, were
listening and I was afraid. So I gulped it down, blood, saliva and all,
and continued. (What powers of endurance I had during those days!
What enthusiasm! What a belief in the rightness of things!) I spoke
even louder in spite of the pain. But still they talked and still they
laughed, as though deaf with cotton in dirty ears. So I spoke with
greater emotional emphasis. I closed my ears and swallowed blood
until I was nauseated. The speech seemed a hundred times as long as
before, but I could not leave out a single word. All had to be said, each
memorized nuance considered, rendered. Nor was that all. Whenever
I uttered a word of three or more syllables a group of voices would yell
for me to repeat it. I used the phrase "social responsibility" and they
yelled:

"What's that word you say, boy?"    69
"Social responsibility," I said.    70
"What?"    71
"Social . . ."    72
"Louder."    73
". . . responsibility."    74
"More!"    75
"Respon—"    76
"Repeat!"    77
"—sibility."    78

The room filled with the uproar of laughter until, no doubt, dis-    79
tracted by having to gulp down my blood, I made a mistake and yelled
a phrase I had often seen denounced in newspaper editorials, heard
debated in private.

"Social . . ."    80
"What?" they yelled.    81
". . . equality—"    82

The laughter hung smokelike in the sudden stillness. I opened my    83
eyes, puzzled. Sounds of displeasure filled the room. The M.C. rushed
forward. They shouted hostile phrases at me. But I did not understand.

A small dry mustached man in the front row blared out, "Say that    84
slowly, son!"

"What, sir?"                                                        85

"What you just said!"                                               86

"Social responsibility, sir," I said.                               87

"You weren't being smart, were you, boy?" he said, not unkindly.    88

"No, sir!"                                                          89

"You sure that about 'equality' was a mistake?"                     90

"Oh, yes, sir," I said. "I was swallowing blood."                   91

"Well, you had better speak more slowly so we can understand.       92
We mean to do right by you, but you've got to know your place at all
times. All right, now, go on with your speech."

I was afraid. I wanted to leave but I wanted also to speak and I was   93
afraid they'd snatch me down.

"Thank you, sir," I said, beginning where I had left off, and having   94
them ignore me as before.

Yet when I finished there was a thunderous applause. I was sur-    95
prised to see the superintendent come forth with a package wrapped
in white tissue paper, and, gesturing for quiet, address the men.

"Gentlemen, you see that I did not overpraise this boy. He makes    96
a good speech and some day he'll lead his people in the proper paths.
And I don't have to tell you that that is important in these days and
times. This is a good, smart boy, and so to encourage him in the right
direction, in the name of the Board of Education I wish to present him
a prize in the form of this . . ."

He paused, removing the tissue paper and revealing a gleaming    97
calfskin brief case.

". . . in the form of this first-class article from Shad Whitmore's   98
shop."

"Boy," he said, addressing me, "take this prize and keep it well.    99
Consider it a badge of office. Prize it. Keep developing as you are and
some day it will be filled with important papers that will help shape the
destiny of your people."

I was so moved that I could hardly express my thanks. A rope of    100
bloody saliva forming a shape like an undiscovered continent drooled
upon the leather and I wiped it quickly away. I felt an importance that
I had never dreamed.

"Open it and see what's inside," I was told.     101

My fingers a-tremble, I complied, smelling the fresh leather and   102
finding an official-looking document inside. It was a scholarship to the
state college for Negroes. My eyes filled with tears and I ran awkwardly off the floor.

I was overjoyed; I did not even mind when I discovered that the   103
gold pieces I had scrambled for were brass pocket tokens advertising
a certain make of automobile.

When I reached home everyone was excited. Next day the neigh-   104
bors came to congratulate me. I even felt safe from grandfather, whose
deathbed curse usually spoiled my triumphs. I stood beneath his photograph with my brief case in hand and smiled triumphantly into his
stolid black peasant's face. It was a face that fascinated me. The eyes
seemed to follow everywhere I went.

That night I dreamed I was at a circus with him and that he   105
refused to laugh at the clowns no matter what they did. Then later he
told me to open my brief case and read what was inside and I did,
finding an official envelope stamped with the state seal; and inside the
envelope I found another and another, endlessly, and I thought I
would fall of weariness. "Them's years," he said. "Now open that
one." And I did and in it I found an engraved document containing a
short message in letters of gold. "Read it," my grandfather said. "Out
loud!"

"To Whom It May Concern," I intoned. "Keep This Nigger-Boy   106
Running."

I awoke with the old man's laughter ringing in my ears.     107

---

# Everything That Rises Must Converge

## FLANNERY O'CONNOR

Her doctor had told Julian's mother that she must lose twenty   1
pounds on account of her blood pressure, so on Wednesday nights
Julian had to take her downtown on the bus for a reducing class at the

Y. The reducing class was designed for working girls over fifty, who weighed from 165 to 200 pounds. His mother was one of the slimmer ones, but she said ladies did not tell their age or weight. She would not ride the buses by herself at night since they had been integrated, and because the reducing class was one of her few pleasures, necessary for her health, and *free*, she said Julian could at least put himself out to take her, considering all she did for him. Julian did not like to consider all she did for him, but every Wednesday night he braced himself and took her.

She was almost ready to go, standing before the hall mirror, put-    2
ting on her hat, while he, his hands behind him, appeared pinned to the door frame, waiting like Saint Sebastian for the arrows to begin piercing him. The hat was new and had cost her seven dollars and a half. She kept saying, "Maybe I shouldn't have paid that for it. No, I shouldn't have. I'll take it off and return it tomorrow. I shouldn't have bought it."

Julian raised his eyes to heaven. "Yes, you should have bought it,"    3
he said. "Put it on and let's go." It was a hideous hat. A purple velvet flap came down on one side of it and stood up on the other; the rest of it was green and looked like a cushion with the stuffing out. He decided it was less comical than jaunty and pathetic. Everything that gave her pleasure was small and depressed him.

She lifted the hat one more time and set it down slowly on top of    4
her head. Two wings of gray hair protruded on either side of her florid face, but her eyes, sky-blue, were as innocent and untouched by experience as they must have been when she was ten. Were it not that she was a widow who had struggled fiercely to feed and clothe and put him through school and who was supporting him still, "until he got on his feet," she might have been a little girl that he had to take to town.

"It's all right, it's all right," he said. "Let's go." He opened the    5
door himself and started down the walk to get her going. The sky was a dying violet and the houses stood out darkly against it, bulbous liver-colored monstrosities of a uniform ugliness though no two were alike. Since this had been a fashionable neighborhood forty years ago, his mother persisted in thinking they did well to have an apartment in it. Each house had a narrow collar of dirt around it in which sat, usually, a grubby child. Julian walked with his hands in his pockets, his head down and thrust forward and his eyes glazed with the determination to make himself completely numb during the time he would be sacrificed to her pleasure.

The door closed and he turned to find the dumpy figure, sur-    6 mounted by the atrocious hat, coming toward him. "Well," she said, "you only live once and paying a little more for it, I at least won't meet myself coming and going."

"Some day I'll start making money," Julian said gloomily—he    7
knew he never would—"and you can have one of those jokes whenever you take the fit." But first they would move. He visualized a place where the nearest neighbors would be three miles away on either side.

"I think you're doing fine," she said, drawing on her gloves.    8
"You've only been out of school a year. Rome wasn't built in a day."

She was one of the few members of the Y reducing class who    9
arrived in hat and gloves and who had a son who had been to college. "It takes time," she said, "and the world is in such a mess. This hat looked better on me than any of the others, though when she brought it out I said, 'Take that thing back. I wouldn't have it on my head,' and she said, 'Now wait till you see it on,' and when she put it on me, I said, 'we-ull,' and she said, 'If you ask me, that hat does something for you and you do something for that hat, and besides,' she said, 'with that hat, you won't meet yourself coming and going.' "

Julian thought he could have stood his lot better if she had been    10
selfish, if she had been an old hag who drank and screamed at him. He walked along, saturated in depression, as if in the midst of his martyrdom he had lost his faith. Catching sight of his long, hopeless, irritated face, she stopped suddenly with a grief-stricken look, and pulled back on his arm. "Wait on me," she said. "I'm going back to the house and take this thing off and tomorrow I'm going to return it. I was out of my head. I can pay the gas bill with the seven-fifty."

He caught her arm in a vicious grip. "You are not going to take it    11
back," he said. "I like it."

"Well," she said, "I don't think I ought . . . ."    12

"Shut up and enjoy it," he muttered, more depressed than ever.    13

"With the world in the mess it's in," she said, "it's a wonder we    14
can enjoy anything. I tell you, the bottom rail is on the top."

Julian sighed.    15

"Of course," she said, "if you know who you are, you can go    16
anywhere." She said this every time he took her to the reducing class. "Most of them in it are not our kind of people," she said, "but I can be gracious to anybody. I know who I am."

"They don't give a damn for your graciousness," Julian said savagely. "Knowing who you are is good for one generation only. You    17
haven't the foggiest idea where you stand now or who you are."

She stopped and allowed her eyes to flash at him. "I most certainly    18

do know who I am," she said, "and if you don't know who you are, I'm
ashamed of you."

"Oh hell," Julian said.                                                    19

"Your great-grandfather was a former governor of this state," she          20
said. "Your grandfather was a prosperous landowner. Your grandmother was a Godhigh."

"Will you look around you," he said tensely, "and see where you            21
are now?" and he swept his arm jerkily out to indicate the neighborhood, which the growing darkness at least made less dingy.

"You remain what you are," she said. "Your great-grandfather               22
had a plantation and two hundred slaves."

"There are no more slaves," he said irritably.                             23

"They were better off when they were," she said. He groaned to             24
see that she was off on that topic. She rolled onto it every few days like
a train on an open track. He knew every stop, every junction, every
swamp along the way, and knew the exact point at which her conclusion would roll majestically into the station: "It's ridiculous. It's simply
not realistic. They should rise, yes, but on their own side of the fence."

"Let's skip it," Julian said.                                              25

"The ones I feel sorry for," she said, "are the ones that are half         26
white. They're tragic."

"Will you skip it?"                                                        27

"Suppose we were half white. We would certainly have mixed                 28
feelings."

"I have mixed feelings now," he groaned.                                   29

"Well let's talk about something pleasant," she said. "I remember          30
going to Grandpa's when I was a little girl. Then the house had double
stairways that went up to what was really the second floor—all the
cooking was done on the first. I used to like to stay down in the kitchen
on account of the way the walls smelled. I would sit with my nose
pressed against the plaster and take deep breaths. Actually the place
belonged to the Godhighs but your grandfather Chestny paid the
mortgage and saved it for them. They were in reduced circumstances,"
she said, "but reduced or not, they never forgot who they were."

"Doubtless that decayed mansion reminded them," Julian mut-               31
tered. He never spoke of it without contempt or thought of it without
longing. He had seen it once when he was a child before it had been
sold. The double stairways had rotted and been torn down. Negroes
were living in it. But it remained in his mind as his mother had known
it. It appeared in his dreams regularly. He would stand on the wide

porch, listening to the rustle of oak leaves, then wander through the high-ceilinged hall into the parlor that opened onto it and gaze at the worn rugs and faded draperies. It occurred to him that it was he, not she, who could have appreciated it. He preferred its threadbare elegance to anything he could name and it was because of it that all the neighborhoods they had lived in had been a torment to him—whereas she had hardly known the difference. She called her insensitivity "being adjustable."

"And I remember the old darky who was my nurse, Caroline.    32
There was no better person in the world. I've always had a great respect for my colored friends," she said. "I'd do anything in the world for them and they'd . . ."

"Will you for God's sake get off that subject?" Julian said. When    33
he got on a bus by himself, he made it a point to sit down beside a Negro, in reparation as it were for his mother's sins.

"You're mighty touchy tonight," she said. "Do you feel all right?"    34

"Yes I feel all right," he said. "Now lay off."    35

She pursed her lips. "Well, you certainly are in a vile humor," she    36
observed. "I just won't speak to you at all."

They had reached the bus stop. There was no bus in sight and    37
Julian, his hands still jammed in his pockets and his head thrust forward, scowled down the empty street. The frustration of having to wait on the bus as well as ride on it began to creep up his neck like a hot hand. The presence of his mother was borne in upon him as she gave a pained sigh. He looked at her bleakly. She was holding herself very erect under the preposterous hat, wearing it like a banner of her imaginary dignity. There was in him an evil urge to break her spirit. He suddenly unloosened his tie and pulled it off and put it in his pocket.

She stiffened. "Why must you look like *that* when you take me to    38
town?" she said. "Why must you deliberately embarrass me?"

"If you'll never learn where you are," he said, "you can at least    39
learn where I am."

"You look like a—thug," she said.    40

"Then I must be one," he murmured.    41

"I'll just go home," she said. "I will not bother you. If you can't do    42
a little thing like that for me . . ."

Rolling his eyes upward, he put his tie back on. "Restored to my    43
class," he muttered. He thrust his face toward her and hissed, "True culture is in the mind, the *mind*," he said, and tapped his head, "the mind."

"It's in the heart," she said, "and in how you do things and how    44
you do things is because of who you *are*."

"Nobody in the damn bus cares who you are."                          45

"I care who I am," she said icily.                                    46

The lighted bus appeared on top of the next hill and as it ap-       47
proached, they moved out into the street to meet it. He put his hand
under her elbow and hoisted her up on the creaking step. She entered
with a little smile, as if she were going into a drawing room where
everyone had been waiting for her. While he put in the tokens, she sat
down on one of the broad front seats for three which faced the aisle.
A thin woman with protruding teeth and long yellow hair was sitting
on the end of it. His mother moved up beside her and left room for
Julian beside herself. He sat down and looked at the floor across the
aisle where a pair of thin feet in red and white canvas sandals were
planted.

His mother immediately began a general conversation meant to        48
attract anyone who felt like talking. "Can it get any hotter?" she said
and removed from her purse a folding fan, black with a Japanese scene
on it, which she began to flutter before her.

"I reckon it might could," the woman with the protruding teeth      49
said, "but I know for a fact my apartment couldn't get no hotter."

"It must get the afternoon sun," his mother said. She sat forward   50
and looked up and down the bus. It was half filled. Everybody was
white. "I see we have the bus to ourselves," she said. Julian cringed.

"For a change," said the woman across the aisle, the owner of the   51
red and white canvas sandals. "I come on one the other day and they
were thick as fleas—up front and all through."

"The world is in a mess everywhere," his mother said. "I don't      52
know how we've let it get in this fix."

"What gets my goat is all those boys from good families stealing    53
automobile tires," the woman with the protruding teeth said. "I told
my boy, I said you may not be rich but you been raised right and if I
ever catch you in any such mess, they can send you on to the reforma-
tory. Be exactly where you belong."

"Training tells," his mother said. "Is your boy in high school?"    54

"Ninth grade," the woman said.                                       55

"My son just finished college last year. He wants to write but he's  56
selling typewriters until he gets started," his mother said.

The woman leaned forward and peered at Julian. He threw her         57
such a malevolent look that she subsided against the seat. On the floor

across the aisle there was an abandoned newspaper. He got up and got it and opened it out in front of him. His mother discreetly continued the conversation in a lower tone but the woman across the aisle said in a loud voice, "Well that's nice. Selling typewriters is close to writing. He can go right from one to the other."

"I tell him," his mother said, "that Rome wasn't built in a day." 58

Behind the newspaper Julian was withdrawing into the inner com- 59 partment of his mind where he spent most of his time. This was a kind of mental bubble in which he established himself when he could not bear to be a part of what was going on around him. From it he could see out and judge but in it he was safe from any kind of penetration from without. It was the only place where he felt free of the general idiocy of his fellows. His mother had never entered it but from it he could see her with absolute clarity.

The old lady was clever enough and he thought that if she had 60 started from any of the right premises, more might have been expected of her. She lived according to the laws of her own fantasy world, outside of which he had never seen her set foot. The law of it was to sacrifice herself for him after she had first created the necessity to do so by making a mess of things. If he had permitted her sacrifices, it was only because her lack of foresight had made them necessary. All of her life had been a struggle to act like a Chestny without the Chestny goods, and to give him everything she thought a Chestny ought to have; but since, said she, it was fun to struggle, why complain? And when you had won, as she had won, what fun to look back on the hard times! He could not forgive her that she had enjoyed the struggle and that she thought *she* had won.

What she meant when she said she had won was that she had 61 brought him up successfully and had sent him to college and that he had turned out so well—good looking (her teeth had gone unfilled so that his could be straightened), intelligent (he realized he was too intelligent to be a success), and with a future ahead of him (there was of course no future ahead of him). She excused his gloominess on the grounds that he was still growing up and his radical ideas on his lack of practical experience. She said he didn't yet know a thing about "life," that he hadn't even entered the real world—when already he was as disenchanted with it as a man of fifty.

The further irony of all this was that in spite of her, he had turned 62 out so well. In spite of going to only a third-rate college, he had, on his own initiative, come out with a first-rate education; in spite of growing up dominated by a small mind, he had ended up with a large one; in spite of all her foolish views, he was free of prejudice and unafraid to face facts. Most miraculous of all, instead of being blinded by love for her as she was for him, he had cut himself emotionally free of her and could see her with complete objectivity. He was not dominated by his mother.

The bus stopped with a sudden jerk and shook him from his 63 meditation. A woman from the back lurched forward with little steps and barely escaped falling in his newspaper as she righted herself. She got off and a large Negro got on. Julian kept his paper lowered to watch. It gave him a certain satisfaction to see injustice in daily operation. It confirmed his view that with a few exceptions there was no one worth knowing within a radius of three hundred miles. The Negro was well dressed and carried a briefcase. He looked around and then sat down on the other end of the seat where the woman with the red and white canvas sandals was sitting. He immediately unfolded a newspaper and obscured himself behind it. Julian's mother's elbow at once prodded insistently into his ribs. "Now you see why I won't ride on these buses by myself," she whispered.

The woman with the red and white canvas sandals had risen at the 64 same time the Negro sat down and had gone further back in the bus and taken the seat of the woman who had got off. His mother leaned forward and cast her an approving look.

Julian rose, crossed the aisle, and sat down in the place of the 65 woman with the canvas sandals. From this position, he looked serenely across at his mother. Her face had turned an angry red. He stared at her, making his eyes the eyes of a stranger. He felt his tension suddenly lift as if he had openly declared war on her.

He would have liked to get in conversation with the Negro and to 66 talk with him about art or politics or any subject that would be above the comprehension of those around them, but the man remained entrenched behind his paper. He was either ignoring the change of seating or had never noticed it. There was no way for Julian to convey his sympathy.

His mother kept her eyes fixed reproachfully on his face. The 67 woman with the protruding teeth was looking at him avidly as if he were a type of monster new to her.

"Do you have a light?" he asked the Negro.                                    68

Without looking away from his paper, the man reached in his 69 pocket and handed him a packet of matches.

"Thanks," Julian said. For a moment he held the matches fool-    70
ishly. A NO SMOKING sign looked down upon him from over the
door. This alone would not have deterred him; he had no cigarettes.
He had quit smoking some months before because he could not afford
it. "Sorry," he muttered and handed back the matches. The Negro
lowered the paper and gave him an annoyed look. He took the matches
and raised the paper again.

His mother continued to gaze at him but she did not take advan-    71
tage of his momentary discomfort. Her eyes retained their battered
look. Her face seemed to be unnaturally red, as if her blood pressure
had risen. Julian allowed no glimmer of sympathy to show on his face.
Having got the advantage, he wanted desperately to keep it and carry
it through. He would have liked to teach her a lesson that would last
her a while, but there seemed no way to continue the point. The Negro
refused to come out from behind his paper.

Julian folded his arms and looked stolidly before him, facing her    72
but as if he did not see her, as if he had ceased to recognize her
existence. He visualized a scene in which, the bus having reached their
stop, he would remain in his seat and when she said, "Aren't you going
to get off?" he would look at her as at a stranger who had rashly
addressed him. The corner they got off on was usually deserted, but it
was well lighted and it would not hurt her to walk by herself the four
blocks to the Y. He decided to wait until the time came and then decide
whether or not he would let her get off by herself. He would have to
be at the Y at ten to bring her back, but he could leave her wondering
if he was going to show up. There was no reason for her to think she
could always depend on him.

He retired again into the high-ceilinged room sparsely settled with    73
large pieces of antique furniture. His soul expanded momentarily but
then he became aware of his mother across from him and the vision
shriveled. He studied her coldly. Her feet in little pumps dangled like
a child's and did not quite reach the floor. She was training on him an
exaggerated look of reproach. He felt completely detached from her.
At that moment he could with pleasure have slapped her as he would
have slapped a particularly obnoxious child in his charge.

He began to imagine various unlikely ways by which he could    74
teach her a lesson. He might make friends with some distinguished
Negro professor or lawyer and bring him home to spend the evening.
He would be entirely justified but her blood pressure would rise to 300.
He could not push her to the extent of making her have a stroke, and

moreover, he had never been successful at making any Negro friends. He had tried to strike up an acquaintance on the bus with some of the better types, with ones that looked like professors or ministers or lawyers. One morning he had sat down next to a distinguished-looking dark brown man who had answered his questions with a sonorous solemnity but who had turned out to be an undertaker. Another day he had sat down beside a cigar-smoking Negro with a diamond ring on his finger, but after a few stilted pleasantries, the Negro had rung the buzzer and risen, slipping two lottery tickets into Julian's hand as he climbed over him to leave.

He imagined his mother lying desperately ill and his being able to    75
secure only a Negro doctor for her. He toyed with that idea for a few minutes and then dropped it for a momentary vision of himself partici- pating as a sympathizer in a sit-in demonstration. This was possible but he did not linger with it. Instead, he approached the ultimate horror. He brought home a beautiful suspiciously Negroid woman. Prepare yourself, he said. There is nothing you can do about it. This is the woman I've chosen. She's intelligent, dignified, even good, and she's suffered and she hasn't thought it *fun*. Now persecute us, go ahead and persecute us. Drive her out of here, but remember, you're driving me too. His eyes were narrowed and through the indignation he had generated, he saw his mother across the aisle, purple-faced, shrunken to the dwarf-like proportions of her moral nature, sitting like a mummy beneath the ridiculous banner of her hat.

He was tilted out of his fantasy again as the bus stopped. The door    76
opened with a sucking hiss and out of the dark a large, gaily dressed, sullen-looking colored woman got on with a little boy. The child, who might have been four, had on a short plaid suit and a Tyrolean hat with a blue feather in it. Julian hoped that he would sit down beside him and that the woman would push in beside his mother. He could think of no better arrangement.

As she waited for her tokens, the woman was surveying the seating    77
possibilities—he hoped with the idea of sitting where she was least wanted. There was something familiar-looking about her but Julian could not place what it was. She was a giant of a woman. Her face was set not only to meet opposition but to seek it out. The downward tilt of her large lower lip was like a warning sign: DON'T TAMPER WITH ME. Her bulging figure was encased in a green crepe dress and her feet overflowed in red shoes. She had on a hideous hat. A purple

velvet flap came down on one side of it and stood up on the other; the rest of it was green and looked like a cushion with the stuffing out. She carried a mammoth red pocketbook that bulged throughout as if it were stuffed with rocks.

To Julian's disappointment, the little boy climbed up on the empty    78
seat beside his mother. His mother lumped all children, black and white, into the common category, "cute," and she thought little Negroes were on the whole cuter than little white children. She smiled at the little boy as he climbed on the seat.

Meanwhile the woman was bearing down upon the empty seat    79
beside Julian. To his annoyance, she squeezed herself into it. He saw his mother's face change as the woman settled herself next to him and he realized with satisfaction that this was more objectionable to her than it was to him. Her face seemed almost gray and there was a look of dull recognition in her eyes, as if suddenly she had sickened at some awful confrontation. Julian saw that it was because she and the woman had, in a sense, swapped sons. Though his mother would not realize the symbolic significance of this, she would feel it. His amusement showed plainly on his face.

The woman next to him muttered something unintelligible to her-    80
self. He was conscious of a kind of bristling next to him, muted growl-ing like that of an angry cat. He could not see anything but the red pocketbook upright on the bulging green thighs. He visualized the woman as she had stood waiting for her tokens—the ponderous figure, rising from the red shoes upward over the solid hips, the mammoth bosom, the haughty face, to the green and purple hat.

His eyes widened.

The vision of the two hats, identical, broke upon him with the    81
radiance of a brilliant sunrise. His face was suddenly lit with joy. He could not believe that Fate had thrust upon his mother such a lesson. He gave a loud chuckle so that she would look at him and see that he saw. She turned her eyes on him slowly. The blue in them seemed to have turned a bruised purple. For a moment he had an uncomfort-able sense of her innocence, but it lasted only a second before princi-ple rescued him. Justice entitled him to laugh. His grin hardened until it said to her as plainly as if he were saying aloud: Your punish-ment exactly fits your pettiness. This should teach you a permanent lesson.

Her eyes shifted to the woman. She seemed unable to bear looking    82 at him and to find the woman preferable. He became conscious again of the bristling presence at his side. The woman was rumbling like a volcano about to become active. His mother's mouth began to twitch slightly at one corner. With a sinking heart, he saw incipient signs of recovery on her face and realized that this was going to strike her suddenly as funny and was going to be no lesson at all. She kept her eyes on the woman and an amused smile came over her face as if the woman were a monkey that had stolen her hat. The little Negro was looking up at her with large fascinated eyes. He had been trying to attract her attention for some time.

"Carver!" the woman said suddenly. "Come heah!"                    83

When he saw that the spotlight was on him at last, Carver drew    84
his feet up and turned himself toward Julian's mother and giggled.

"Carver!" the woman said. "You heah me? Come heah!"              85

Carver slid down from the seat but remained squatting with his    86
back against the base of it, his head turned slyly around toward Julian's mother, who was smiling at him. The woman reached a hand across the aisle and snatched him to her. He righted himself and hung backwards on her knees, grinning at Julian's mother. "Isn't he cute?" Julian's mother said to the woman with the protruding teeth.

"I reckon he is," the woman said without conviction.              87

The Negress yanked him upright but he eased out of her grip and    88
shot across the aisle and scrambled, giggling wildly, onto the seat beside his love.

"I think he likes me," Julian's mother said, and smiled at the    89
woman. It was the smile she used when she was being particularly gracious to an inferior. Julian saw everything lost. The lesson had rolled off her like rain on a roof.

The woman stood up and yanked the little boy off the seat as if she    90
were snatching him from contagion. Julian could feel the rage in her at having no weapon like his mother's smile. She gave the child a sharp slap across his leg. He howled once and then thrust his head into her stomach and kicked his feet against her shins. "Behave," she said vehemently.

The bus stopped and the Negro who had been reading the news-    91
paper got off. The woman moved over and set the little boy down with a thump between herself and Julian. She held him firmly by the knee. In a moment he put his hands in front of his face and peeped at Julian's mother through his fingers.

"I see yooooooo!" she said and put her hand in front of her face    92
and peeped at him.

The woman slapped his hand down. "Quit yo' foolishness," she    93
said, "before I knock the living Jesus out of you!"

Julian was thankful that the next stop was theirs. He reached up    94
and pulled the cord. The woman reached up and pulled it at the same
time. Oh my God, he thought. He had the terrible intuition that when
they got off the bus together, his mother would open her purse and give
the little boy a nickel. The gesture would be as natural to her as
breathing. The bus stopped and the woman got up and lunged to the
front, dragging the child, who wished to stay on, after her. Julian and
his mother got up and followed. As they neared the door, Julian tried
to relieve her of her pocketbook.

"No," she murmured, "I want to give the little boy a nickel."    95

"No!" Julian hissed. "No!"    96

She smiled down at the child and opened her bag. The bus door    97
opened and the woman picked him up by the arm and descended with
him, hanging at her hip. Once in the street she set him down and shook
him.

Julian's mother had to close her purse while she got down the bus    98
step but as soon as her feet were on the ground, she opened it again
and began to rummage inside. "I can't find but a penny," she whispered, "but it looks like a new one."

"Don't do it!" Julian said fiercely between his teeth. There was a    99
streetlight on the corner and she hurried to get under it so that she
could better see into her pocketbook. The woman was heading off
rapidly down the street with the child still hanging backward on her
hand.

"Oh little boy!" Julian's mother called and took a few quick steps    100
and caught up with them just beyond the lamppost. "Here's a bright
new penny for you," and she held out the coin, which shone bronze in
the dim light.

The huge woman turned and for a moment stood, her shoulders    101
lifted and her face frozen with frustrated rage, and stared at Julian's
mother. Then all at once she seemed to explode like a piece of machinery that had been given one ounce of pressure too much. Julian saw the
black fist swing out with the red pocketbook. He shut his eyes and
cringed as he heard the woman shout, "He don't take nobody's pennies!" When he opened his eyes, the woman was disappearing down

the street with the little boy staring wide-eyed over her shoulder. Julian's mother was sitting on the sidewalk.

"I told you not to do that," Julian said angrily. "I told you not to      102
do that!"

He stood over her for a minute, gritting his teeth. Her legs were         103
stretched out in front of her and her hat was on her lap. He squatted down and looked at her in the face. It was totally expressionless. "You got exactly what you deserved," he said. "Now get up."

He picked up her pocketbook and put what had fallen out back in           104
it. He picked the hat up off her lap. The penny caught his eye on the sidewalk and he picked that up and let it drop before her eyes into the purse. Then he stood up and leaned over and held his hands out to pull her up. She remained immobile. He sighed. Rising above them on either side were black apartment buildings, marked with irregular rectangles of light. At the end of the block a man came out of a door and walked off in the opposite direction. "All right," he said, "suppose somebody happens by and wants to know why you're sitting on the sidewalk?"

She took the hand and, breathing hard, pulled heavily up on it and        105
then stood for a moment, swaying slightly as if the spots of light in the darkness were circling around her. Her eyes, shadowed and confused, finally settled on his face. He did not try to conceal his irritation. "I hope this teaches you a lesson," he said. She leaned forward and her eyes raked his face. She seemed trying to determine his identity. Then, as if she found nothing familiar about him, she started off with a headlong movement in the wrong direction.

"Aren't you going on to the Y?" he asked.                                 106

"Home," she muttered.                                                     107

"Well, are we walking?"                                                   108

For answer she kept going. Julian followed along, his hands be-           109
hind him. He saw no reason to let the lesson she had had go without backing it up with an explanation of its meaning. She might as well be made to understand what had happened to her. "Don't think that was just an uppity Negro woman," he said. "That was the whole colored race which will no longer take your condescending pennies. That was your black double. She can wear the same hat as you, and to be sure," he added gratuitously (because he thought it was funny), "it looked better on her than it did on you.

What all this means," he said, "is that the old world is gone. The old manners are obsolete and your graciousness is not worth a damn." He thought bitterly of the house that had been lost for him. "You aren't who you think you are," he said.

She continued to plow ahead, paying no attention to him. Her hair    110
had come undone on one side. She dropped her pocketbook and took no notice. He stopped and picked it up and handed it to her but she did not take it.

"You needn't act as if the world had come to an end," he said,    111
"because it hasn't. From now on you've got to live in a new world and face a few realities for a change. Buck up," he said, "it won't kill you."

She was breathing fast.    112

"Let's wait on the bus," he said.    113

"Home," she said thickly.    114

"I hate to see you behave like this," he said. "Just like a child. I    115
should be able to expect more of you." He decided to stop where he was and make her stop and wait for a bus. "I'm not going any farther," he said, stopping. "We're going on the bus."

She continued to go on as if she had not heard him. He took a few    116
steps and caught her arm and stopped her. He looked into her face and caught his breath. He was looking into a face he had never seen before. "Tell Grandpa to come get me," she said.

He stared, stricken.    117

"Tell Caroline to come get me," she said.    118

Stunned, he let her go and she lurched forward again, walking    119
as if one leg were shorter than the other. A tide of darkness seemed to be sweeping her from him. "Mother!" he cried. "Darling, sweet-heart, wait!" Crumpling, she fell to the pavement. He dashed for-ward and fell at her side, crying, "Mamma, Mamma!" He turned her over. Her face was fiercely distorted. One eye, large and star-ing, moved slightly to the left as if it had become unmoored. The other remained fixed on him, raked his face again, found nothing and closed.

"Wait here, wait here!" he cried and jumped up and began to    120
run for help toward a cluster of lights he saw in the distance ahead of him. "Help, help!" he shouted, but his voice was thin, scarcely a thread of sound. The lights drifted farther away the faster he ran

and his feet moved numbly as if they carried him nowhere. The tide of darkness seemed to sweep him back to her, postponing from moment to moment his entry into the world of guilt and sorrow.

---

# Yellow Woman

## LESLIE MARMON SILKO

### I

My thigh clung to his with dampness, and I watched the sun rising   1 up through the tamaracks and willows. The small brown water birds came to the river and hopped across the mud, leaving brown scratches in the alkali-white crust. They bathed in the river silently. I could hear the water, almost at our feet where the narrow fast channel bubbled and washed green ragged moss and fern leaves. I looked at him beside me, rolled in the red blanket on the white river sand. I cleaned the sand out of the cracks between my toes, squinting because the sun was above the willow trees. I looked at him for the last time, sleeping on the white river sand.

I felt hungry and followed the river south the way we had come   2 the afternoon before, following our footprints that were already blurred by lizard tracks and bug trails. The horses were still lying down, and the black one whinnied when he saw me but he did not get up—maybe it was because the corral was made out of thick cedar branches and the horses had not yet felt the sun like I had. I tried to look beyond the pale red mesas to the pueblo. I knew it was there, even if I could not see it, on the sandrock hill above the river, the same river that moved past me now and had reflected the moon last night.

The horse felt warm underneath me. He shook his head and   3 pawed the sand. The bay whinnied and leaned against the gate trying to follow, and I remembered him asleep in the red blanket beside the river. I slid off the horse and tied him close to the other horse. I walked north with the river again, and the white sand broke loose in footprints over footprints.

"Wake up." 4

He moved in the blanket and turned his face to me with his eyes 5
still closed. I knelt down to touch him.

"I'm leaving." 6

He smiled now, eyes still closed. "You are coming with me, re- 7
member?" He sat up now with his bare dark chest and belly in the sun.

"Where?" 8

"To my place." 9

"And will I come back?" 10

He pulled his pants on. I walked away from him, feeling him 11
behind me and smelling the willows.

"Yellow Woman," he said. 12

I turned to face him. "Who are you?" I asked. 13

He laughed and knelt on the low, sandy bank, washing his face in 14
the river. "Last night you guessed my name, and you knew why I had
come."

I stared past him at the shallow moving water and tried to remem- 15
ber the night, but I could only see the moon in the water and remember
his warmth around me.

"But I only said that you were him and that I was Yellow 16
Woman—I'm not really her—I have my own name and I come from
the pueblo on the other side of the mesa. Your name is Silva and you
are a stranger I met by the river yesterday afternoon."

He laughed softly. "What happened yesterday has nothing to do 17
with what you will do today, Yellow Woman."

"I know—that's what I'm saying—the old stories about the 18
ka'tsina spirit and Yellow Woman can't mean us."

My old grandpa liked to tell those stories best. There is one about 19
Badger and Coyote who went hunting and were gone all day, and
when the sun was going down they found a house. There was a girl
living there alone, and she had light hair and eyes and she told them
that they could sleep with her. Coyote wanted to be with her all night
so he sent Badger into a prairie-dog hole, telling him he thought he saw
something in it. As soon as Badger crawled in, Coyote blocked up the
entrance with rocks and hurried back to Yellow Woman.

"Come here," he said gently. 20

He touched my neck and I moved close to him to feel his breathing 21
and to hear his heart. I was wondering if Yellow Woman had known
who she was—if she knew that she would become part of the stories.
Maybe she'd had another name that her husband and relatives called

her so that only the ka'tsina from the north and the storytellers would know her as Yellow Woman. But I didn't go on; I felt him all around me, pushing me down into the white river sand.

Yellow Woman went away with the spirit from the north and lived    22
with him and his relatives. She was gone for a long time, but then one day she came back and she brought twin boys.

"Do you know the story?"                                          23

"What story?" He smiled and pulled me close to him as he said    24
this. I was afraid lying there on the red blanket. All I could know was the way he felt, warm, damp, his body beside me. This is the way it happens in the stories, I was thinking, with no thought beyond the moment she meets the ka'tsina spirit and they go.

"I don't have to go. What they tell in stories was real only then,    25
back in time immemorial, like they say."

He stood up and pointed at my clothes tangled in the blanket.    26
"Let's go," he said.

I walked beside him, breathing hard because he walked fast, his    26
hand around my wrist. I had stopped trying to pull away from him, because his hand felt cool and the sun was high, drying the river bed into alkali. I will see someone, eventually I will see someone, and then I will be certain that he is only a man—some man from nearby—and I will be sure that I am not Yellow Woman. Because she is from out of time past and I live now and I've been to school and there are highways and pickup trucks that Yellow Woman never saw.

It was an easy ride north on horseback. I watched the change from    28
the cottonwood trees along the river to the junipers that brushed past us in the foothills, and finally there were only piñons, and when I looked up at the rim of the mountain plateau I could see pine trees growing on the edge. Once I stopped to look down, but the pale sandstone had disappeared and the river was gone and the dark lava hills were all around. He touched my hand, not speaking, but always singing softly a mountain song and looking into my eyes.

I felt hungry and wondered what they were doing at home now—    29
my mother, my grandmother, my husband, and the baby. Cooking breakfast, saying, "Where did she go?—maybe kidnapped," and Al going to the tribal police with the details: "She went walking along the river."

The house was made with black lava rock and red mud. It was high    30
above the spreading miles of arroyos and long mesas. I smelled a mountain smell of pitch and buck brush. I stood there beside the black

horse, looking down on the small, dim country we had passed, and I shivered.

"Yellow Woman, come inside where it's warm."             31

## II

He lit a fire in the stove. It was an old stove with a round belly and   32 an enamel coffeepot on top. There was only the stove, some faded Navajo blankets, and a bedroll and cardboard box. The floor was made of smooth adobe plaster, and there was one small window facing east. He pointed at the box.

"There's some potatoes and the frying pan." He sat on the floor   33 with his arms around his knees pulling them close to his chest and he watched me fry the potatoes. I didn't mind him watching me because he was always watching me—he had been watching me since I came upon him sitting on the river bank trimming leaves from a willow twig with his knife. We ate from the pan and he wiped the grease from his fingers on his Levis.

"Have you brought women here before?" He smiled and kept   34 chewing, so I said, "Do you always use the same tricks?"

"What tricks?" He looked at me like he didn't understand.   35

"The story about being a ka'tsina from the mountains. The story   36 about Yellow Woman."

Silva was silent; his face was calm.   37

"I don't believe it. Those stories couldn't happen now," I said.   38

He shook his head and said softly, "But someday they will talk   39 about us, and they will say, 'Those two lived long ago when things like that happened.'"

He stood up and went out. I ate the rest of the potatoes and   40 thought about things—about the noise the stove was making and the sound of the mountain wind outside. I remembered yesterday and the day before, and then I went outside.

I walked past the corral to the edge where the narrow trail cut   41 through the black rim rock. I was standing in the sky with nothing around me but the wind that came down from the blue mountain peak behind me. I could see faint mountain images in the distance miles across the vast spread of mesas and valleys and plains. I wondered who was over there to feel the mountain wind on those sheer blue edges— who walks on the pine needles in those blue mountains.

"Can you see the pueblo?" Silva was standing behind me.   42

I shook my head. "We're too far away."                                          43

"From here I can see the world." He stepped out on the edge.                     44
"The Navajo reservation begins over there." He pointed to the east.
"The Pueblo boundaries are over here." He looked below us to the
south, where the narrow trail seemed to come from. "The Texans have
their ranches over there, starting with that valley, the Concho Valley.
The Mexicans run some cattle over there too."

"Do you ever work for them?"                                                     45

"I steal from them," Silva answered. The sun was dropping behind       46
us and shadows were filling the land below. I turned away from the
edge that dropped forever into the valleys below.

"I'm cold," I said; "I'm going inside." I started wondering about       47
this man who could speak the Pueblo language so well but who lived
on a mountain and rustled cattle. I decided that this man Silva must be
Navajo, because Pueblo men didn't do things like that.

"You must be a Navajo."                                                          48

Silva shook his head gently. "Little Yellow Woman," he said, "you      49
never give up, do you? I have told you who I am. The Navajo people
know me, too." He knelt down and unrolled the bedroll and spread the
extra blankets out on a piece of canvas. The sun was down, and the
only light in the house came from outside—the dim orange light from
sundown.

I stood there and waited for him to crawl under the blankets.           50

"What are you waiting for?" he said, and I lay down beside him.       51
He undressed me slowly like the night before beside the river—kissing
my face gently and running his hands up and down my belly and legs.
He took off my pants and then he laughed.

"Why are you laughing?"                                                          52

"You are breathing so hard."                                                     53

I pulled away from him and turned my back to him.                                54

He pulled me around and pinned me down with his arms and       55
chest. "You don't understand, do you, little Yellow Woman? You will
do what I want."

And again he was all around me with his skin slippery against       56
mine, and I was afraid because I understood that his strength could
hurt me. I lay underneath him and I knew that he could destroy me.
But later, while he slept beside me, I touched his face and I had a
feeling—the kind of feeling for him that overcame me that morning along the river. I kissed him on the forehead and he reached out
for me.

When I woke up in the morning he was gone. It gave me a strange    57
feeling because for a long time I sat there on the blankets and looked
around the little house for some object of his—some proof that he had
been there or maybe that he was coming back. Only the blankets and
the cardboard box remained. The .30–30 that had been leaning in the
corner was gone, and so was the knife I had used the night before. He
was gone, and I had my chance to go now. But first I had to eat,
because I knew it would be a long walk home.

I found some dried apricots in the cardboard box, and I sat down    58
on a rock at the edge of the plateau rim. There was no wind and the
sun warmed me. I was surrounded by silence. I drowsed with apricots
in my mouth, and I didn't believe that there were highways or rail-
roads or cattle to steal.

When I woke up, I stared down at my feet in the black mountain    59
dirt. Little black ants were swarming over the pine needles around my
foot. They must have smelled the apricots. I thought about my family
far below me. They would be wondering about me, because this had
never happened to me before. The tribal police would file a report. But
if old Grandpa weren't dead he would tell them what happened—he
would laugh and say, "Stolen by a ka'tsina, a mountain spirit. She'll
come home—they usually do." There are enough of them to handle
things. My mother and grandmother will raise the baby like they raised
me. Al will find someone else, and they will go on like before, except
that there will be a story about the day I disappeared while I was
walking along the river. Silva had come for me; he said he had. I did
not decide to go. I just went. Moonflowers blossom in the sand hills
before dawn, just as I followed him. That's what I was thinking as I
wandered along the trail through the pine trees.

It was noon when I got back. When I saw the stone house I    60
remembered that I had meant to go home. But that didn't seem important any more, maybe because there were little blue flowers growing
in the meadow behind the stone house and the gray squirrels were
playing in the pines next to the house. The horses were standing in the
corral, and there was a beef carcass hanging on the shady side of a big
pine in front of the house. Flies buzzed around the clotted blood that
hung from the carcass. Silva was washing his hands in a bucket full of
water. He must have heard me coming because he spoke to me without
turning to face me.

"I've been waiting for you."    61

"I went walking in the big pine trees."    62

I looked into the bucket full of bloody water with brown-and-white    63
animal hairs floating in it. Silva stood there letting his hand drip,
examining me intently.

"Are you coming with me?"                                            64

"Where?" I asked him.                                                65

"To sell the meat in Marquez."                                       66

"If you're sure it's O.K."                                           67

"I wouldn't ask you if it wasn't," he answered.                      68

He sloshed the water around in the bucket before he dumped it        69
out and set the bucket upside down near the door. I followed him to
the corral and watched him saddle the horses. Even beside the horses
he looked tall, and I asked him again if he wasn't Navajo. He didn't say
anything; he just shook his head and kept cinching up the saddle.

"But Navajos are tall."                                              70

"Get on the horse," he said, "and let's go."                         71

The last thing he did before we started down the steep trail was     72
to grab the .30–30 from the corner. He slid the rifle into the scabbard
that hung from his saddle.

"Do they ever try to catch you?" I asked.                            73

"They don't know who I am."                                          74

"Then why did you bring the rifle?"                                  75

"Because we are going to Marquez where the Mexicans live."           76

## III

The trail leveled out on a narrow ridge that was steep on both sides    77
like an animal spine. On one side I could see where the trail went
around the rocky gray hills and disappeared into the southeast where
the pale sandrock mesas stood in the distance near my home. On the
other side was a trail that went west, and as I looked far into the
distance I thought I saw the little town. But Silva said no, that I was
looking in the wrong place, that I just thought I saw houses. After that
I quit looking off into the distance; it was hot and the wildflowers were
closing up their deep-yellow petals. Only the waxy cactus flowers
bloomed in the bright sun, and I saw every color that a cactus blossom
can be; the white ones and the red ones were still buds, but the purple
and the yellow were blossoms, open full and the most beautiful of all.

Silva saw him before I did. The white man was riding a big gray       78
horse, coming up the trail toward us. He was traveling fast and the
gray horse's feet sent rocks rolling off the trail into the dry tum-

bleweeds. Silva motioned for me to stop and we watched the white man. He didn't see us right away, but finally his horse whinnied at our horses and he stopped. He looked at us briefly before he loped the gray horse across the three hundred yards that separated us. He stopped his horse in front of Silva, and his young fat face was shadowed by the brim of his hat. He didn't look mad, but his small, pale eyes moved from the blood-soaked gunny sacks hanging from my saddle to Silva's face and then back to my face.

"Where did you get the fresh meat?" the white man asked. 79

"I've been hunting," Silva said, and when he shifted his weight in 80 the saddle the leather creaked.

"The hell you have, Indian. You've been rustling cattle. We've 81 been looking for the thief for a long time."

The rancher was fat, and sweat began to soak through his white 82 cowboy shirt and the wet cloth stuck to the thick rolls of belly fat. He almost seemed to be panting from the exertion of talking, and he smelled rancid, maybe because Silva scared him.

Silva turned to me and smiled. "Go back up the mountain, Yellow 83 Woman."

The white man got angry when he heard Silva speak in a language 84 he couldn't understand. "Don't try anything, Indian. Just keep riding to Marquez. We'll call the state police from there."

The rancher must have been unarmed because he was very fright- 85 ened and if he had a gun he would have pulled it out then. I turned my horse around and the rancher yelled, "Stop!" I looked at Silva for an instant and there was something ancient and dark—something I could feel in my stomach—in his eyes, and when I glanced at his hand I saw his finger on the trigger of the .30–30 that was still in the saddle scabbard. I slapped my horse across the flank and the sacks of raw meat swung against my knees as the horse leaped up the trail. It was hard to keep my balance, and once I thought I felt the saddle slipping backward; it was because of this that I could not look back.

I didn't stop until I reached the ridge where the trail forked. The 86 horse was breathing deep gasps and there was a dark film of sweat on its neck. I looked down in the direction I had come from, but I couldn't see the place. I waited. The wind came up and pushed warm air past me. I looked up at the sky, pale blue and full of thin clouds and fading vapor trails left by jets.

I think four shots were fired—I remember hearing four hollow 87 explosions that reminded me of deer hunting. There could have been more shots after that, but I couldn't have heard them because my horse was running again and the loose rocks were making too much noise as they scattered around his feet.

Horses have a hard time running downhill, but I went that way          88
instead of uphill to the mountain because I thought it was safer. I felt better with the horse running southeast past the round gray hills that were covered with cedar trees and black lava rock. When I got to the plain in the distance I could see the dark green patches of tamaracks that grew along the river; and beyond the river I could see the beginning of the pale sandrock mesas. I stopped the horse and looked back to see if anyone was coming; then I got off the horse and turned the horse around, wondering if it would go back to its corral under the pines of the mountain. It looked back at me for a moment and then plucked a mouthful of green tumbleweeds before it trotted back up the trail with its ears pointed forward, carrying its head daintily to one side to avoid stepping on the dragging reins. When the horse disappeared over the last hill, the gunny sacks full of meat were still swinging and bouncing.

## IV

I walked toward the river on a woodhauler's road that I knew          89
would eventually lead to the paved road. I was thinking about waiting beside the road for someone to drive by, but by the time I got to the pavement I had decided it wasn't very far to walk if I followed the river back the way Silva and I had come.

The river water tasted good, and I sat in the shade under a cluster          90
of silvery willows. I thought about Silva, and I felt sad at leaving him; still, there was something strange about him, and I tried to figure it out all the way back home.

I came back to the place on the river bank where he had been          91
sitting the first time I saw him. The green willow leaves that he had trimmed from the branch were still lying there, wilted in the sand. I saw the leaves and I wanted to go back to him—to kiss him and to touch him—but the mountains were too far away now. And I told myself, because I believe it, he will come back sometime and be waiting again by the river.

I followed the path up from the river into the village. The sun          92
was getting low, and I could smell supper cooking when I got to the

screen door of my house. I could hear their voices inside—my mother was telling my grandmother how to fix the Jell-o and my husband, Al, was playing with the baby. I decided to tell them that some Navajo had kidnapped me, but I was sorry that old Grandpa wasn't alive to hear my story because it was the Yellow Woman stories he liked to tell best.

# Poetry

## *When I Heard the Learn'd Astronomer*

### WALT WHITMAN

When I heard the learn'd astronomer,                                      1
When the proofs, the figures, were ranged in columns before me,
When I was shown the charts and diagrams, to add, divide, and
    measure them,
When I sitting heard the astronomer where he lectured with much
    applause in the lecture-room,
How soon unaccountable I became tired and sick,                          5
Till rising and gliding out I wander'd off by myself,
In the mystical moist night-air, and from time to time,
Look'd up in perfect silence at the stars.

## *since feeling is first*

### e. e. cummings

since feeling is first                                                    1
who pays any attention
to the syntax of things
will never wholly kiss you;

wholly to be a fool                                                       5
while Spring is in the world

my blood approves,
and kisses are a better fate
than wisdom
lady i swear by all flowers. Don't cry                                    10
—the best gesture of my brain is less than
your eyelids' flutter which says

we are for each other: then
laugh, leaning back in my arms
for life's not a paragraph                                                15

And death i think is no parenthesis

---

# The Deer Lay Down Their Bones

## ROBINSON JEFFERS

I followed the narrow cliffside trail half way up the mountain          1
Above the deep river-canyon. There was a little cataract crossed
    the path, flinging itself
Over tree roots and rocks, shaking the jeweled fern-fronds, bright
    bubbling water
Pure from the mountain, but a bad smell came up. Wondering at
    it I clambered down the steep stream
Some forty feet, and found in the midst of bush-oak and laurel,         5
Hung like a bird's nest on the precipice brink a small hidden
    clearing,
Grass and a shallow pool. But all about there were bones lying in
    the grass, clean bones and stinking bones,
Antlers and bones: I understood that the place was a refuge for
    wounded deer; there are so many
Hurt ones escape the hunters and limp away to lie hidden; here
    they have water for the awful thirst
And peace to die in; dense green laurel and grim cliff                   10
Make sanctuary, and a sweet wind blows upward from the deep
    gorge.—I wish my bones were with theirs.
But that's a foolish thing to confess, and a little cowardly. We
    know that life

Is on the whole quite equally good and bad, mostly gray neutral,
    and can be endured
To the dim end, no matter what magic of grass, water and
    precipice, and pain of wounds,
Makes death look dear. We have been given life and have used            15
    it—not a great gift perhaps—but in honesty
Should use it all. Mine's empty since my love died— Empty? The
    flame-haired grandchild with great blue eyes
That look like hers?—What can I do for the child? I gaze at her
    and wonder what sort of man
In the fall of the world . . . I am growing old, that is the trouble.
    My children and little grandchildren
Will find their way, and why should I wait ten years yet, having       20
    lived sixty-seven, ten years more or less,
Before I crawl out on a ledge of rock and die snapping, like a
    wolf
Who has lost his mate?—I am bound by my own thirty-year-old
    decision: who drinks the wine
Should take the dregs; even in the bitter lees and sediment
New discovery may lie. The deer in that beautiful place lay
    down their bones: I must wear mine.

---

# Spring and All

## WILLIAM CARLOS WILLIAMS

By the road to the contagious hospital                                  1
under the surge of the blue
mottled clouds driven from the
northeast—a cold wind. Beyond, the
waste of broad, muddy fields                                            5
brown with dried weeds, standing and fallen

patches of standing water
the scattering of tall trees

All along the road the reddish
purplish, forked, upstanding, twiggy                                    10

stuff of bushes and small trees
with dead, brown leaves under them
leafless vines—

Lifeless in appearance, sluggish
dazed spring approaches—                                         15

They enter the new world naked,
cold, uncertain of all
save that they enter. All about them
the cold, familiar wind—

Now the grass, tomorrow                                          20
the stiff curl of wildcarrot leaf
One by one objects are defined—
It quickens: clarity, outline of leaf

But now the stark dignity of
entrance—Still, the profound change                             25
has come upon them: rooted, they
grip down and begin to awaken

---

# For the Dead

## ADRIENNE RICH

I dreamed I called you on the telephone                          1
to say: *Be kinder to yourself*
but you were sick and would not answer

The waste of my love goes on this way
trying to save you from yourself                                 5

I have always wondered about the leftover
energy, water rushing down a hill
long after the rains have stopped

or the fire you want to go to bed from
but cannot leave, burning-down but not burnt-down                10

the red coals more extreme, more curious
in their flashing and dying
than you wish they were
sitting there long after midnight

---

# *Postscript*

## ROSARIO CASTELLAÑOS

My antagonist (who I always am) says to me:                           1
Very simple. You've solved your problem
like Spinoza, *more geometricum:*
a place, a form to last,
and a function, perhaps, to fulfill.                                  5

But you've forgotten to say who supervises
the exact coincidence
between the cog and everything else: who signs
the official approval for the deeds. Who . . .
and, in any case, for what? Or why?                                   10

Well, obviously, you've never thought about this
but just about getting by
and getting on with living
as though it were necessary. In short, very
     feminine.

But for God's sake, aren't you ashamed of that                       15
     crumb
you chew on so laboriously from one day to the
     next?
Don't you rebel against this circular task
of a mule around a grindstone? At least
put blinders on so you can't see that you're
always in the same place.                                            20

You know what? Metaphysics makes everything
   look good.
It's good adhesive, the same as ethics.
Don't belittle it: you're not so young anymore.
You'll need it, just like religion
or any other drug when                                          25
the real moment of dying comes.

Jacob Bronowski. "Science and Imagination," from *Science and Human Values*. Copyright © 1956, 1965 by J. Bronowski, renewed © 1984 by Rita Bronowski. Reprinted by permission of Julian Messner, a division of Simon & Schuster, Inc.

Susan Brownmiller. "Vulnerability: A Feminine Emotion," from *Femininity*. Copyright © 1984 by Susan Brownmiller. Reprinted by permission of Linden Press, a division of Simon & Schuster, Inc.

Truman Capote. "A Lamp in a Window," from *Music for Chamelons* by Truman Capote. Copyright © 1975, 1977, 1979, 1980 by Truman Capote. Reprinted by permission of Random House, Inc.

Rosario Castellaños. "Postscript." Reprinted by permission of the author. D. R. © 1972 Fondo de Cultura Económica.

e. e. cummings. "since feeling is first," from *IS 5 poems* by e. e. cummings, edited by George James Firmage, by permission of Liveright Publishing Corporation. Copyright © 1985 by e. e. cummings Trust. Copyright 1926 by Horace Liveright. Copyright © 1954 by e. e. cummings. Copyright © 1985 by George James Firmage.

Joan Didion. "Getting the Vegas Willies." Reprinted by permission of Wallace Literary Agency, Inc. Copyright © 1977 by Joan Didion, first appeared in *Esquire*.

Annie Dillard. "Bring on the Lions." Excerpt from *The Writing Life* by Annie Dillard. Copyright © 1989 by Annie Dillard. Reprinted by permission of HarperCollins Publishers, Inc.

Loren Eiseley. "The Angry Winter." Excerpt from "The Angry Winter" in *The Unexpected Universe*. Copyright © 1968 by Loren Eiseley. Reprinted by permission of Harcourt Brace Jovanovich, Inc.

Ralph Ellison. "Battle Royal," from *Invisible Man* by Ralph Ellison. Copyright 1948 by Ralph Ellison. Reprinted by permission of Random House, Inc.

Nora Ephron. "A Few Words about Breasts." Reprinted by permission of International Creative Management, Inc. Copyright © 1972 by Nora Ephron.

Marc Feigen Fasteau. "Friendships among Men," from *The Male Machine* by Marc Feigen Fasteau. Copyright © 1974 by McGraw-Hill Publishing Company. Reproduced by permission of McGraw-Hill Publishing Company.

Paul Fussell. "About the House," from *Class*. Copyright © 1983 by Paul Fussell. Reprinted by permission of Summit Books, a division of Simon & Schuster, Inc.

William Golding. "Thinking as a Hobby." Copyright © 1961 by William Golding. Renewed. Reprinted by permission of Curtis Brown, Ltd.

Ellen Goodman. "Casualties of Commitment," from *Keeping in Touch* "Casualties of Commitment." Copyright © 1985 by the Washington Post Company. Reprinted by permission of Summit Books, a division of Simon & Schuster, Inc. "The Fate of the Dinosaur," from *Keeping in Touch*. Copyright © 1985 by the Washington Post Company. Reprinted by permission of Summit Books, a division of Simon & Schuster, Inc.

Stephen Jay Gould. "The Terrifying Normalcy of AIDS." Copyright © 1987 by the New York Times Company. Reprinted by permission.

S. I. Hayakawa. "Sexual Fantasy and the 1957 Car." Copyright © 1962 by S. I. Hayakawa; Copyright 1952, 1953, 1954, 1955, 1956, 1957, 1958, by the International Society for General Semantics. Reprinted with permission of S. I. Hayakawa.

Michael Herr. From *Dispatches* by Michael Herr. Copyright © 1968, 1969, 1970, 1977 by Michael Herr. Reprinted by permission of Alfred A. Knopf, Inc.

Robinson Jeffers. "The Deer Lay Down Their Bones," from *The Selected Poetry of*

Epistemology." Copyright © 1964 by Harvard University Press. Reprinted by permission.

Robert Pirsig. An excerpt from *Zen and the Art of Motorcycle Maintenance*. Copyright © 1974 by Robert Pirsig. Published by Bantam Books. Used by permission of William Morrow and Company, Inc., Publishers, New York, N.Y.

Adrienne Rich. "Split at the Root: An Essay on Jewish Identity," slightly abridged, is reprinted from *Blood, Bread, and Poetry, Selected Prose 1979–1985* by Adrienne Rich. Reprinted by permission of the author and W. W. Norton & Company, Inc. Copyright © 1986 by Adrienne Rich. "For the Dead," from *The Fact of a Doorframe, Poems Old and New, 1950–1984*, by Adrienne Rich, by permission of W. W. Norton & Company, Inc. Copyright © 1984 by Adrienne Rich, Copyright © 1975, 1978 by W. W. Norton & Company, Inc. Copyright © 1981 by Adrienne Rich.

Richard Rodriguez. "Aria: A Memoir of a Bilingual Childhood," from *Hunger of Memory* by Richard Rodriguez. Copyright © 1982 by Richard Rodriguez. Reprinted by permission of David R. Godine, Publisher.

Mike Rose. "Entering the Conversation of the University." Reprinted with permission of the Free Press, a division of Macmillan, Inc. From *Lives on the Boundary: The Struggles and Achievements of America's Underprepared* by Mike Rose. Copyright © 1989 by Mike Rose. "Rigid Rules, Inflexible Plans, and the Stifling of Language: A Cognitivist Analysis of Writer's Block." From *College Composition and Communication*, December 1980, by the National Council of Teachers of English. Reprinted with permission.

Bertrand Russell. "The Superior Virtue of the Oppressed," from *Unpopular Essays*. Copyright © 1950 by Bertrand Russell. Reprinted by permission of Simon & Schuster, Inc.

Jonathan Schell. "Nuclear Peril: The Choice," from *The Fate of the Earth* by Jonathan Schell. Copyright © 1982 by Jonathan Schell. Reprinted by permission of Alfred A. Knopf, Inc. Originally appeared in *The New Yorker*.

Delmore Schwartz. "In Dreams Begin Responsibilities," from *In Dreams Begin Responsibilities*. Copyright © 1978 by New Directions Publishing Corporation. Reprinted by permission of New Directions Publishing Corporation.

Felice N. Schwartz. "Management Women and the New Facts of Life." Reprinted by permission of *Harvard Business Review*, Jan/Feb issue 1989. Copyright © 1989 by the President and Fellows of Harvard College; all rights reserved.

Leslie Marmon Silko. "Yellow Woman," from *The Man to Send Rain Clouds*. Ed. Kenneth Rosen. By permission of Leslie Marmon Silko.

Susan Sontag. "Metaphoric Uses of TB and Cancer." An excerpt from *Illness as a Metaphor* by Susan Sontag. Retitled "Metaphoric Uses of TB and Cancer." Copyright © 1977, 1978 by Susan Sontag.

Lewis Thomas. "On Natural Death," from *The Medusa and the Snail* by Lewis Thomas. Copyright © 1979 by Lewis Thomas. Reprinted by permission of Viking Penguin, a division of Penguin Books USA, Inc. "The Attic of the Brain," from *Late Night Thoughts on Listening to Mahler's Ninth* by Lewis Thomas. Copyright © 1980 by Lewis Thomas. Used by permission of Harcourt Brace Jovanovich, Inc.

Judith Viorst. "Good as Guilt," from *Necessary Losses*. Copyright © 1986 by Judith Viorst. Reprinted by permission of Simon & Schuster, Inc.

Rebecca West. "The Sin of Self-Sacrifice." Reprinted by permission of the Peters Fraser & Dunlop Group, Ltd.

Joseph Williams and Gregory G. Colomb. "The Novice Writer." Reprinted with permission from Joseph M. Williams and Gregory G. Colomb. From *Programs That Work:* edited by Toby Fulwiler and Art Young (Boynton/Cook Publishers, Portsmouth NH, 1990) and Heinemann Educational Books, Inc.

William Carlos Williams. "The Use of Force," from *William Carlos Williams: The Doctor Stories.* Copyright 1933, 1938 by William Carlos Williams. Reprinted by permission of New Directions Publishing Corporation. "Spring and All," from *The Collected Poems of William Carlos Williams, 1909–1939* vol. I. Copyright © 1938 by New Directions Publishing Corporation. Reprinted by permission of New Directions Publishing Corporation.

Tom Wolfe. "O Rotten Gotham—Sliding Down into the Behavioral Sink," from *The Pump House Gang* by Tom Wolfe. Copyright © 1968 by Tom Wolfe. Reprinted by permission of Farrar, Straus, and Giroux, Inc.

William Zinsser. "College Pressures." Originally published in Blair and Ketchum's *Country Journal*, April 1979. Copyright © Cowles Magazines, Inc.

# Index